SLEEPY PRINCESS IN THE DEMON CASTLE

7

Story & Art by
KAGIJI KUMANOMATA

NIGHTS

79TH NIGHT Reincarnation at the Church 3

80TH NIGHT Love Me ♡ Princess Mandrake 17

81ST NIGHT She Goes Castle Hopping Again 29

82ND NIGHT Do You Seriously Think
I Can Keep a Low Profile? 43

83RD NIGHT Don't Forget Bussy!... 55

84TH NIGHT The Sleepy Princess's Speech 67

85TH NIGHT Quilly and Me 83

86TH NIGHT Comforter (Stalker) 95

87TH NIGHT A Movie Isn't a Movie Without Popcorn 107

88TH NIGHT Homemade Chocolate Pudding Inside ♡ 119

89TH NIGHT You Didn't Create a Ko-tatsu,
You Dug Your Own Grave 131

90TH NIGHT Don't You Dare "This May Sting a Bit" Me! 143

91ST NIGHT One-on-One in the Hospital Room 155

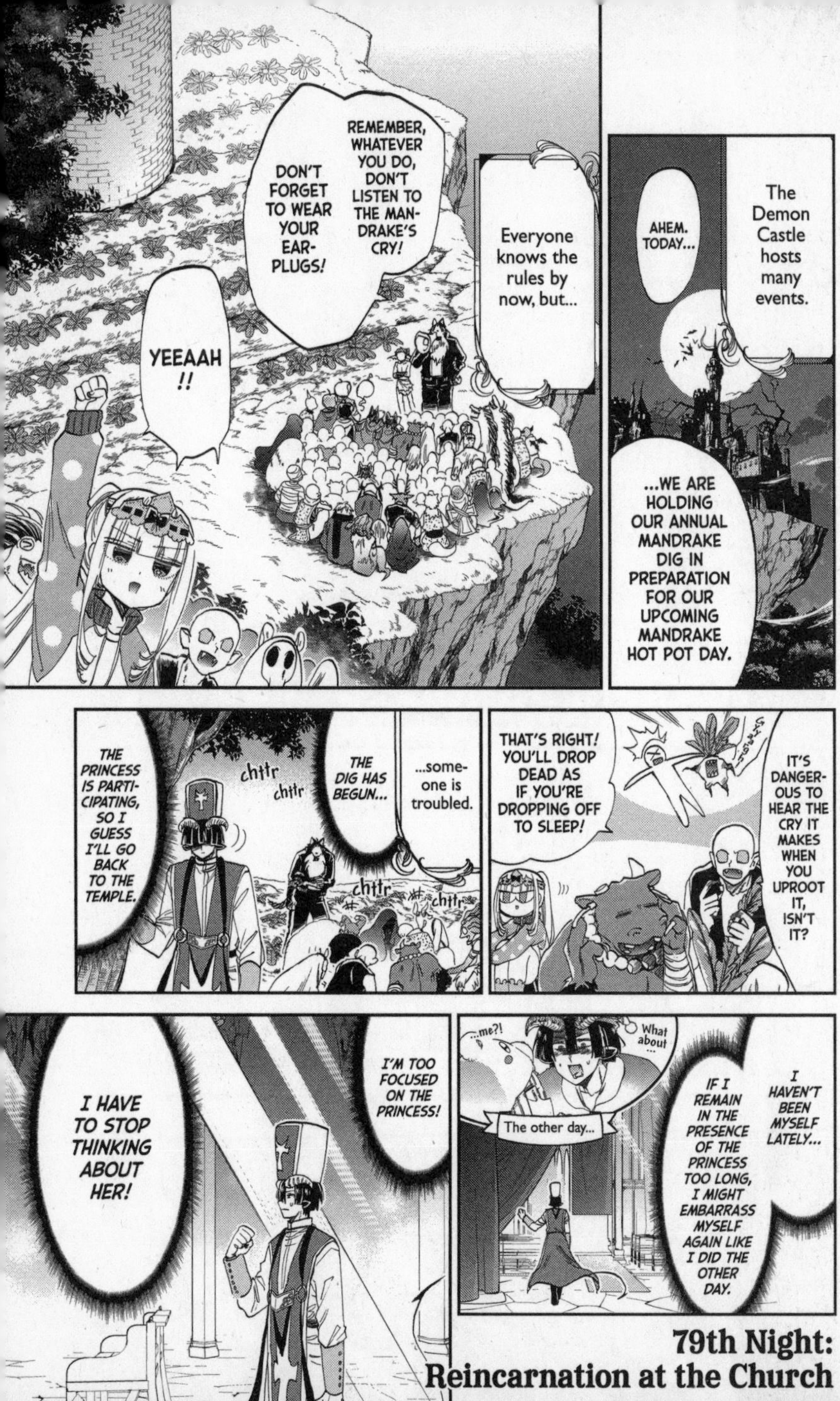
The Demon Castle hosts many events.
AHEM. TODAY...
...WE ARE HOLDING OUR ANNUAL MANDRAKE DIG IN PREPARATION FOR OUR UPCOMING MANDRAKE HOT POT DAY.
Everyone knows the rules by now, but...
REMEMBER, WHATEVER YOU DO, DON'T LISTEN TO THE MAN-DRAKE'S CRY!
DON'T FORGET TO WEAR YOUR EAR-PLUGS!
YEEAAH !!
IT'S DANGER-OUS TO HEAR THE CRY IT MAKES WHEN YOU UPROOT IT, ISN'T IT?
THAT'S RIGHT! YOU'LL DROP DEAD AS IF YOU'RE DROPPING OFF TO SLEEP!
...some-one is troubled.
THE DIG HAS BEGUN...
chttr chttr
chttr chttr
THE PRINCESS IS PARTI-CIPATING, SO I GUESS I'LL GO BACK TO THE TEMPLE.
I HAVEN'T BEEN MYSELF LATELY...
What about ...
...me?!
IF I REMAIN IN THE PRESENCE OF THE PRINCESS TOO LONG, I MIGHT EMBARRASS MYSELF AGAIN LIKE I DID THE OTHER DAY.
The other day...
I'M TOO FOCUSED ON THE PRINCESS!
I HAVE TO STOP THINKING ABOUT HER!

79th Night: Reincarnation at the Church

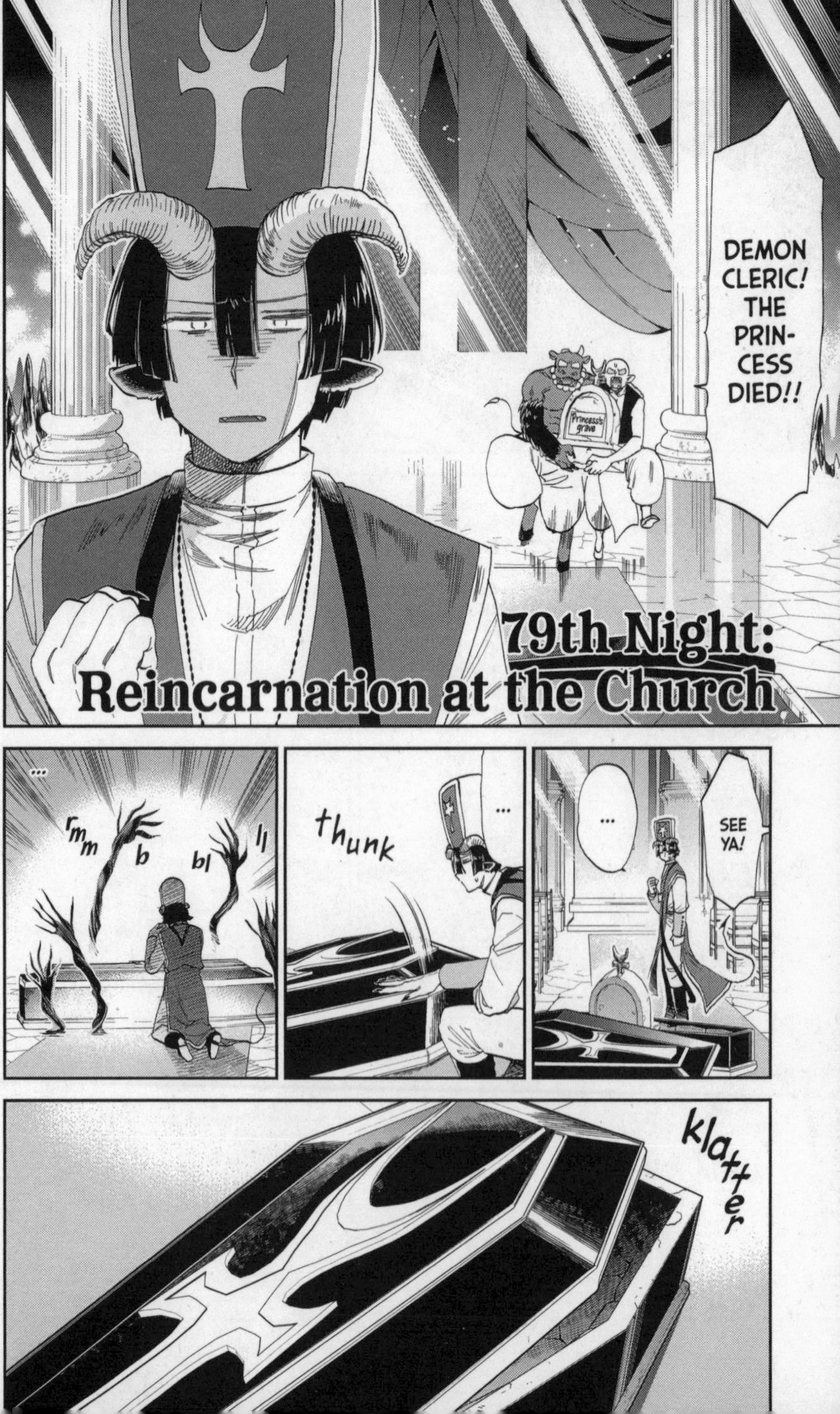
DEMON CLERIC! THE PRIN-CESS DIED!!
Princess's grave
79th Night: Reincarnation at the Church
SEE YA!
...
...
thunk
...
rmm b bl ll
klatter

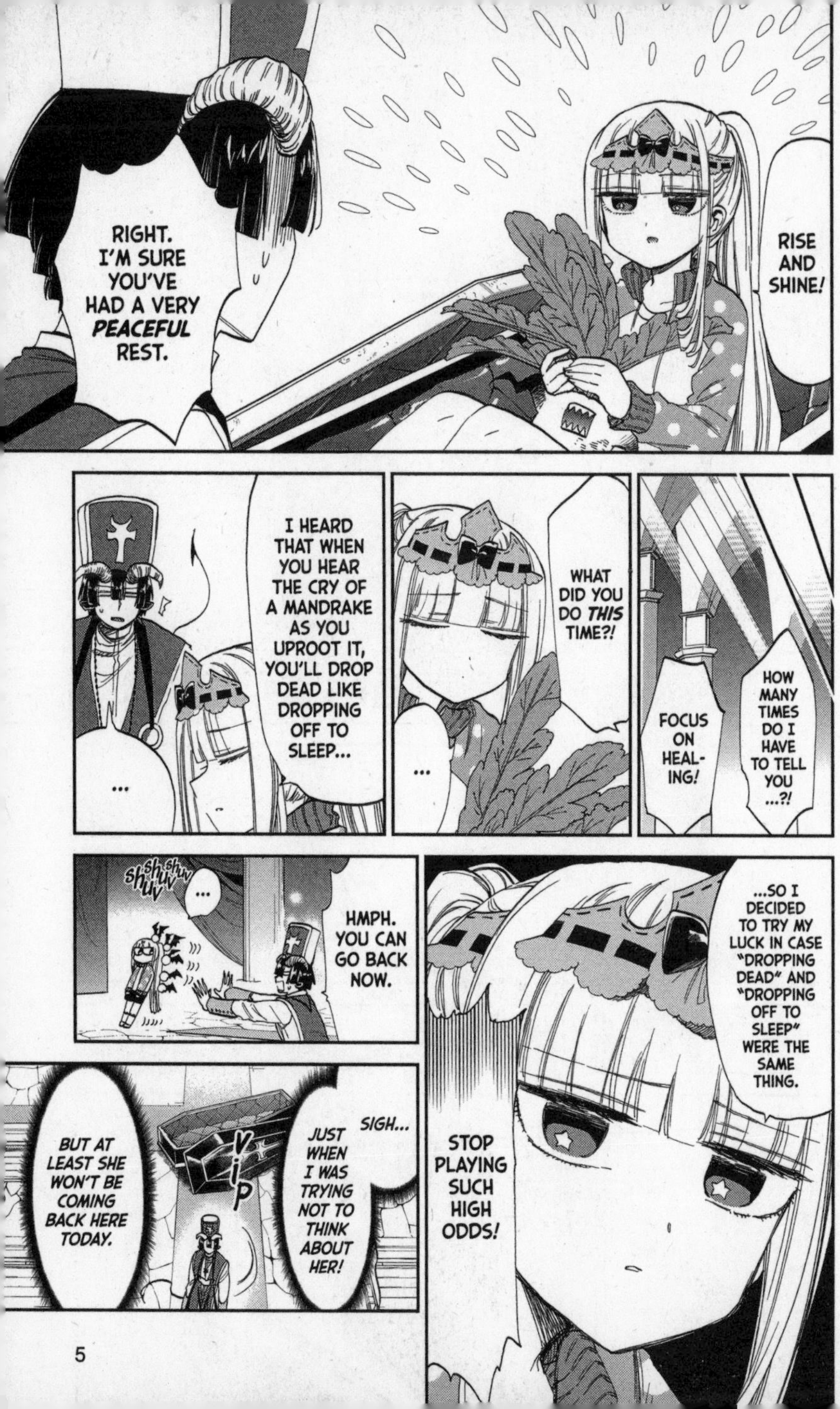
RISE AND SHINE!
RIGHT. I'M SURE YOU'VE HAD A VERY *PEACEFUL* REST.
HOW MANY TIMES DO I HAVE TO TELL YOU ...?!
FOCUS ON HEAL-ING!
WHAT DID YOU DO *THIS* TIME?!
...
I HEARD THAT WHEN YOU HEAR THE CRY OF A MANDRAKE AS YOU UPROOT IT, YOU'LL DROP DEAD LIKE DROPPING OFF TO SLEEP...
...
...SO I DECIDED TO TRY MY LUCK IN CASE "DROPPING DEAD" AND "DROPPING OFF TO SLEEP" WERE THE SAME THING.
STOP PLAYING SUCH HIGH ODDS!
HMPH. YOU CAN GO BACK NOW.
...
shuv shuv shuv
SIGH...
JUST WHEN I WAS TRYING NOT TO THINK ABOUT HER!
vip
BUT AT LEAST SHE WON'T BE COMING BACK HERE TODAY.

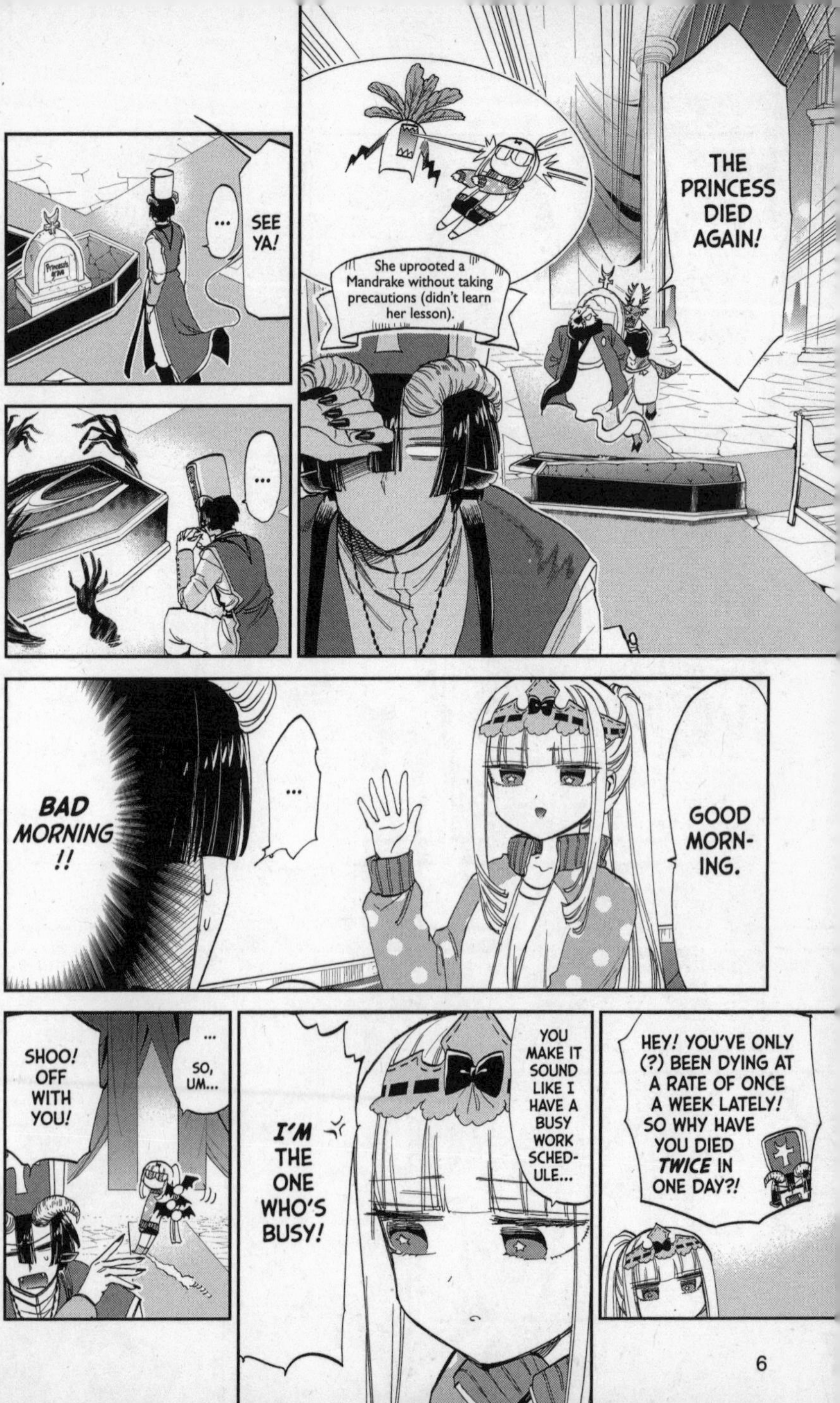
THE PRINCESS DIED AGAIN!
She uprooted a Mandrake without taking precautions (didn't learn her lesson).
SEE YA!
...
...
GOOD MORNING.
...
BAD MORNING!!
HEY! YOU'VE ONLY (?) BEEN DYING AT A RATE OF ONCE A WEEK LATELY! SO WHY HAVE YOU DIED TWICE IN ONE DAY?!
YOU MAKE IT SOUND LIKE I HAVE A BUSY WORK SCHEDULE...
I'M THE ONE WHO'S BUSY!
... SO, UM...
SHOO! OFF WITH YOU!

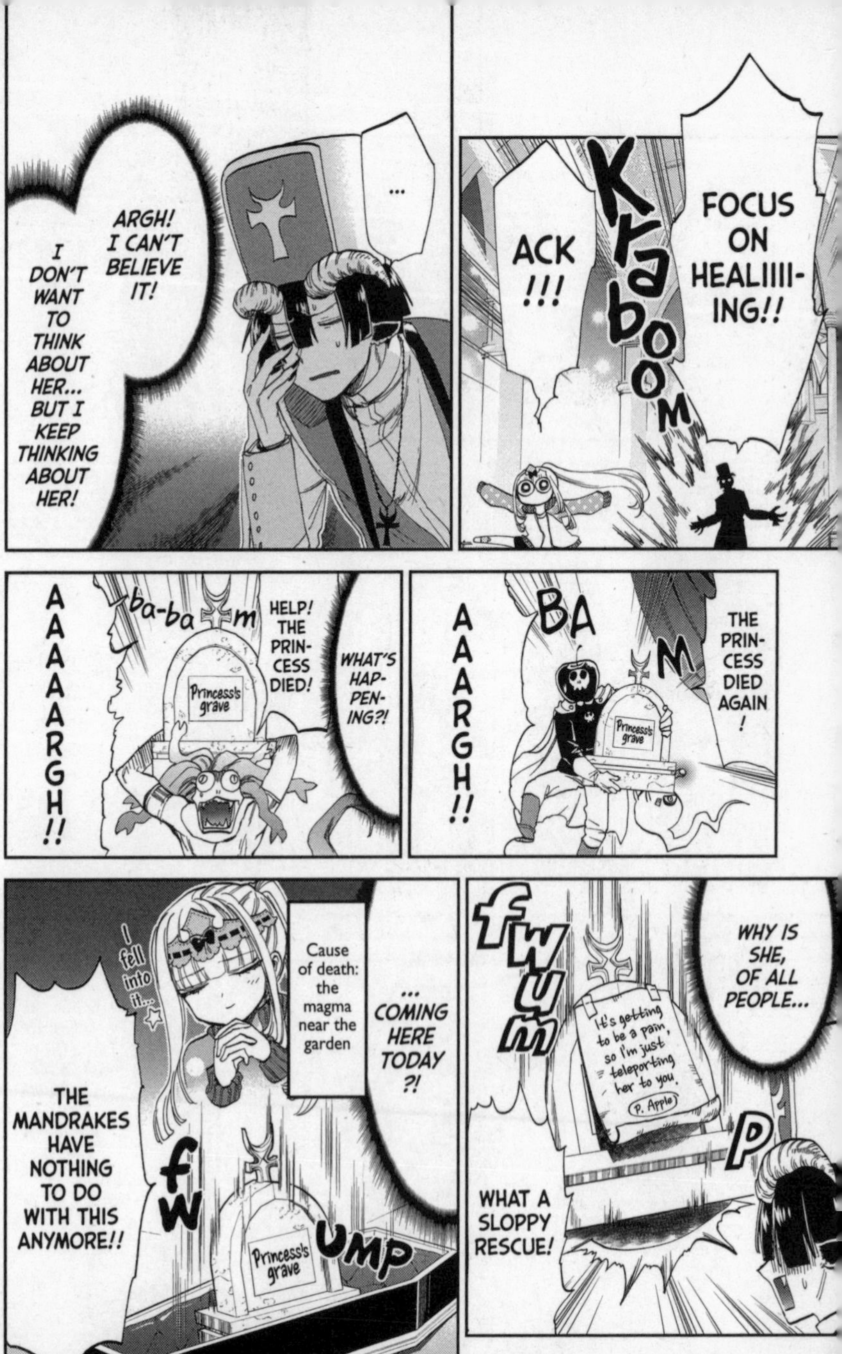
FOCUS ON HEALIIIII-ING!!
Kraboom
ACK!!!
...
ARGH! I CAN'T BELIEVE IT!
I DON'T WANT TO THINK ABOUT HER... BUT I KEEP THINKING ABOUT HER!
THE PRIN-CESS DIED AGAIN!
BAM
Princess's grave
AAAARGH!!
WHAT'S HAP-PEN-ING?!
HELP! THE PRIN-CESS DIED!
ba-bam
Princess's grave
AAAAAARGH!!
WHY IS SHE, OF ALL PEOPLE...
fwum
It's getting to be a pain, so I'm just teleporting her to you.
P. Apple
P
WHAT A SLOPPY RESCUE!
... COMING HERE TODAY?!
Cause of death: the magma near the garden
I fell into it...
THE MANDRAKES HAVE NOTHING TO DO WITH THIS ANYMORE!!
fwUMP
Princess's grave

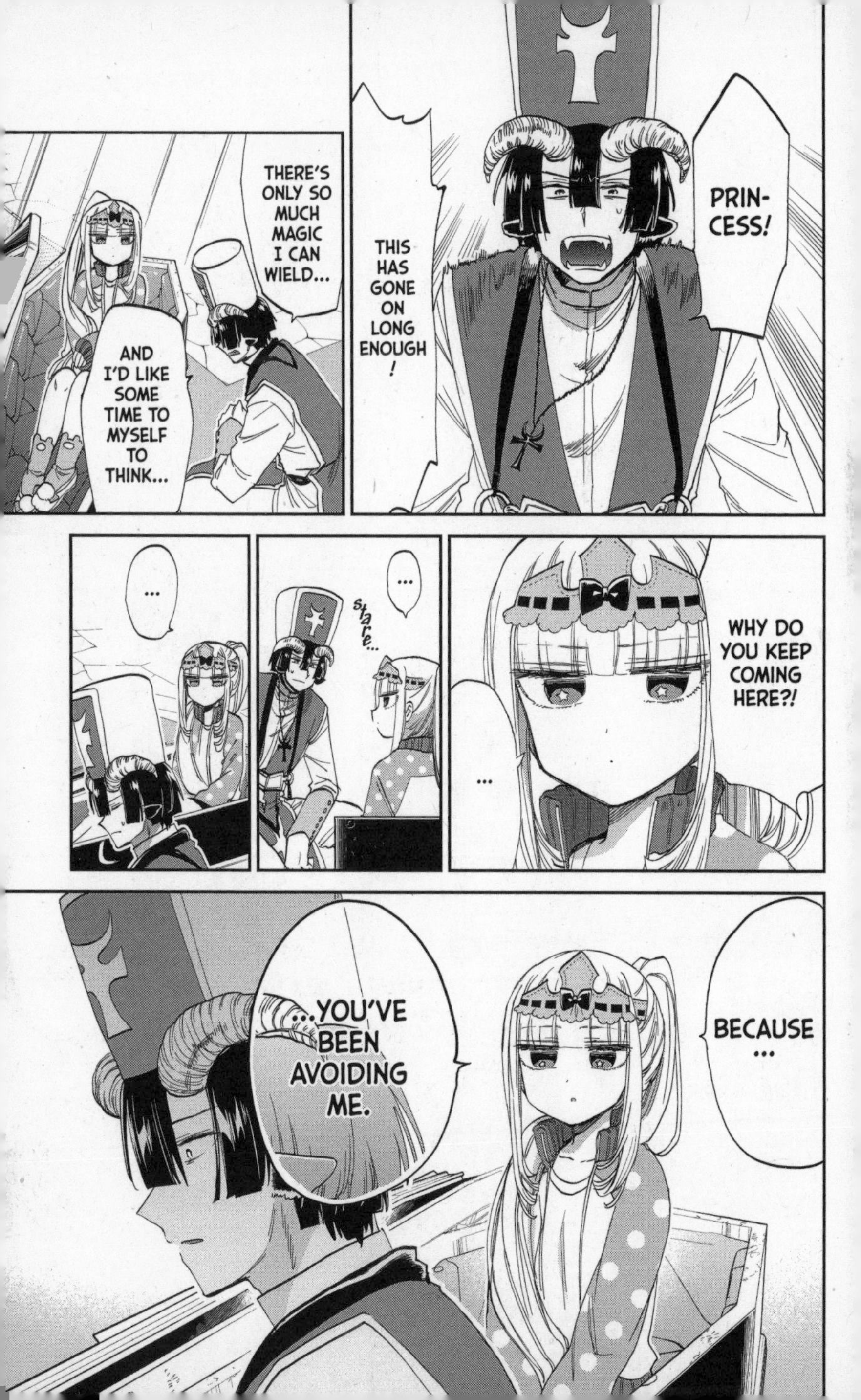
PRIN-CESS!
THIS HAS GONE ON LONG ENOUGH!
THERE'S ONLY SO MUCH MAGIC I CAN WIELD...
AND I'D LIKE SOME TIME TO MYSELF TO THINK...
WHY DO YOU KEEP COMING HERE?!
...
...
stare...
...
BECAUSE...
...YOU'VE BEEN AVOIDING ME.

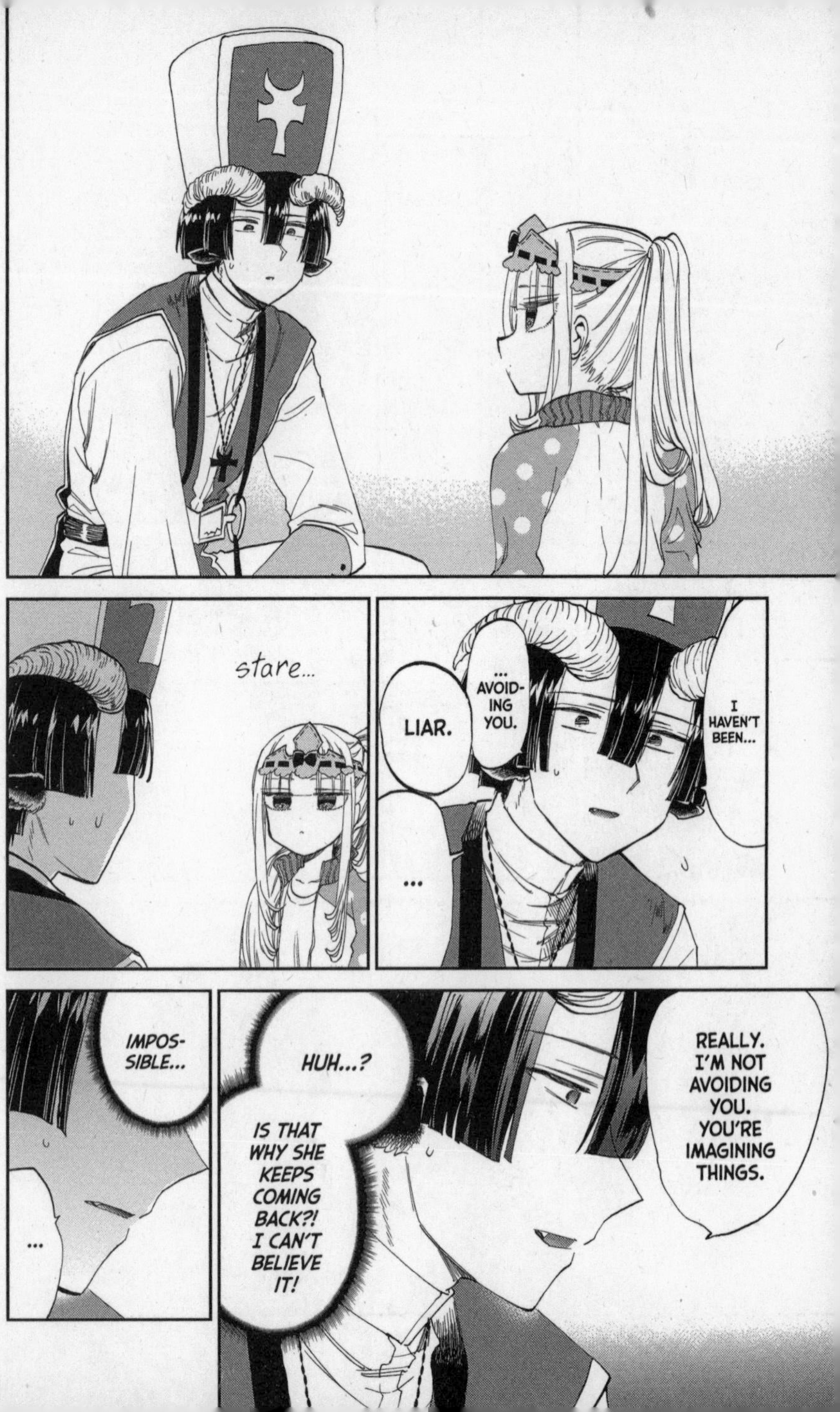
I HAVEN'T BEEN...
... AVOIDING YOU.
LIAR.
...
stare...
REALLY. I'M NOT AVOIDING YOU. YOU'RE IMAGINING THINGS.
HUH...?
IS THAT WHY SHE KEEPS COMING BACK?! I CAN'T BELIEVE IT!
IMPOS-SIBLE...
...

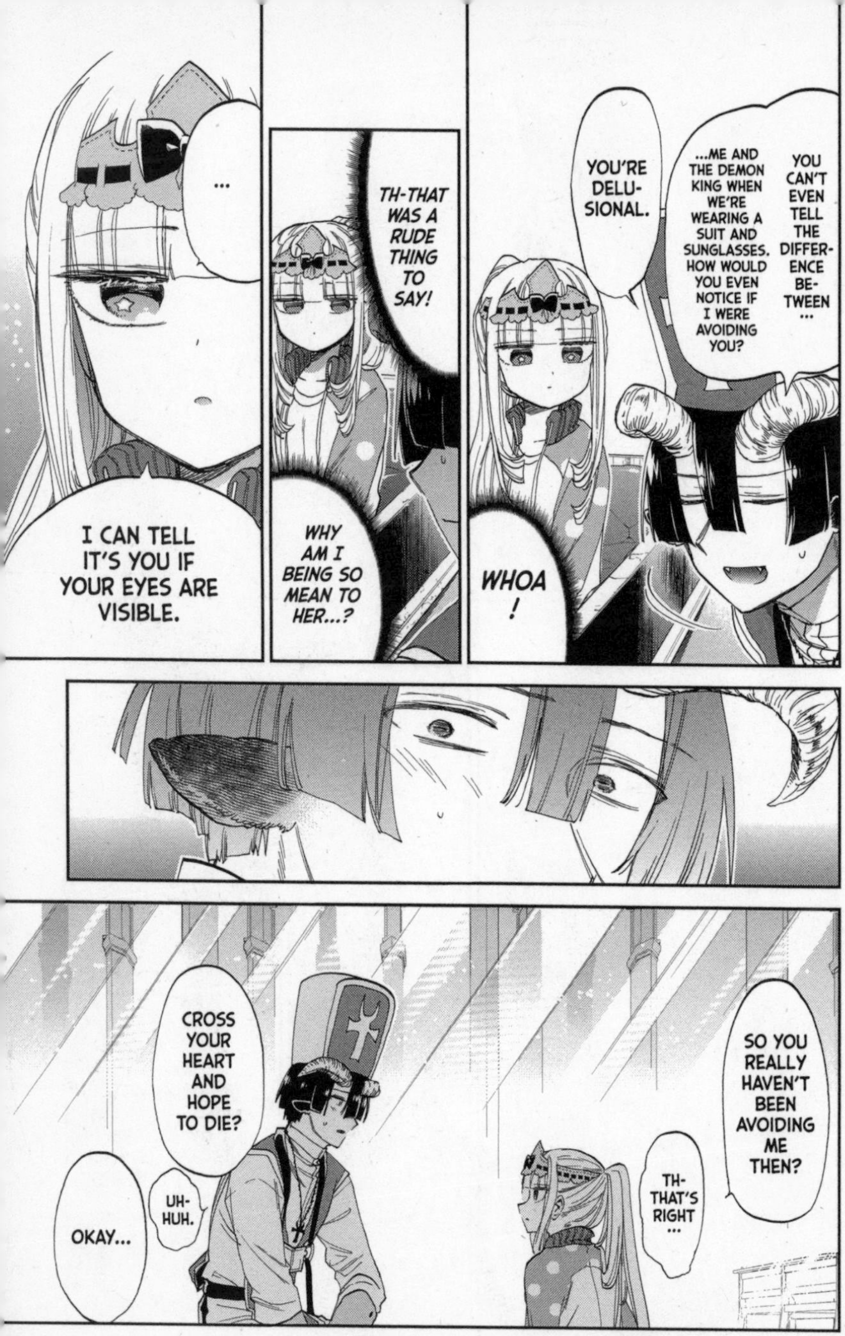
YOU CAN'T EVEN TELL THE DIFFERENCE BETWEEN...
...ME AND THE DEMON KING WHEN WE'RE WEARING A SUIT AND SUNGLASSES. HOW WOULD YOU EVEN NOTICE IF I WERE AVOIDING YOU?
YOU'RE DELUSIONAL.
WHOA!
TH-THAT WAS A RUDE THING TO SAY!
WHY AM I BEING SO MEAN TO HER...?
...
I CAN TELL IT'S YOU IF YOUR EYES ARE VISIBLE.
SO YOU REALLY HAVEN'T BEEN AVOIDING ME THEN?
TH-THAT'S RIGHT...
CROSS YOUR HEART AND HOPE TO DIE?
UH-HUH.
OKAY...

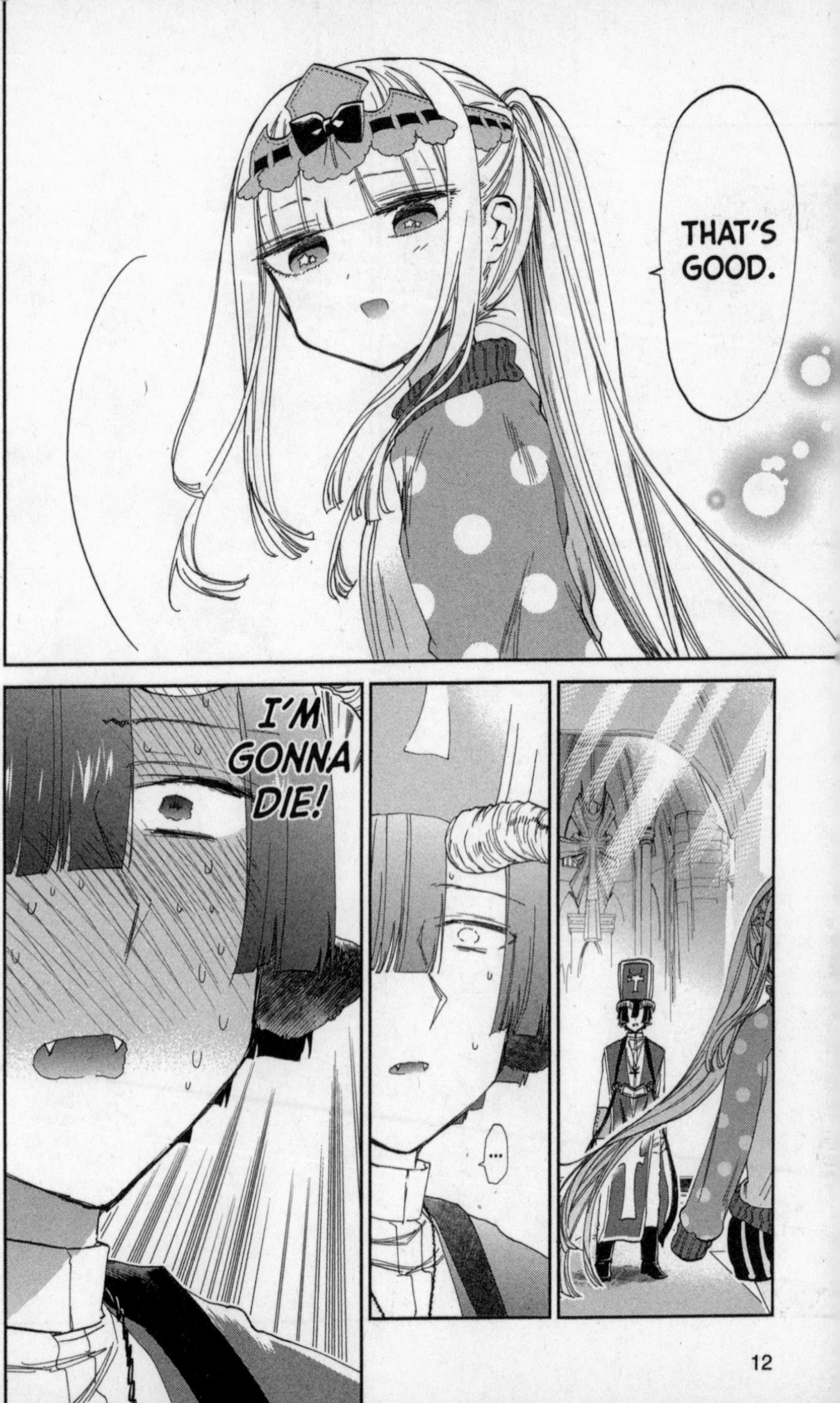
THAT'S GOOD.
...
I'M GONNA DIE!

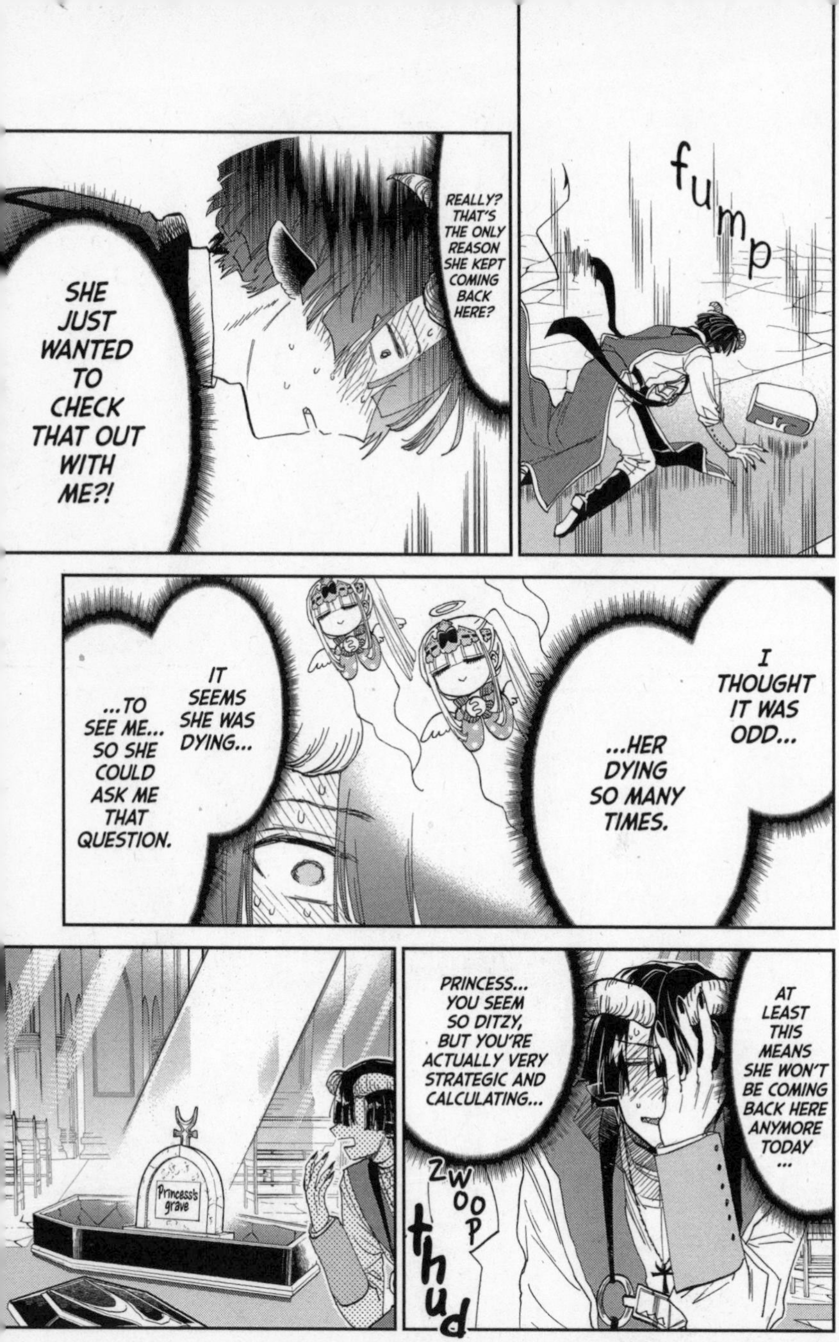
fump
REALLY? THAT'S THE ONLY REASON SHE KEPT COMING BACK HERE?
SHE JUST WANTED TO CHECK THAT OUT WITH ME?!
I THOUGHT IT WAS ODD...
...HER DYING SO MANY TIMES.
IT SEEMS SHE WAS DYING...
...TO SEE ME... SO SHE COULD ASK ME THAT QUESTION.
AT LEAST THIS MEANS SHE WON'T BE COMING BACK HERE ANYMORE TODAY ...
PRINCESS... YOU SEEM SO DITZY, BUT YOU'RE ACTUALLY VERY STRATEGIC AND CALCULATING...
zwoop
thud
Princess's grave

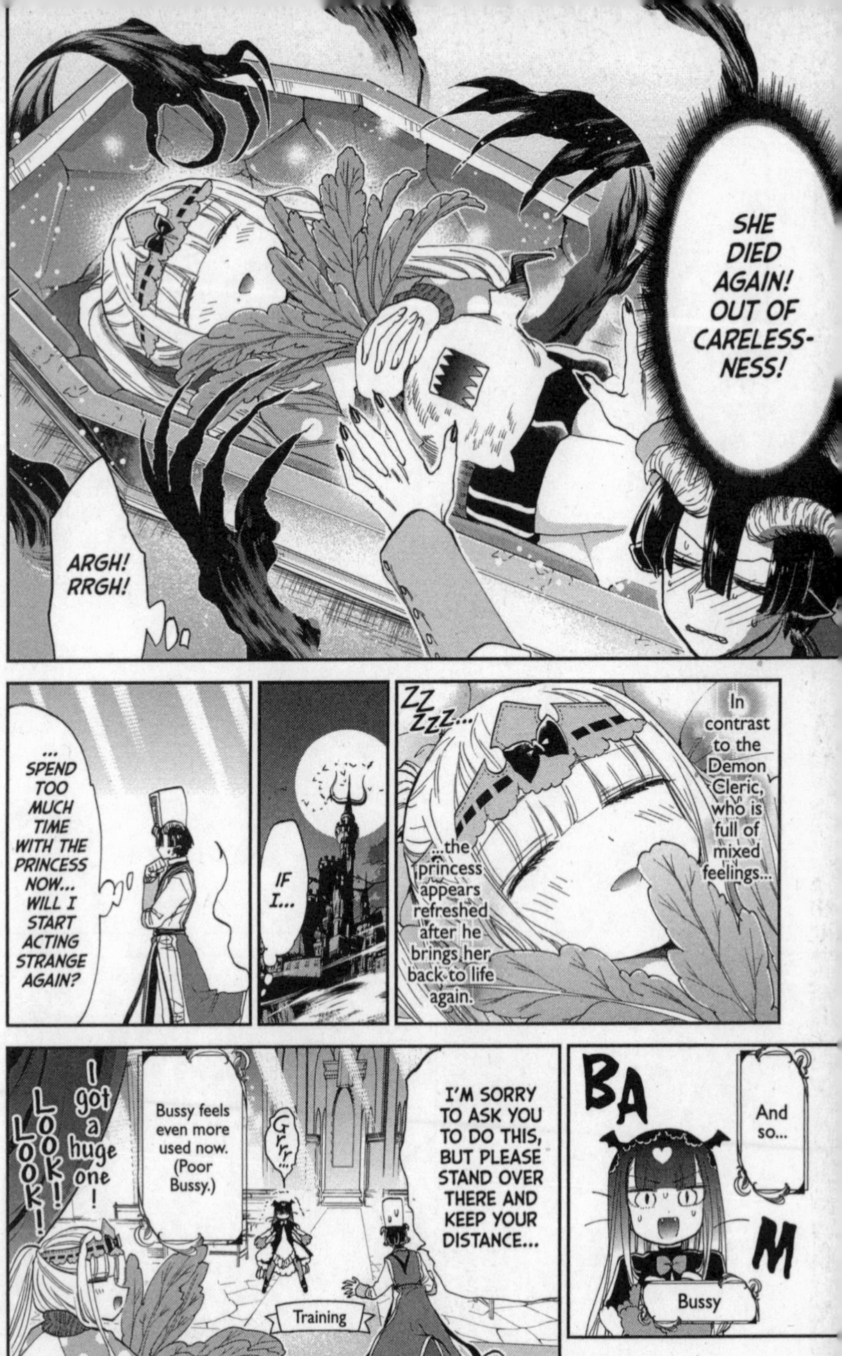
SHE DIED AGAIN! OUT OF CARELESS-NESS!
ARGH! RRGH!
ZZZZZ...
In contrast to the Demon Cleric, who is full of mixed feelings...
...the princess appears refreshed after he brings her back to life again.
IF I...
...SPEND TOO MUCH TIME WITH THE PRINCESS NOW... WILL I START ACTING STRANGE AGAIN?
And so...
BAM
Bussy
I'M SORRY TO ASK YOU TO DO THIS, BUT PLEASE STAND OVER THERE AND KEEP YOUR DISTANCE...
Grrr...
Bussy feels even more used now. (Poor Bussy.)
I got a huge one!
LOOK! LOOK!
Training

Mandrake

Dangerousness: ☆☆☆☆☆☆
Tastiness: ☆☆☆☆☆☆☆☆

They taste good grated too!

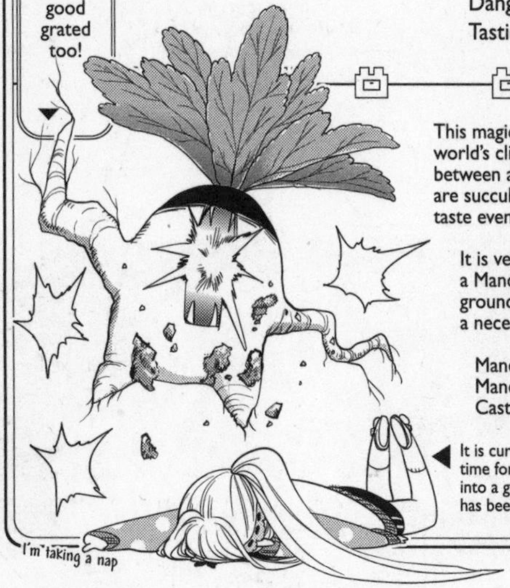
I'm taking a nap

This magical plant grows well in the demon world's climate. The flavor is somewhere between a gourd and a daikon radish. They are succulent and can be eaten raw, but they taste even better cooked.

It is very dangerous to hear the cry of a Mandrake when it is pulled out of the ground. Their scream is fatal. Earplugs are a necessity when harvesting them.

Mandrakes are the featured item on Mandrake Hot Pot Day at the Demon Castle.

It is currently taking some time for the princess to turn into a gravestone because she has been dying so often.

The Mandrake Dig

Top 3 Deaths

-Aurora Sya Lis Goodereste
"I dropped dead."

-Frankenzombie
"Can you believe that an undead can die?"

-Great Red Siberian
"That was before I took on humanoid form!"

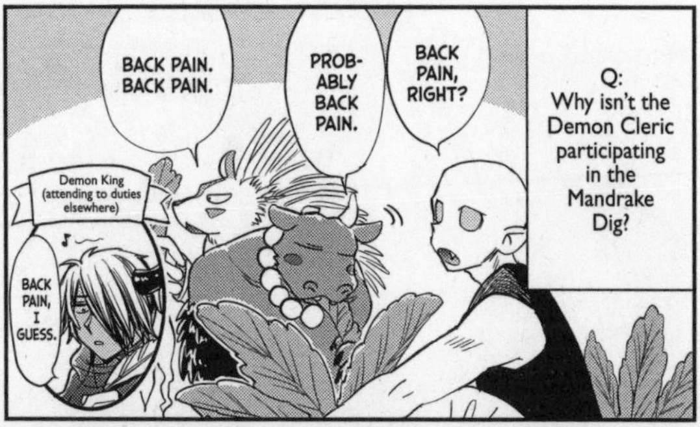
Q:
Why isn't the Demon Cleric participating in the Mandrake Dig?
BACK PAIN, RIGHT?
PROB-ABLY BACK PAIN.
BACK PAIN. BACK PAIN.
Demon King (attending to duties elsewhere)
BACK PAIN, I GUESS.

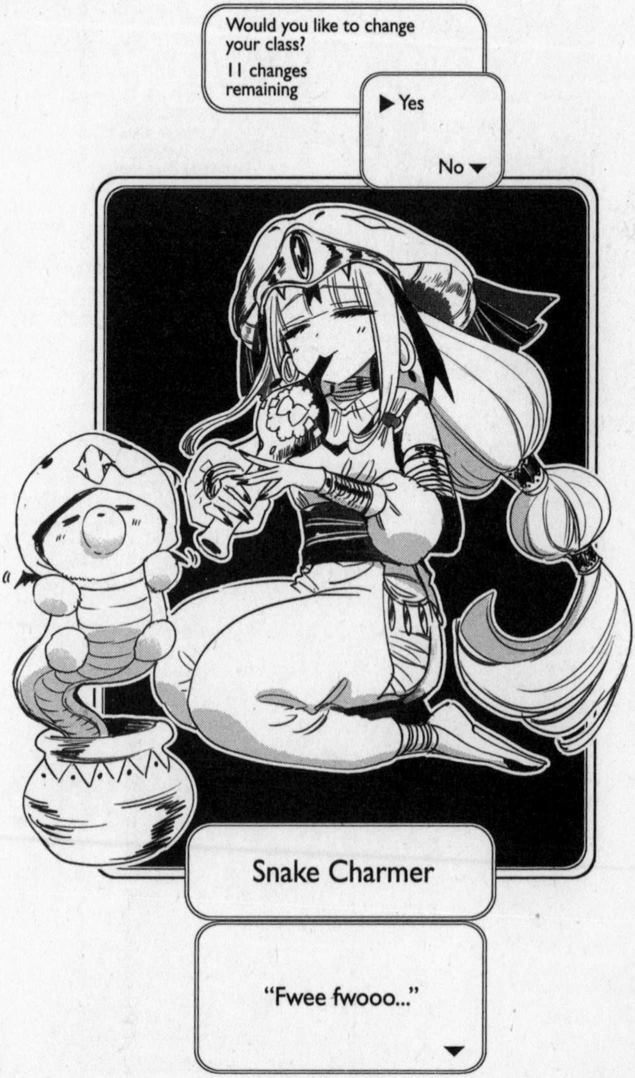
Would you like to change your class?
11 changes remaining
▶Yes
No ▼
Snake Charmer
"Fwee fwooo..."

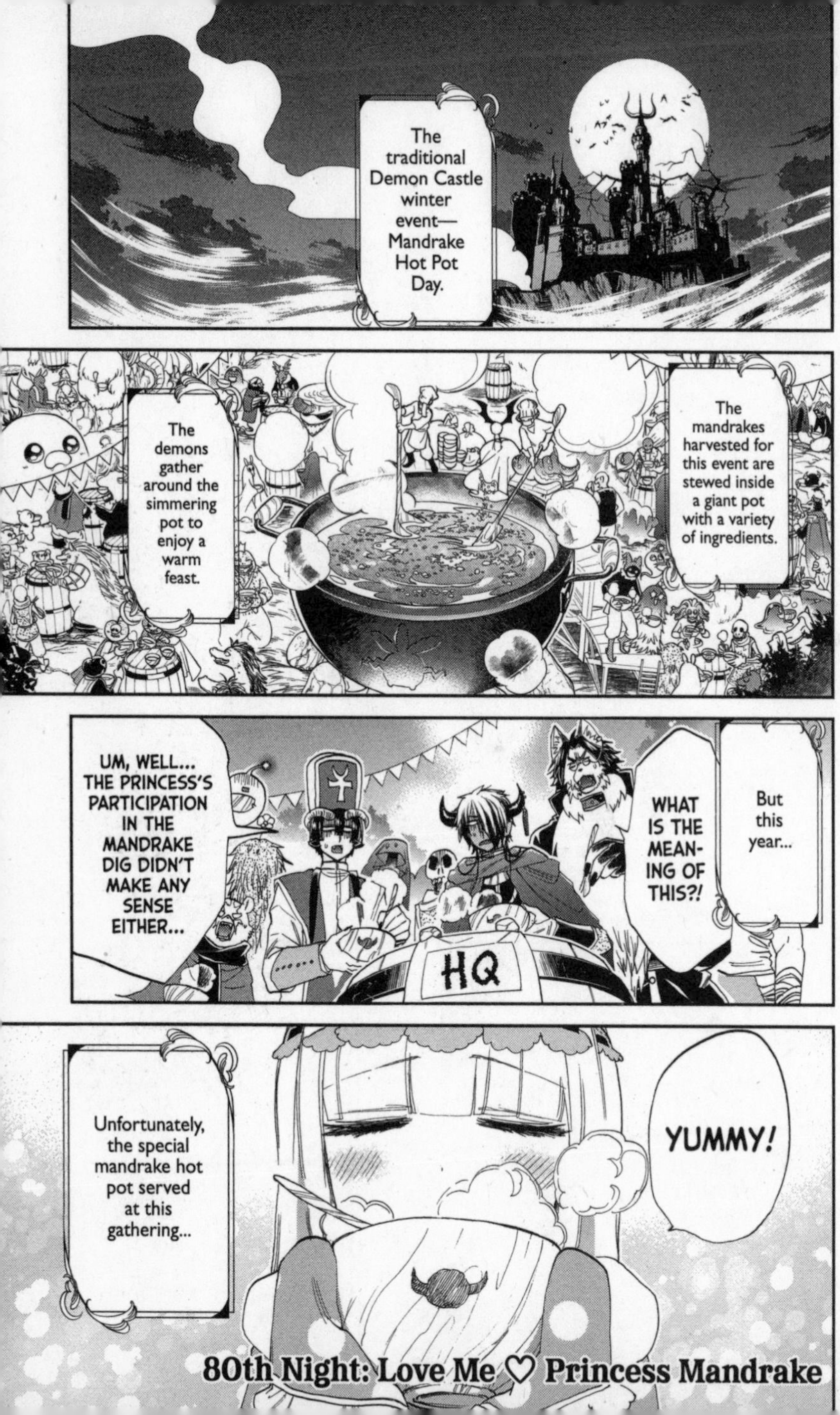
The traditional Demon Castle winter event—Mandrake Hot Pot Day.
The mandrakes harvested for this event are stewed inside a giant pot with a variety of ingredients.
The demons gather around the simmering pot to enjoy a warm feast.
But this year...
WHAT IS THE MEAN-ING OF THIS?!
UM, WELL... THE PRINCESS'S PARTICIPATION IN THE MANDRAKE DIG DIDN'T MAKE ANY SENSE EITHER...
HQ
YUMMY!
Unfortunately, the special mandrake hot pot served at this gathering...
80th Night: Love Me ♡ Princess Mandrake

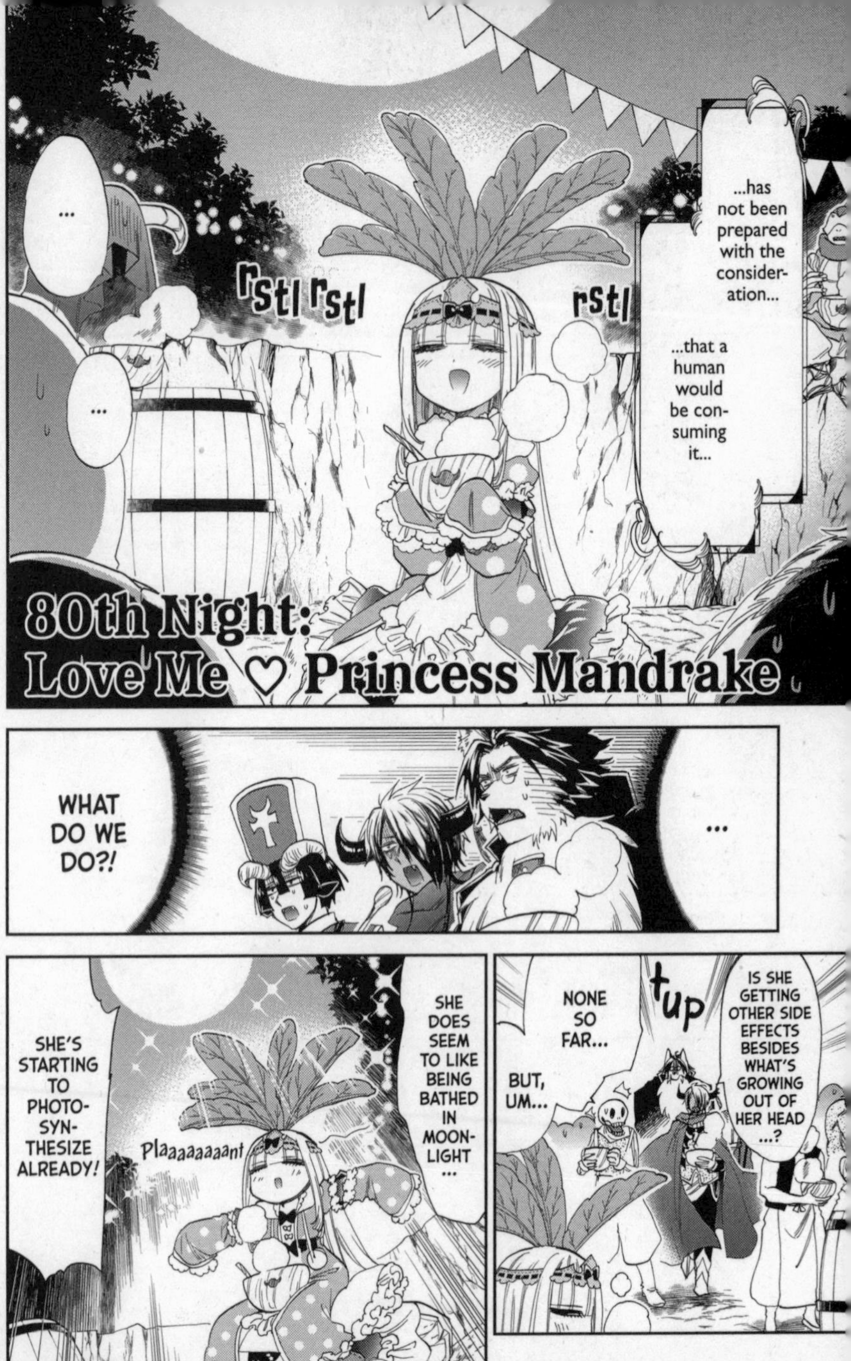
...has not been prepared with the consideration...
...that a human would be consuming it...
rstl
rstl rstl
...
...
80th Night: Love Me ♡ Princess Mandrake
...
WHAT DO WE DO?!
IS SHE GETTING OTHER SIDE EFFECTS BESIDES WHAT'S GROWING OUT OF HER HEAD ...?
tup
NONE SO FAR...
BUT, UM...
SHE DOES SEEM TO LIKE BEING BATHED IN MOONLIGHT ...
Plaaaaaaaant
SHE'S STARTING TO PHOTOSYNTHESIZE ALREADY!

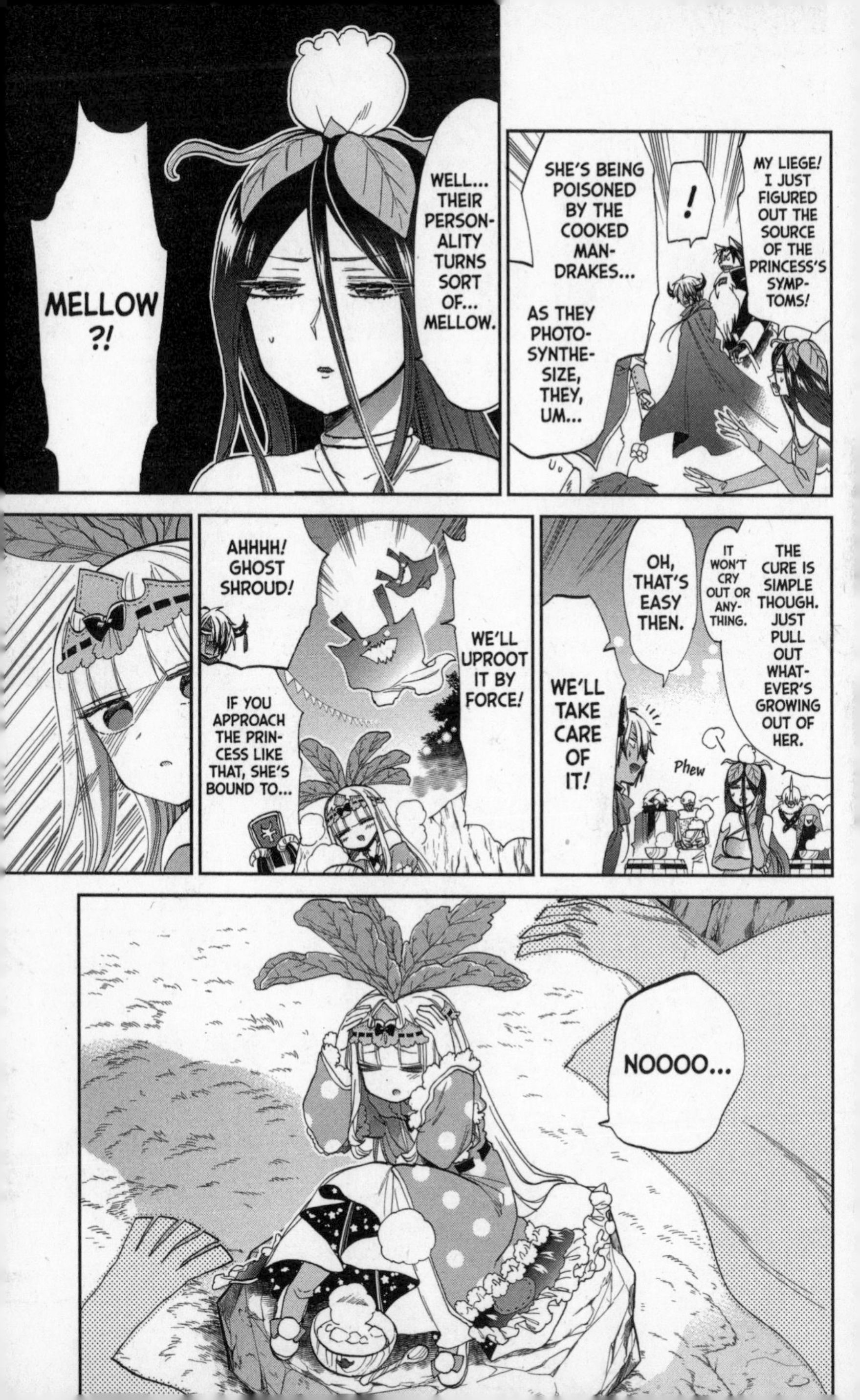

MY LIEGE! I JUST FIGURED OUT THE SOURCE OF THE PRINCESS'S SYMPTOMS!
!
SHE'S BEING POISONED BY THE COOKED MANDRAKES...
AS THEY PHOTOSYNTHESIZE, THEY, UM...
WELL... THEIR PERSONALITY TURNS SORT OF... MELLOW.
MELLOW ?!
THE CURE IS SIMPLE THOUGH. JUST PULL OUT WHATEVER'S GROWING OUT OF HER.
IT WON'T CRY OUT OR ANYTHING.
OH, THAT'S EASY THEN.
Phew
WE'LL TAKE CARE OF IT!
WE'LL UPROOT IT BY FORCE!
AHHHH! GHOST SHROUD!
IF YOU APPROACH THE PRINCESS LIKE THAT, SHE'S BOUND TO...
NOOOO...

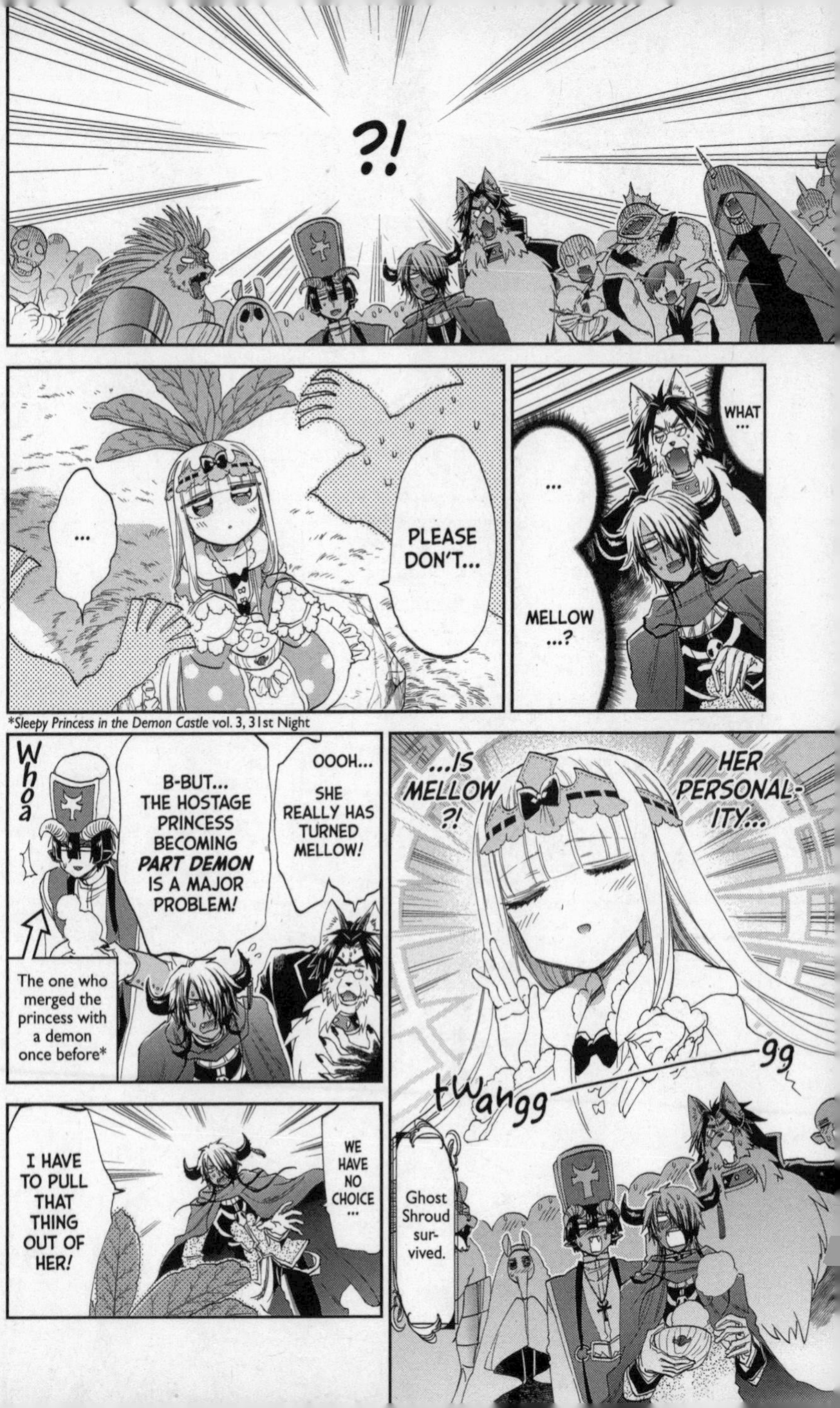
?!
WHAT ...
...
MELLOW ...?
PLEASE DON'T...
...
HER PERSONAL-ITY...
...IS MELLOW ?!
twangg
Ghost Shroud sur-vived.
OOOH... SHE REALLY HAS TURNED MELLOW!
B-BUT... THE HOSTAGE PRINCESS BECOMING PART DEMON IS A MAJOR PROBLEM!
Whoa
The one who merged the princess with a demon once before*
WE HAVE NO CHOICE ...
I HAVE TO PULL THAT THING OUT OF HER!

**Sleepy Princess in the Demon Castle* vol. 3, 31st Night

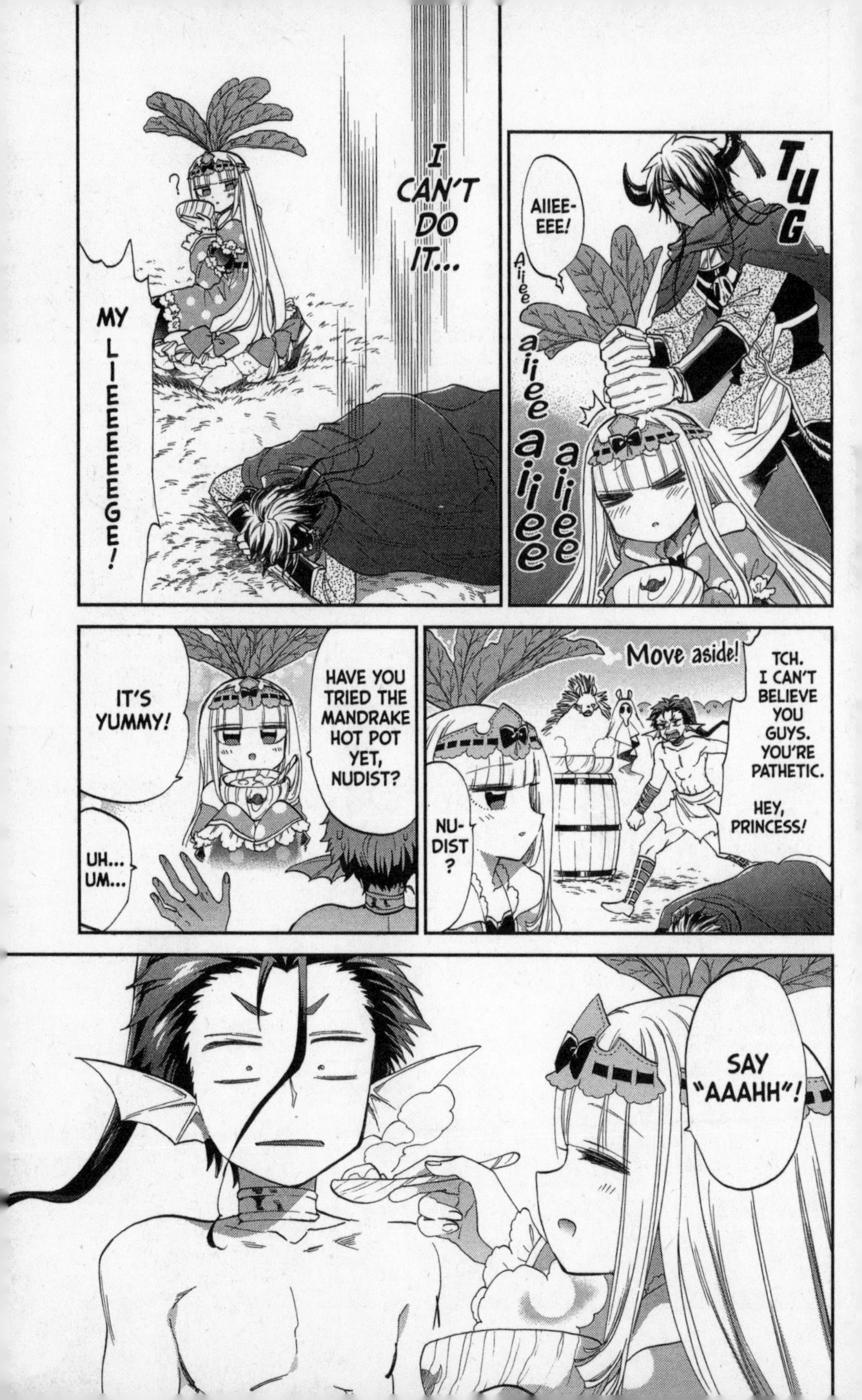
TUG
AIIEE-EEE!
Aiiee aiiee aiiee aiiee
I CAN'T DO IT...
MY LIEEEEEEGE!
TCH. I CAN'T BELIEVE YOU GUYS. YOU'RE PATHETIC.
HEY, PRINCESS!
Move aside!
NU-DIST?
HAVE YOU TRIED THE MANDRAKE HOT POT YET, NUDIST?
IT'S YUMMY!
UH... UM...
SAY "AAAHH"!

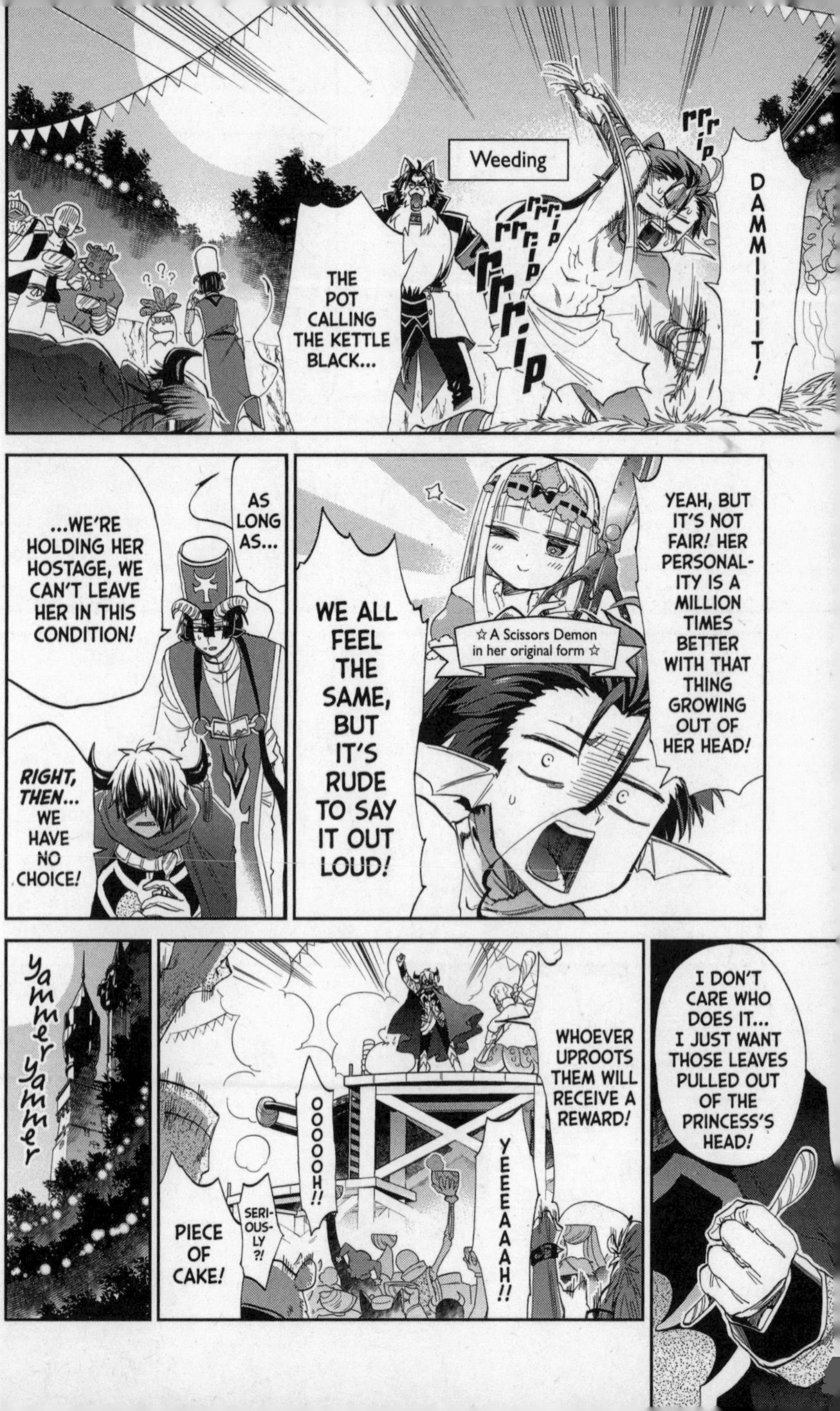
DAMMIIIIT!
rrrip
rrrrip
rrrrrip
rrrrrrip
Weeding
THE POT CALLING THE KETTLE BLACK...
YEAH, BUT IT'S NOT FAIR! HER PERSONAL-ITY IS A MILLION TIMES BETTER WITH THAT THING GROWING OUT OF HER HEAD!
☆ A Scissors Demon in her original form ☆
WE ALL FEEL THE SAME, BUT IT'S RUDE TO SAY IT OUT LOUD!
AS LONG AS...
...WE'RE HOLDING HER HOSTAGE, WE CAN'T LEAVE HER IN THIS CONDITION!
RIGHT, THEN... WE HAVE NO CHOICE!
I DON'T CARE WHO DOES IT... I JUST WANT THOSE LEAVES PULLED OUT OF THE PRINCESS'S HEAD!
WHOEVER UPROOTS THEM WILL RECEIVE A REWARD!
YEEEAAAH!!
OOOOOOH!!
SERI-OUS-LY?!
PIECE OF CAKE!
Yammer yammer

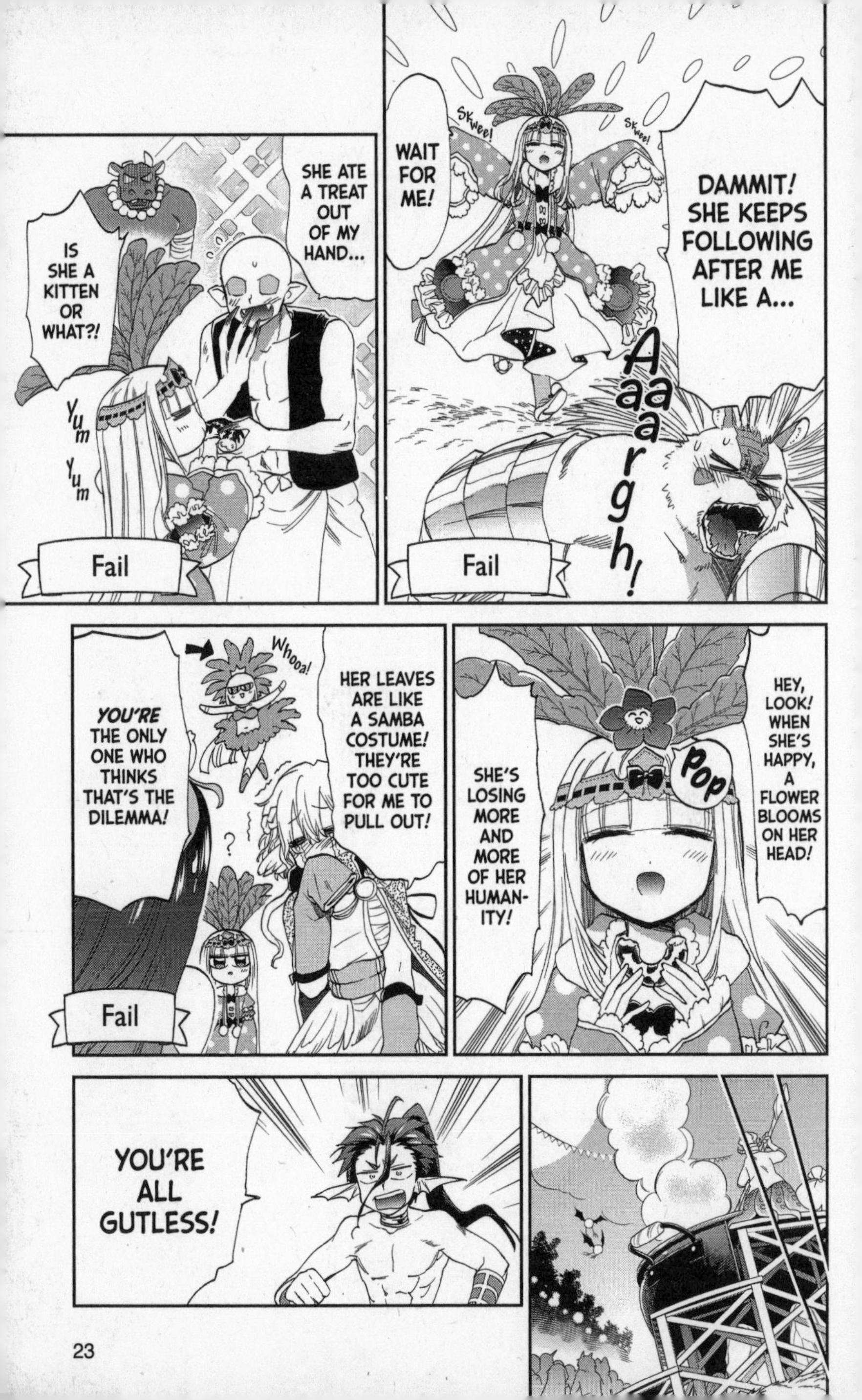
DAMMIT! SHE KEEPS FOLLOWING AFTER ME LIKE A...
Skwee!
Skwee!
WAIT FOR ME!
Aaaargh!
Fail
SHE ATE A TREAT OUT OF MY HAND...
IS SHE A KITTEN OR WHAT?!
Yum Yum
Fail
HEY, LOOK! WHEN SHE'S HAPPY, A FLOWER BLOOMS ON HER HEAD!
Pop
SHE'S LOSING MORE AND MORE OF HER HUMAN-ITY!
HER LEAVES ARE LIKE A SAMBA COSTUME! THEY'RE TOO CUTE FOR ME TO PULL OUT!
Whooa!
YOU'RE THE ONLY ONE WHO THINKS THAT'S THE DILEMMA!
?
Fail
YOU'RE ALL GUTLESS!

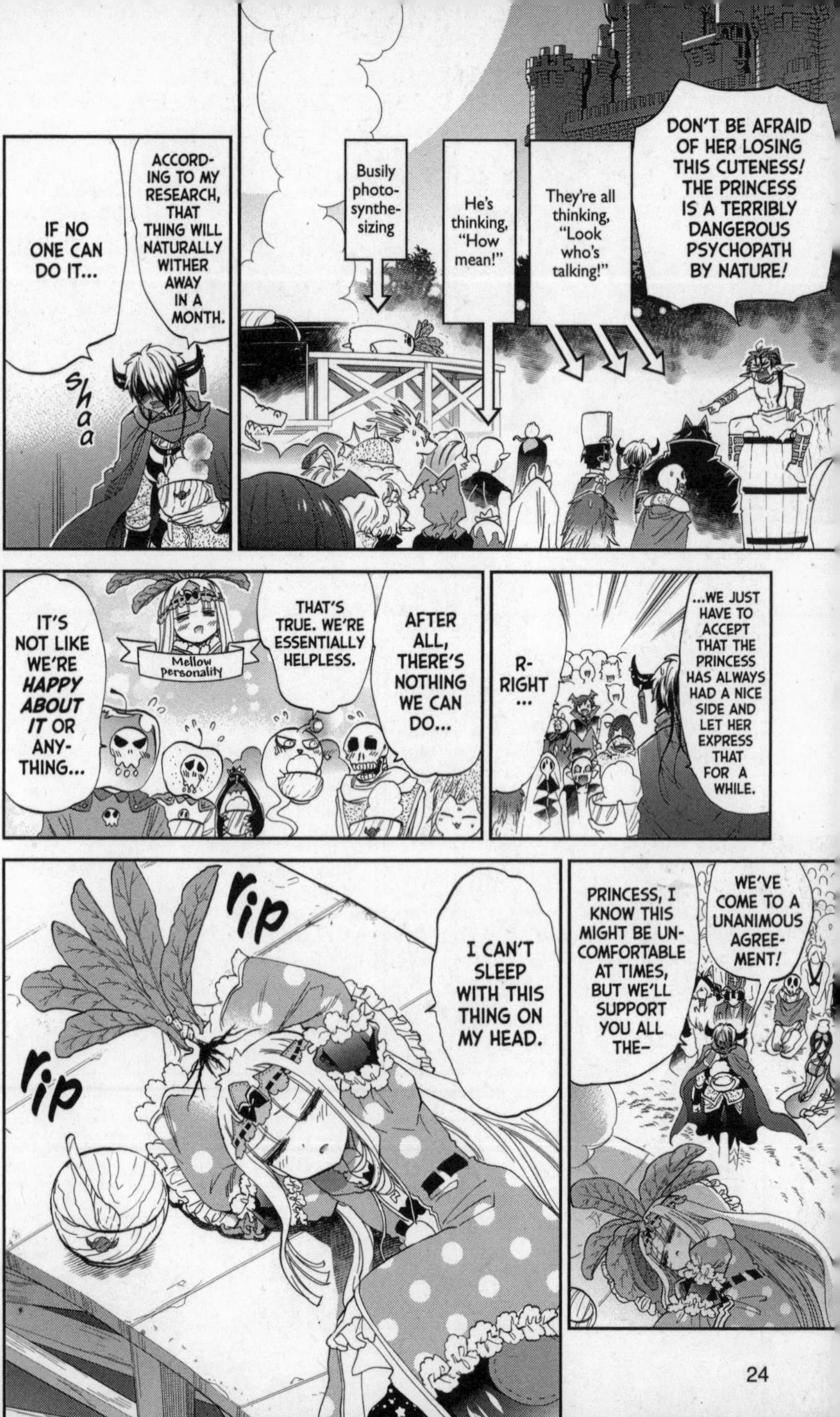
DON'T BE AFRAID OF HER LOSING THIS CUTENESS! THE PRINCESS IS A TERRIBLY DANGEROUS PSYCHOPATH BY NATURE!
They're all thinking, "Look who's talking!"
He's thinking, "How mean!"
Busily photo-synthe-sizing
ACCORD-ING TO MY RESEARCH, THAT THING WILL NATURALLY WITHER AWAY IN A MONTH.
IF NO ONE CAN DO IT...
Shaa
...WE JUST HAVE TO ACCEPT THAT THE PRINCESS HAS ALWAYS HAD A NICE SIDE AND LET HER EXPRESS THAT FOR A WHILE.
R-RIGHT...
AFTER ALL, THERE'S NOTHING WE CAN DO...
THAT'S TRUE. WE'RE ESSENTIALLY HELPLESS.
Mellow Personality
IT'S NOT LIKE WE'RE *HAPPY ABOUT IT* OR ANY-THING...
WE'VE COME TO A UNANIMOUS AGREE-MENT!
PRINCESS, I KNOW THIS MIGHT BE UN-COMFORTABLE AT TIMES, BUT WE'LL SUPPORT YOU ALL THE-
I CAN'T SLEEP WITH THIS THING ON MY HEAD.
rip
rip

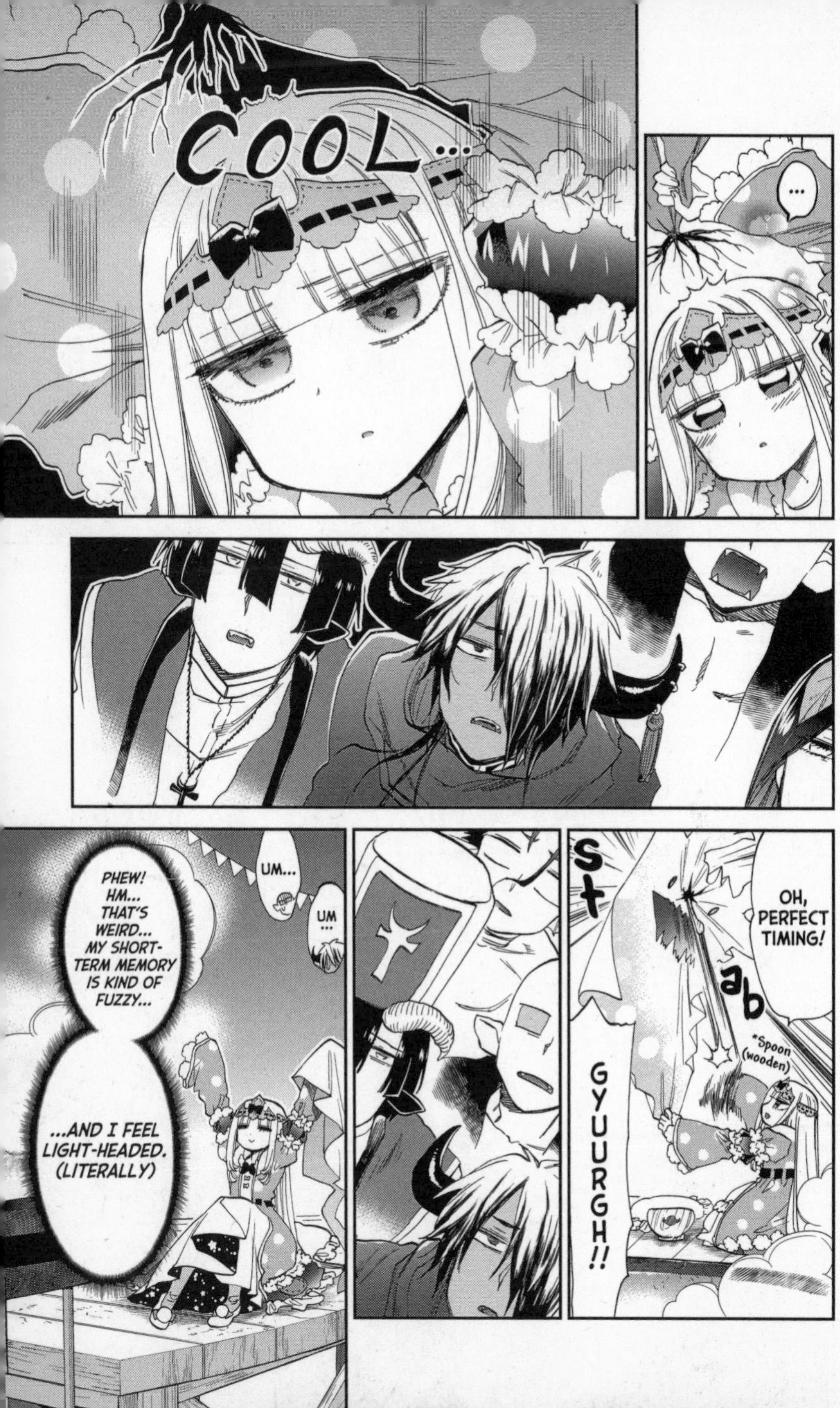
...
COOL...
OH, PERFECT TIMING!
St
ab
*Spoon (wooden)
GYUURGH!!
UM...
UM...
PHEW! HM... THAT'S WEIRD... MY SHORT-TERM MEMORY IS KIND OF FUZZY...
...AND I FEEL LIGHT-HEADED. (LITERALLY)

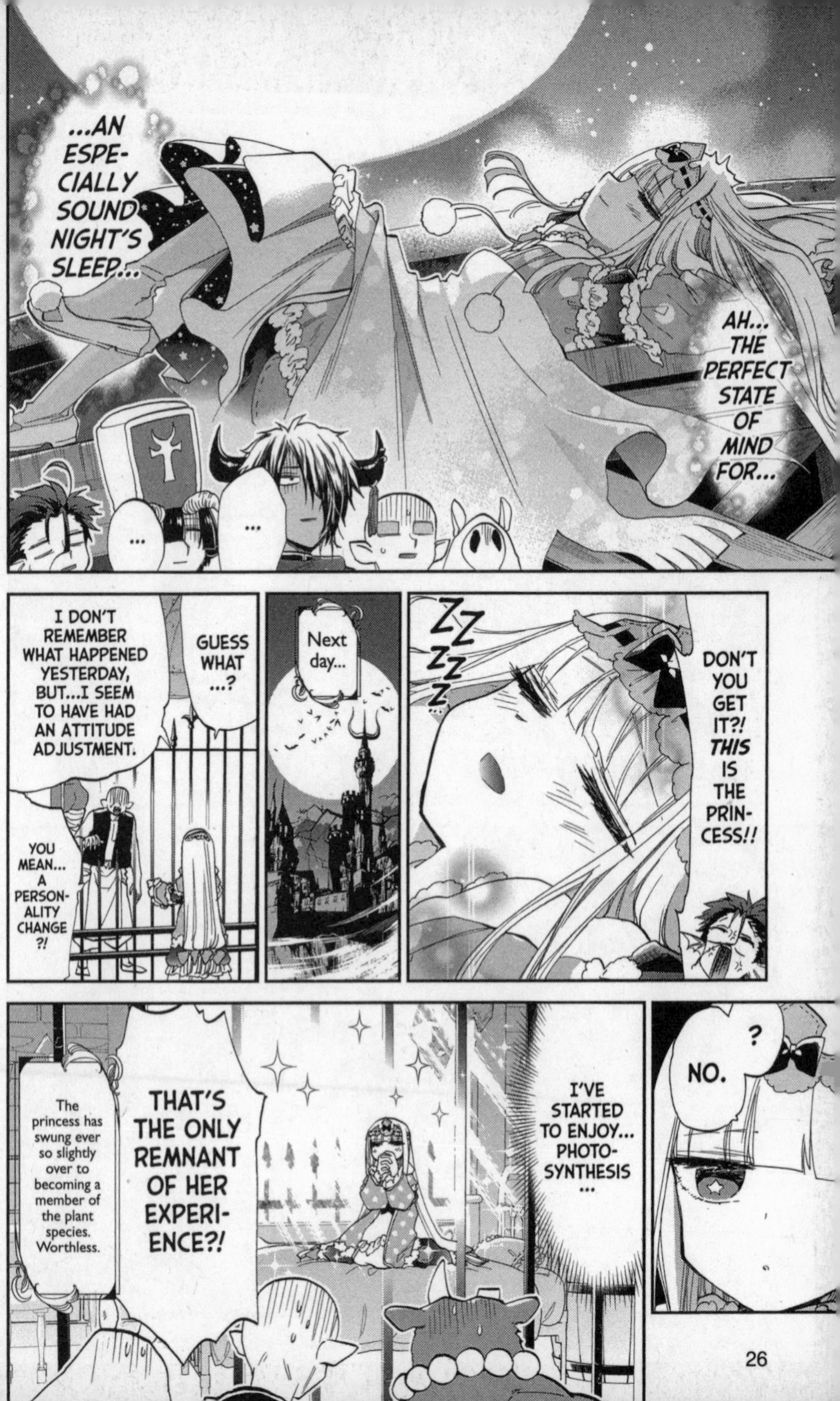
AH... THE PERFECT STATE OF MIND FOR...
...AN ESPECIALLY SOUND NIGHT'S SLEEP...
...
...
ZZZ...
DON'T YOU GET IT?! THIS IS THE PRINCESS!!
Next day...
GUESS WHAT...?
I DON'T REMEMBER WHAT HAPPENED YESTERDAY, BUT...I SEEM TO HAVE HAD AN ATTITUDE ADJUSTMENT.
YOU MEAN... A PERSONALITY CHANGE?!
?
NO.
I'VE STARTED TO ENJOY... PHOTOSYNTHESIS...
THAT'S THE ONLY REMNANT OF HER EXPERIENCE?!
The princess has swung ever so slightly over to becoming a member of the plant species. Worthless.

Mandrake Hot Pot Feast

Participation: ☆☆☆☆☆☆☆☆☆
Fillingness: ☆☆☆☆☆☆☆☆☆☆

The miso fans and the soy sauce fans are always in conflict.

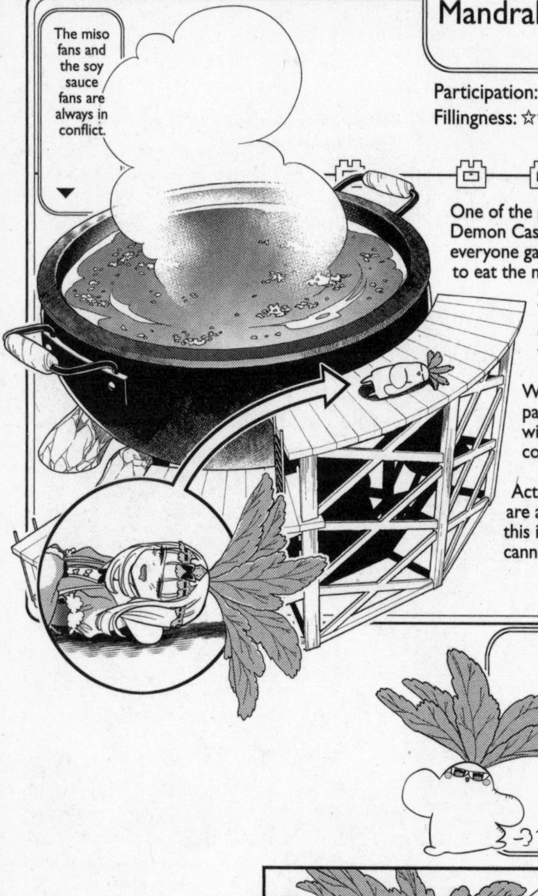

One of the periodic events held at the Demon Castle is a hot pot feast in which everyone gathers around a huge cauldron to eat the mandrakes that have been grown on the Demon Castle grounds. The purpose of this traditional event is to build community through a shared meal.

When a human accidentally took part in the event, the demons witnessed the side effects of cooked mandrake poisoning.

Actually, specieswise, mandrakes are a relative of Neo-Alraune, so this is actually a seriously cannibalistic party. Scary!

!Warning!

The mandrake that was pulled out of the princess's head has gone missing. It is possibly ambulatory and dangerous.

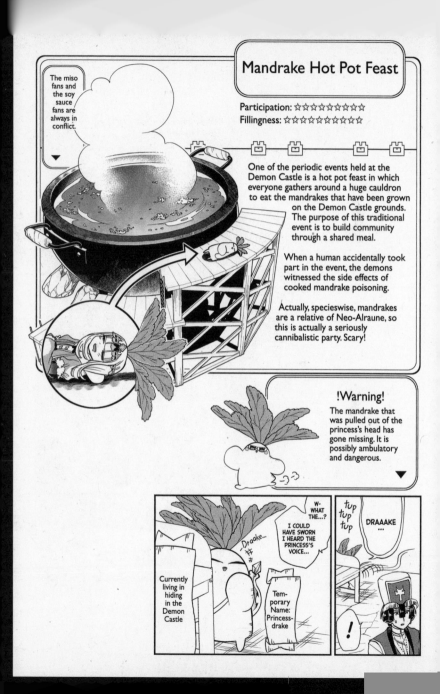

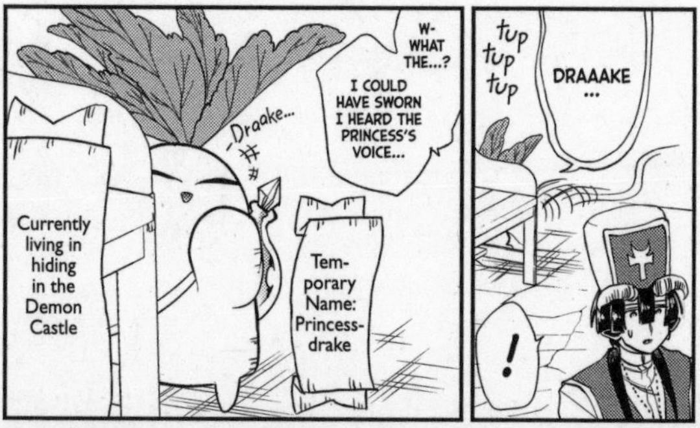
tup tup tup
DRAAAKE...
!
W-WHAT THE...?
I COULD HAVE SWORN I HEARD THE PRINCESS'S VOICE...
Draake...
Currently living in hiding in the Demon Castle
Temporary Name: Princess-drake

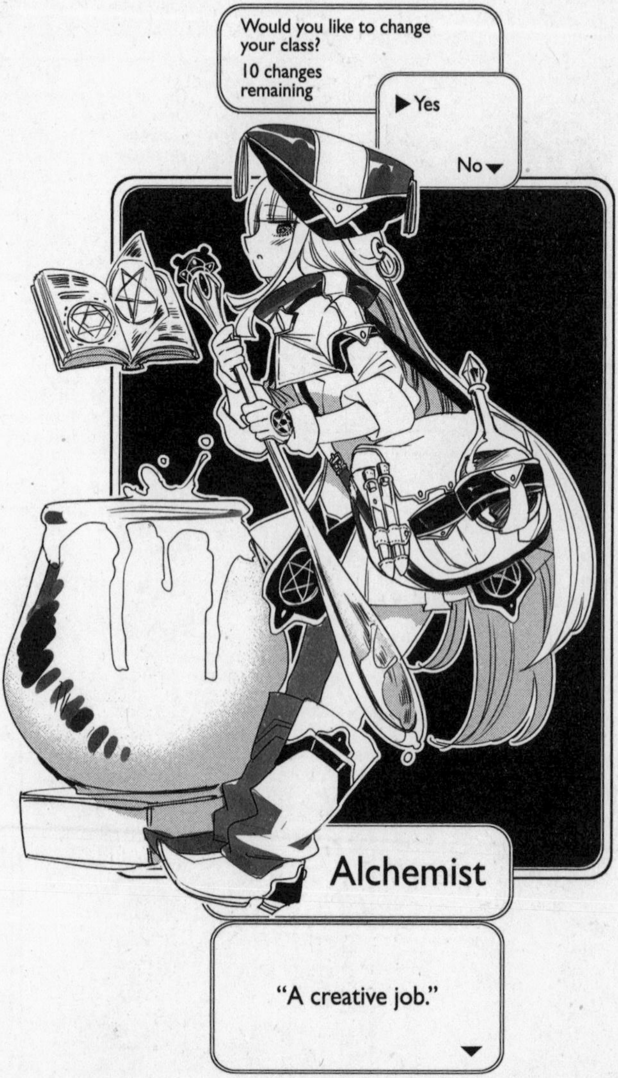

Would you like to change your class?
10 changes remaining
▶Yes
No
Alchemist
"A creative job."

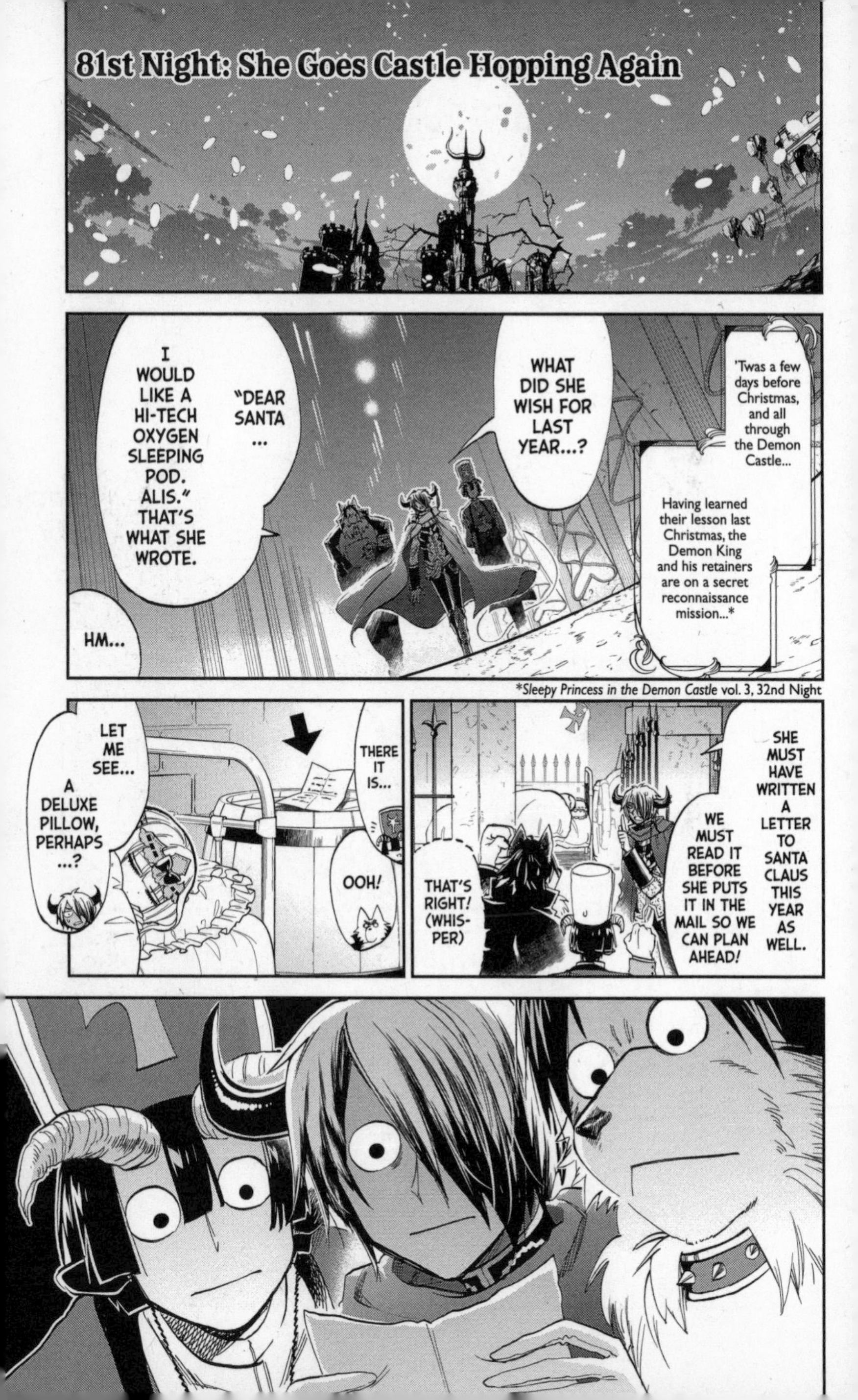
81st Night: She Goes Castle Hopping Again
'Twas a few days before Christmas, and all through the Demon Castle...
Having learned their lesson last Christmas, the Demon King and his retainers are on a secret reconnaissance mission...*
WHAT DID SHE WISH FOR LAST YEAR...?
"DEAR SANTA ...
I WOULD LIKE A HI-TECH OXYGEN SLEEPING POD. ALIS." THAT'S WHAT SHE WROTE.
HM...
SHE MUST HAVE WRITTEN A LETTER TO SANTA CLAUS THIS YEAR AS WELL.
WE MUST READ IT BEFORE SHE PUTS IT IN THE MAIL SO WE CAN PLAN AHEAD!
THAT'S RIGHT! (WHIS-PER)
THERE IT IS...
OOH!
LET ME SEE... A DELUXE PILLOW, PERHAPS ...?
**Sleepy Princess in the Demon Castle* vol. 3, 32nd Night

81st Night: She Goes Castle Hopping Again

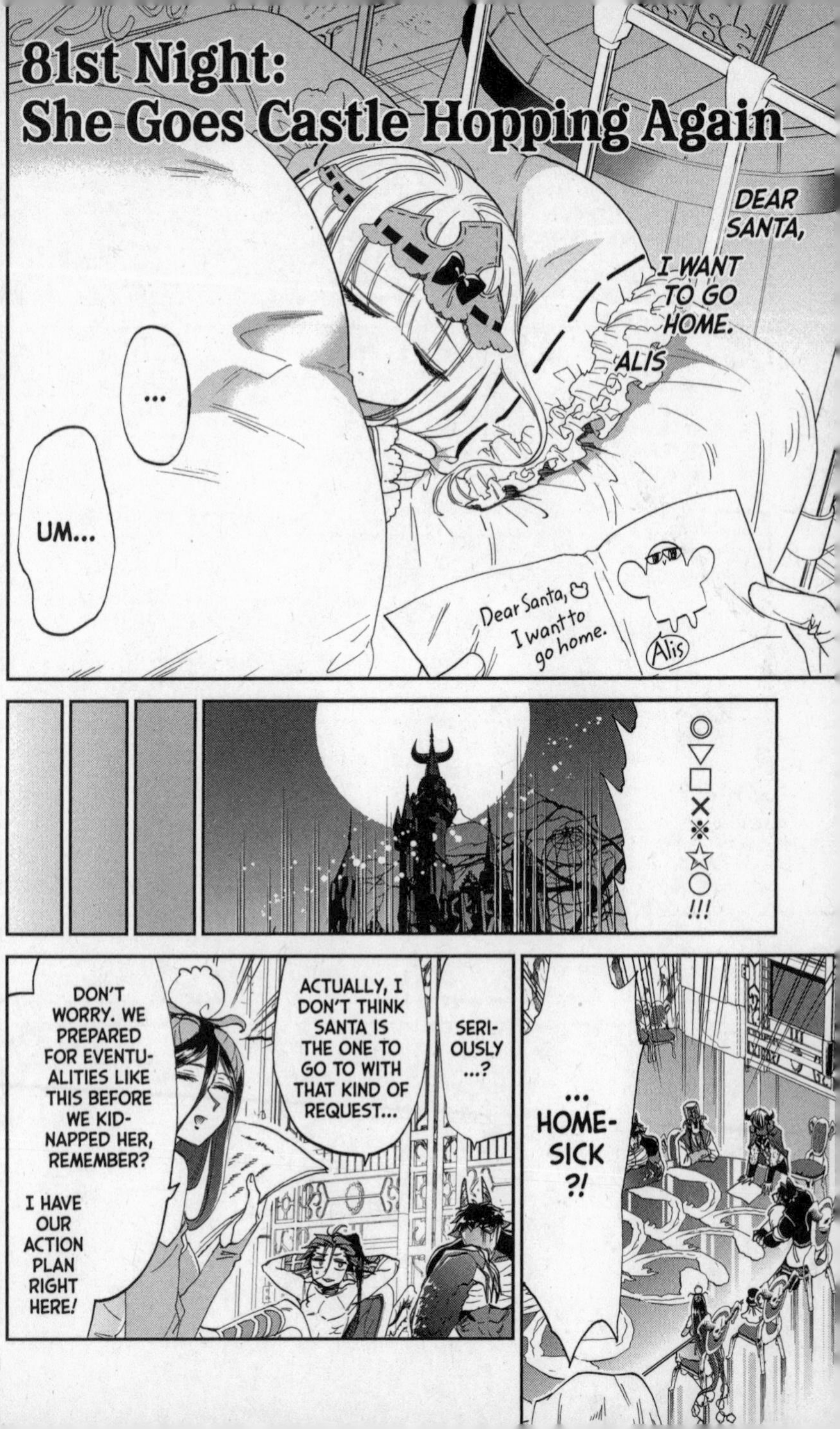
DEAR SANTA,
I WANT TO GO HOME.
ALIS
Dear Santa, I want to go home.
Alis
...
UM...
◎▽□×※☆○!!!
... HOME-SICK?!
SERI-OUSLY...?
ACTUALLY, I DON'T THINK SANTA IS THE ONE TO GO TO WITH THAT KIND OF REQUEST...
DON'T WORRY. WE PREPARED FOR EVENTU-ALITIES LIKE THIS BEFORE WE KID-NAPPED HER, REMEMBER?
I HAVE OUR ACTION PLAN RIGHT HERE!

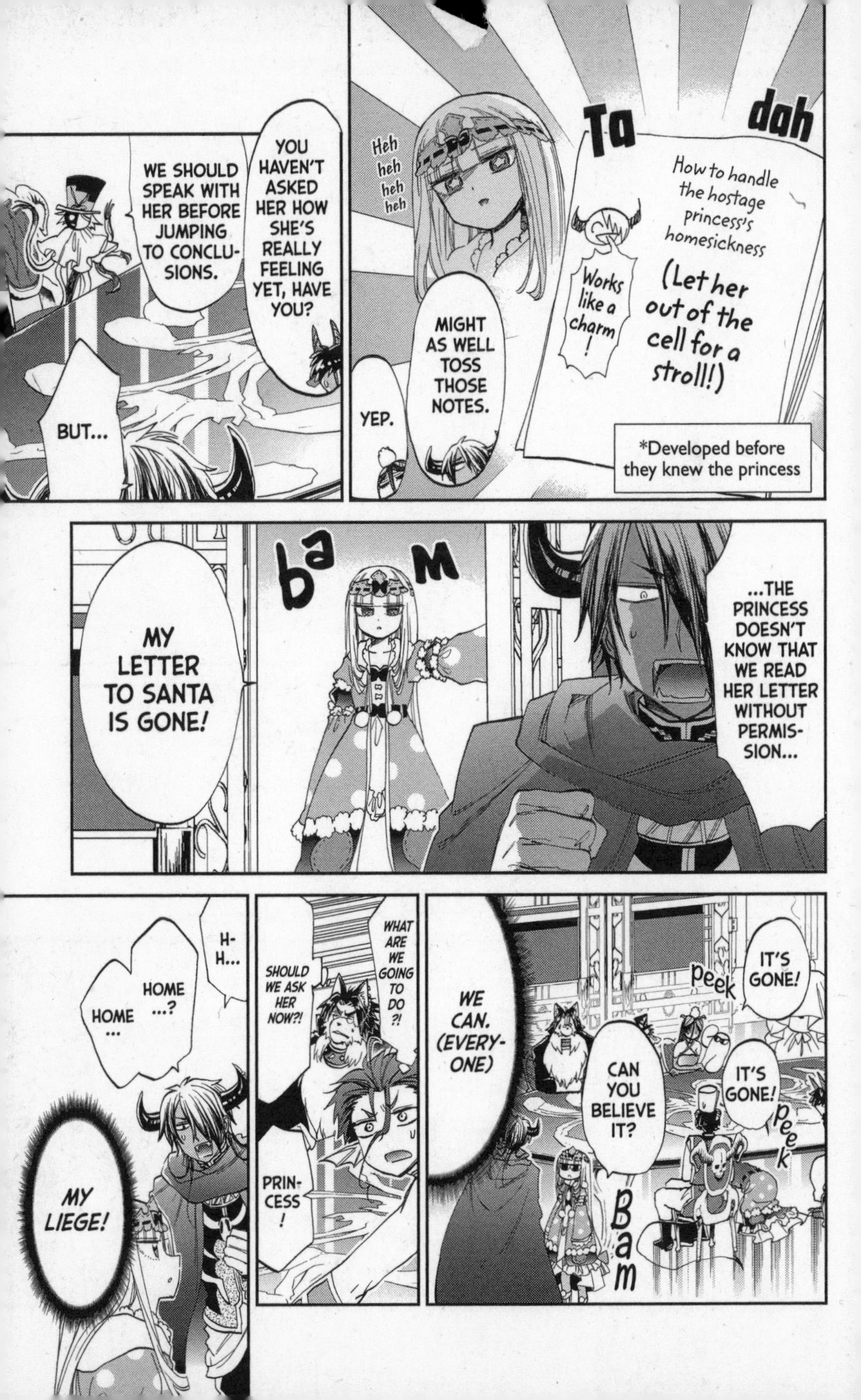
Ta dah
How to handle the hostage princess's homesickness
(Let her out of the cell for a stroll!)
Works like a charm!
Heh heh heh heh
MIGHT AS WELL TOSS THOSE NOTES.
YEP.
*Developed before they knew the princess
YOU HAVEN'T ASKED HER HOW SHE'S REALLY FEELING YET, HAVE YOU?
WE SHOULD SPEAK WITH HER BEFORE JUMPING TO CONCLUSIONS.
BUT...
...THE PRINCESS DOESN'T KNOW THAT WE READ HER LETTER WITHOUT PERMISSION...
baM
MY LETTER TO SANTA IS GONE!
IT'S GONE!
peek
IT'S GONE!
peek
CAN YOU BELIEVE IT?
Bam
WE CAN. (EVERYONE)
WHAT ARE WE GOING TO DO?!
SHOULD WE ASK HER NOW?!
PRINCESS!
H-H...
HOME...?
HOME...
MY LIEGE!

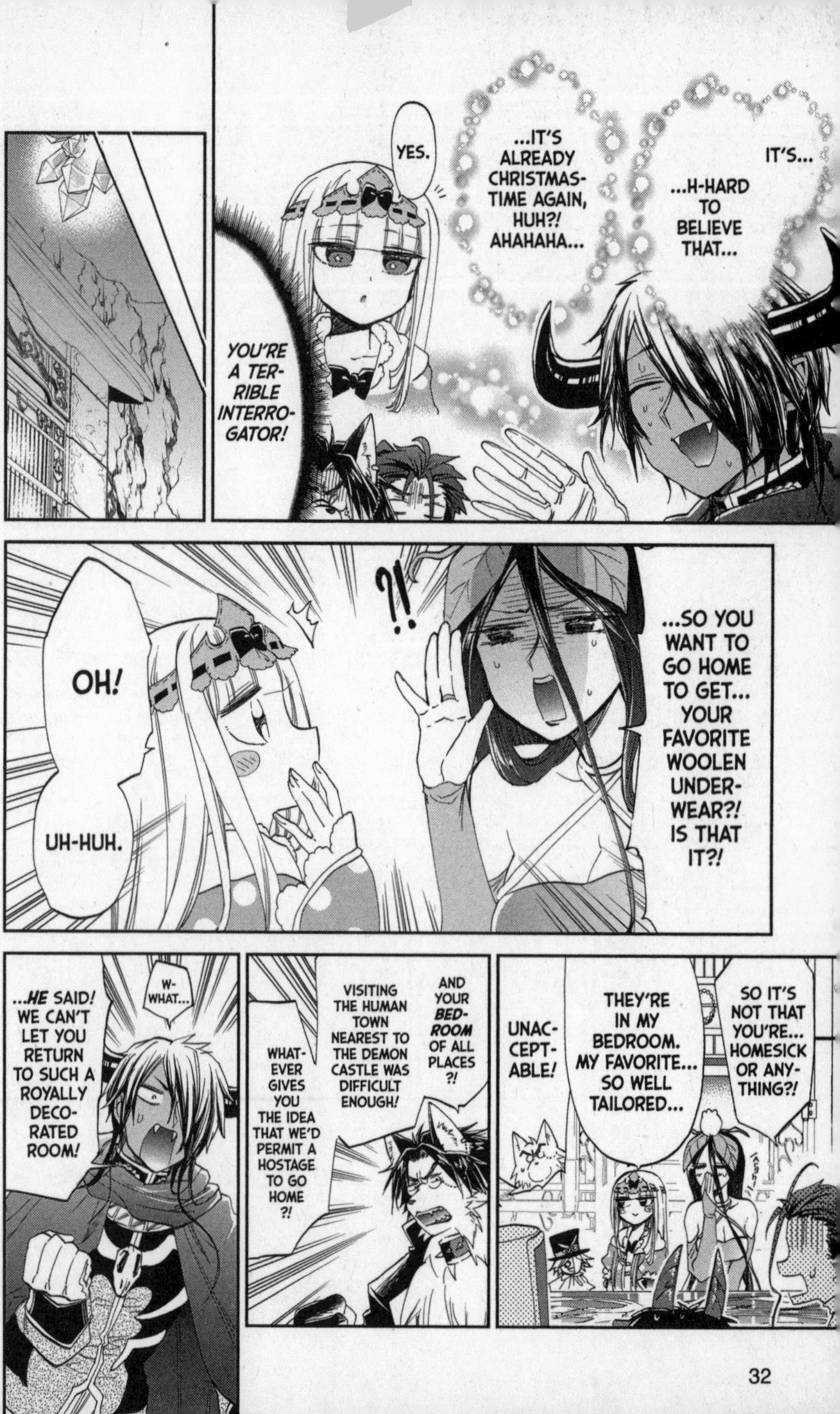
IT'S...
...H-HARD TO BELIEVE THAT...
...IT'S ALREADY CHRISTMAS-TIME AGAIN, HUH?! AHAHAHA...
YES.
YOU'RE A TERRIBLE INTERROGATOR!
...SO YOU WANT TO GO HOME TO GET... YOUR FAVORITE WOOLEN UNDERWEAR?! IS THAT IT?!
?!
OH!
UH-HUH.
SO IT'S NOT THAT YOU'RE... HOMESICK OR ANYTHING?!
THEY'RE IN MY BEDROOM. MY FAVORITE... SO WELL TAILORED...
UNACCEPTABLE!
AND YOUR BEDROOM OF ALL PLACES?!
VISITING THE HUMAN TOWN NEAREST TO THE DEMON CASTLE WAS DIFFICULT ENOUGH!
WHATEVER GIVES YOU THE IDEA THAT WE'D PERMIT A HOSTAGE TO GO HOME?!
W-WHAT...
...HE SAID! WE CAN'T LET YOU RETURN TO SUCH A ROYALLY DECORATED ROOM!

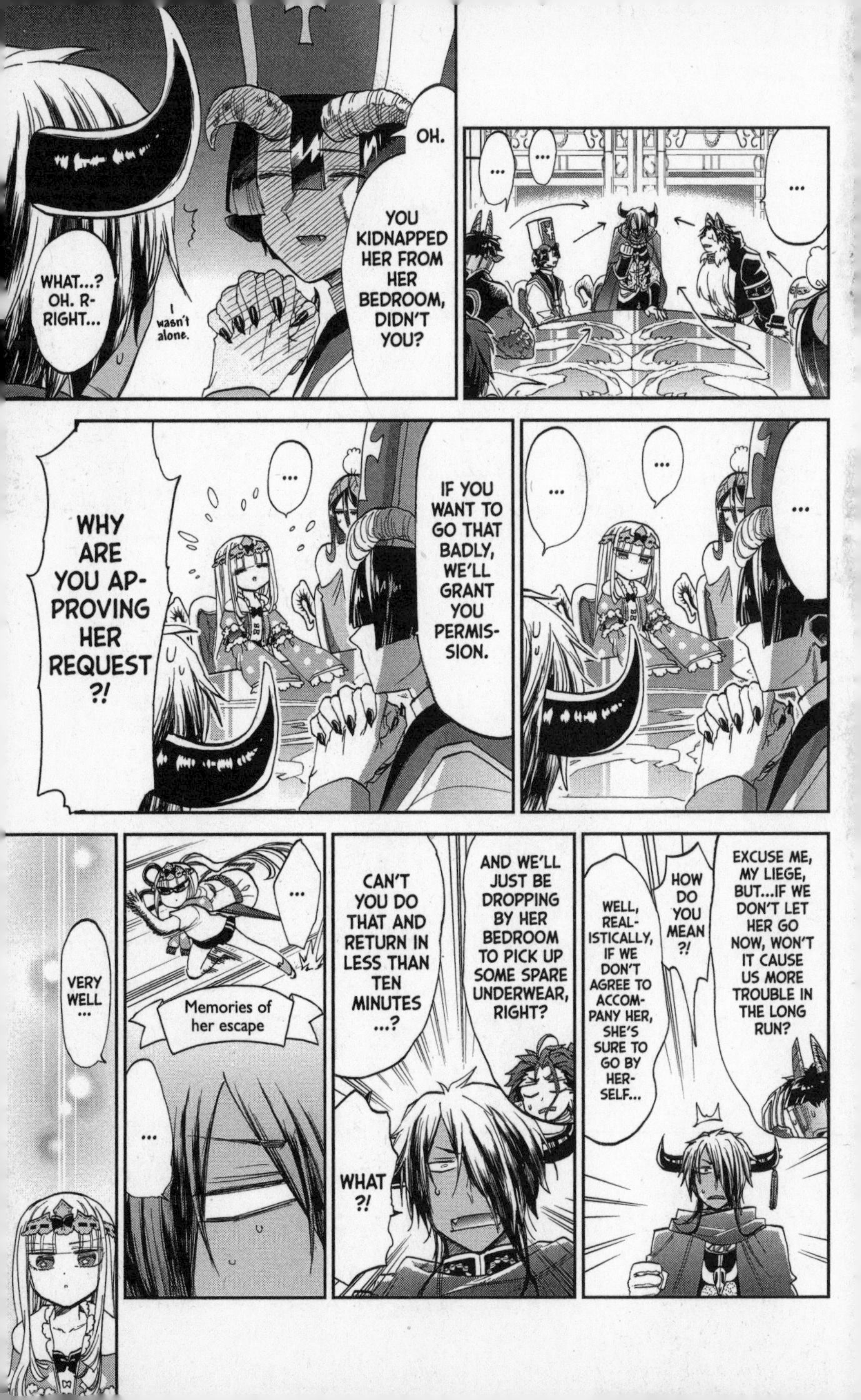
...
...
...
OH.
YOU KIDNAPPED HER FROM HER BEDROOM, DIDN'T YOU?
I wasn't alone.
WHAT...? OH. R-RIGHT...
...
...
...
IF YOU WANT TO GO THAT BADLY, WE'LL GRANT YOU PERMISSION.
...
WHY ARE YOU APPROVING HER REQUEST?!
EXCUSE ME, MY LIEGE, BUT...IF WE DON'T LET HER GO NOW, WON'T IT CAUSE US MORE TROUBLE IN THE LONG RUN?
HOW DO YOU MEAN?!
WELL, REALISTICALLY, IF WE DON'T AGREE TO ACCOMPANY HER, SHE'S SURE TO GO BY HERSELF...
AND WE'LL JUST BE DROPPING BY HER BEDROOM TO PICK UP SOME SPARE UNDERWEAR, RIGHT?
CAN'T YOU DO THAT AND RETURN IN LESS THAN TEN MINUTES...?
WHAT?!
...
Memories of her escape
...
VERY WELL...

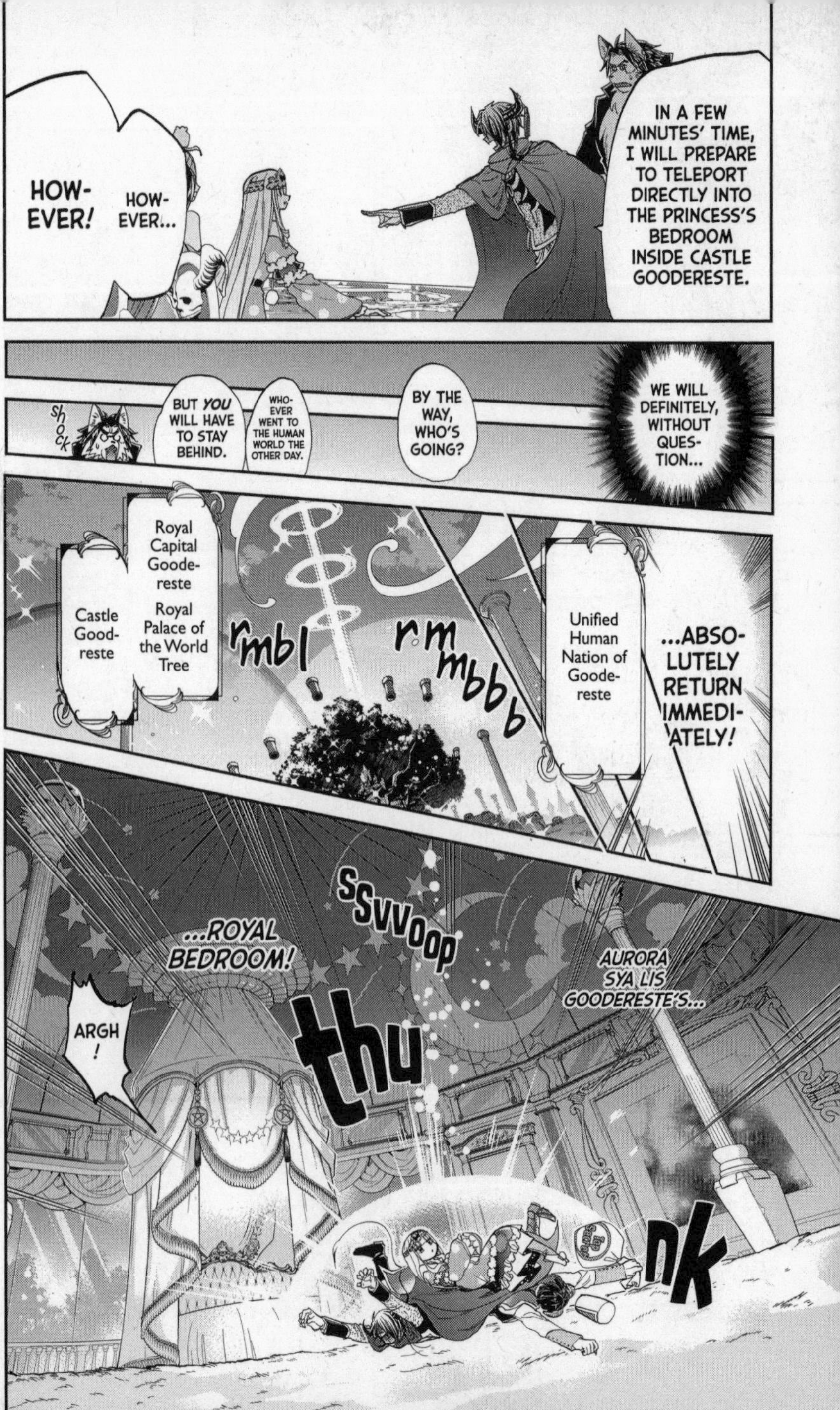
IN A FEW MINUTES' TIME, I WILL PREPARE TO TELEPORT DIRECTLY INTO THE PRINCESS'S BEDROOM INSIDE CASTLE GOODERESTE.
HOW-EVER...
HOW-EVER!
WE WILL DEFINITELY, WITHOUT QUES-TION...
BY THE WAY, WHO'S GOING?
WHO-EVER WENT TO THE HUMAN WORLD THE OTHER DAY.
BUT *YOU* WILL HAVE TO STAY BEHIND.
shock
...ABSO-LUTELY RETURN IMMEDI-ATELY!
Unified Human Nation of Goode-reste
rmmbbb
rmbl
Royal Capital Goode-reste
Royal Palace of the World Tree
Castle Good-reste
AURORA SYA LIS GOODERESTE'S...
SSVVOOP
...ROYAL BEDROOM!
thunk
ARGH!

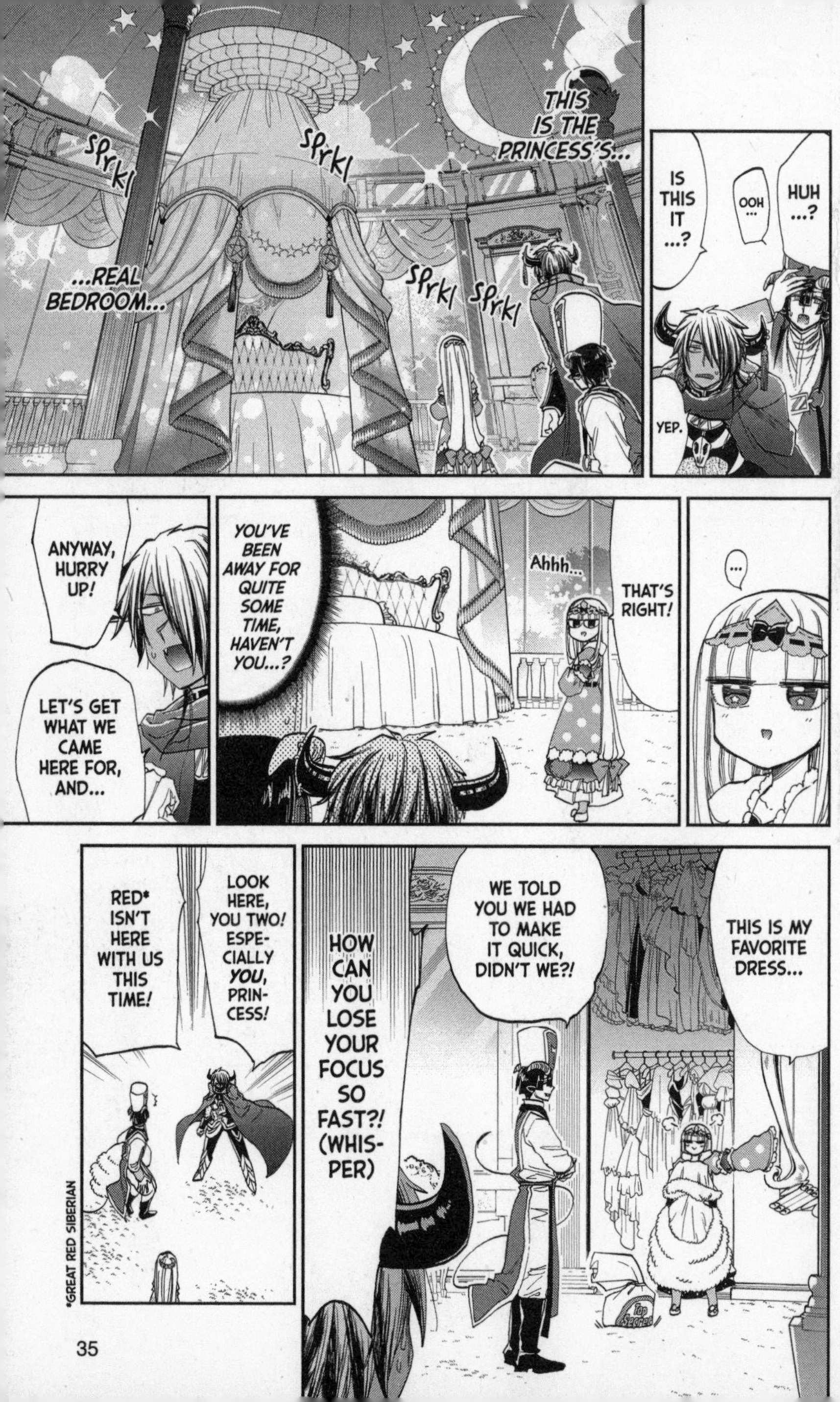
HUH ...?
OOH ...
IS THIS IT ...?
YEP.
THIS IS THE PRINCESS'S...
SPRKL
SPRKL
SPRKL SPRKL
...REAL BEDROOM...
...
THAT'S RIGHT!
Ahhh...
YOU'VE BEEN AWAY FOR QUITE SOME TIME, HAVEN'T YOU...?
ANYWAY, HURRY UP!
LET'S GET WHAT WE CAME HERE FOR, AND...
THIS IS MY FAVORITE DRESS...
WE TOLD YOU WE HAD TO MAKE IT QUICK, DIDN'T WE?!
HOW CAN YOU LOSE YOUR FOCUS SO FAST?! (WHISPER)
LOOK HERE, YOU TWO! ESPECIALLY *YOU*, PRINCESS!
RED* ISN'T HERE WITH US THIS TIME!

*GREAT RED SIBERIAN

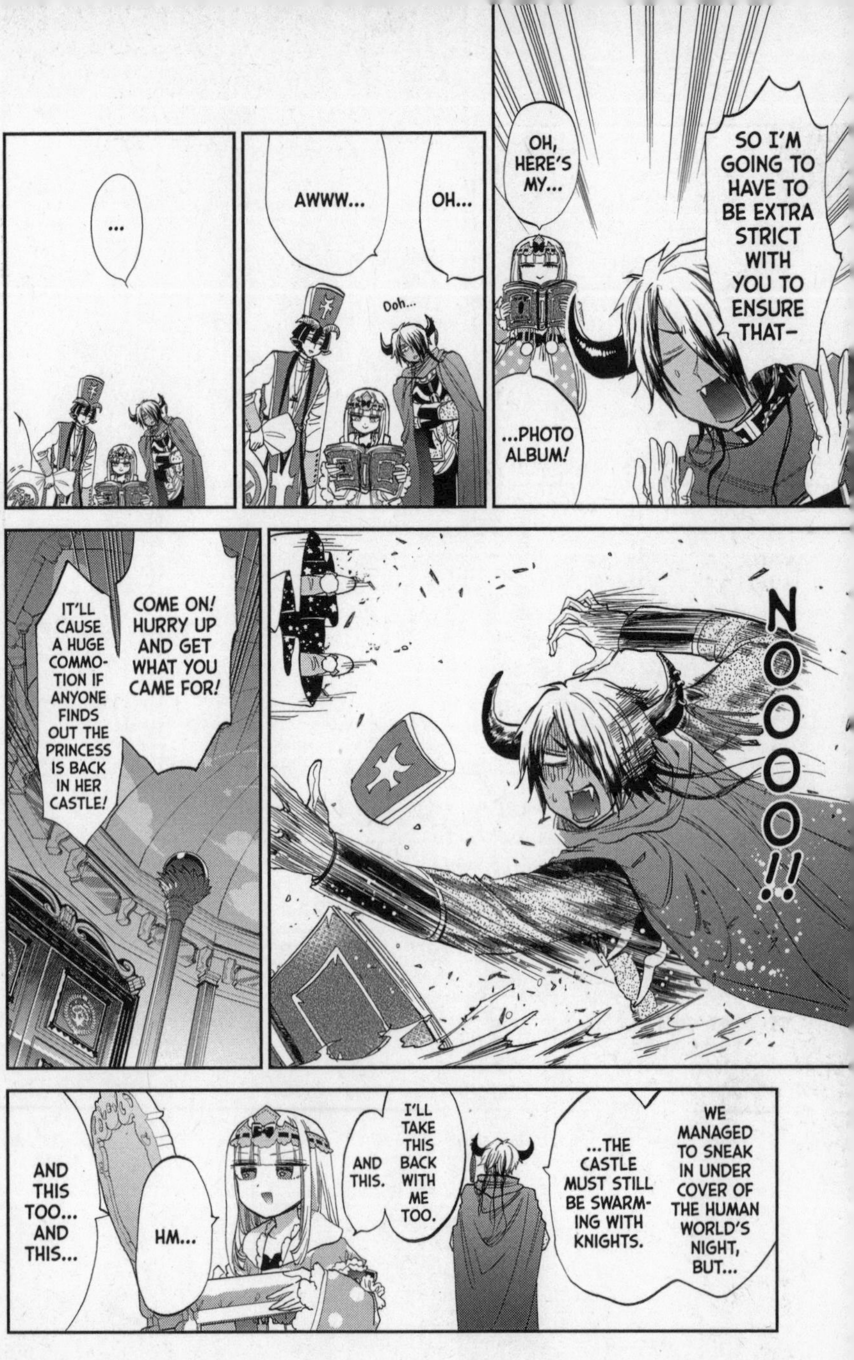
SO I'M GOING TO HAVE TO BE EXTRA STRICT WITH YOU TO ENSURE THAT—
OH, HERE'S MY...
...PHOTO ALBUM!
OH...
AWWW...
Ooh...
...
NOOOOO!!
COME ON! HURRY UP AND GET WHAT YOU CAME FOR!
IT'LL CAUSE A HUGE COMMOTION IF ANYONE FINDS OUT THE PRINCESS IS BACK IN HER CASTLE!
WE MANAGED TO SNEAK IN UNDER COVER OF THE HUMAN WORLD'S NIGHT, BUT...
...THE CASTLE MUST STILL BE SWARMING WITH KNIGHTS.
I'LL TAKE THIS BACK WITH ME TOO.
AND THIS.
HM...
AND THIS TOO... AND THIS...

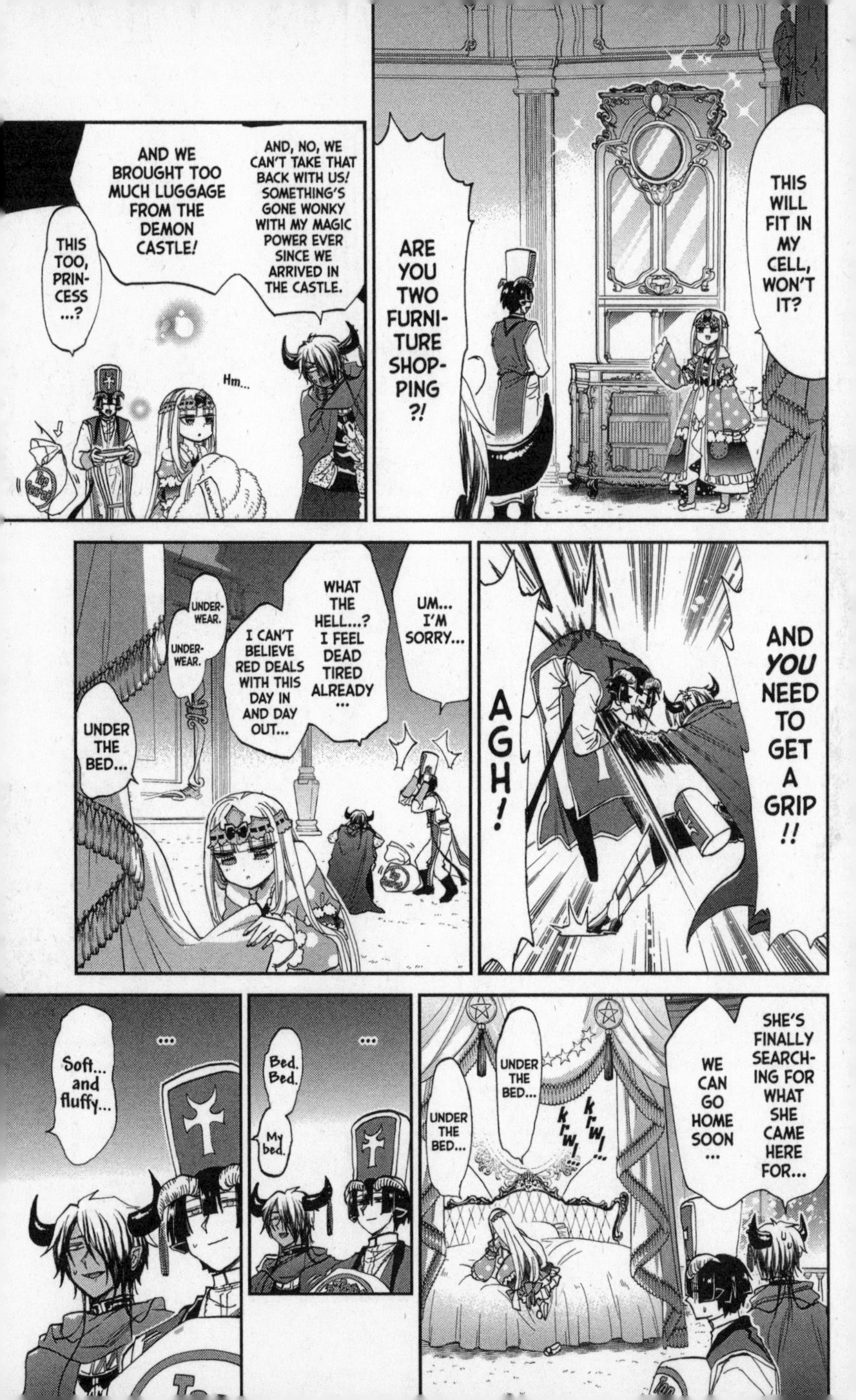
THIS WILL FIT IN MY CELL, WON'T IT?
ARE YOU TWO FURNITURE SHOPPING?!
AND, NO, WE CAN'T TAKE THAT BACK WITH US! SOMETHING'S GONE WONKY WITH MY MAGIC POWER EVER SINCE WE ARRIVED IN THE CASTLE.
AND WE BROUGHT TOO MUCH LUGGAGE FROM THE DEMON CASTLE!
THIS TOO, PRINCESS...?
Hm...
AND YOU NEED TO GET A GRIP!!
AGH!
UM... I'M SORRY...
WHAT THE HELL...? I FEEL DEAD TIRED ALREADY...
I CAN'T BELIEVE RED DEALS WITH THIS DAY IN AND DAY OUT...
UNDERWEAR.
UNDERWEAR.
UNDER THE BED...
SHE'S FINALLY SEARCHING FOR WHAT SHE CAME HERE FOR...
WE CAN GO HOME SOON...
krwl krwl...
UNDER THE BED...
UNDER THE BED...
...
Bed. Bed.
My bed.
...
Soft... and fluffy...

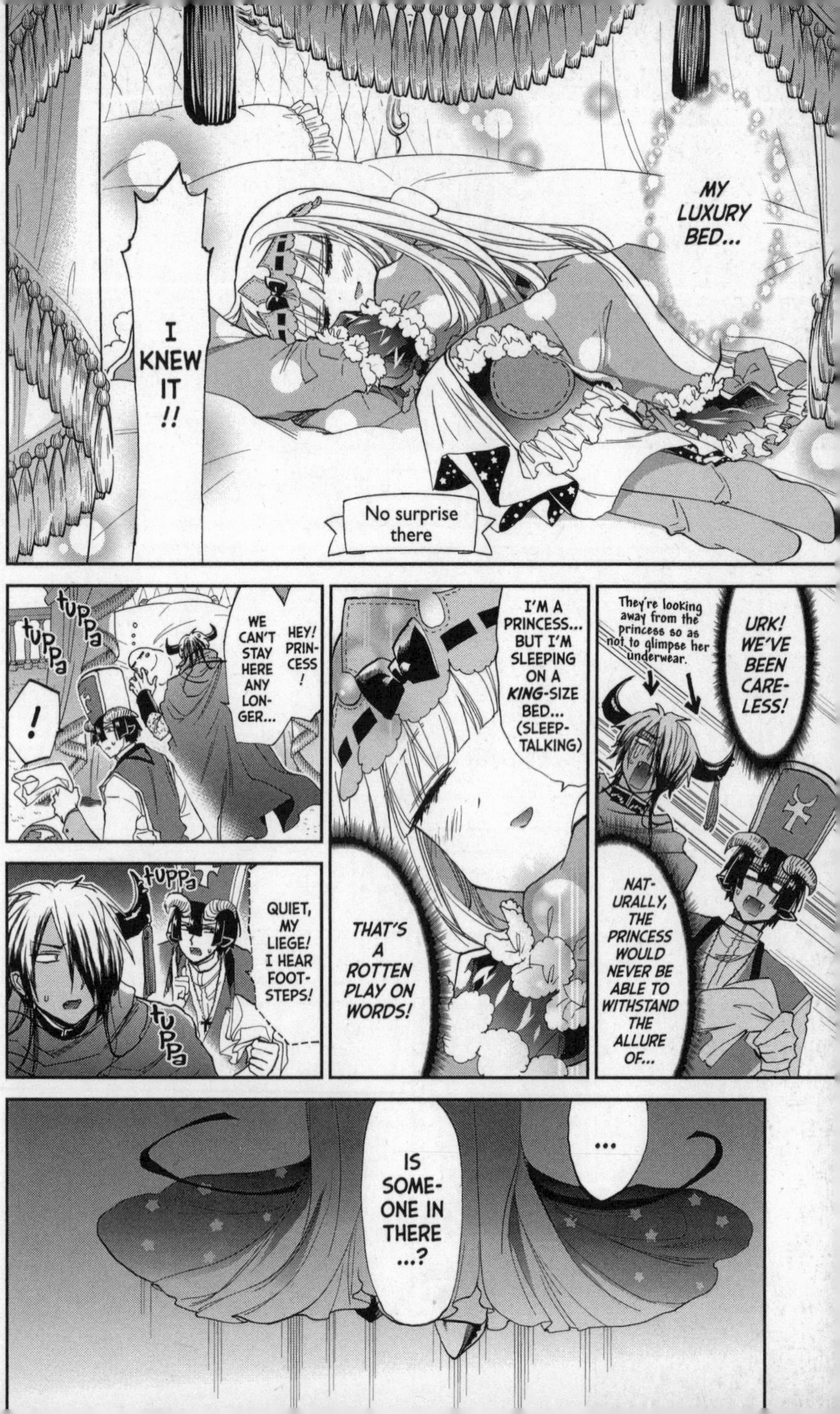
MY LUXURY BED...
I KNEW IT!!
No surprise there
URK! WE'VE BEEN CARE-LESS!
They're looking away from the princess so as not to glimpse her underwear.
NAT-URALLY, THE PRINCESS WOULD NEVER BE ABLE TO WITHSTAND THE ALLURE OF...
I'M A PRINCESS... BUT I'M SLEEPING ON A *KING*-SIZE BED... (SLEEP-TALKING)
THAT'S A ROTTEN PLAY ON WORDS!
HEY! PRIN-CESS!
WE CAN'T STAY HERE ANY LON-GER...
tuppa
tuppa
...
!
QUIET, MY LIEGE! I HEAR FOOT-STEPS!
tuppa
tuppa
...
IS SOME-ONE IN THERE ...?

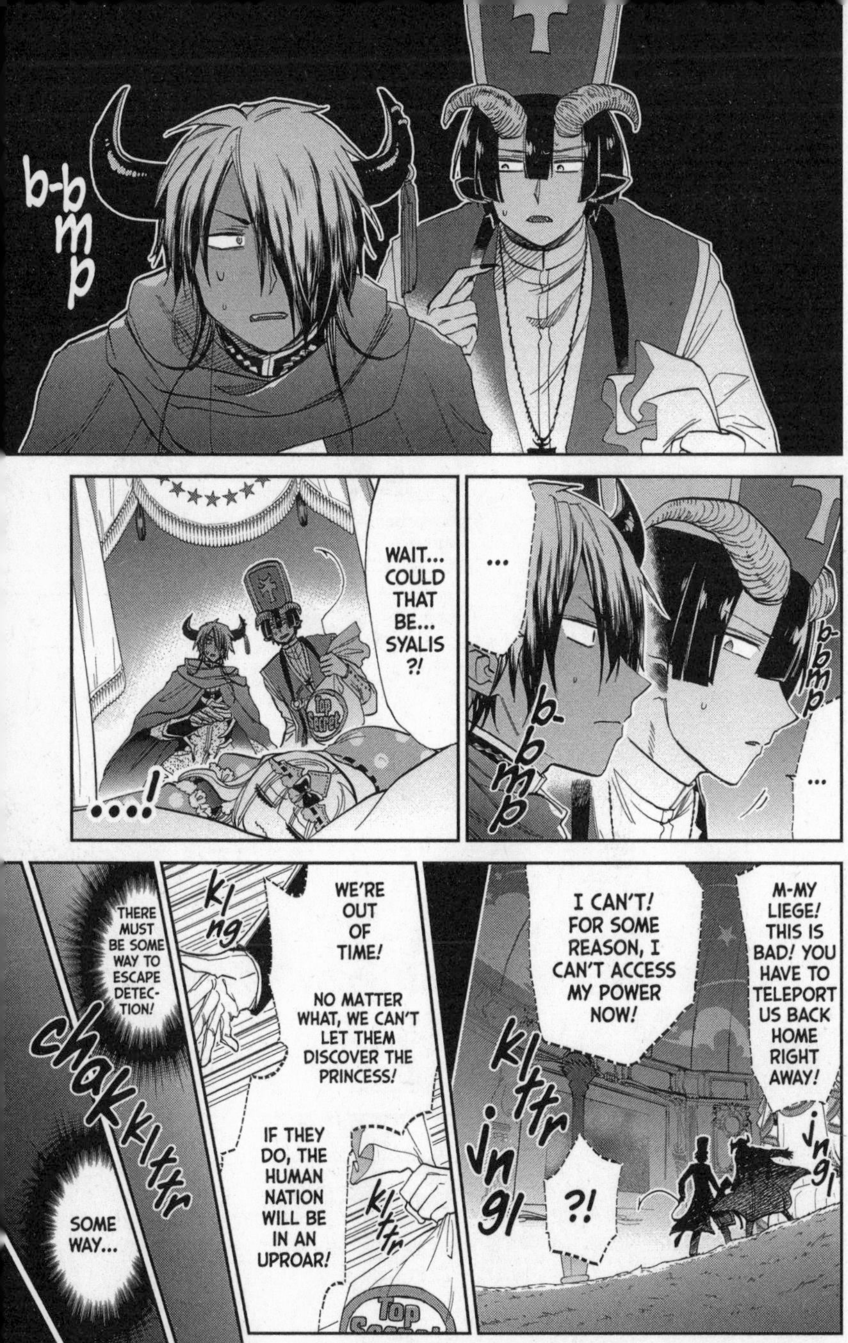
b-bmp
...
b-bmp
b-bmp
...
WAIT... COULD THAT BE... SYALIS?!
...!
M-MY LIEGE! THIS IS BAD! YOU HAVE TO TELEPORT US BACK HOME RIGHT AWAY!
I CAN'T! FOR SOME REASON, I CAN'T ACCESS MY POWER NOW!
jngl
?!
klttr
jngl
WE'RE OUT OF TIME!
NO MATTER WHAT, WE CAN'T LET THEM DISCOVER THE PRINCESS!
klng
IF THEY DO, THE HUMAN NATION WILL BE IN AN UPROAR!
klttr
THERE MUST BE SOME WAY TO ESCAPE DETECTION!
chakklttr
SOME WAY...

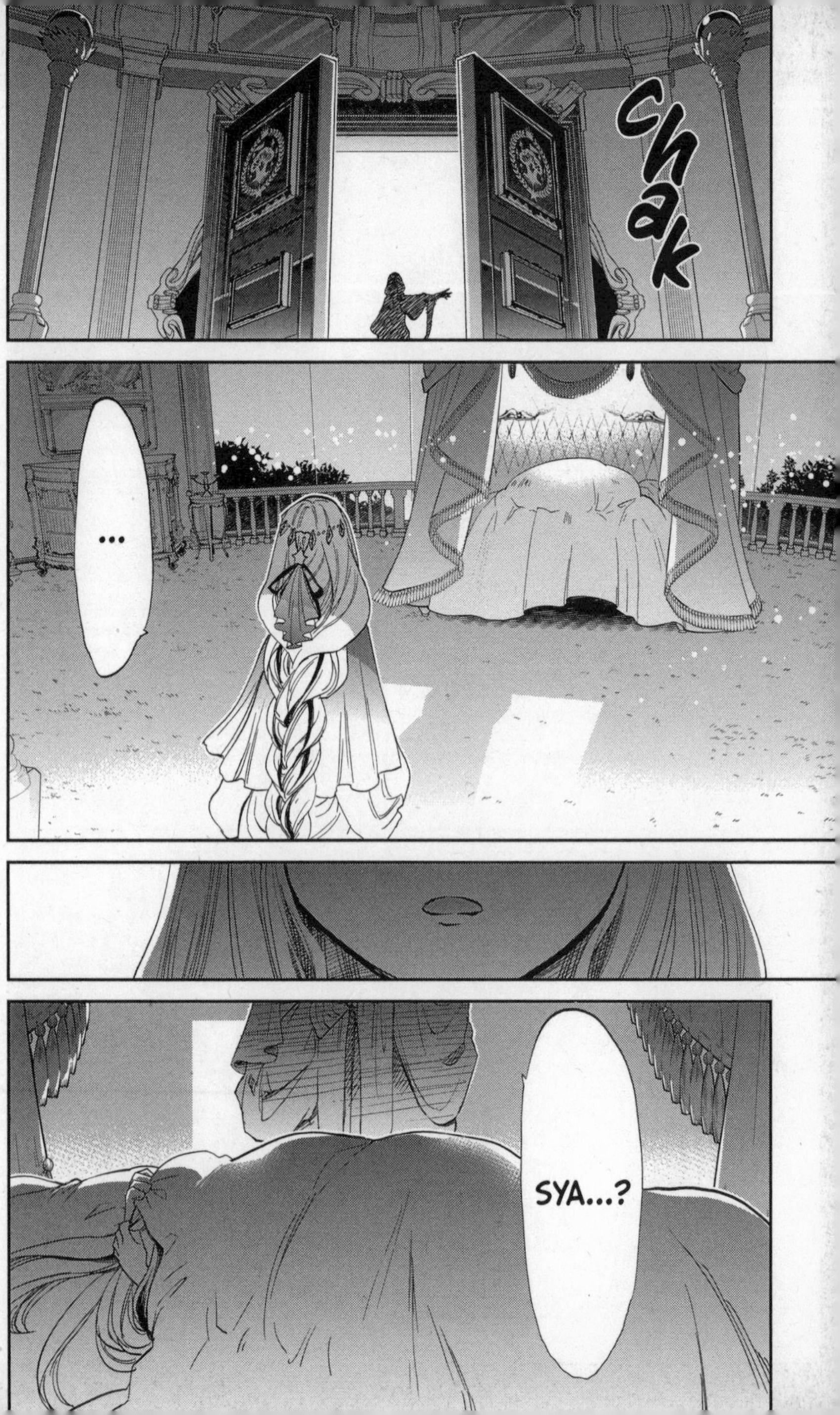
Chak
...
SYA...?

Princess Aurora Sya Lis Goodereste's Bedroom

Quality of Sleep: ☆☆☆☆☆☆☆☆☆
Luxuriousness: ☆☆☆☆☆☆☆☆☆☆☆

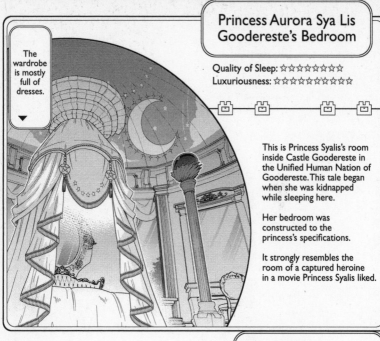

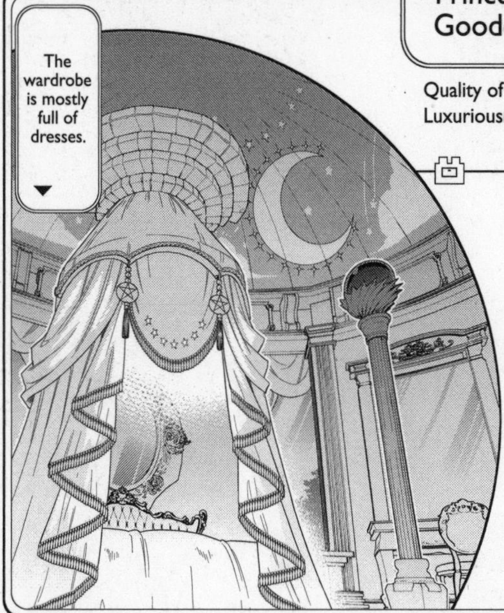
The wardrobe is mostly full of dresses.

This is Princess Syalis's room inside Castle Goodereste in the Unified Human Nation of Goodereste. This tale began when she was kidnapped while sleeping here.

Her bedroom was constructed to the princess's specifications.

It strongly resembles the room of a captured heroine in a movie Princess Syalis liked.

Former problem:
"I should have asked them to create a hidden chamber or something."

Problem a few years later:
"I wish my life were like that movie."

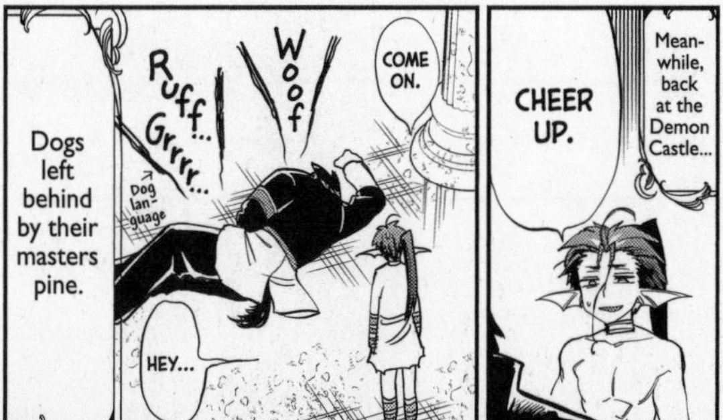
Meanwhile, back at the Demon Castle...
CHEER UP.
COME ON.
Woof
Ruff...
Grrrr...
Dog language
HEY...
Dogs left behind by their masters pine.

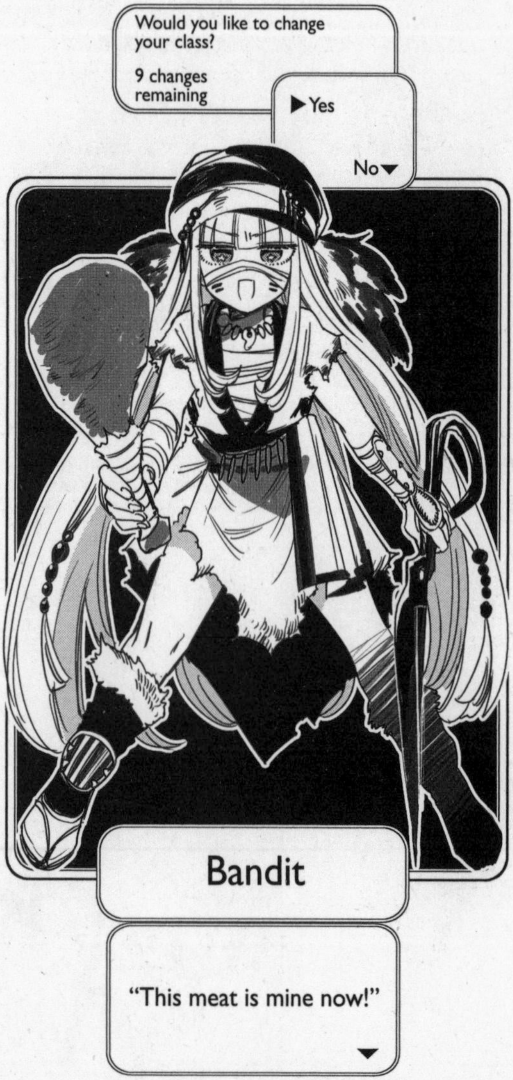
Would you like to change your class?
9 changes remaining
▶Yes
No▼
Bandit
"This meat is mine now!"

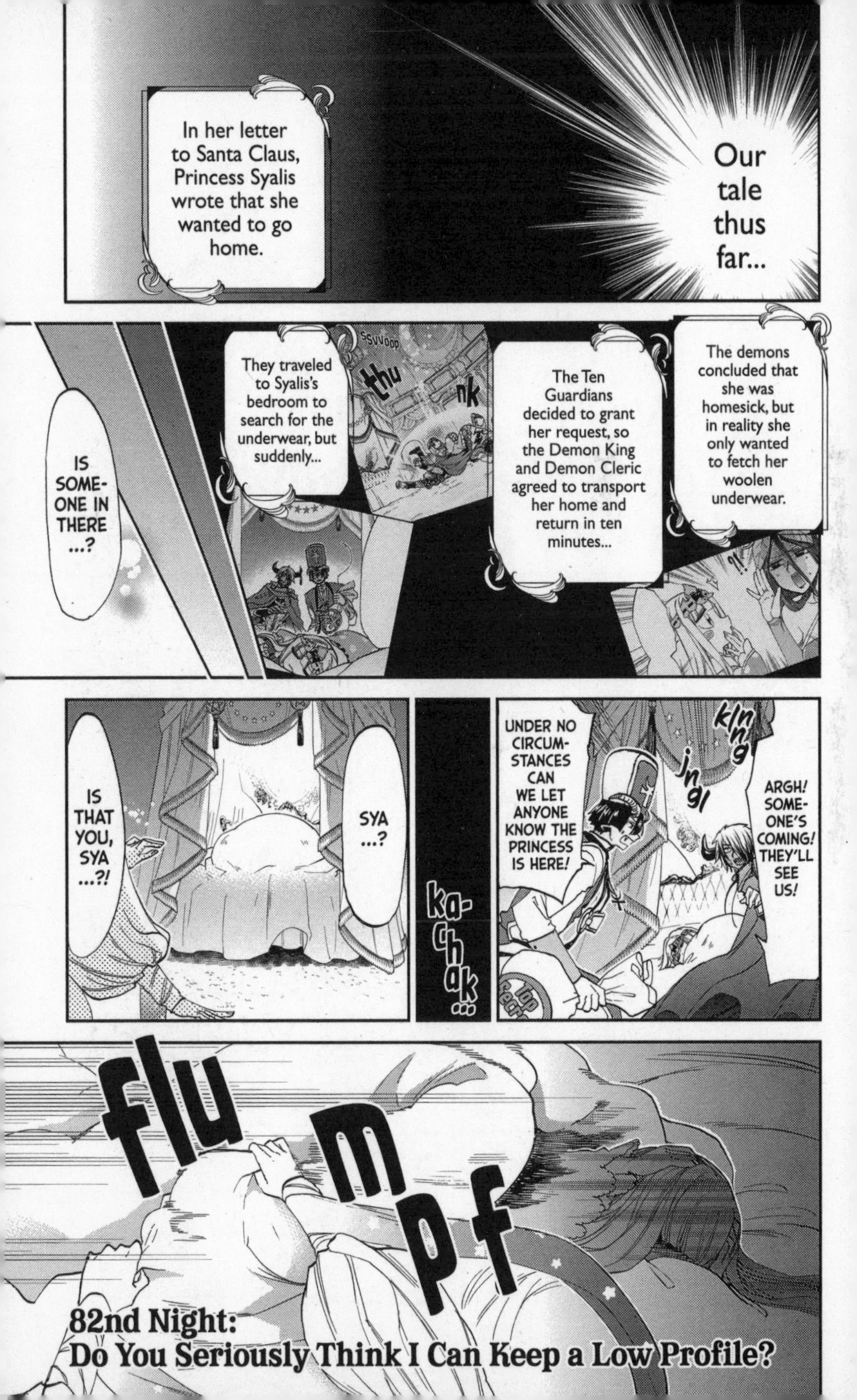
Our tale thus far...
In her letter to Santa Claus, Princess Syalis wrote that she wanted to go home.
The demons concluded that she was homesick, but in reality she only wanted to fetch her woolen underwear.
?!
The Ten Guardians decided to grant her request, so the Demon King and Demon Cleric agreed to transport her home and return in ten minutes...
SSVVOOP
thunk
They traveled to Syalis's bedroom to search for the underwear, but suddenly...
IS SOMEONE IN THERE...?
kling
jingl
ARGH! SOMEONE'S COMING! THEY'LL SEE US!
UNDER NO CIRCUMSTANCES CAN WE LET ANYONE KNOW THE PRINCESS IS HERE!
ka-chak..
SYA...?
IS THAT YOU, SYA...?!
flumpf
82nd Night:
Do You Seriously Think I Can Keep a Low Profile?

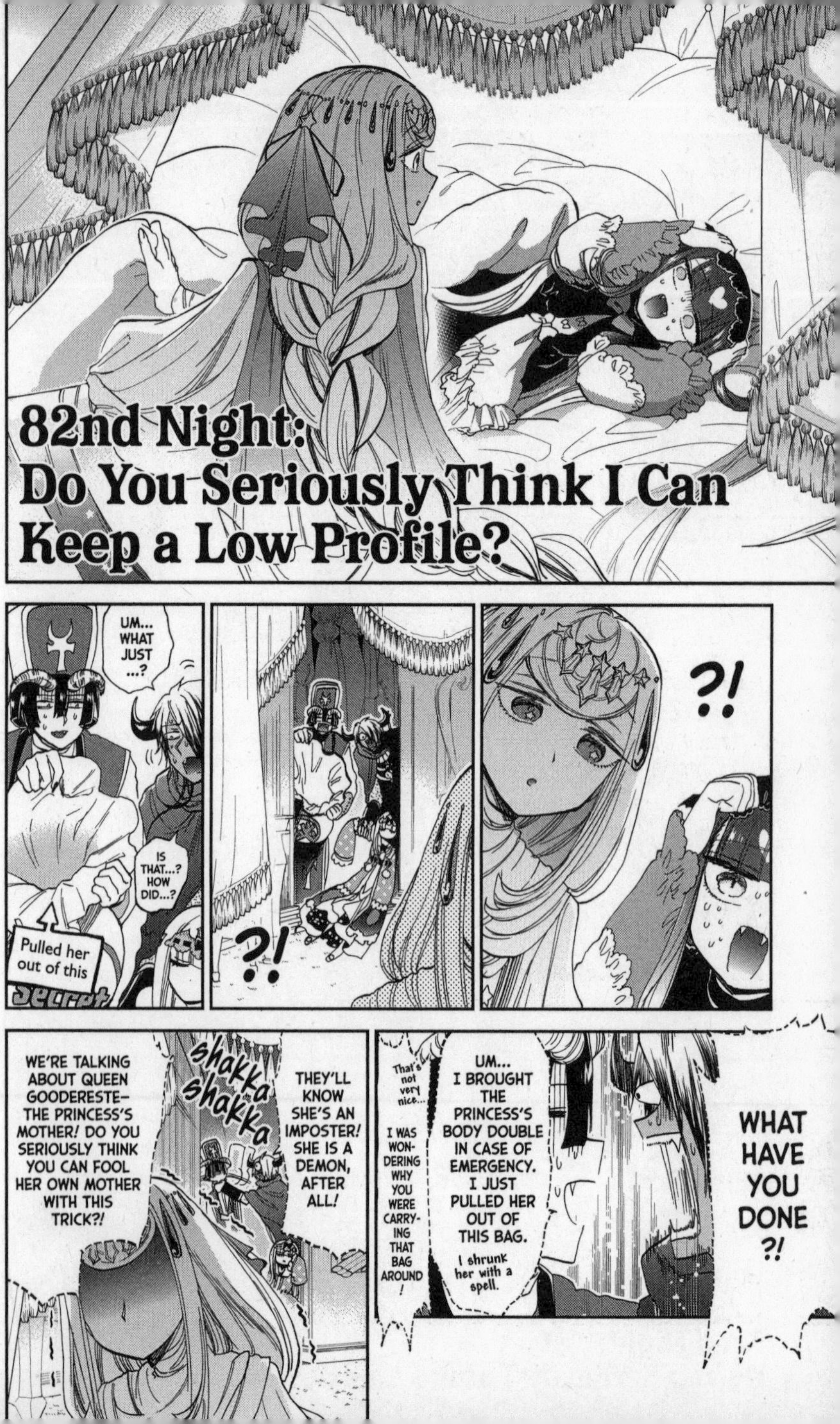
82nd Night:
Do You Seriously Think I Can Keep a Low Profile?
?!
?!
UM... WHAT JUST ...?
IS THAT...? HOW DID...?
Pulled her out of this
WHAT HAVE YOU DONE ?!
UM... I BROUGHT THE PRINCESS'S BODY DOUBLE IN CASE OF EMERGENCY. I JUST PULLED HER OUT OF THIS BAG.
I shrunk her with a spell.
That's not very nice...
I WAS WON-DERING WHY YOU WERE CARRY-ING THAT BAG AROUND!
shakka shakka
THEY'LL KNOW SHE'S AN IMPOSTER! SHE IS A DEMON, AFTER ALL!
WE'RE TALKING ABOUT QUEEN GOODERESTE—THE PRINCESS'S MOTHER! DO YOU SERIOUSLY THINK YOU CAN FOOL HER OWN MOTHER WITH THIS TRICK?!

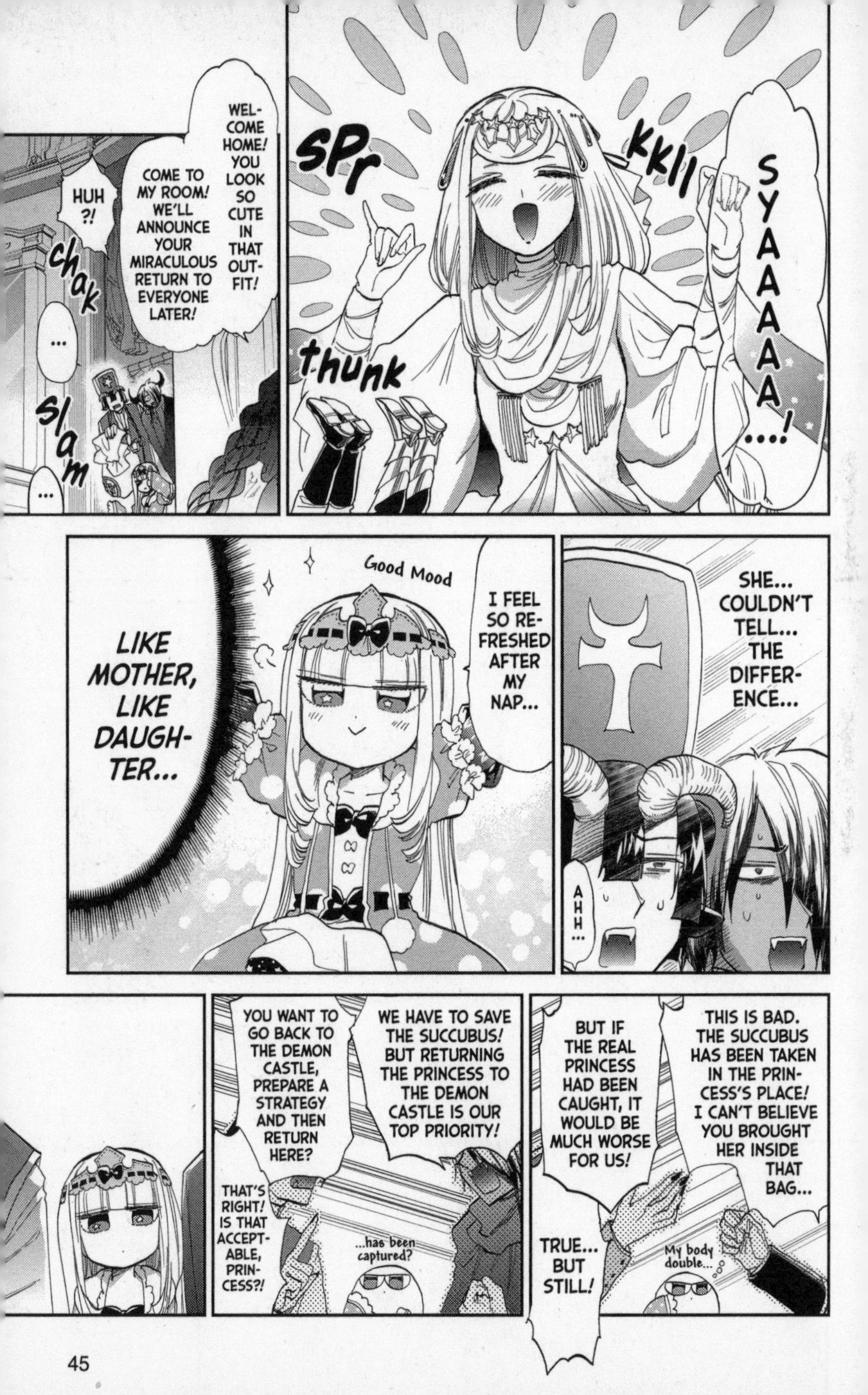
SYAAAAA...!
kkll
SPr
thunk
WEL-COME HOME! YOU LOOK SO CUTE IN THAT OUT-FIT!
COME TO MY ROOM! WE'LL ANNOUNCE YOUR MIRACULOUS RETURN TO EVERYONE LATER!
HUH?!
chak
...
slam
...
SHE... COULDN'T TELL... THE DIFFER-ENCE...
AHH...
Good Mood
I FEEL SO RE-FRESHED AFTER MY NAP...
LIKE MOTHER, LIKE DAUGH-TER...
THIS IS BAD. THE SUCCUBUS HAS BEEN TAKEN IN THE PRIN-CESS'S PLACE! I CAN'T BELIEVE YOU BROUGHT HER INSIDE THAT BAG...
BUT IF THE REAL PRINCESS HAD BEEN CAUGHT, IT WOULD BE MUCH WORSE FOR US!
TRUE... BUT STILL!
My body double...
WE HAVE TO SAVE THE SUCCUBUS! BUT RETURNING THE PRINCESS TO THE DEMON CASTLE IS OUR TOP PRIORITY!
YOU WANT TO GO BACK TO THE DEMON CASTLE, PREPARE A STRATEGY AND THEN RETURN HERE?
...has been captured?
THAT'S RIGHT! IS THAT ACCEPT-ABLE, PRIN-CESS?!

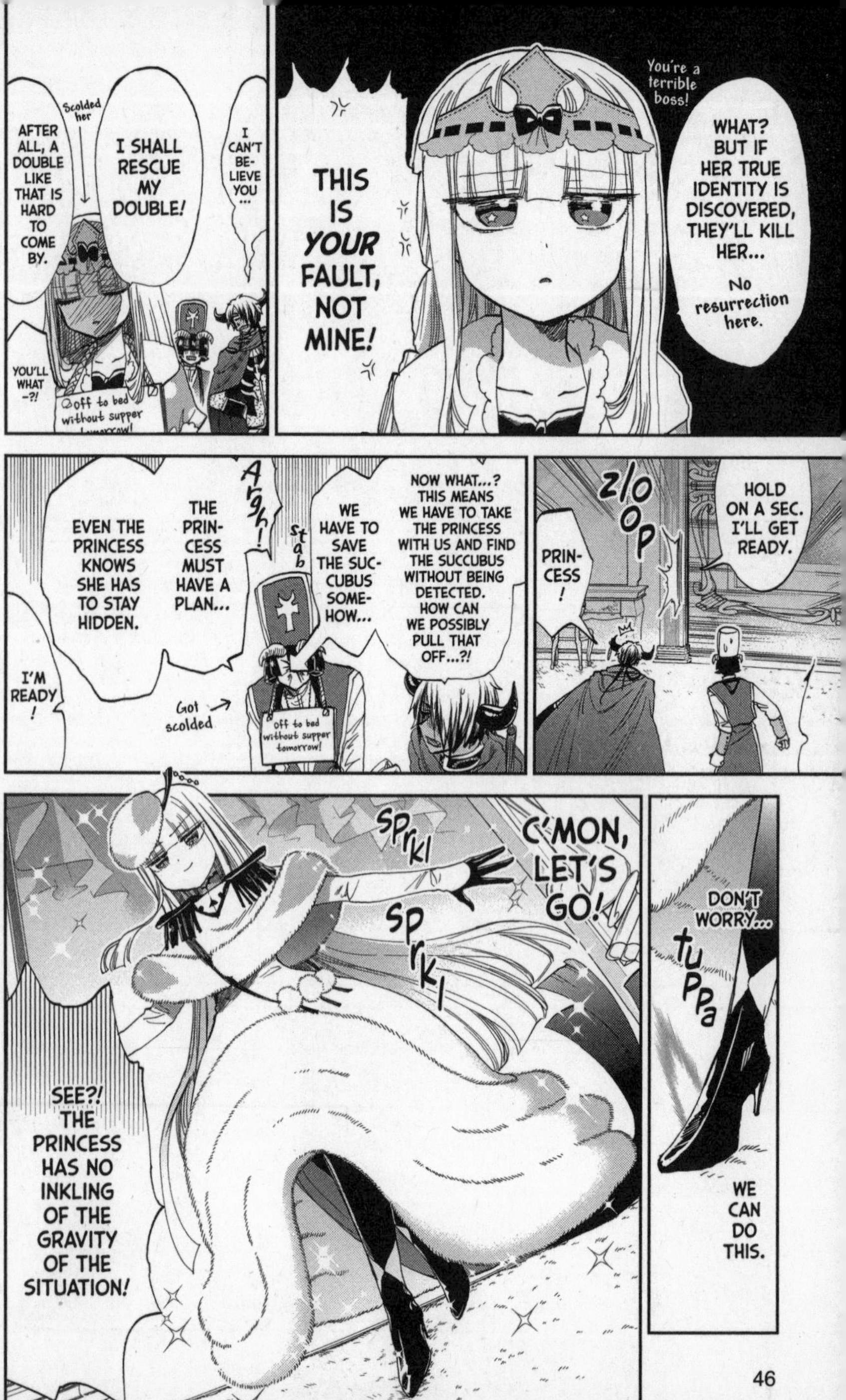
You're a terrible boss!
WHAT? BUT IF HER TRUE IDENTITY IS DISCOVERED, THEY'LL KILL HER...
No resurrection here.
THIS IS YOUR FAULT, NOT MINE!
I CAN'T BE-LIEVE YOU...
I SHALL RESCUE MY DOUBLE!
Scolded her
AFTER ALL, A DOUBLE LIKE THAT IS HARD TO COME BY.
YOU'LL WHAT—?!
off to bed without supper
HOLD ON A SEC. I'LL GET READY.
ZLOOP
PRIN-CESS!
NOW WHAT...? THIS MEANS WE HAVE TO TAKE THE PRINCESS WITH US AND FIND THE SUCCUBUS WITHOUT BEING DETECTED. HOW CAN WE POSSIBLY PULL THAT OFF...?!
WE HAVE TO SAVE THE SUC-CUBUS SOME-HOW...
stab
Argh!
THE PRIN-CESS MUST HAVE A PLAN...
EVEN THE PRINCESS KNOWS SHE HAS TO STAY HIDDEN.
I'M READY!
Got scolded
off to bed without supper tomorrow!
DON'T WORRY...
tuppa
WE CAN DO THIS.
C'MON, LET'S GO!
sprkl
sprkl
SEE?! THE PRINCESS HAS NO INKLING OF THE GRAVITY OF THE SITUATION!

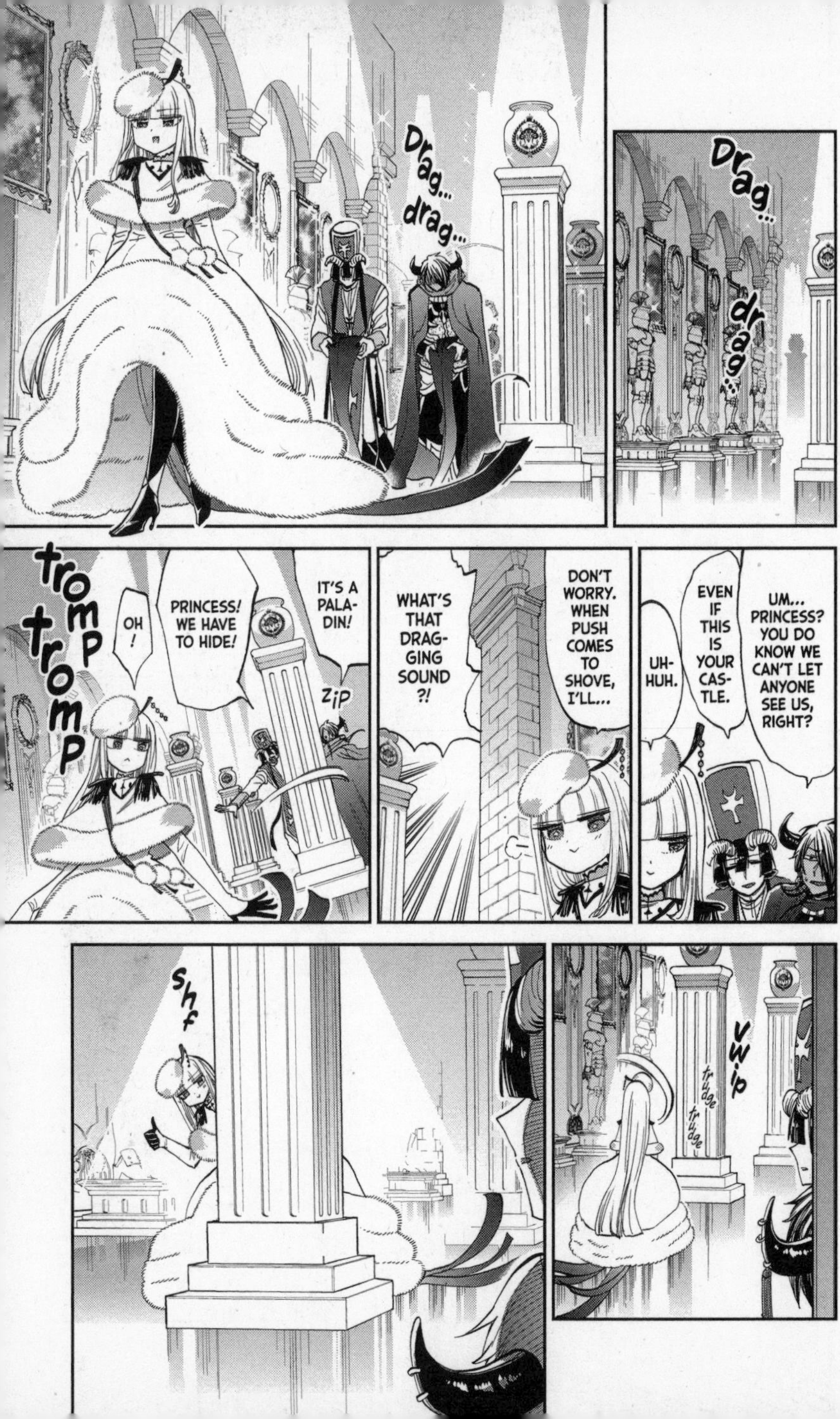
Drag... drag...
Drag... drag...
UM... PRINCESS? YOU DO KNOW WE CAN'T LET ANYONE SEE US, RIGHT?
EVEN IF THIS IS YOUR CAS-TLE.
UH-HUH.
DON'T WORRY. WHEN PUSH COMES TO SHOVE, I'LL...
WHAT'S THAT DRAG-GING SOUND?!
IT'S A PALA-DIN!
zip
PRINCESS! WE HAVE TO HIDE!
OH!
tromp tromp tromp
vwip
trudge trudge
shf

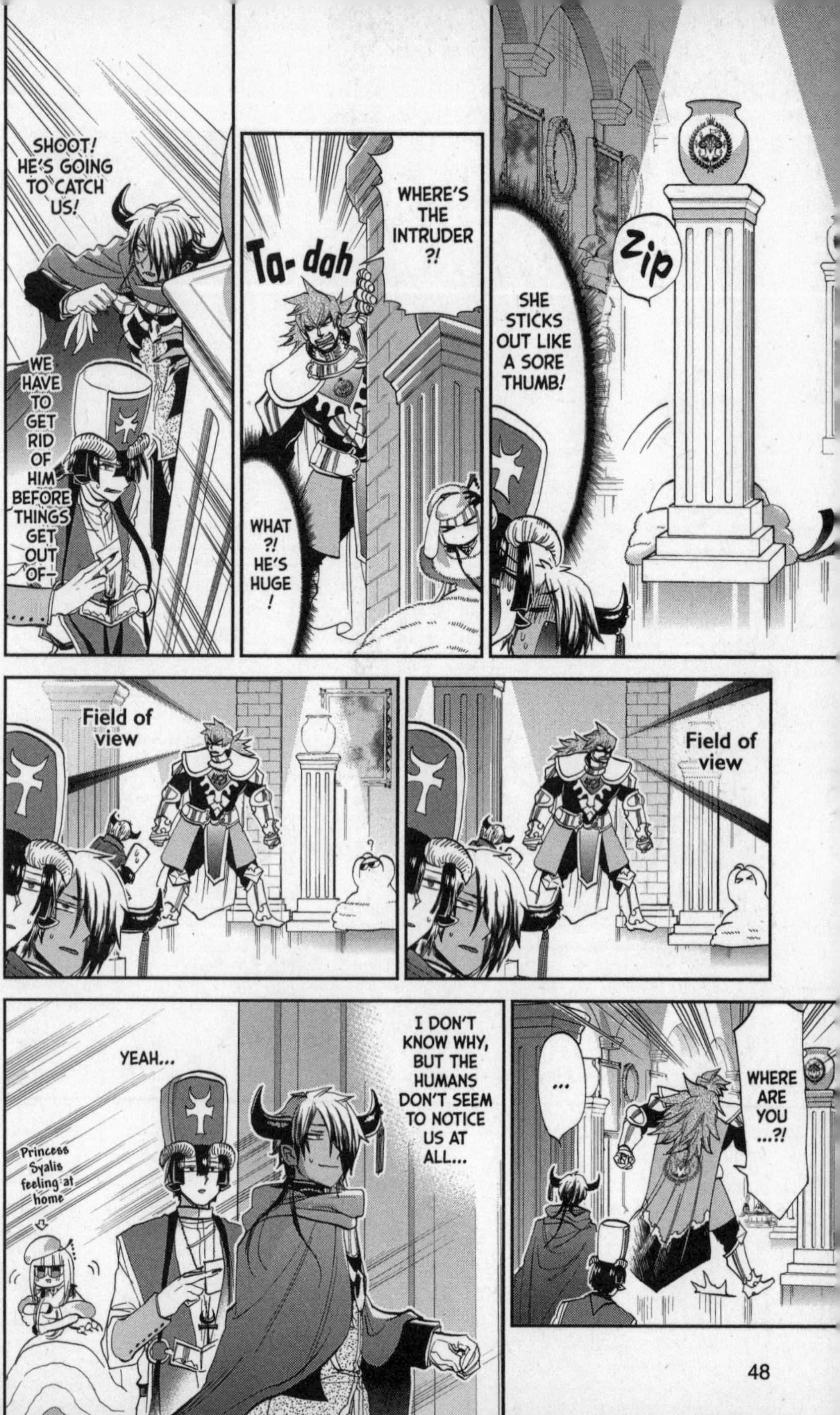
Zip
SHE STICKS OUT LIKE A SORE THUMB!
WHERE'S THE INTRUDER?!
Ta-dah
WHAT?! HE'S HUGE!
SHOOT! HE'S GOING TO CATCH US!
WE HAVE TO GET RID OF HIM BEFORE THINGS GET OUT OF—
Field of view
Field of view
WHERE ARE YOU...?!
...
I DON'T KNOW WHY, BUT THE HUMANS DON'T SEEM TO NOTICE US AT ALL...
YEAH...
Princess Syalis feeling at home

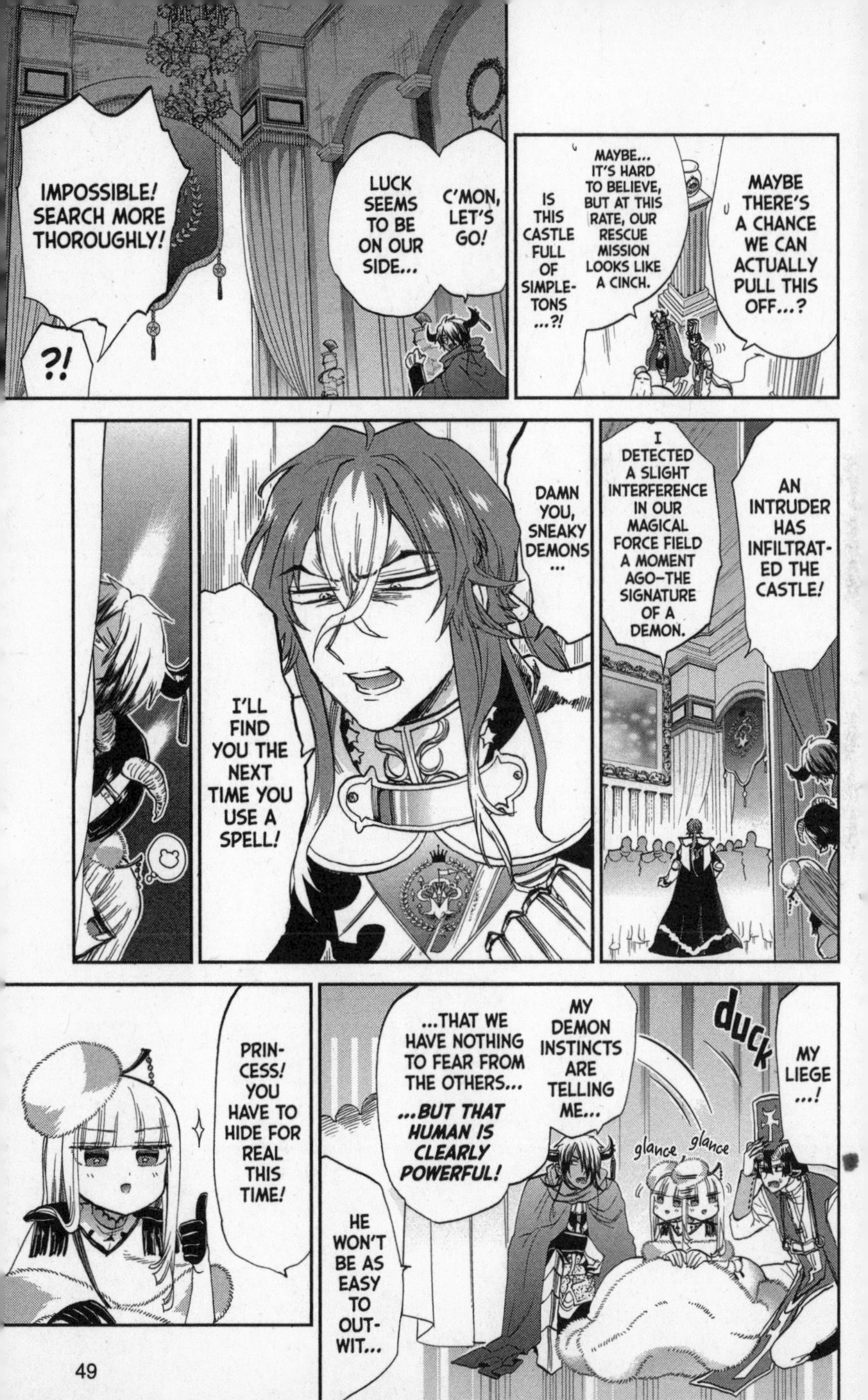
MAYBE THERE'S A CHANCE WE CAN ACTUALLY PULL THIS OFF...?
MAYBE... IT'S HARD TO BELIEVE, BUT AT THIS RATE, OUR RESCUE MISSION LOOKS LIKE A CINCH.
IS THIS CASTLE FULL OF SIMPLE-TONS...?!
C'MON, LET'S GO!
LUCK SEEMS TO BE ON OUR SIDE...
IMPOSSIBLE! SEARCH MORE THOROUGHLY!
?!
AN INTRUDER HAS INFILTRAT-ED THE CASTLE!
I DETECTED A SLIGHT INTERFERENCE IN OUR MAGICAL FORCE FIELD A MOMENT AGO—THE SIGNATURE OF A DEMON.
DAMN YOU, SNEAKY DEMONS...
I'LL FIND YOU THE NEXT TIME YOU USE A SPELL!
MY LIEGE...!
duck
MY DEMON INSTINCTS ARE TELLING ME...
...THAT WE HAVE NOTHING TO FEAR FROM THE OTHERS...
...BUT THAT HUMAN IS CLEARLY POWERFUL!
glance glance
HE WON'T BE AS EASY TO OUT-WIT...
PRIN-CESS! YOU HAVE TO HIDE FOR REAL THIS TIME!

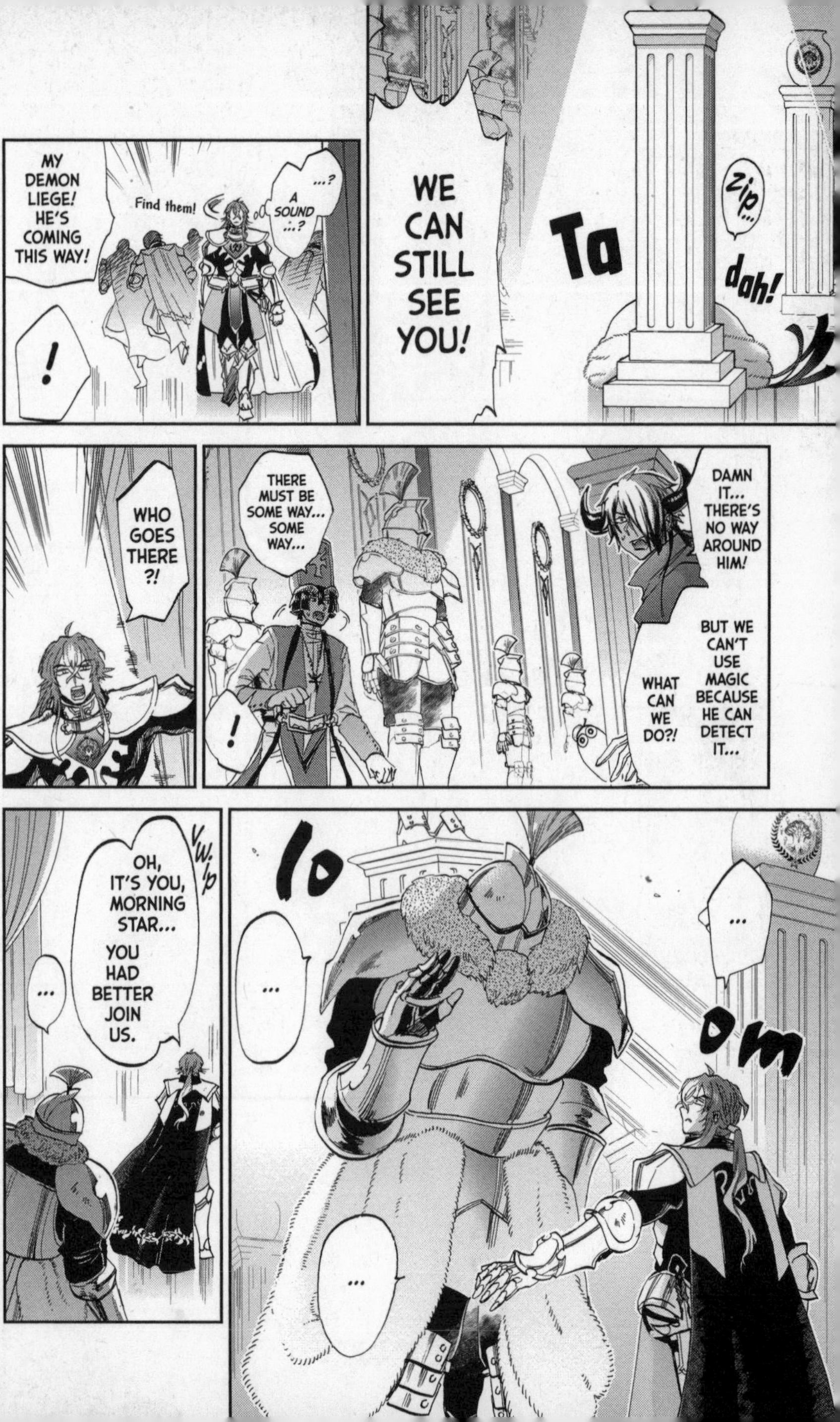
Zip...
Ta
dah!
WE CAN STILL SEE YOU!
...?
A SOUND ...?
Find them!
MY DEMON LIEGE! HE'S COMING THIS WAY!
!
DAMN IT... THERE'S NO WAY AROUND HIM!
BUT WE CAN'T USE MAGIC BECAUSE HE CAN DETECT IT...
WHAT CAN WE DO?!
THERE MUST BE SOME WAY... SOME WAY...
!
WHO GOES THERE?!
lo
om
...
...
...
Vwip
OH, IT'S YOU, MORNING STAR...
YOU HAD BETTER JOIN US.
...

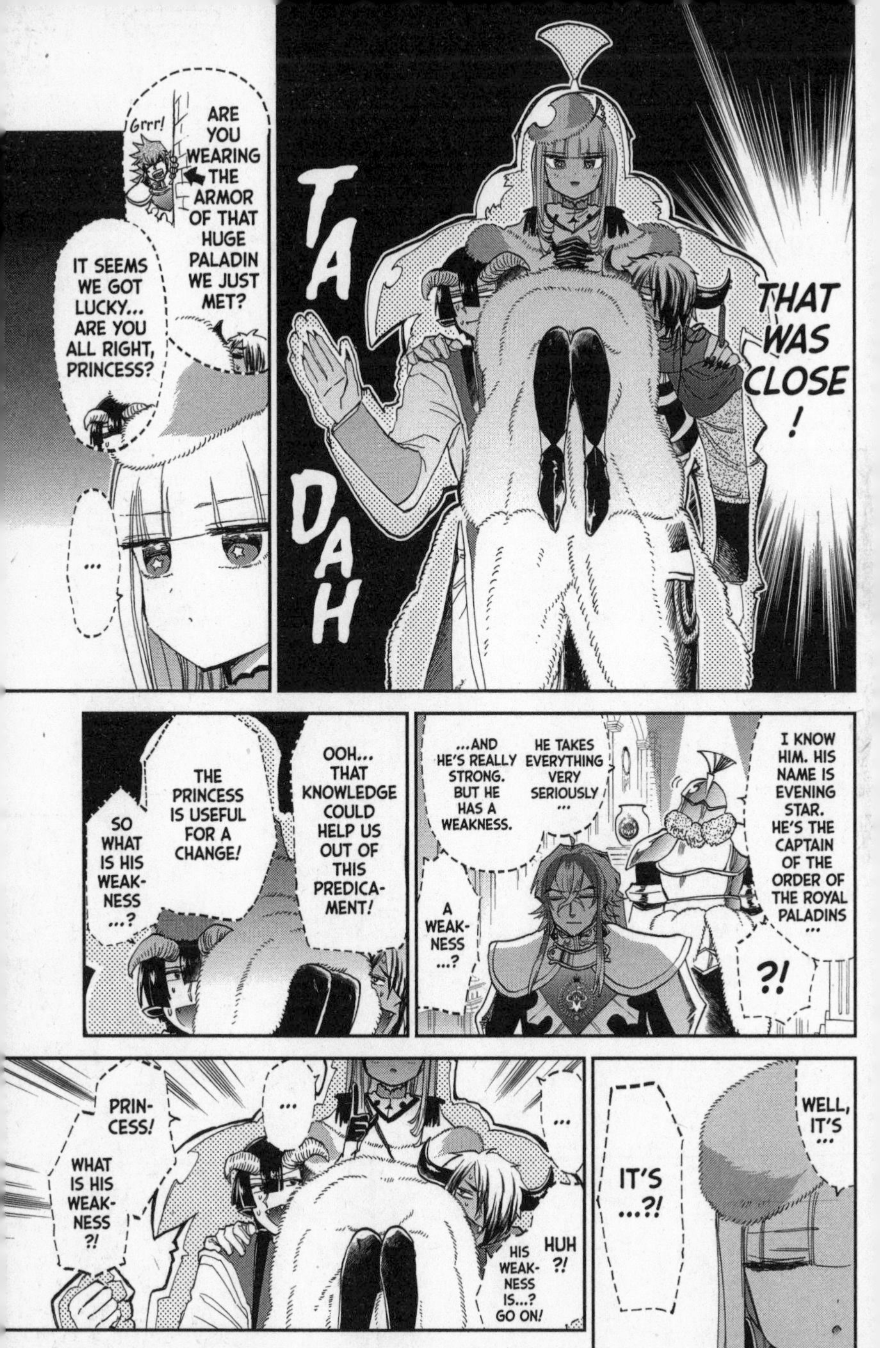
THAT WAS CLOSE!
TA DAH
ARE YOU WEARING THE ARMOR OF THAT HUGE PALADIN WE JUST MET?
Grrr!
IT SEEMS WE GOT LUCKY... ARE YOU ALL RIGHT, PRINCESS?
...
I KNOW HIM. HIS NAME IS EVENING STAR. HE'S THE CAPTAIN OF THE ORDER OF THE ROYAL PALADINS...
?!
HE TAKES EVERYTHING VERY SERIOUSLY...
...AND HE'S REALLY STRONG. BUT HE HAS A WEAKNESS.
A WEAKNESS...?
OOH... THAT KNOWLEDGE COULD HELP US OUT OF THIS PREDICAMENT!
THE PRINCESS IS USEFUL FOR A CHANGE!
SO WHAT IS HIS WEAKNESS...?
WELL, IT'S...
IT'S...?!
...
...
HUH?!
HIS WEAKNESS IS...? GO ON!
PRINCESS! WHAT IS HIS WEAKNESS?!

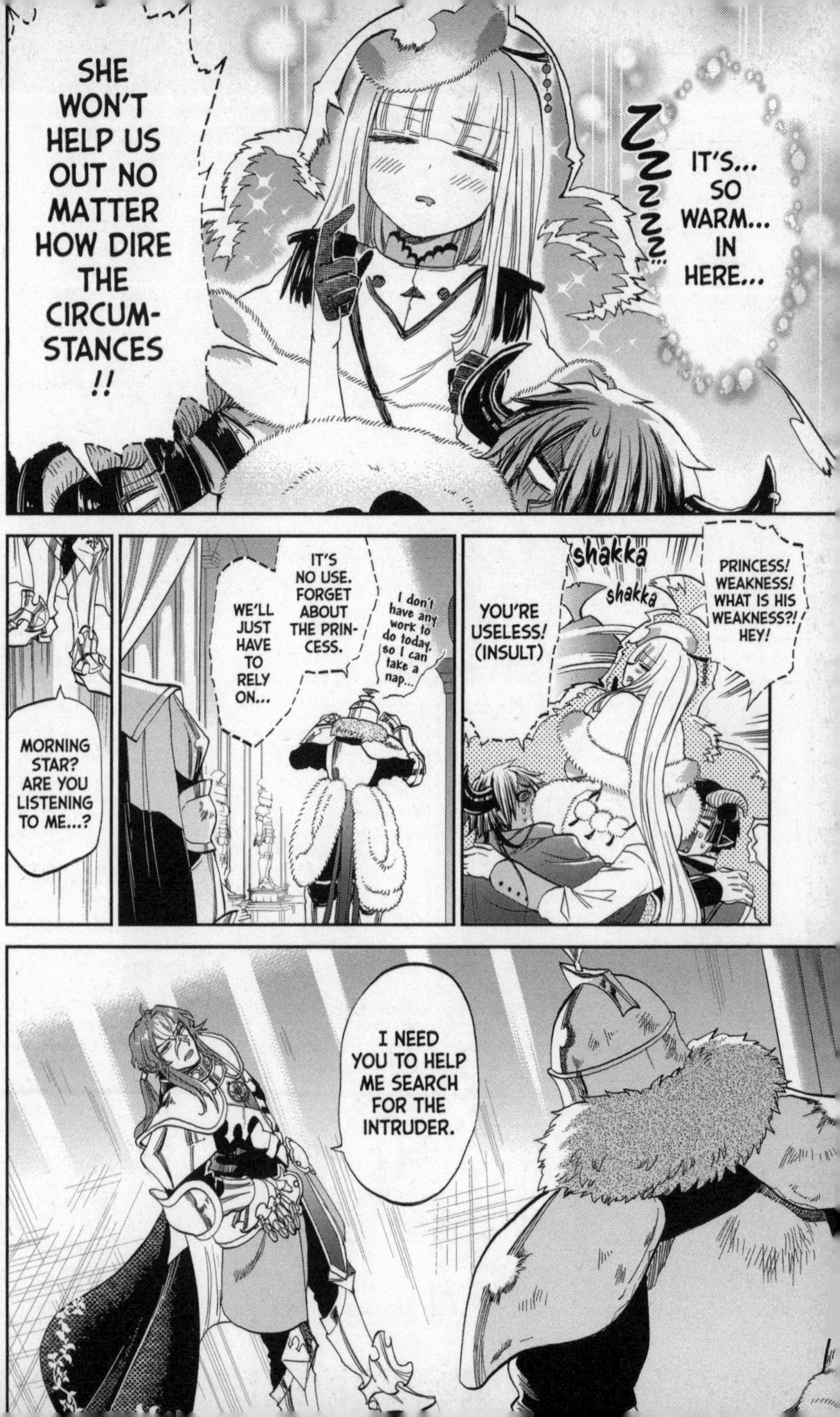
IT'S... SO WARM... IN HERE...
ZZZZZ...
SHE WON'T HELP US OUT NO MATTER HOW DIRE THE CIRCUM-STANCES!!
PRINCESS! WEAKNESS! WHAT IS HIS WEAKNESS?! HEY!
shakka
shakka
YOU'RE USELESS! (INSULT)
I don't have any work to do today, so I can take a nap...
IT'S NO USE. FORGET ABOUT THE PRIN-CESS.
WE'LL JUST HAVE TO RELY ON...
MORNING STAR? ARE YOU LISTENING TO ME...?
I NEED YOU TO HELP ME SEARCH FOR THE INTRUDER.

I still perform my duties.

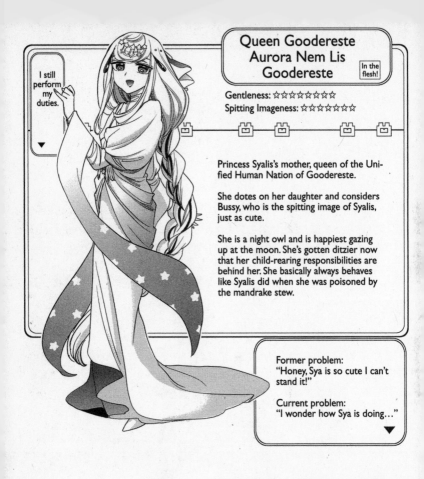

Queen Goodereste Aurora Nem Lis Goodereste

In the flesh!

Gentleness: ☆☆☆☆☆☆☆☆☆

Spitting Imageness: ☆☆☆☆☆☆☆☆

Princess Syalis's mother, queen of the Unified Human Nation of Goodereste.

She dotes on her daughter and considers Bussy, who is the spitting image of Syalis, just as cute.

She is a night owl and is happiest gazing up at the moon. She's gotten ditzier now that her child-rearing responsibilities are behind her. She basically always behaves like Syalis did when she was poisoned by the mandrake stew.

Former problem:
"Honey, Sya is so cute I can't stand it!"

Current problem:
"I wonder how Sya is doing…"

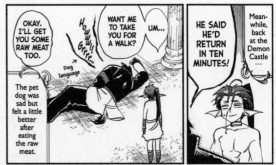

Meanwhile, back at the Demon Castle…
HE SAID HE'D RETURN IN TEN MINUTES!
UM...
WANT ME TO TAKE YOU FOR A WALK?
Howwl!! Grrrr...
Dog language
OKAY. I'LL GET YOU SOME RAW MEAT TOO.
The pet dog was sad but felt a little better after eating the raw meat.

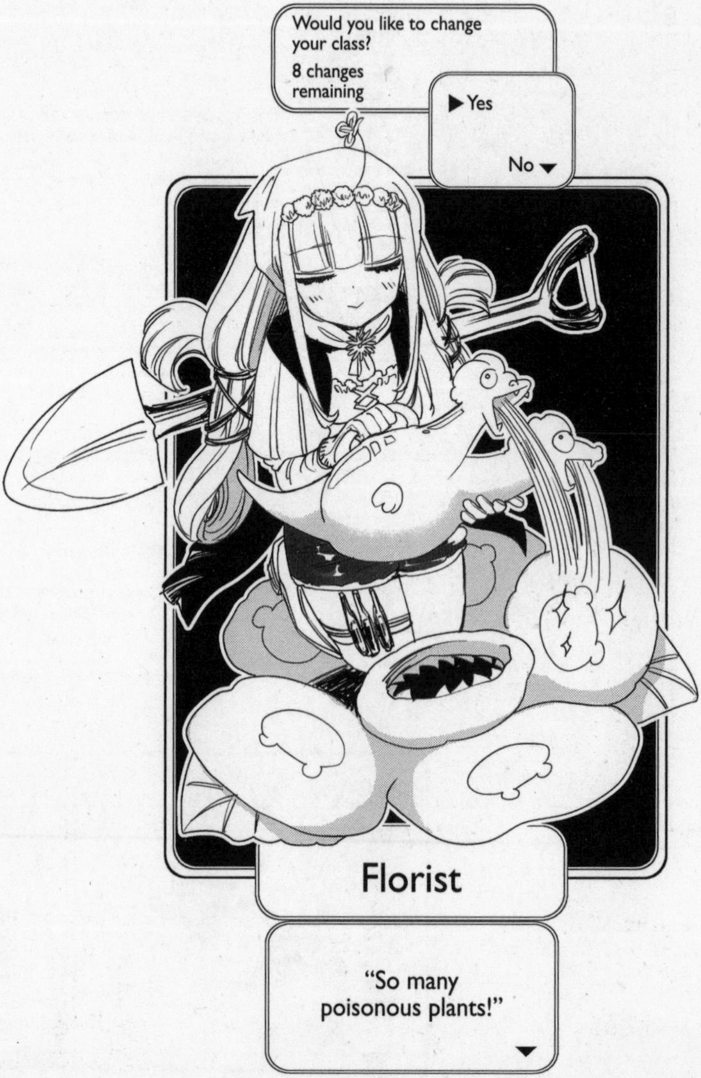
Would you like to change your class?
8 changes remaining
▶Yes
No
Florist
"So many poisonous plants!"

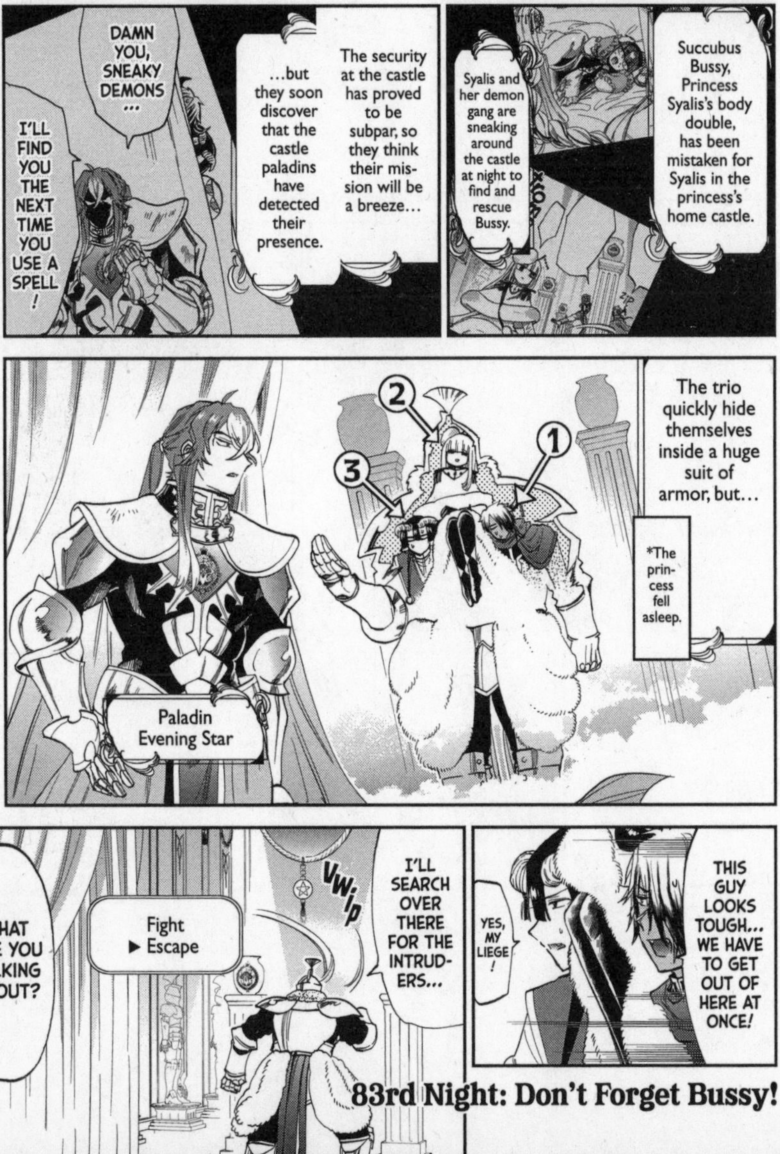
Succubus Bussy, Princess Syalis's body double, has been mistaken for Syalis in the princess's home castle.
Syalis and her demon gang are sneaking around the castle at night to find and rescue Bussy.
The security at the castle has proved to be subpar, so they think their mission will be a breeze…
…but they soon discover that the castle paladins have detected their presence.
DAMN YOU, SNEAKY DEMONS…
I'LL FIND YOU THE NEXT TIME YOU USE A SPELL!
The trio quickly hide themselves inside a huge suit of armor, but…
*The princess fell asleep.
1
2
3
Paladin Evening Star
THIS GUY LOOKS TOUGH… WE HAVE TO GET OUT OF HERE AT ONCE!
YES, MY LIEGE!
I'LL SEARCH OVER THERE FOR THE INTRUDERS…
VWip
Fight
▶ Escape
WHAT ARE YOU TALKING ABOUT?

83rd Night: Don't Forget Bussy!

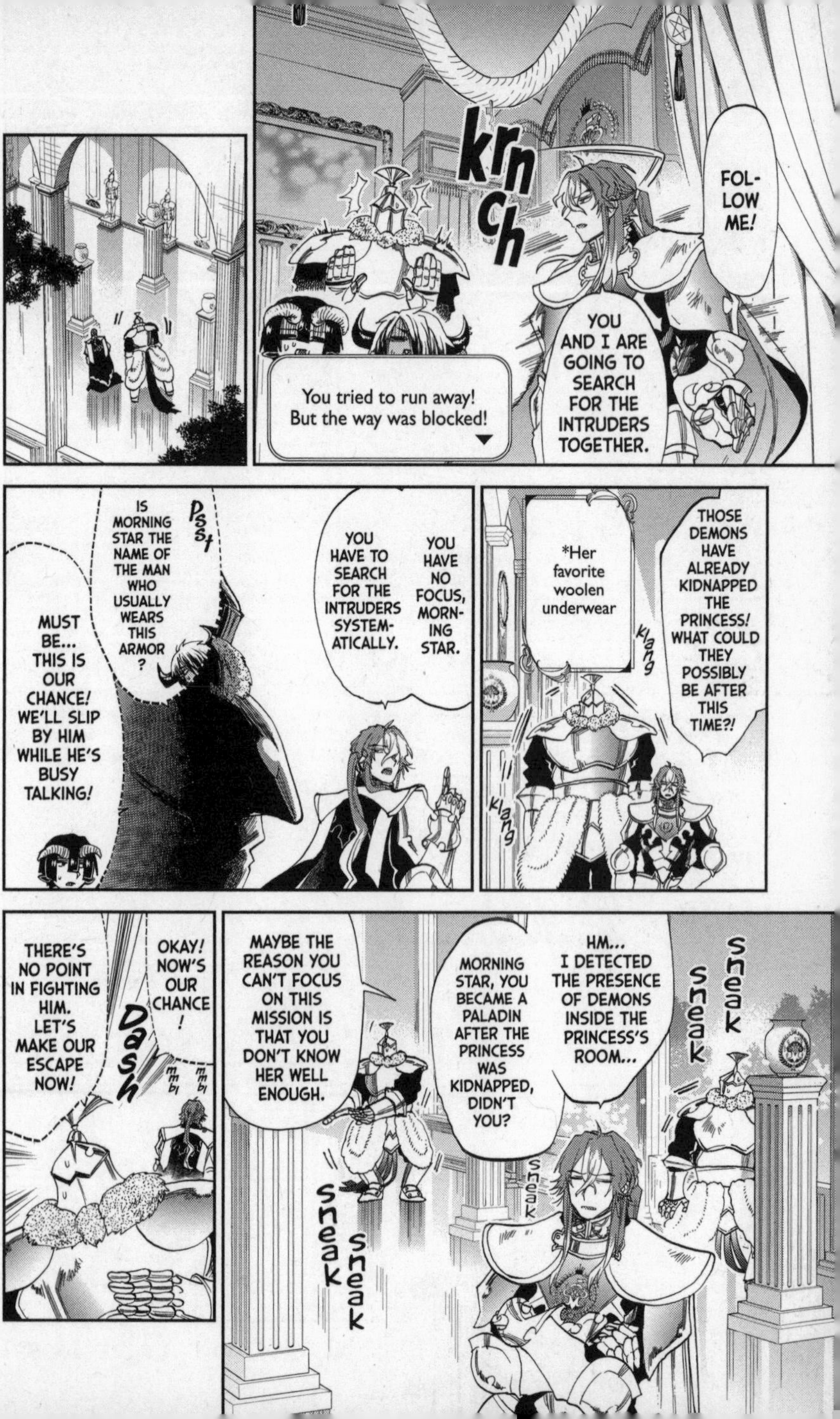
FOL-
LOW
ME!
YOU AND I ARE GOING TO SEARCH FOR THE INTRUDERS TOGETHER.
krnch
You tried to run away! But the way was blocked!
THOSE DEMONS HAVE ALREADY KIDNAPPED THE PRINCESS! WHAT COULD THEY POSSIBLY BE AFTER THIS TIME?!
*Her favorite woolen underwear
klang
klang
YOU HAVE NO FOCUS, MORN-
ING STAR.
YOU HAVE TO SEARCH FOR THE INTRUDERS SYSTEM-
ATICALLY.
Psst
IS MORNING STAR THE NAME OF THE MAN WHO USUALLY WEARS THIS ARMOR?
MUST BE... THIS IS OUR CHANCE! WE'LL SLIP BY HIM WHILE HE'S BUSY TALKING!
HM... I DETECTED THE PRESENCE OF DEMONS INSIDE THE PRINCESS'S ROOM...
sneak
sneak
MORNING STAR, YOU BECAME A PALADIN AFTER THE PRINCESS WAS KIDNAPPED, DIDN'T YOU?
sneak
MAYBE THE REASON YOU CAN'T FOCUS ON THIS MISSION IS THAT YOU DON'T KNOW HER WELL ENOUGH.
sneak
sneak
OKAY! NOW'S OUR CHANCE!
THERE'S NO POINT IN FIGHTING HIM. LET'S MAKE OUR ESCAPE NOW!
Dash
mmbl
mmbl

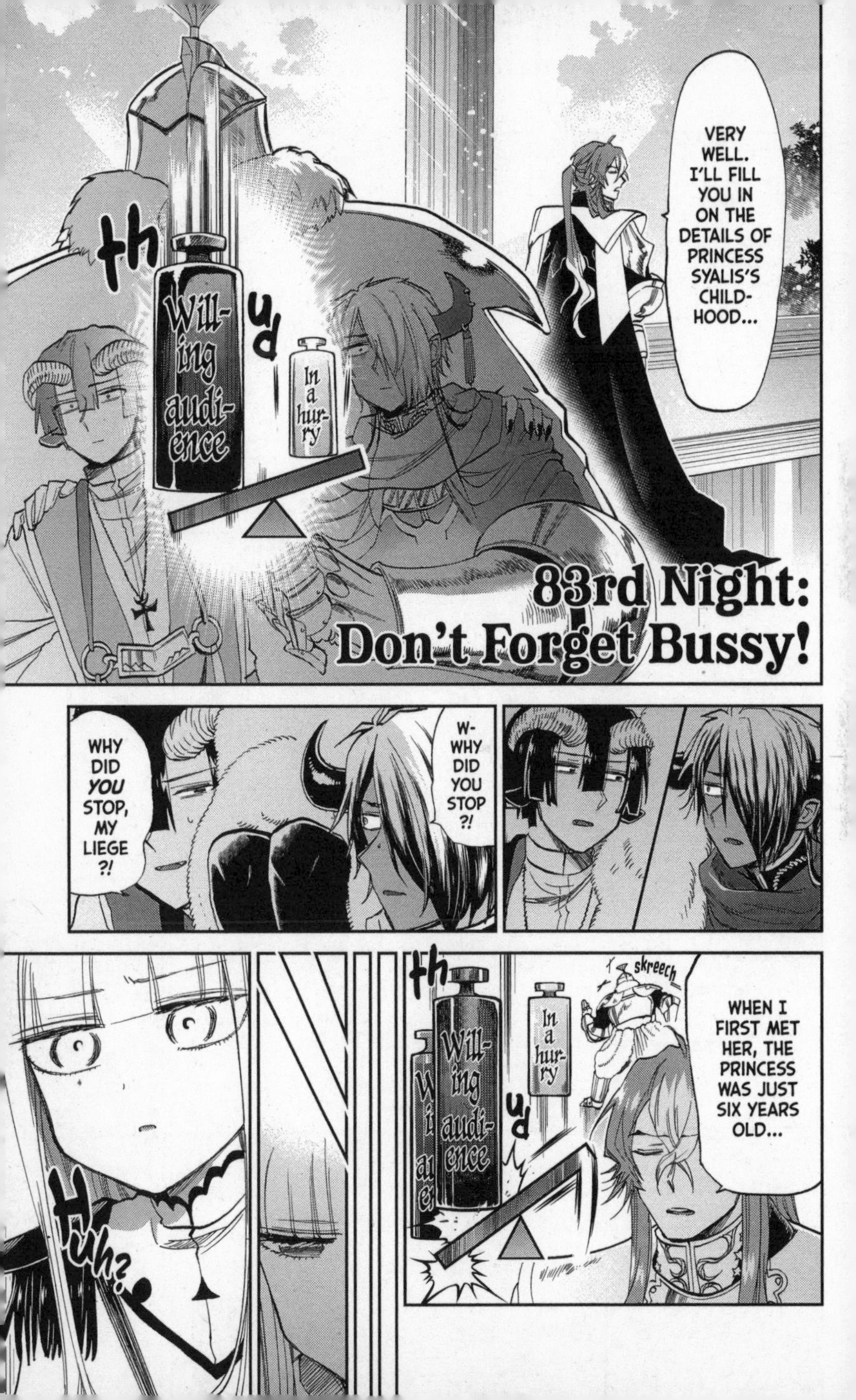
VERY WELL. I'LL FILL YOU IN ON THE DETAILS OF PRINCESS SYALIS'S CHILDHOOD...
83rd Night: Don't Forget Bussy!
thud
Willing audience
In a hurry
W-WHY DID YOU STOP?!
WHY DID *YOU* STOP, MY LIEGE?!
WHEN I FIRST MET HER, THE PRINCESS WAS JUST SIX YEARS OLD...
skreech
thud
In a hurry
Willing audience
Huh?

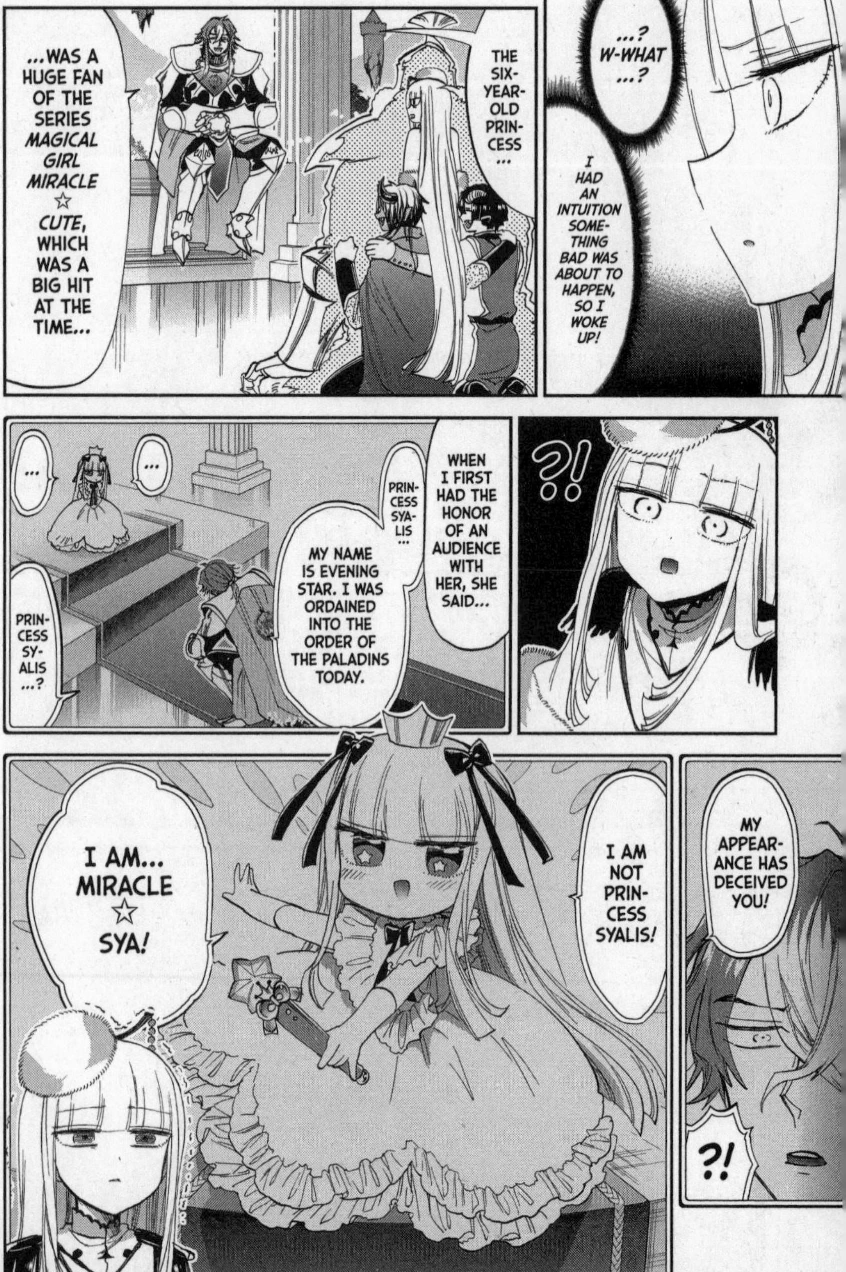
...? W-WHAT ...?
I HAD AN INTUITION SOMETHING BAD WAS ABOUT TO HAPPEN, SO I WOKE UP!
THE SIX-YEAR-OLD PRINCESS ...
...WAS A HUGE FAN OF THE SERIES *MAGICAL GIRL MIRACLE ☆ CUTE*, WHICH WAS A BIG HIT AT THE TIME...
?!
WHEN I FIRST HAD THE HONOR OF AN AUDIENCE WITH HER, SHE SAID...
PRINCESS SYALIS ...
MY NAME IS EVENING STAR. I WAS ORDAINED INTO THE ORDER OF THE PALADINS TODAY.
...
...
PRINCESS SYALIS ...?
MY APPEARANCE HAS DECEIVED YOU!
?!
I AM NOT PRINCESS SYALIS!
I AM... MIRACLE ☆ SYA!

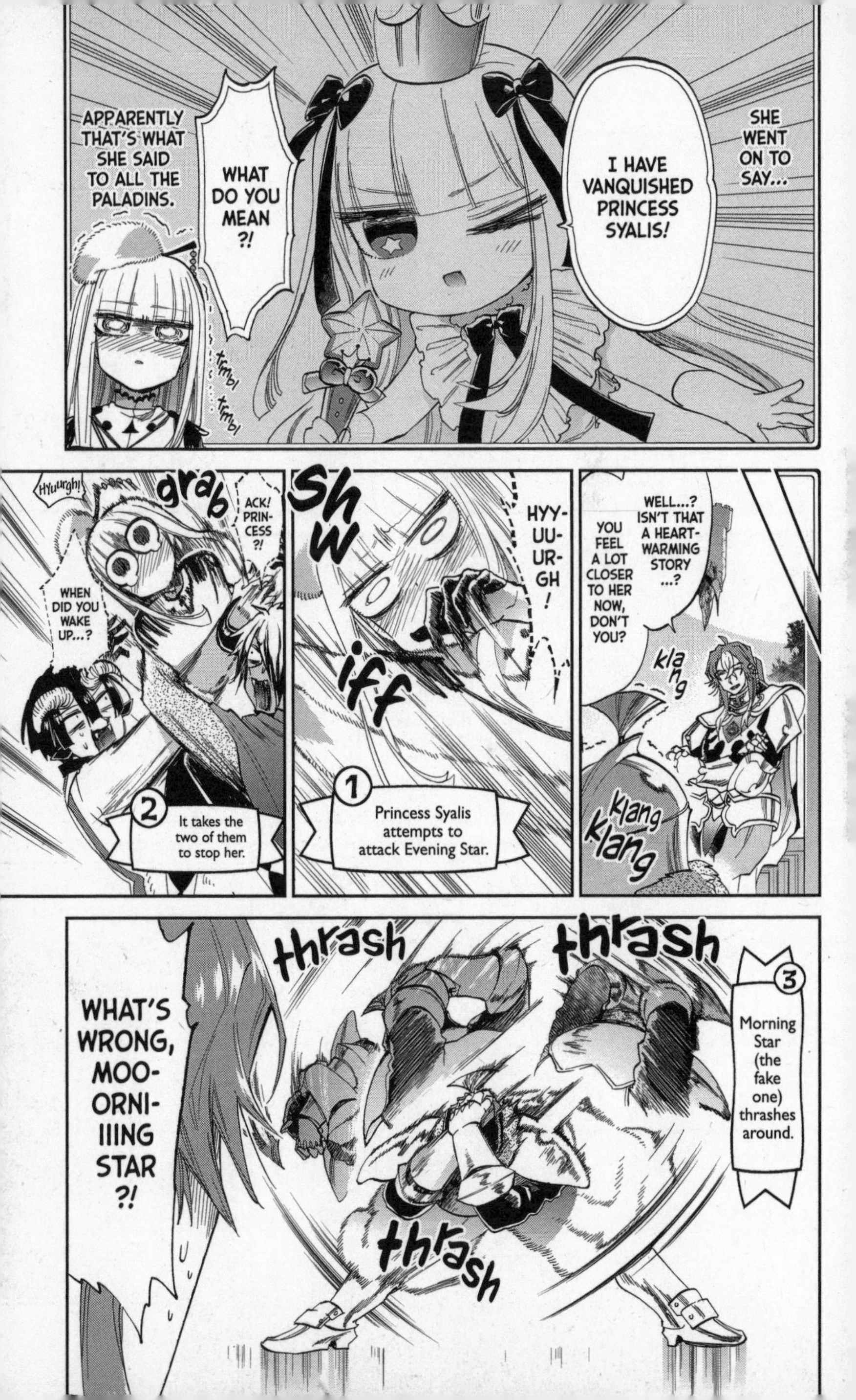
SHE WENT ON TO SAY...
I HAVE VANQUISHED PRINCESS SYALIS!
WHAT DO YOU MEAN ?!
APPARENTLY THAT'S WHAT SHE SAID TO ALL THE PALADINS.
trmbl
trmbl
WELL...? ISN'T THAT A HEART-WARMING STORY ...?
YOU FEEL A LOT CLOSER TO HER NOW, DON'T YOU?
klang
klang
klang
shw
iff
HYY-UU-URGH!
1
Princess Syalis attempts to attack Evening Star.
grab
ACK! PRIN-CESS ?!
HYuurgh!
WHEN DID YOU WAKE UP...?
2
It takes the two of them to stop her.
3
Morning Star (the fake one) thrashes around.
thrash
thrash
WHAT'S WRONG, MOO-ORNI-IIING STAR ?!
thrash

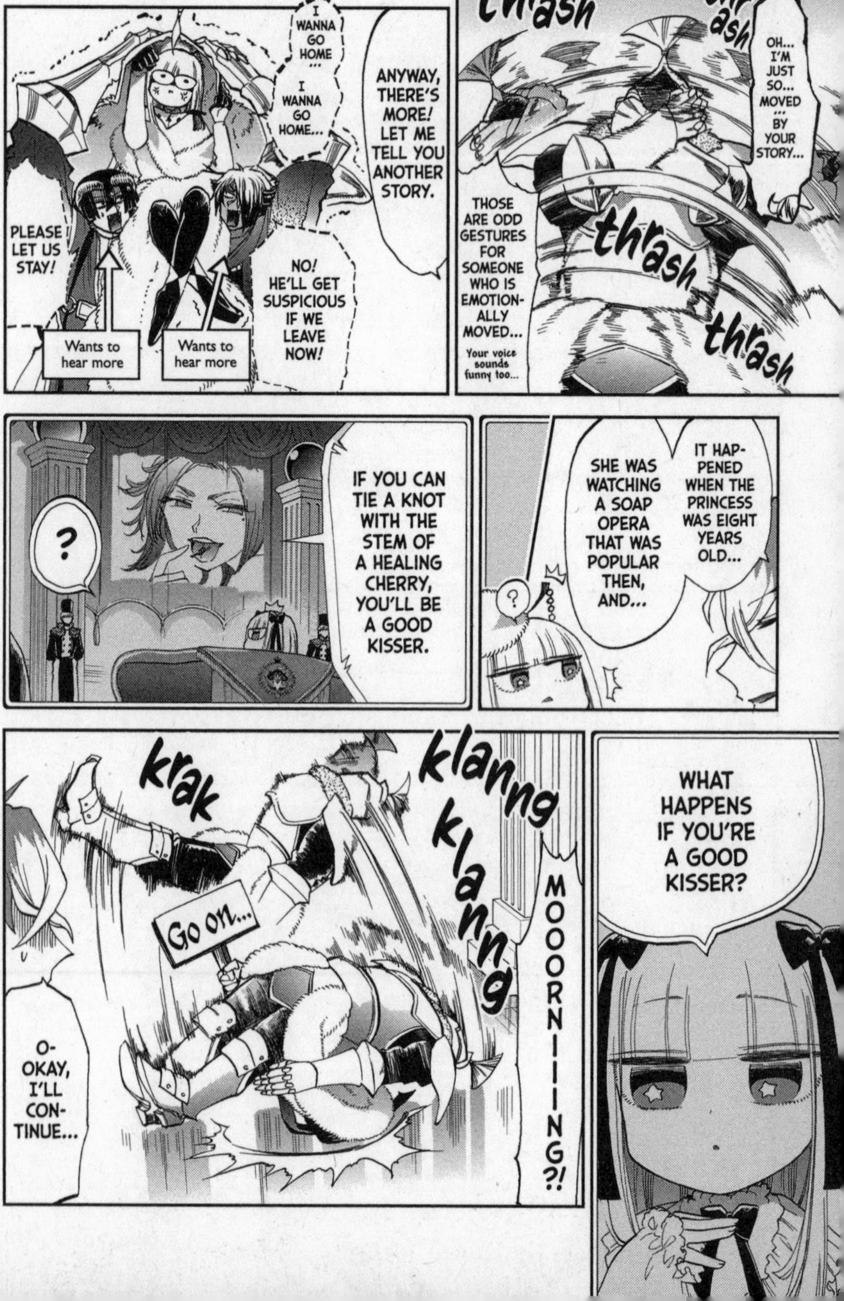
thrash
thrash
OH... I'M JUST SO... MOVED... BY YOUR STORY...
thrash
thrash
THOSE ARE ODD GESTURES FOR SOMEONE WHO IS EMOTIONALLY MOVED...
Your voice sounds funny too...
ANYWAY, THERE'S MORE! LET ME TELL YOU ANOTHER STORY.
I WANNA GO HOME...
I WANNA GO HOME...
NO! HE'LL GET SUSPICIOUS IF WE LEAVE NOW!
PLEASE LET US STAY!
Wants to hear more
Wants to hear more
IT HAPPENED WHEN THE PRINCESS WAS EIGHT YEARS OLD...
SHE WAS WATCHING A SOAP OPERA THAT WAS POPULAR THEN, AND...
?
IF YOU CAN TIE A KNOT WITH THE STEM OF A HEALING CHERRY, YOU'LL BE A GOOD KISSER.
?
WHAT HAPPENS IF YOU'RE A GOOD KISSER?
klanng
klanng
krak
MOOORNIIING?!
Go on...
O-OKAY, I'LL CONTINUE...

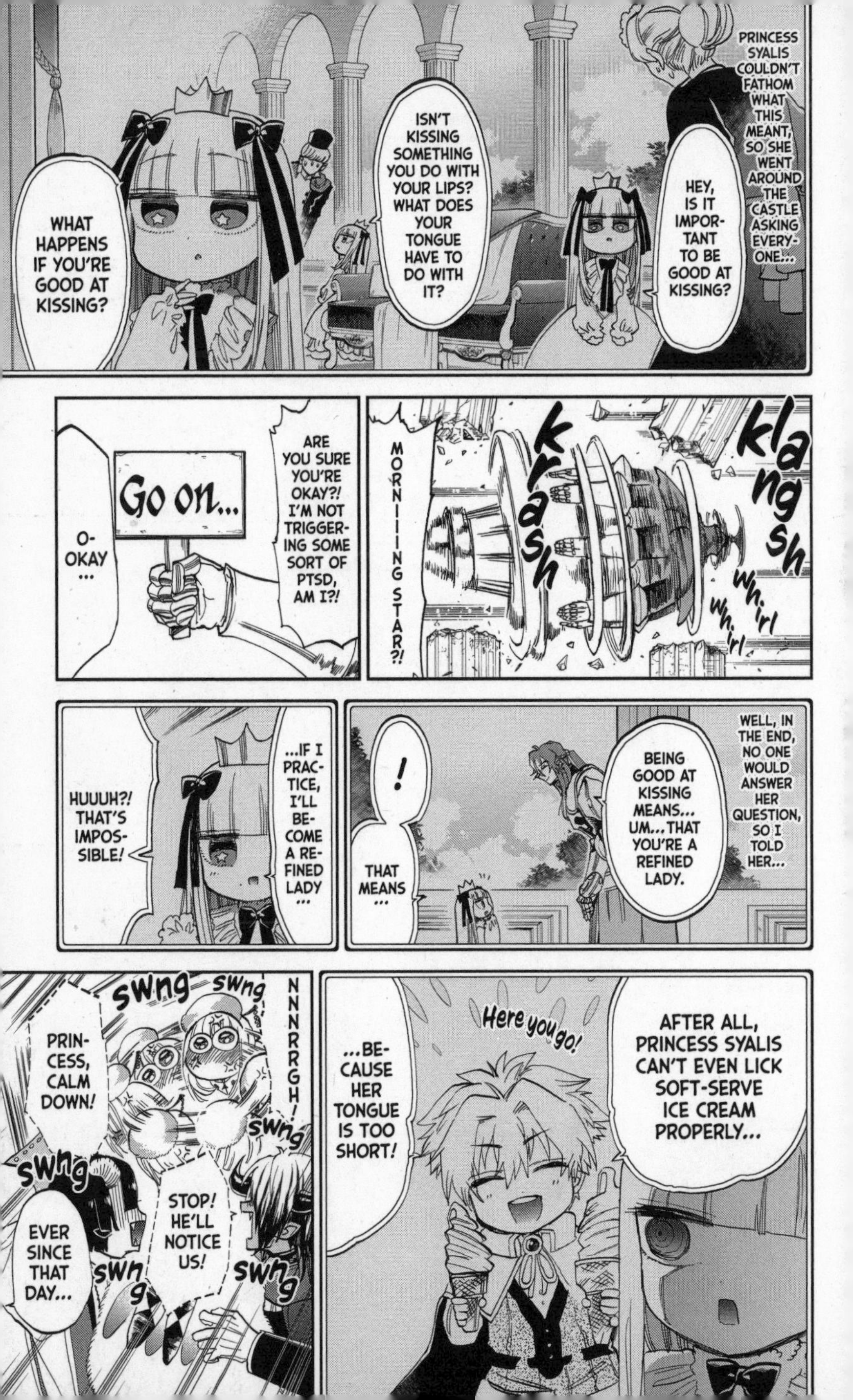
PRINCESS SYALIS COULDN'T FATHOM WHAT THIS MEANT, SO SHE WENT AROUND THE CASTLE ASKING EVERYONE...
HEY, IS IT IMPORTANT TO BE GOOD AT KISSING?
ISN'T KISSING SOMETHING YOU DO WITH YOUR LIPS? WHAT DOES YOUR TONGUE HAVE TO DO WITH IT?
WHAT HAPPENS IF YOU'RE GOOD AT KISSING?
klangsh
krash
whirl
whirl
MORNIIING STAR?!
ARE YOU SURE YOU'RE OKAY?! I'M NOT TRIGGERING SOME SORT OF PTSD, AM I?!
Go on...
O-OKAY...
WELL, IN THE END, NO ONE WOULD ANSWER HER QUESTION, SO I TOLD HER...
BEING GOOD AT KISSING MEANS... UM...THAT YOU'RE A REFINED LADY.
!
THAT MEANS...
...IF I PRACTICE, I'LL BECOME A REFINED LADY...
HUUUH?! THAT'S IMPOSSIBLE!
AFTER ALL, PRINCESS SYALIS CAN'T EVEN LICK SOFT-SERVE ICE CREAM PROPERLY...
Here you go!
...BECAUSE HER TONGUE IS TOO SHORT!
NNNRRGH!
swng
swng
PRINCESS, CALM DOWN!
swng
swng
STOP! HE'LL NOTICE US!
EVER SINCE THAT DAY...
swng
swng

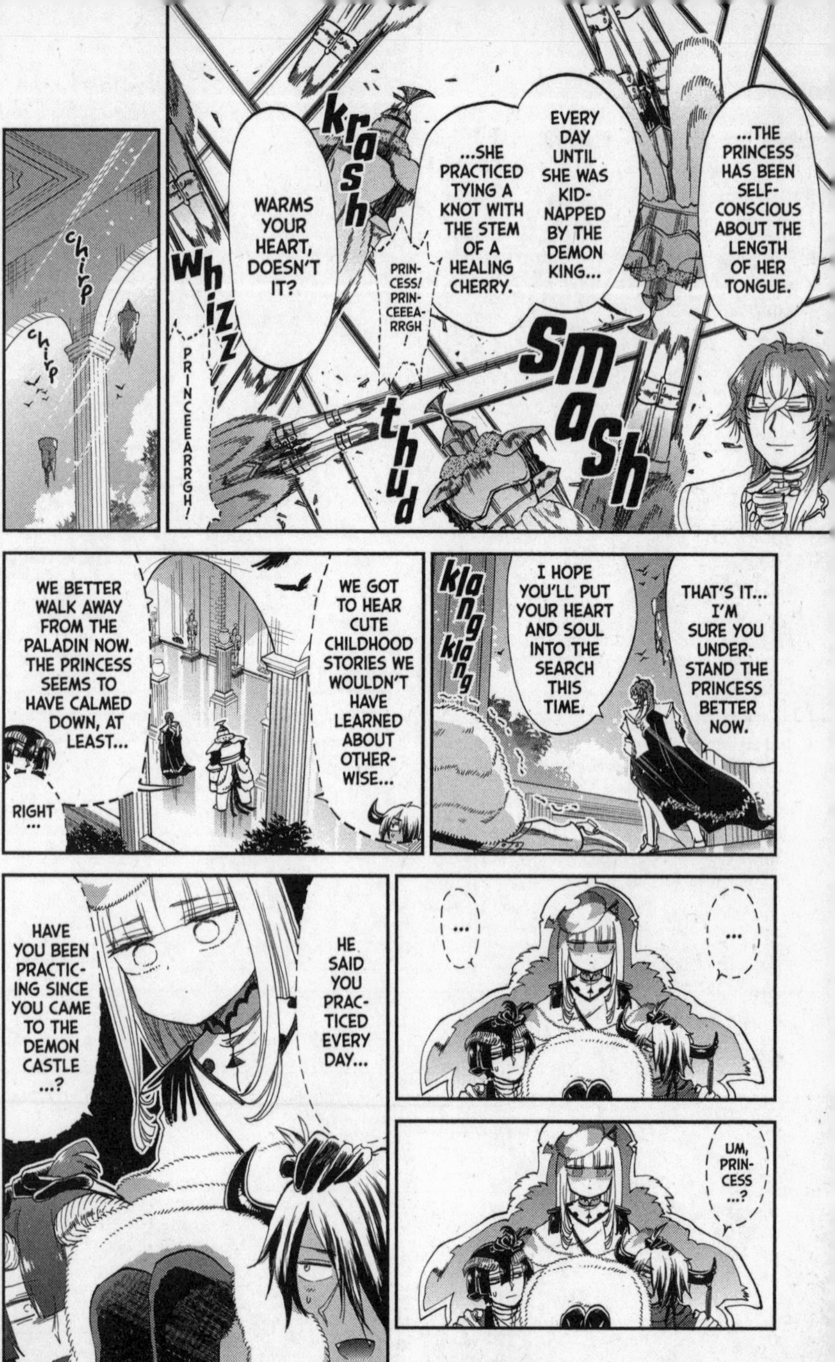
...THE PRINCESS HAS BEEN SELF-CONSCIOUS ABOUT THE LENGTH OF HER TONGUE.
EVERY DAY UNTIL SHE WAS KIDNAPPED BY THE DEMON KING...
...SHE PRACTICED TYING A KNOT WITH THE STEM OF A HEALING CHERRY.
SMASH
PRINCESS! PRINCEEEA-ARRGH!
krash
WARMS YOUR HEART, DOESN'T IT?
thud
Whizz
PRINCEEARRGH!
chirp
chirp
THAT'S IT... I'M SURE YOU UNDERSTAND THE PRINCESS BETTER NOW.
I HOPE YOU'LL PUT YOUR HEART AND SOUL INTO THE SEARCH THIS TIME.
klang klang
WE GOT TO HEAR CUTE CHILDHOOD STORIES WE WOULDN'T HAVE LEARNED ABOUT OTHERWISE...
WE BETTER WALK AWAY FROM THE PALADIN NOW. THE PRINCESS SEEMS TO HAVE CALMED DOWN, AT LEAST...
RIGHT...
...
...
UM, PRINCESS...?
HE SAID YOU PRACTICED EVERY DAY...
HAVE YOU BEEN PRACTICING SINCE YOU CAME TO THE DEMON CASTLE...?

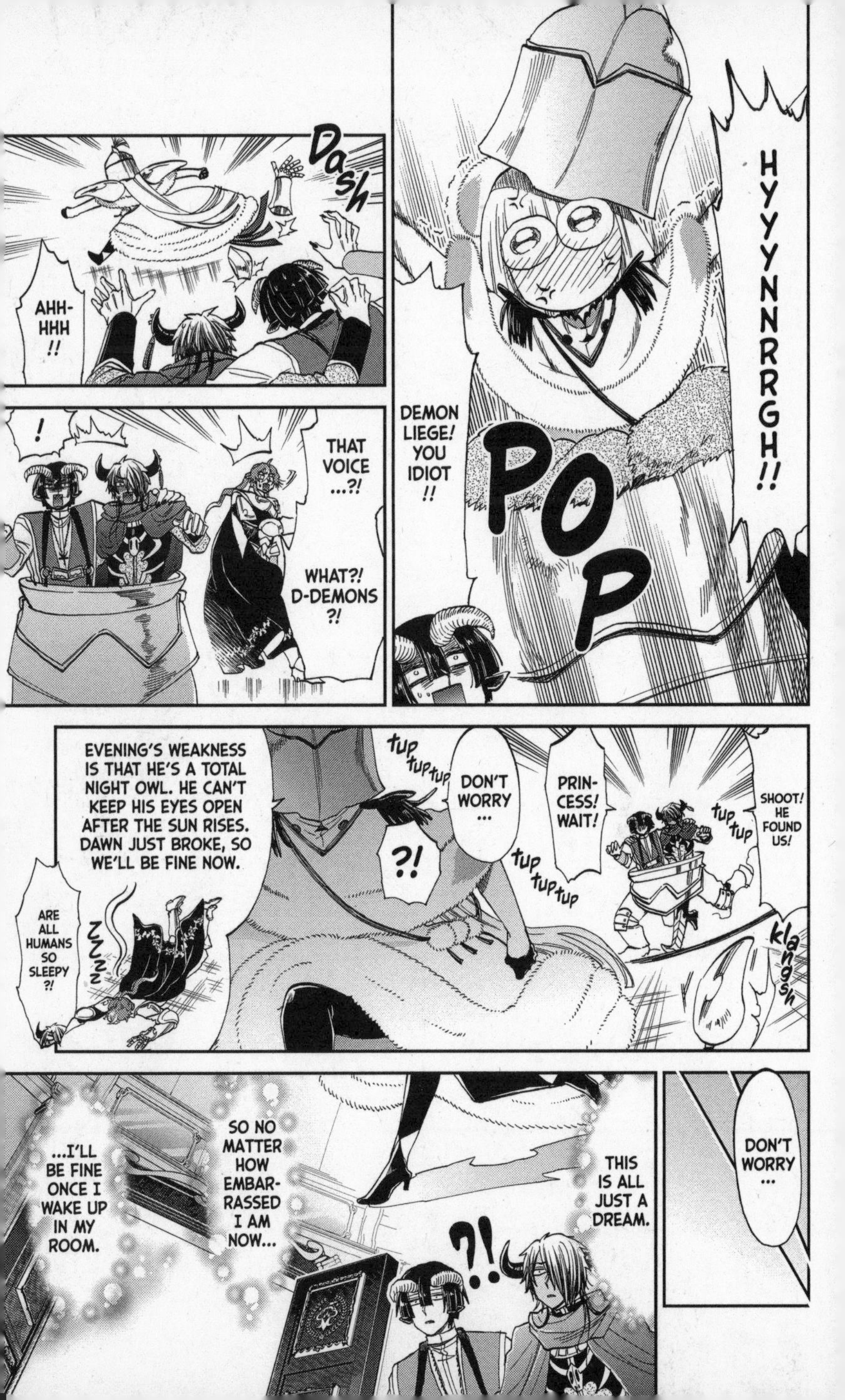
HYYYNNRRGH!!
DEMON LIEGE! YOU IDIOT!!
POP
Dash
AHH-HHH!!
THAT VOICE ...?!
!
WHAT?! D-DEMONS?!
SHOOT! HE FOUND US!
tup tup
klangsh
PRIN-CESS! WAIT!
tup tup tup
DON'T WORRY ...
tup tup tup
?!
EVENING'S WEAKNESS IS THAT HE'S A TOTAL NIGHT OWL. HE CAN'T KEEP HIS EYES OPEN AFTER THE SUN RISES. DAWN JUST BROKE, SO WE'LL BE FINE NOW.
ARE ALL HUMANS SO SLEEPY?!
ZZZZ
DON'T WORRY ...
THIS IS ALL JUST A DREAM.
SO NO MATTER HOW EMBAR-RASSED I AM NOW...
...I'LL BE FINE ONCE I WAKE UP IN MY ROOM.
?!

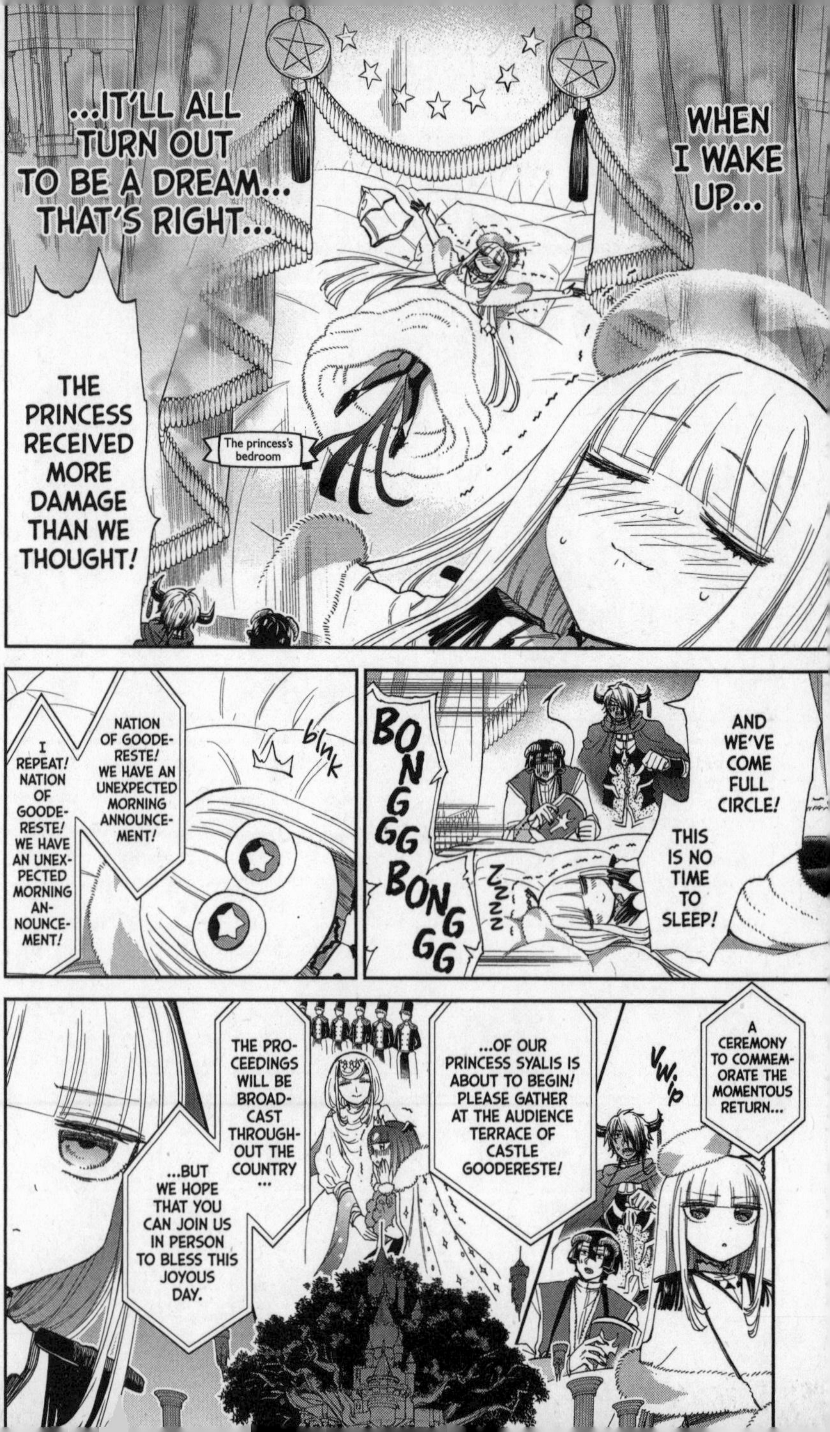
WHEN I WAKE UP...
...IT'LL ALL TURN OUT TO BE A DREAM... THAT'S RIGHT...
The princess's bedroom
THE PRINCESS RECEIVED MORE DAMAGE THAN WE THOUGHT!
AND WE'VE COME FULL CIRCLE!
THIS IS NO TIME TO SLEEP!
BONGGG BONGGG
Zzzz
blink
NATION OF GOODERESTE! WE HAVE AN UNEXPECTED MORNING ANNOUNCEMENT!
I REPEAT! NATION OF GOODERESTE! WE HAVE AN UNEXPECTED MORNING ANNOUNCEMENT!
A CEREMONY TO COMMEMORATE THE MOMENTOUS RETURN...
VWip
...OF OUR PRINCESS SYALIS IS ABOUT TO BEGIN! PLEASE GATHER AT THE AUDIENCE TERRACE OF CASTLE GOODERESTE!
THE PROCEEDINGS WILL BE BROADCAST THROUGHOUT THE COUNTRY...
...BUT WE HOPE THAT YOU CAN JOIN US IN PERSON TO BLESS THIS JOYOUS DAY.

Extreme night owl.

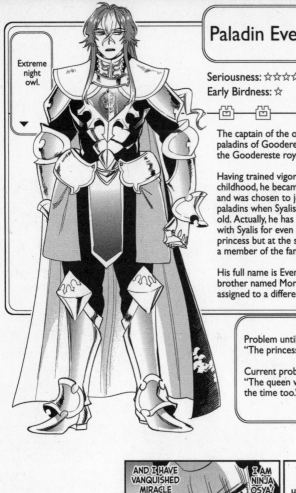

Paladin Evening Star

Seriousness: ☆☆☆☆☆☆☆☆☆☆

Early Birdness: ☆

The captain of the order of the paladins of Goodereste, who serve the Goodereste royal family.

Having trained vigorously since early childhood, he became an imperial guard and was chosen to join the order of the paladins when Syalis was just six years old. Actually, he has been acquainted with Syalis for even longer. He serves the princess but at the same considers her a member of the family.

His full name is Evening Star. He has a brother named Morning Star who is assigned to a different detail.

Problem until ten or so years ago:
"The princess keeps disappearing."

Current problem:
"The queen wanders off all the time too."

AH, PRINCESS ...
Memory
SHOULD I CALL HER BY THE NAME SHE USED THE OTHER DAY?
UM... YOUR HIGHNESS MIRACLE ☆ SYA...
NO ...
I AM NINJA OSYA!
AND I HAVE VANQUISHED MIRACLE ☆ SYA!
MY APOLOGIES, YOUR HIGHNESS OSYA.
An adult willing to humor children

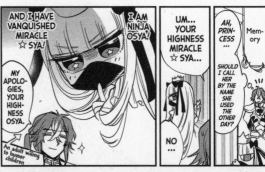

Would you like to change your class?

7 changes remaining

▶ Yes

No ▼

Auctioneer

"Hammer price!"

▼

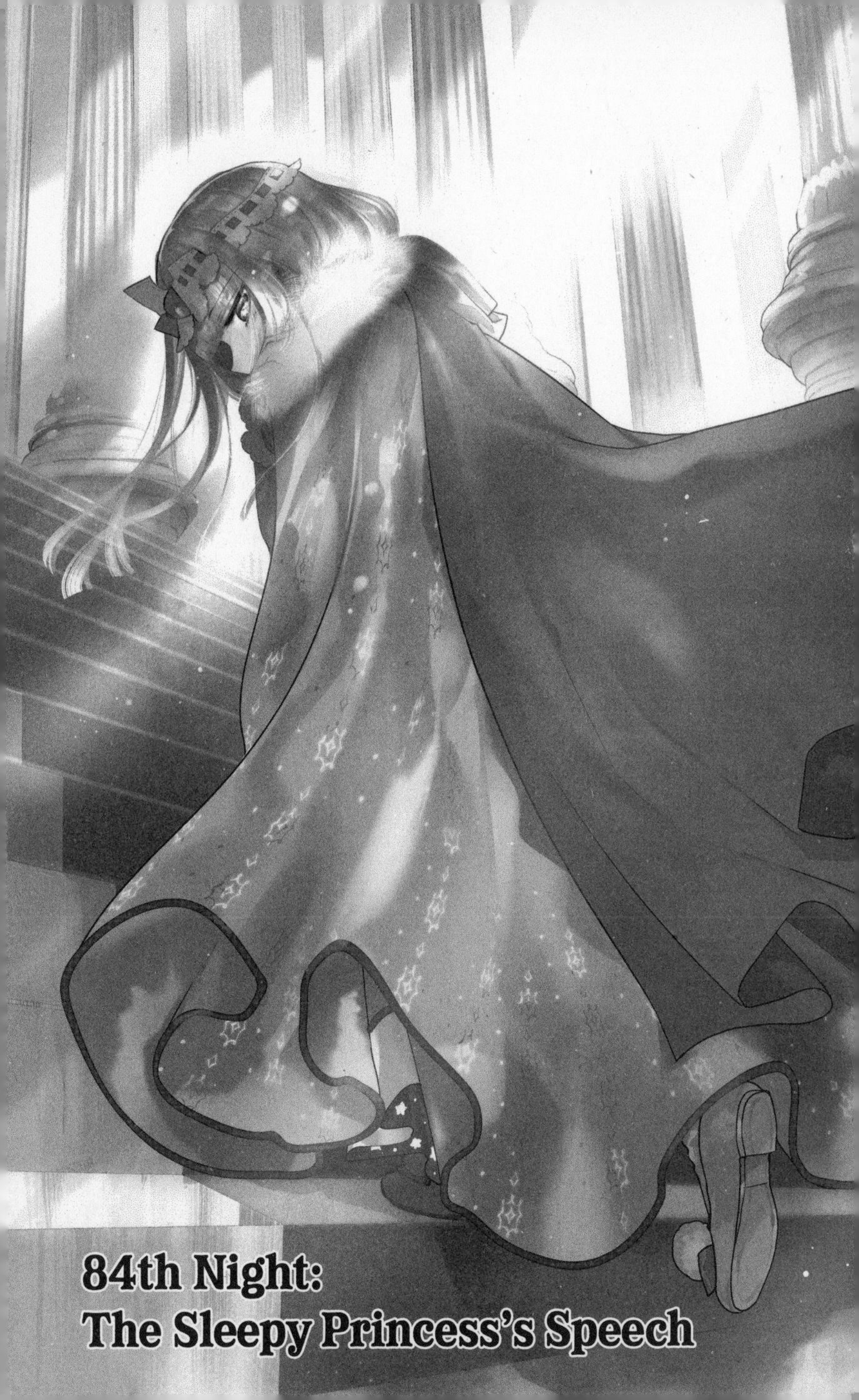

84th Night: The Sleepy Princess's Speech

SLEEPY PRINCESS
IN THE DEMON CASTLE

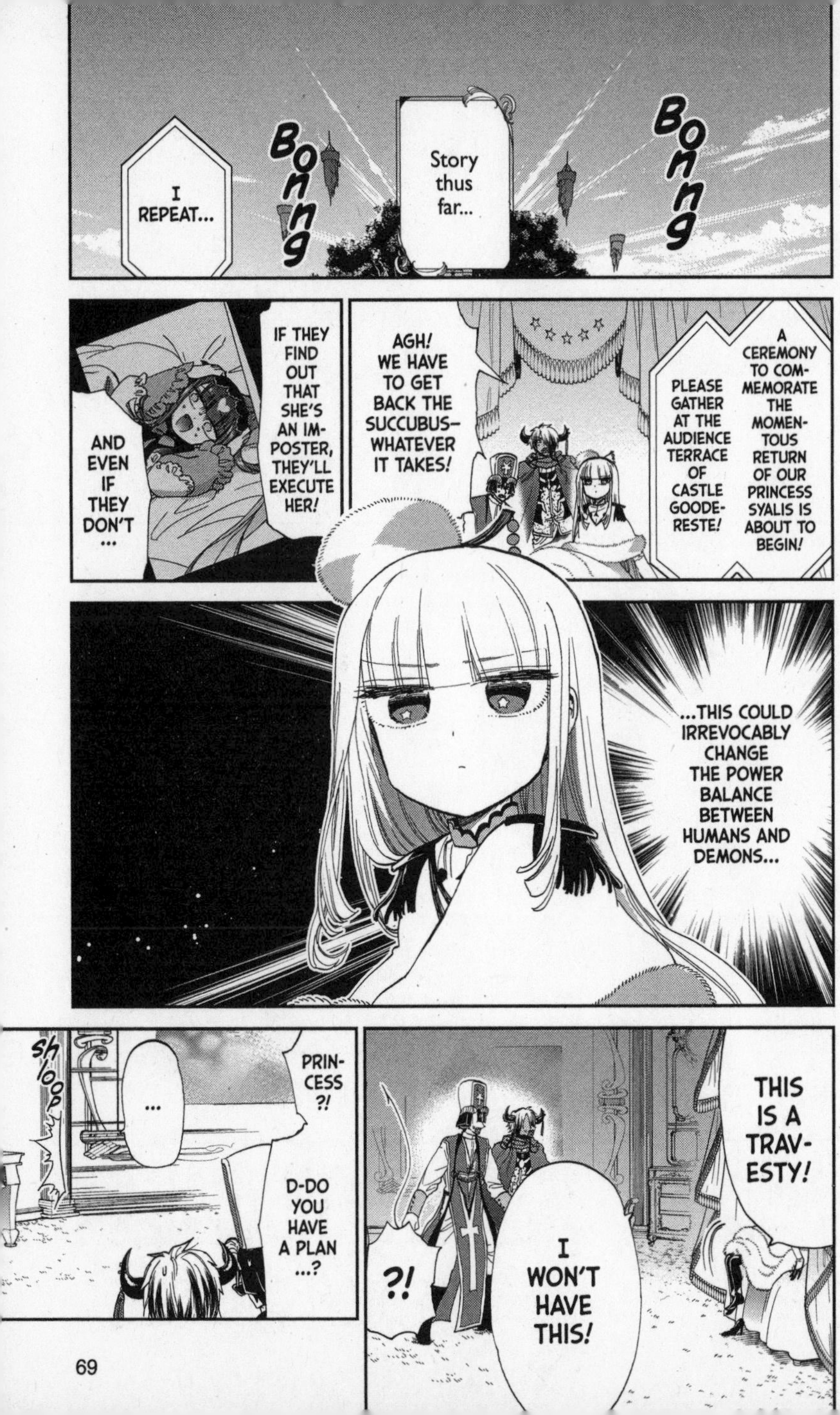
Bonng
Story thus far...
Bonng
I REPEAT...
A CEREMONY TO COMMEMORATE THE MOMENTOUS RETURN OF OUR PRINCESS SYALIS IS ABOUT TO BEGIN!
PLEASE GATHER AT THE AUDIENCE TERRACE OF CASTLE GOODERESTE!
AGH! WE HAVE TO GET BACK THE SUCCUBUS—WHATEVER IT TAKES!
IF THEY FIND OUT THAT SHE'S AN IMPOSTER, THEY'LL EXECUTE HER!
AND EVEN IF THEY DON'T...
...THIS COULD IRREVOCABLY CHANGE THE POWER BALANCE BETWEEN HUMANS AND DEMONS...
THIS IS A TRAVESTY!
I WON'T HAVE THIS!
?!
PRINCESS?!
D-DO YOU HAVE A PLAN...?
...
shloop

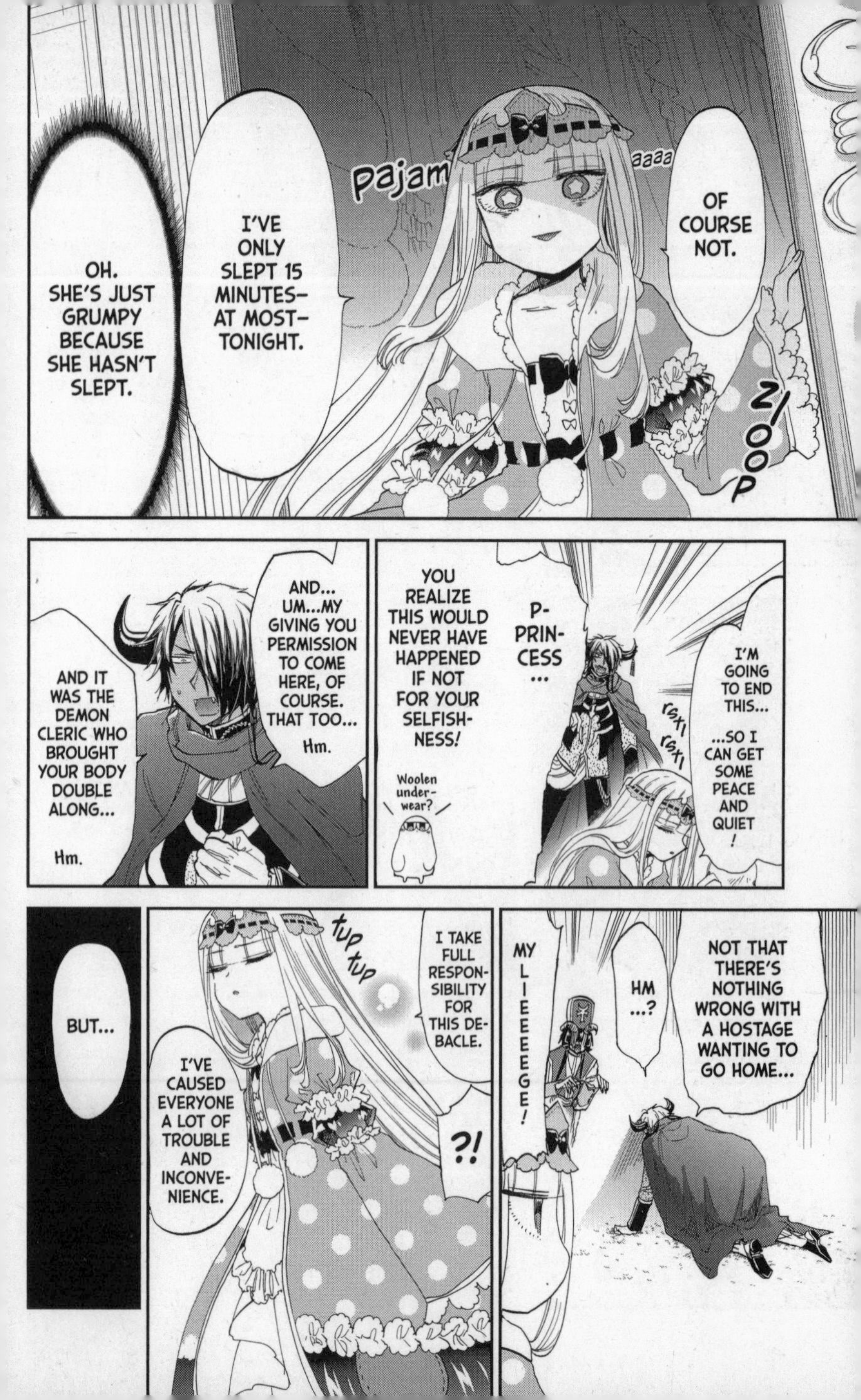
OF COURSE NOT.
Pajamaaaa
I'VE ONLY SLEPT 15 MINUTES—AT MOST—TONIGHT.
OH. SHE'S JUST GRUMPY BECAUSE SHE HASN'T SLEPT.
ZIOOP
I'M GOING TO END THIS...
...SO I CAN GET SOME PEACE AND QUIET!
rsxl rsxl
P-PRINCESS...
YOU REALIZE THIS WOULD NEVER HAVE HAPPENED IF NOT FOR YOUR SELFISHNESS!
Woolen underwear?
AND... UM...MY GIVING YOU PERMISSION TO COME HERE, OF COURSE. THAT TOO...
Hm.
AND IT WAS THE DEMON CLERIC WHO BROUGHT YOUR BODY DOUBLE ALONG...
Hm.
NOT THAT THERE'S NOTHING WRONG WITH A HOSTAGE WANTING TO GO HOME...
HM...?
MY LIEEEEEGE!
I TAKE FULL RESPONSIBILITY FOR THIS DEBACLE.
tup tup
?!
I'VE CAUSED EVERYONE A LOT OF TROUBLE AND INCONVENIENCE.
BUT...

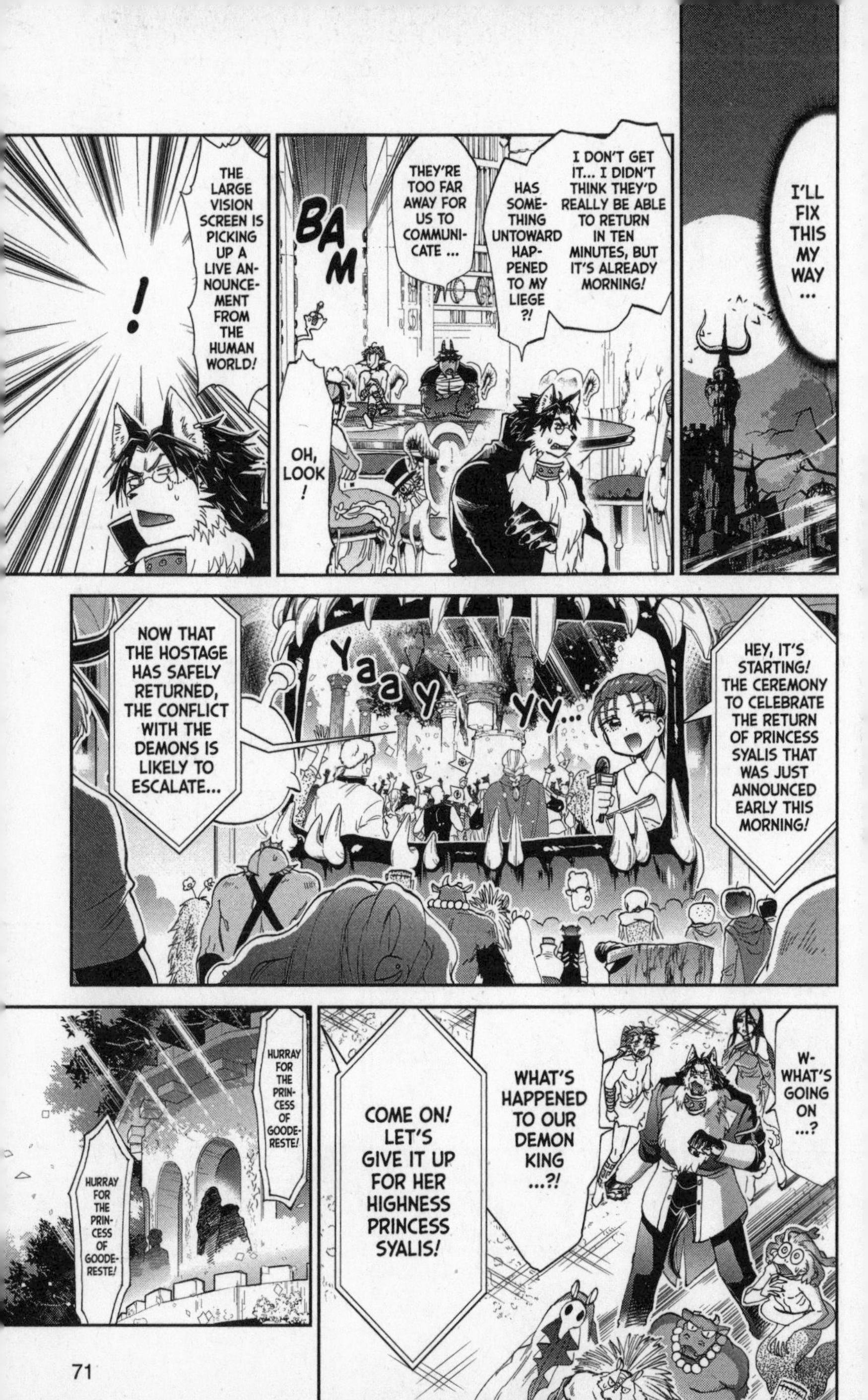
I'LL FIX THIS MY WAY...
I DON'T GET IT... I DIDN'T THINK THEY'D REALLY BE ABLE TO RETURN IN TEN MINUTES, BUT IT'S ALREADY MORNING!
HAS SOMETHING UNTOWARD HAPPENED TO MY LIEGE?!
THEY'RE TOO FAR AWAY FOR US TO COMMUNICATE...
BAM
OH, LOOK!
THE LARGE VISION SCREEN IS PICKING UP A LIVE ANNOUNCEMENT FROM THE HUMAN WORLD!
!
HEY, IT'S STARTING! THE CEREMONY TO CELEBRATE THE RETURN OF PRINCESS SYALIS THAT WAS JUST ANNOUNCED EARLY THIS MORNING!
Yaaayyy...
NOW THAT THE HOSTAGE HAS SAFELY RETURNED, THE CONFLICT WITH THE DEMONS IS LIKELY TO ESCALATE...
W-WHAT'S GOING ON...?
WHAT'S HAPPENED TO OUR DEMON KING...?!
COME ON! LET'S GIVE IT UP FOR HER HIGHNESS PRINCESS SYALIS!
HURRAY FOR THE PRINCESS OF GOODERESTE!
HURRAY FOR THE PRINCESS OF GOODERESTE!

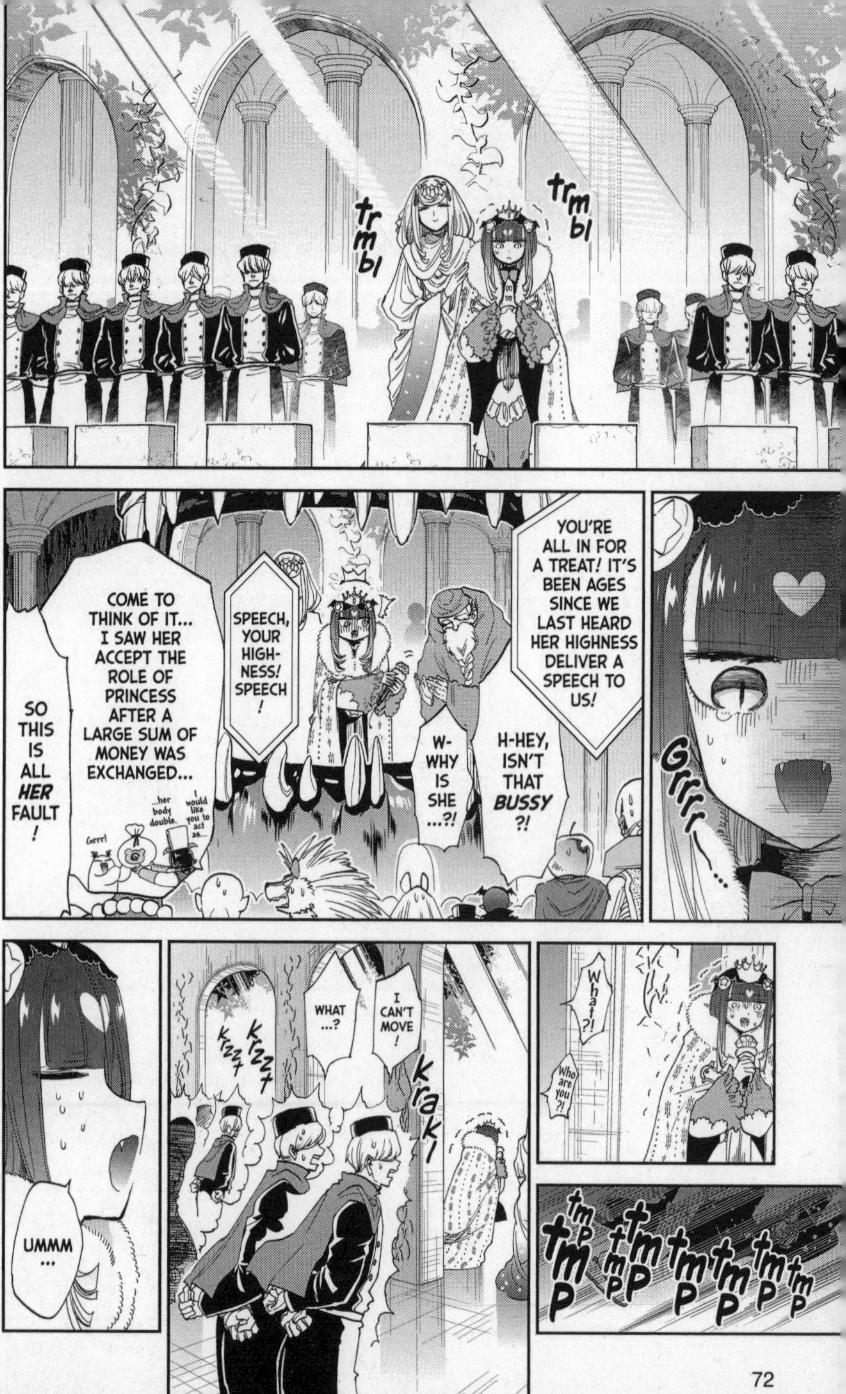
trmbl
trmbl
Grrrr...
YOU'RE ALL IN FOR A TREAT! IT'S BEEN AGES SINCE WE LAST HEARD HER HIGHNESS DELIVER A SPEECH TO US!
H-HEY, ISN'T THAT *BUSSY*?!
W-WHY IS SHE...?!
SPEECH, YOUR HIGHNESS! SPEECH!
COME TO THINK OF IT... I SAW HER ACCEPT THE ROLE OF PRINCESS AFTER A LARGE SUM OF MONEY WAS EXCHANGED...
I would like you to act as...
...her body double.
Grrr!
SO THIS IS ALL *HER* FAULT!
What?!
Who are you?!
tmp tmp tmp tmp tmp tmp tmp tmp
I CAN'T MOVE!
WHAT...?
kraki
krzzt krzzt
UMMM...

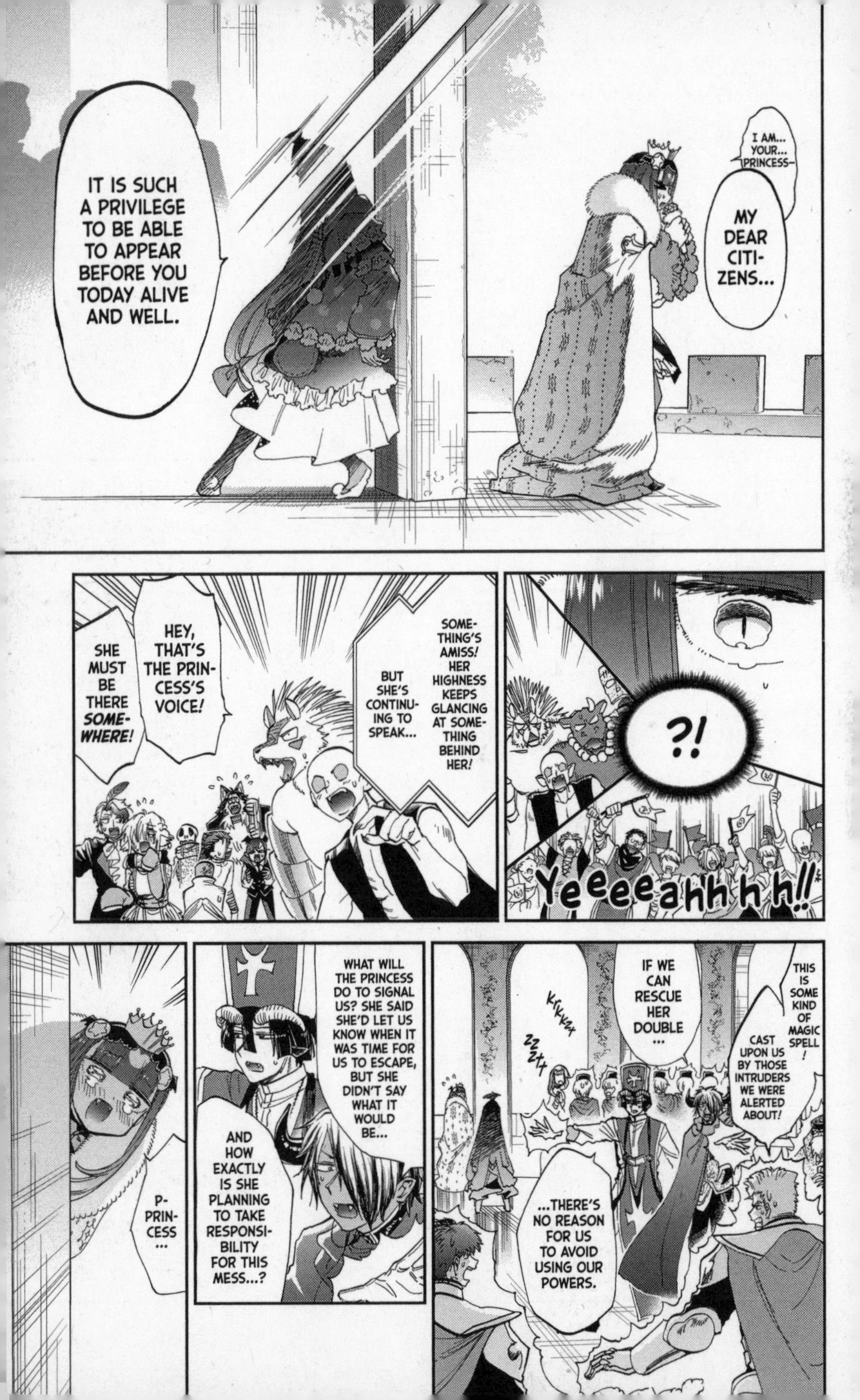
I AM... YOUR... PRINCESS—
MY DEAR CITIZENS...
IT IS SUCH A PRIVILEGE TO BE ABLE TO APPEAR BEFORE YOU TODAY ALIVE AND WELL.
?!
Yeeeeahhhh!!
SOMETHING'S AMISS! HER HIGHNESS KEEPS GLANCING AT SOMETHING BEHIND HER!
BUT SHE'S CONTINUING TO SPEAK...
HEY, THAT'S THE PRINCESS'S VOICE!
SHE MUST BE THERE *SOMEWHERE!*
THIS IS SOME KIND OF MAGIC SPELL!
CAST UPON US BY THOSE INTRUDERS WE WERE ALERTED ABOUT!
IF WE CAN RESCUE HER DOUBLE...
...THERE'S NO REASON FOR US TO AVOID USING OUR POWERS.
WHAT WILL THE PRINCESS DO TO SIGNAL US? SHE SAID SHE'D LET US KNOW WHEN IT WAS TIME FOR US TO ESCAPE, BUT SHE DIDN'T SAY WHAT IT WOULD BE...
AND HOW EXACTLY IS SHE PLANNING TO TAKE RESPONSIBILITY FOR THIS MESS...?
P-PRINCESS...

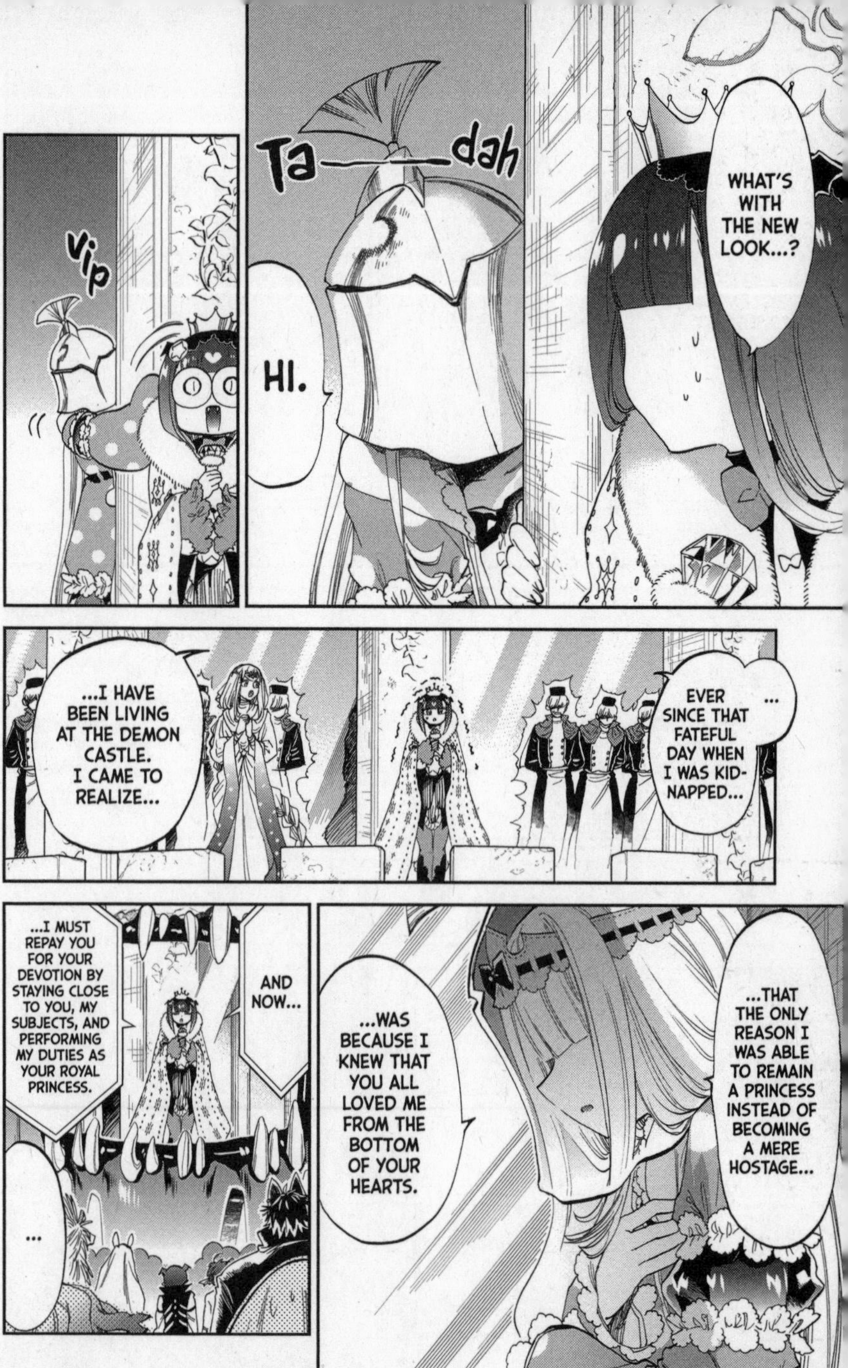
WHAT'S WITH THE NEW LOOK...?
Ta——dah
HI.
Vip
...
EVER SINCE THAT FATEFUL DAY WHEN I WAS KID-NAPPED...
...I HAVE BEEN LIVING AT THE DEMON CASTLE. I CAME TO REALIZE...
...THAT THE ONLY REASON I WAS ABLE TO REMAIN A PRINCESS INSTEAD OF BECOMING A MERE HOSTAGE...
...WAS BECAUSE I KNEW THAT YOU ALL LOVED ME FROM THE BOTTOM OF YOUR HEARTS.
AND NOW...
...I MUST REPAY YOU FOR YOUR DEVOTION BY STAYING CLOSE TO YOU, MY SUBJECTS, AND PERFORMING MY DUTIES AS YOUR ROYAL PRINCESS.
...

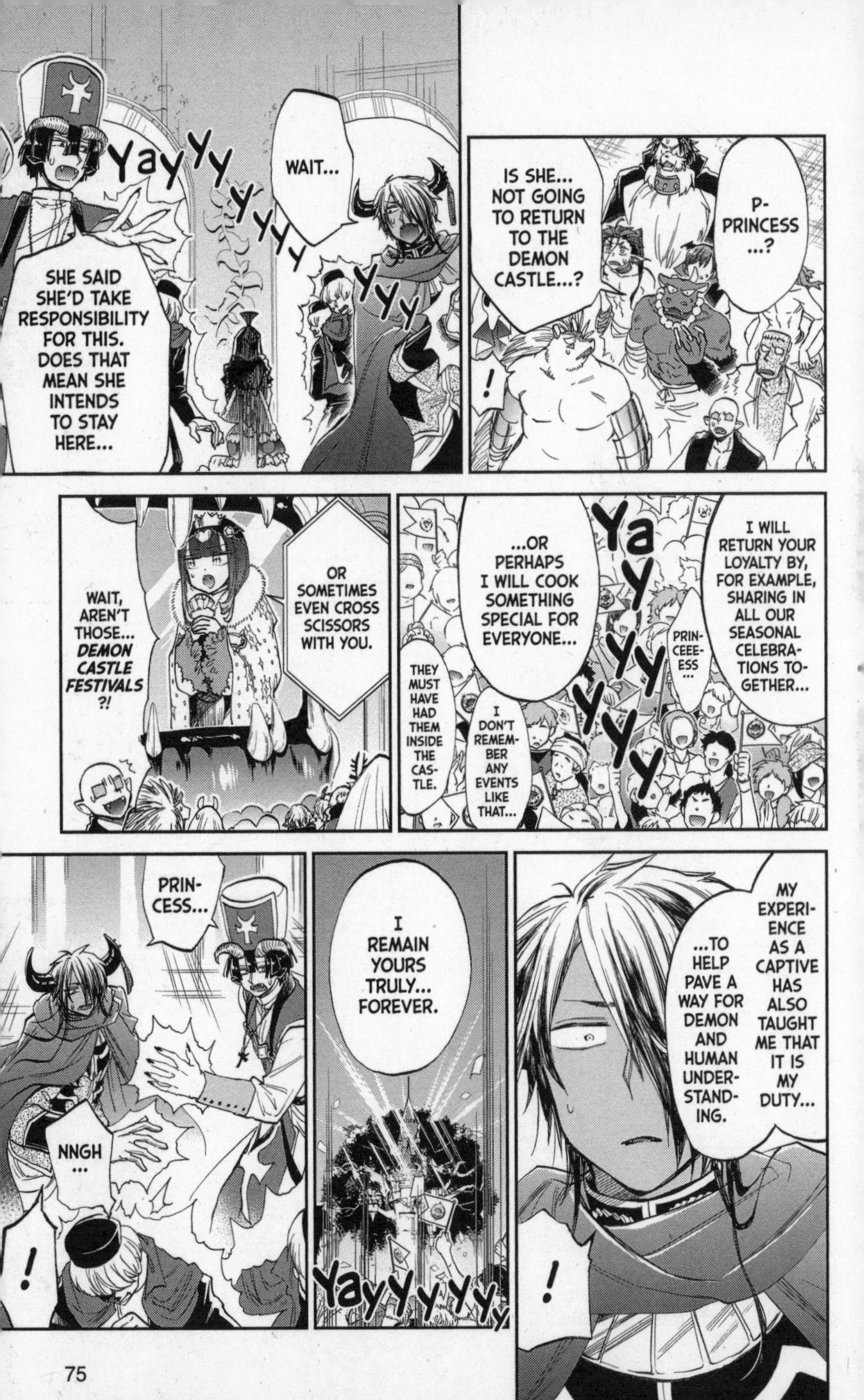
P-PRINCESS ...?
IS SHE... NOT GOING TO RETURN TO THE DEMON CASTLE...?
!
WAIT...
Yayyyyyyyyy
SHE SAID SHE'D TAKE RESPONSIBILITY FOR THIS. DOES THAT MEAN SHE INTENDS TO STAY HERE...
I WILL RETURN YOUR LOYALTY BY, FOR EXAMPLE, SHARING IN ALL OUR SEASONAL CELEBRATIONS TOGETHER...
...OR PERHAPS I WILL COOK SOMETHING SPECIAL FOR EVERYONE...
PRINCEEE-ESS...
Yayyyyyy
I DON'T REMEMBER ANY EVENTS LIKE THAT...
THEY MUST HAVE HAD THEM INSIDE THE CASTLE.
OR SOMETIMES EVEN CROSS SCISSORS WITH YOU.
WAIT, AREN'T THOSE... *DEMON CASTLE FESTIVALS*?!
MY EXPERIENCE AS A CAPTIVE HAS ALSO TAUGHT ME THAT IT IS MY DUTY...
...TO HELP PAVE A WAY FOR DEMON AND HUMAN UNDERSTANDING.
!
I REMAIN YOURS TRULY... FOREVER.
Yayyyyyyy
PRINCESS...
NNGH...
!

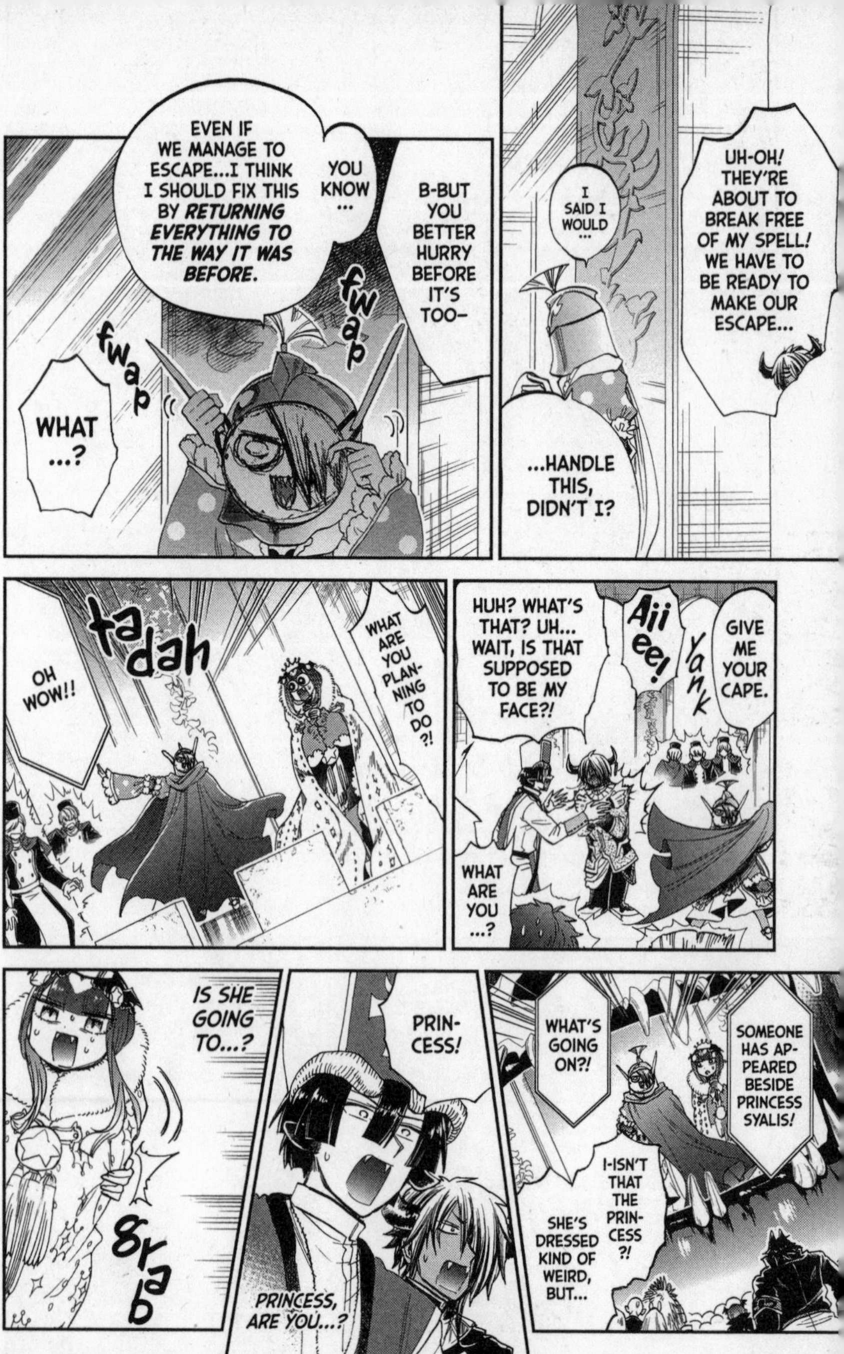
UH-OH! THEY'RE ABOUT TO BREAK FREE OF MY SPELL! WE HAVE TO BE READY TO MAKE OUR ESCAPE...
I SAID I WOULD...
...HANDLE THIS, DIDN'T I?
B-BUT YOU BETTER HURRY BEFORE IT'S TOO—
fwap
YOU KNOW...
EVEN IF WE MANAGE TO ESCAPE...I THINK I SHOULD FIX THIS BY *RETURNING EVERYTHING TO THE WAY IT WAS BEFORE.*
fwap
WHAT...?
GIVE ME YOUR CAPE.
Yank
Aiieee!
HUH? WHAT'S THAT? UH... WAIT, IS THAT SUPPOSED TO BE MY FACE?!
WHAT ARE YOU...?
WHAT ARE YOU PLAN-NING TO DO?!
tadah
OH WOW!!
SOMEONE HAS AP-PEARED BESIDE PRINCESS SYALIS!
WHAT'S GOING ON?!
I-ISN'T THAT THE PRIN-CESS?!
SHE'S DRESSED KIND OF WEIRD, BUT...
PRIN-CESS!
PRINCESS, ARE YOU...?
IS SHE GOING TO...?
grab

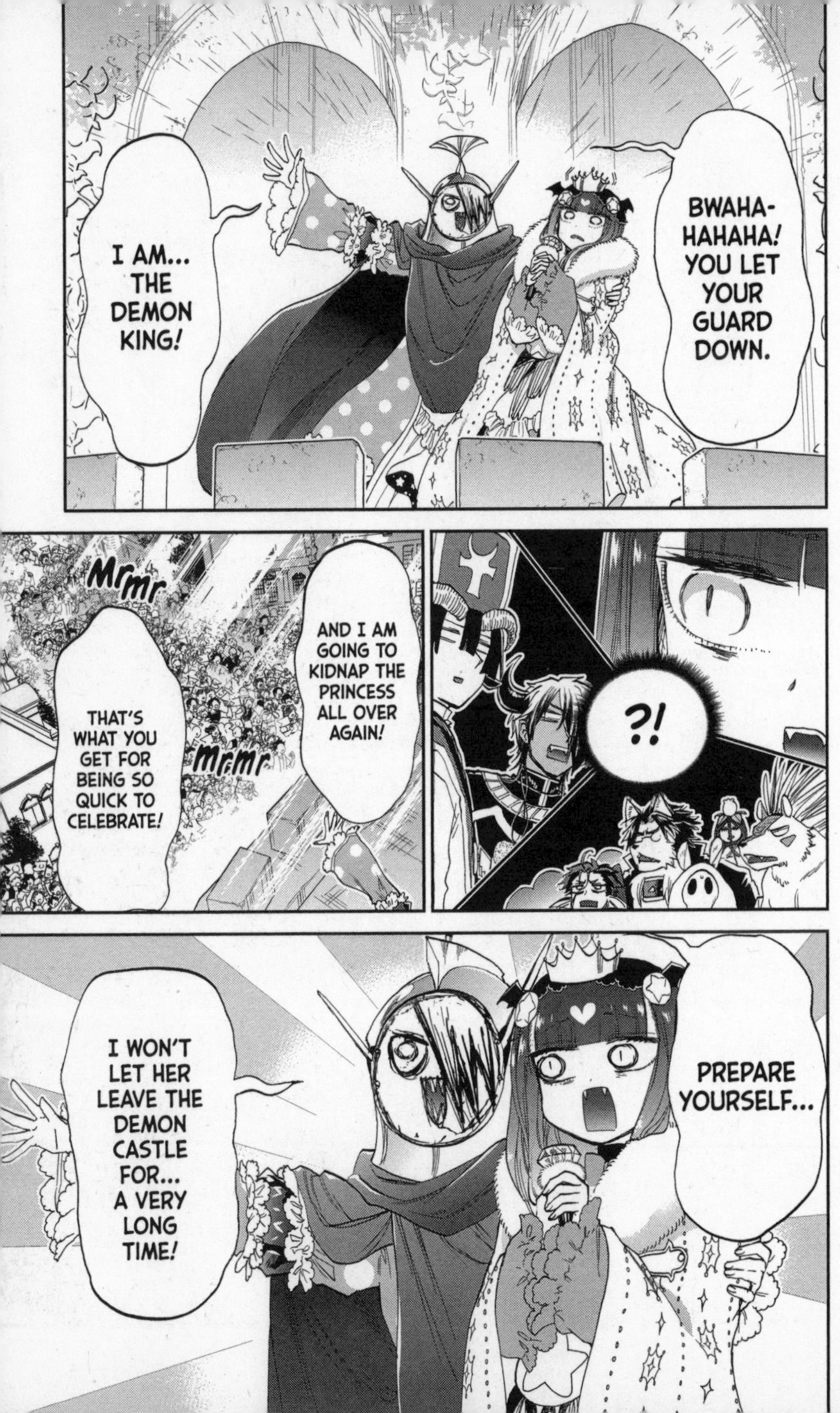
BWAHA-HAHAHA! YOU LET YOUR GUARD DOWN.
I AM... THE DEMON KING!
?!
AND I AM GOING TO KIDNAP THE PRINCESS ALL OVER AGAIN!
Mrmr
THAT'S WHAT YOU GET FOR BEING SO QUICK TO CELEBRATE!
mrmr
PREPARE YOURSELF...
I WON'T LET HER LEAVE THE DEMON CASTLE FOR... A VERY LONG TIME!

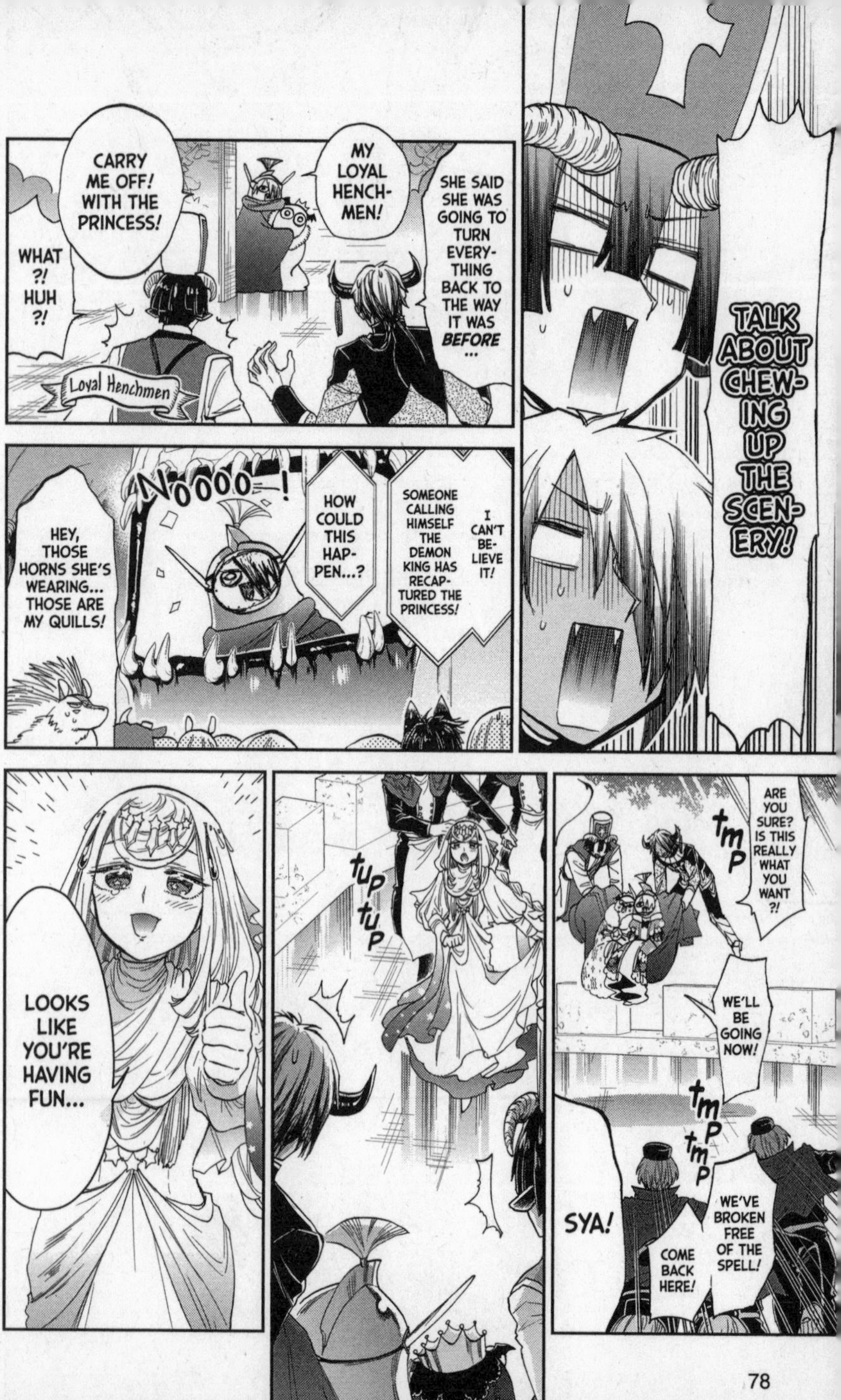
TALK ABOUT CHEWING UP THE SCENERY!
SHE SAID SHE WAS GOING TO TURN EVERYTHING BACK TO THE WAY IT WAS *BEFORE*...
MY LOYAL HENCHMEN!
CARRY ME OFF! WITH THE PRINCESS!
WHAT?! HUH?!
Loyal Henchmen
I CAN'T BELIEVE IT!
SOMEONE CALLING HIMSELF THE DEMON KING HAS RECAPTURED THE PRINCESS!
HOW COULD THIS HAPPEN...?
NOOOO—!
HEY, THOSE HORNS SHE'S WEARING... THOSE ARE MY QUILLS!
ARE YOU SURE? IS THIS REALLY WHAT YOU WANT?!
tmp
WE'LL BE GOING NOW!
tmp tmp
WE'VE BROKEN FREE OF THE SPELL!
COME BACK HERE!
SYA!
tup tup
LOOKS LIKE YOU'RE HAVING FUN...

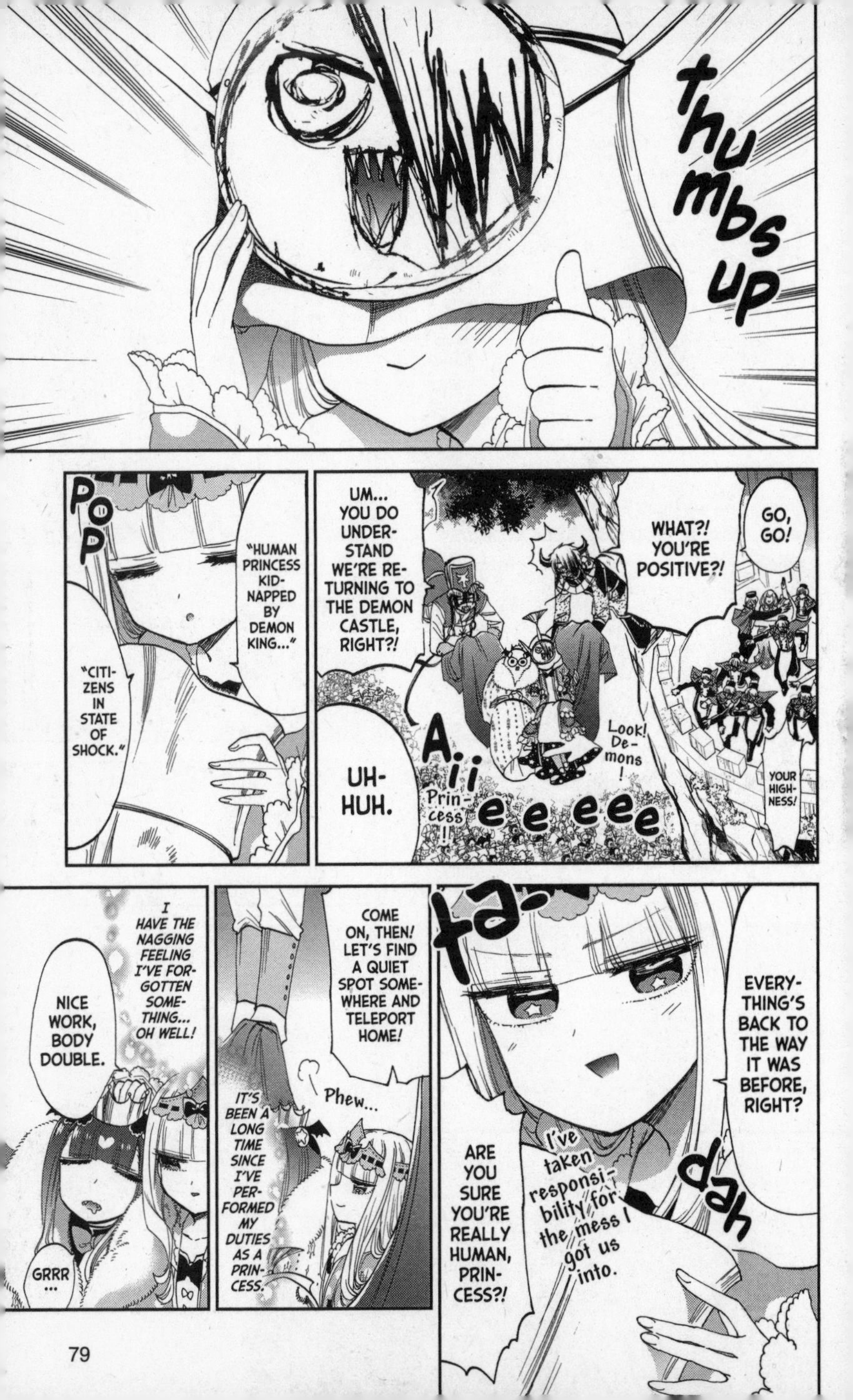
thumbs up
GO, GO!
WHAT?! YOU'RE POSITIVE?!
UM... YOU DO UNDERSTAND WE'RE RETURNING TO THE DEMON CASTLE, RIGHT?!
UH-HUH.
Look! Demons!
YOUR HIGHNESS!
Aiieeeee
Princess!!
POP
"HUMAN PRINCESS KIDNAPPED BY DEMON KING..."
"CITIZENS IN STATE OF SHOCK."
ta-
EVERYTHING'S BACK TO THE WAY IT WAS BEFORE, RIGHT?
dah
I've taken responsibility for the mess I got us into.
ARE YOU SURE YOU'RE REALLY HUMAN, PRINCESS?!
COME ON, THEN! LET'S FIND A QUIET SPOT SOMEWHERE AND TELEPORT HOME!
Phew...
IT'S BEEN A LONG TIME SINCE I'VE PERFORMED MY DUTIES AS A PRINCESS.
I HAVE THE NAGGING FEELING I'VE FORGOTTEN SOMETHING... OH WELL!
NICE WORK, BODY DOUBLE.
GRRR...

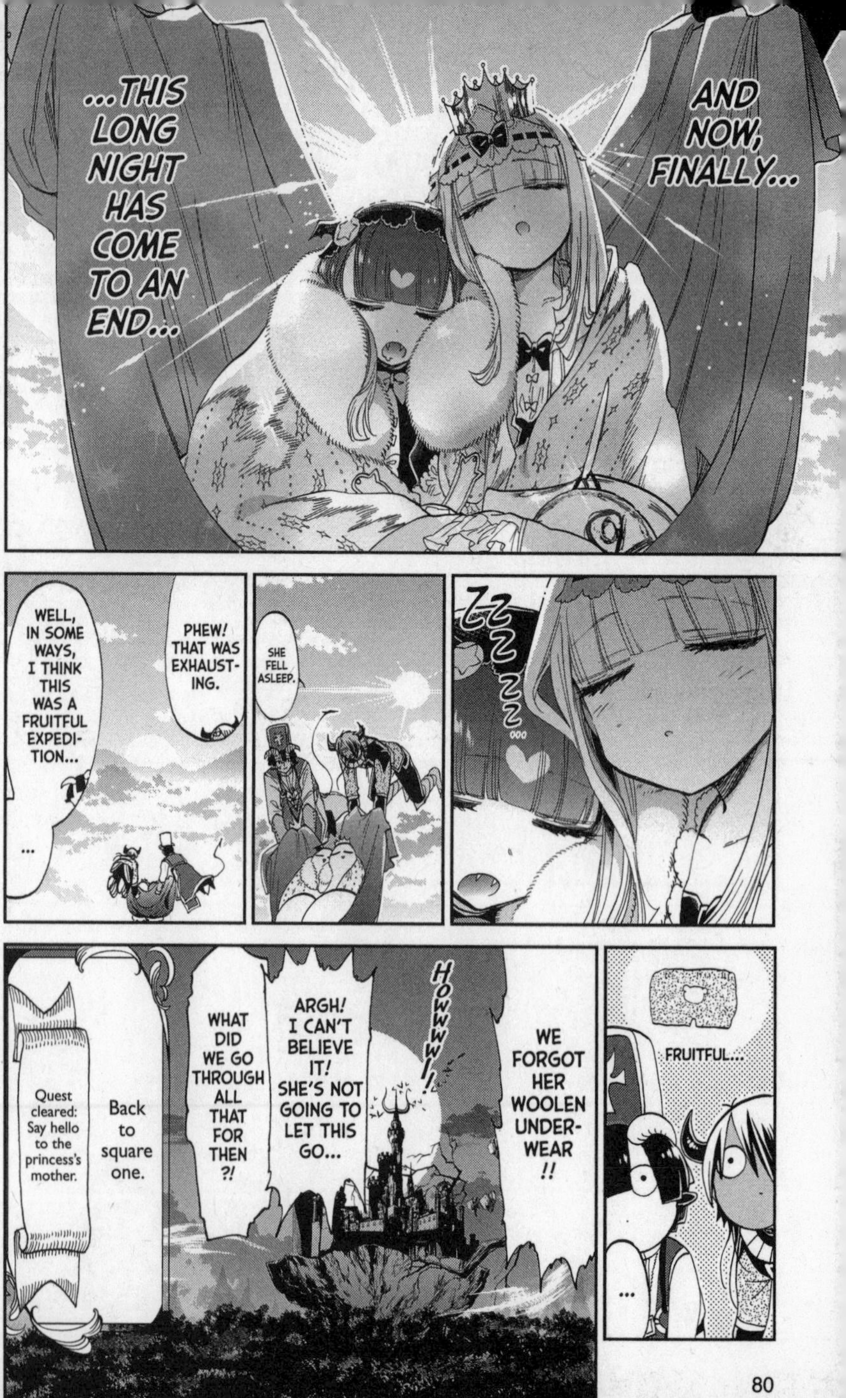
AND NOW, FINALLY...
...THIS LONG NIGHT HAS COME TO AN END...
SHE FELL ASLEEP.
PHEW! THAT WAS EXHAUST-ING.
WELL, IN SOME WAYS, I THINK THIS WAS A FRUITFUL EXPEDI-TION...
...
FRUITFUL...
...
HOWWWW!!
WE FORGOT HER WOOLEN UNDER-WEAR!!
ARGH! I CAN'T BELIEVE IT! SHE'S NOT GOING TO LET THIS GO...
WHAT DID WE GO THROUGH ALL THAT FOR THEN?!
Back to square one.
Quest cleared: Say hello to the princess's mother.

The princess's home castle.

Royal Palace of the World Tree
Castle Goodereste

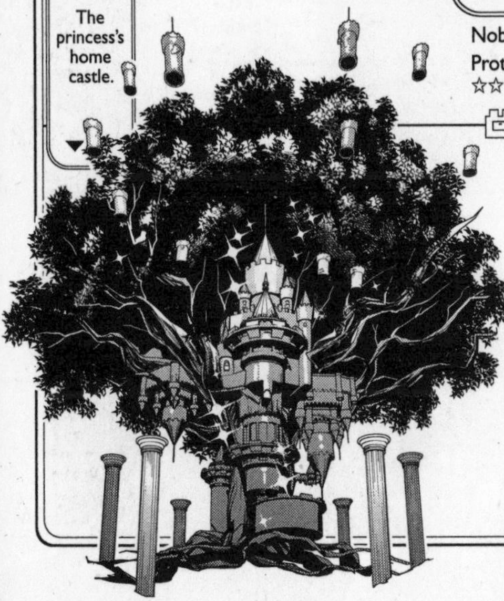

Noblesse Oblige: ☆☆☆☆☆☆☆☆☆☆☆

Protection of the World Tree: ☆☆☆☆☆☆☆☆☆☆☆

This royal palace was built inside a sacred tree at the time of the founding of the Unified Human Nation. It has been chosen as a Human World Heritage site due to its cultural importance.

The protective spells placed upon the sacred tree are extremely powerful, and thus most attack spells cast inside the castle are rendered impotent.

However, it is said that spells that the sacred tree deems beneficial to humanity are permitted. Could that be true...?

Problem until ten or so years ago: "This place is too big! I keep getting lost!"

Problem as of a few years ago: "I just go back and forth between my bedroom and my office."

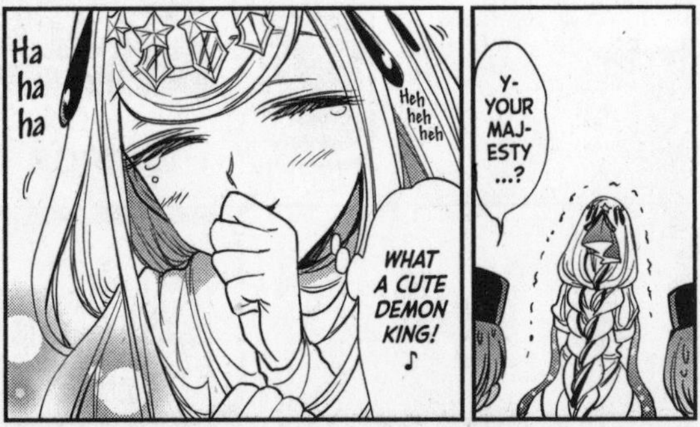
Y- YOUR MAJ- ESTY ...?
Ha ha ha
Heh heh heh
WHAT A CUTE DEMON KING! ♪

85th Night: Quilly and Me

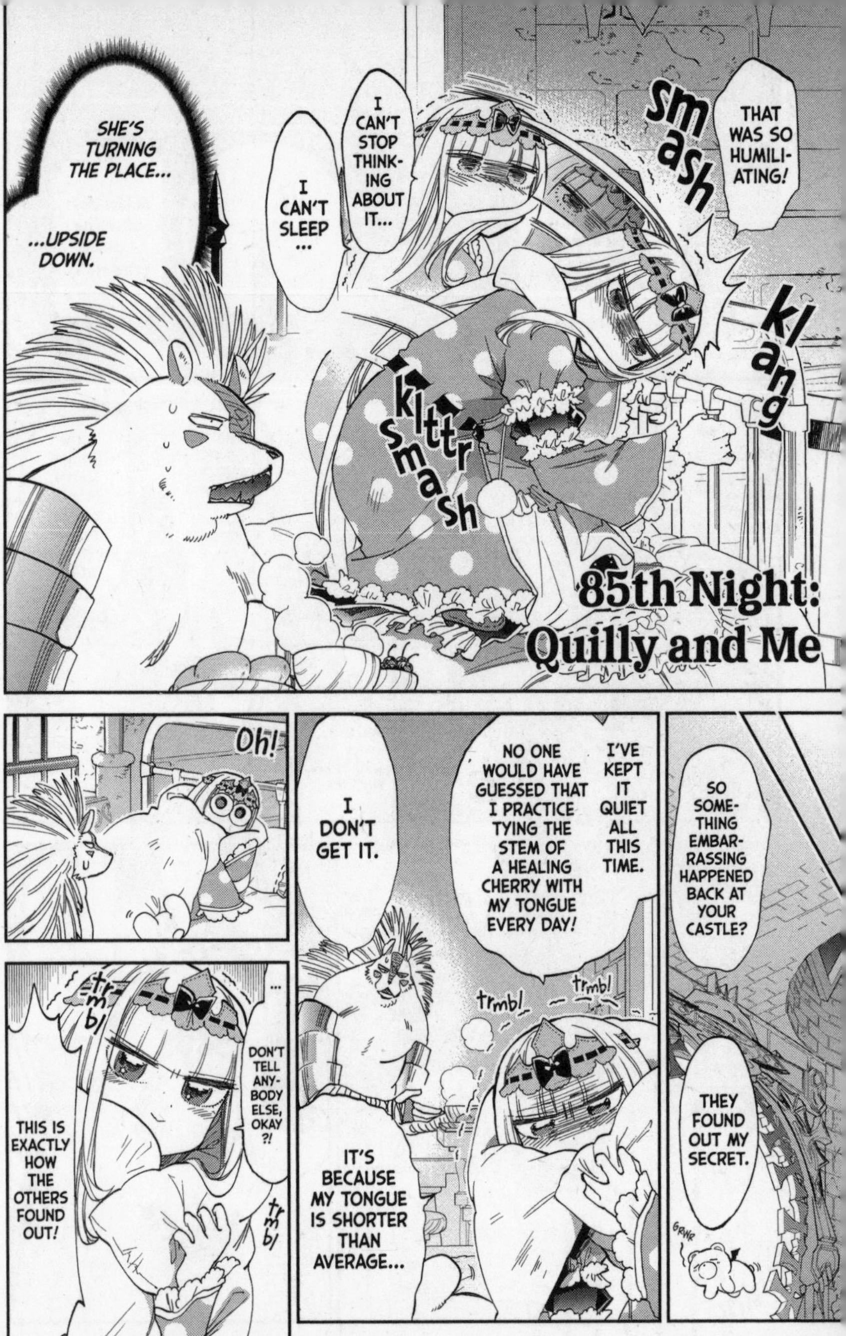
THAT WAS SO HUMILIATING!
smash
klang
I CAN'T STOP THINKING ABOUT IT...
I CAN'T SLEEP...
kltttr
smash
SHE'S TURNING THE PLACE...
...UPSIDE DOWN.
SO SOMETHING EMBARRASSING HAPPENED BACK AT YOUR CASTLE?
THEY FOUND OUT MY SECRET.
GRWR
I'VE KEPT IT QUIET ALL THIS TIME.
NO ONE WOULD HAVE GUESSED THAT I PRACTICE TYING THE STEM OF A HEALING CHERRY WITH MY TONGUE EVERY DAY!
I DON'T GET IT.
trmbl
trmbl
IT'S BECAUSE MY TONGUE IS SHORTER THAN AVERAGE...
Oh!
...
DON'T TELL ANYBODY ELSE, OKAY?!
trmbl
THIS IS EXACTLY HOW THE OTHERS FOUND OUT!
trmbl

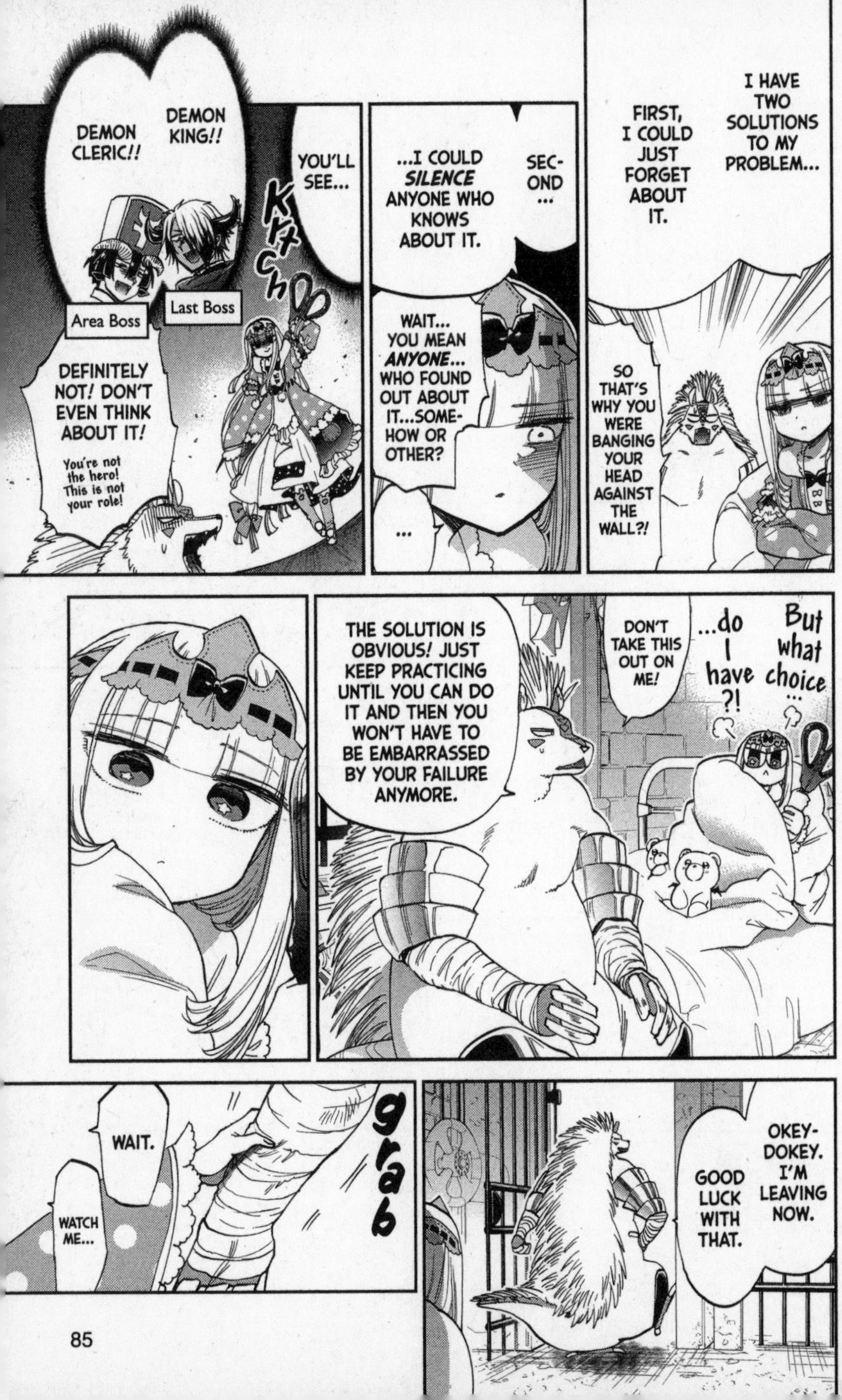
I HAVE TWO SOLUTIONS TO MY PROBLEM...
FIRST, I COULD JUST FORGET ABOUT IT.
SO THAT'S WHY YOU WERE BANGING YOUR HEAD AGAINST THE WALL?!
SEC-OND...
...I COULD *SILENCE* ANYONE WHO KNOWS ABOUT IT.
WAIT... YOU MEAN *ANYONE*... WHO FOUND OUT ABOUT IT...SOME-HOW OR OTHER?
...
YOU'LL SEE...
Kktch
DEMON KING!!
DEMON CLERIC!!
Last Boss
Area Boss
DEFINITELY NOT! DON'T EVEN THINK ABOUT IT!
You're not the hero! This is not your role!
But what choice...
...do I have?!
DON'T TAKE THIS OUT ON ME!
THE SOLUTION IS OBVIOUS! JUST KEEP PRACTICING UNTIL YOU CAN DO IT AND THEN YOU WON'T HAVE TO BE EMBARRASSED BY YOUR FAILURE ANYMORE.
OKEY-DOKEY. I'M LEAVING NOW.
GOOD LUCK WITH THAT.
grab
WAIT.
WATCH ME...

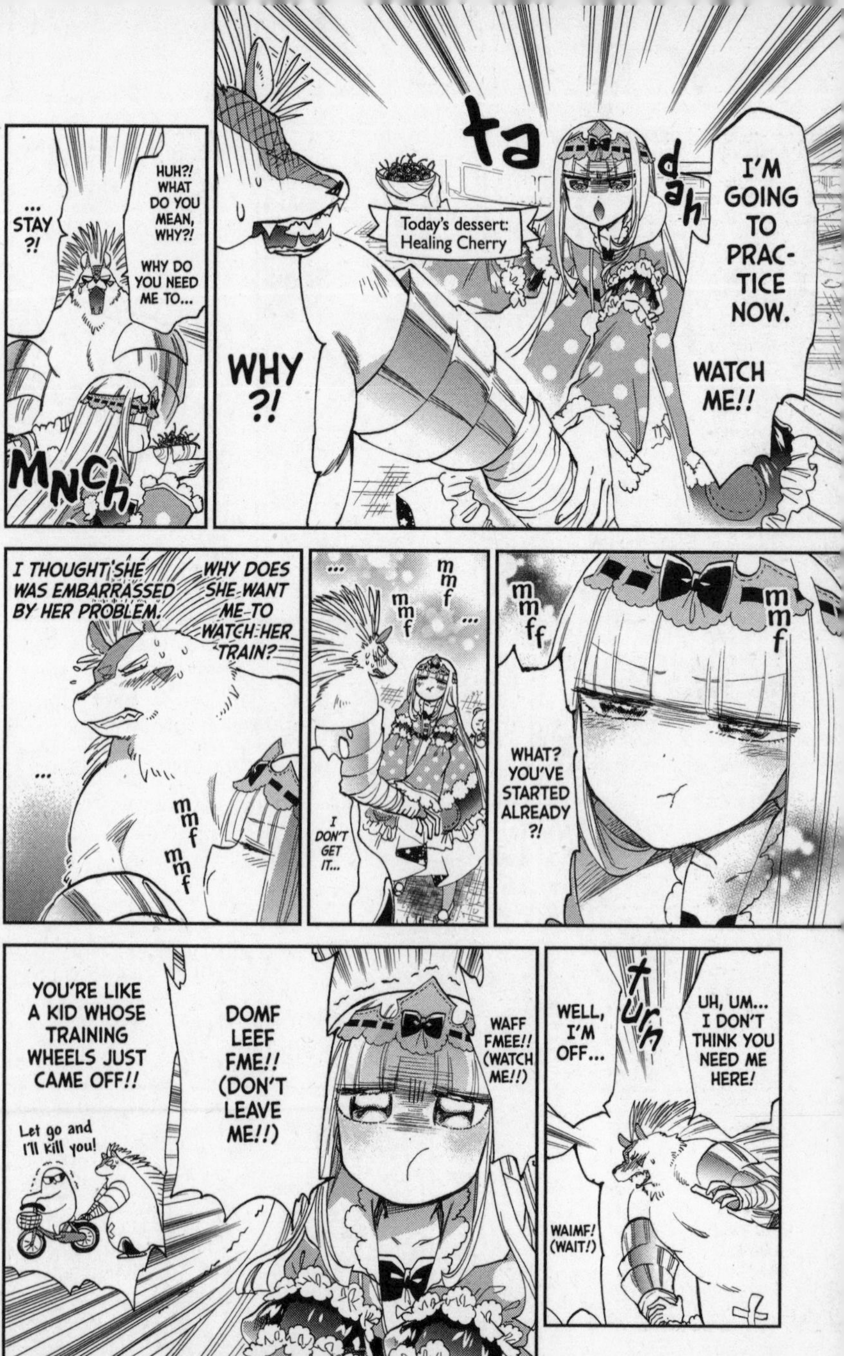
ta
dah
I'M GOING TO PRACTICE NOW.
WATCH ME!!
Today's dessert: Healing Cherry
WHY?!
HUH?! WHAT DO YOU MEAN, WHY?!
WHY DO YOU NEED ME TO...
... STAY?!
MNCh
mmff
mmf
WHAT? YOU'VE STARTED ALREADY?!
...
mmf
mmf
...
I DON'T GET IT...
WHY DOES SHE WANT ME TO WATCH HER TRAIN?
I THOUGHT SHE WAS EMBARRASSED BY HER PROBLEM.
...
mmf
mmf
UH, UM... I DON'T THINK YOU NEED ME HERE!
turn
WELL, I'M OFF...
WAIMF! (WAIT!)
WAFF FMEE!! (WATCH ME!!)
DOMF LEEF FME!! (DON'T LEAVE ME!!)
YOU'RE LIKE A KID WHOSE TRAINING WHEELS JUST CAME OFF!!
Let go and I'll kill you!

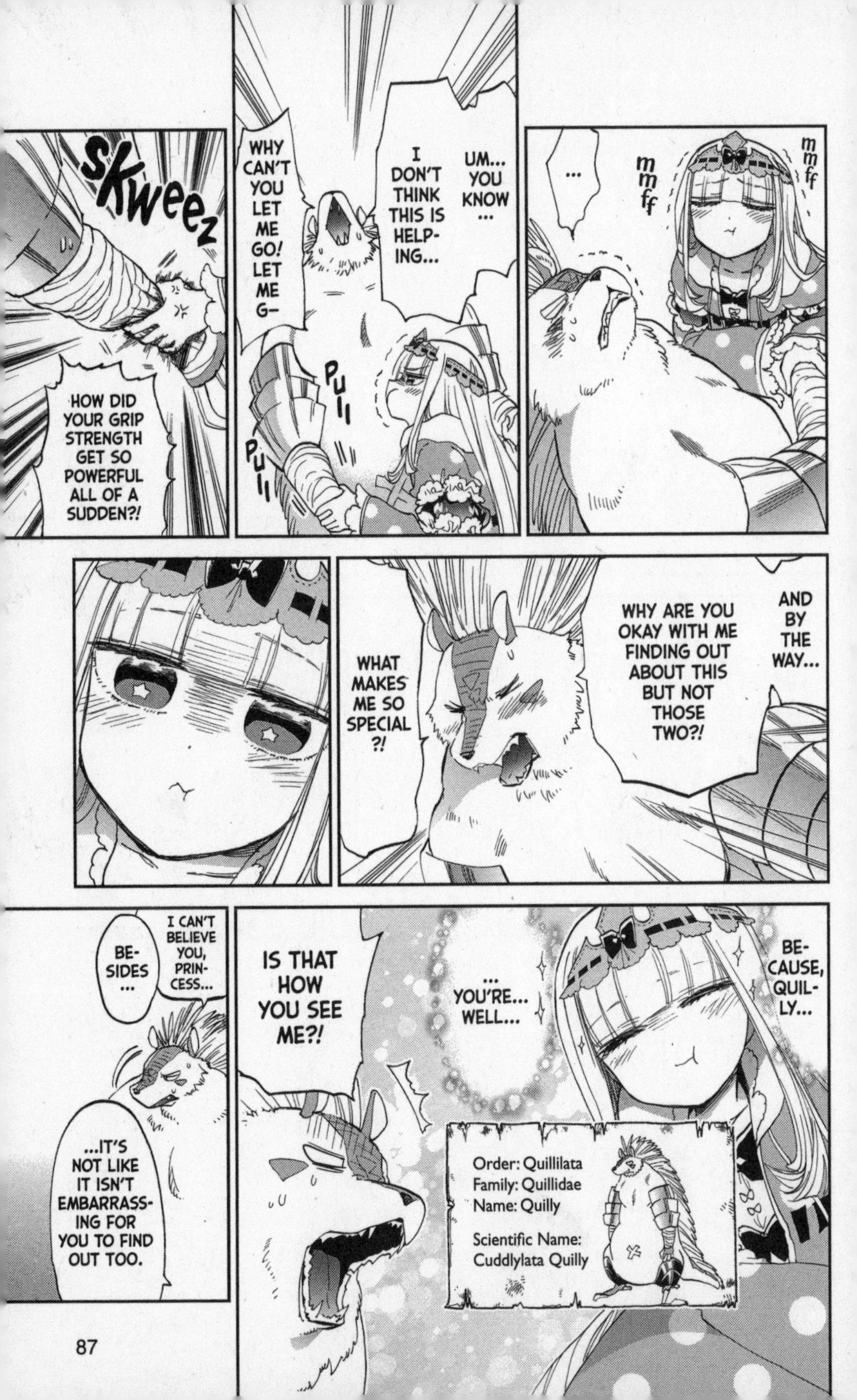
mmff
mmff
...
UM... YOU KNOW ...
I DON'T THINK THIS IS HELP-ING...
WHY CAN'T YOU LET ME GO! LET ME G-
PULL
PULL
SKWEEZ
HOW DID YOUR GRIP STRENGTH GET SO POWERFUL ALL OF A SUDDEN?!
AND BY THE WAY...
WHY ARE YOU OKAY WITH ME FINDING OUT ABOUT THIS BUT NOT THOSE TWO?!
WHAT MAKES ME SO SPECIAL ?!
BE-CAUSE, QUILL-LY...
... YOU'RE... WELL...
IS THAT HOW YOU SEE ME?!
Order: Quillilata
Family: Quillidae
Name: Quilly
Scientific Name: Cuddlylata Quilly
I CAN'T BELIEVE YOU, PRIN-CESS...
BE-SIDES ...
...IT'S NOT LIKE IT ISN'T EMBARRASS-ING FOR YOU TO FIND OUT TOO.

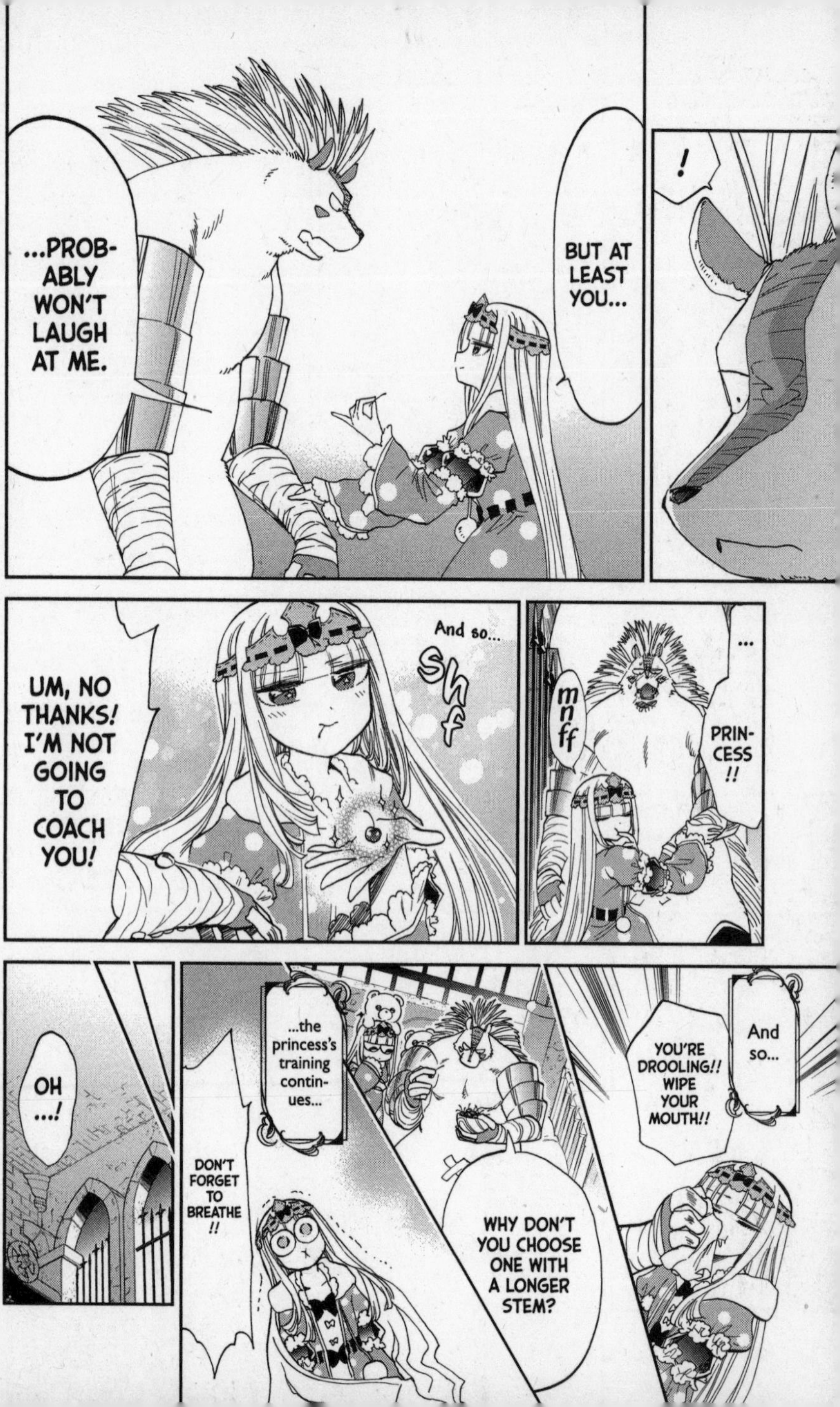
!
BUT AT LEAST YOU...
...PROB-ABLY WON'T LAUGH AT ME.
...
PRIN-CESS!!
mnff
And so...
Shf
UM, NO THANKS! I'M NOT GOING TO COACH YOU!
And so...
YOU'RE DROOLING!! WIPE YOUR MOUTH!!
...the princess's training contin-ues...
WHY DON'T YOU CHOOSE ONE WITH A LONGER STEM?
DON'T FORGET TO BREATHE!!
OH ...!

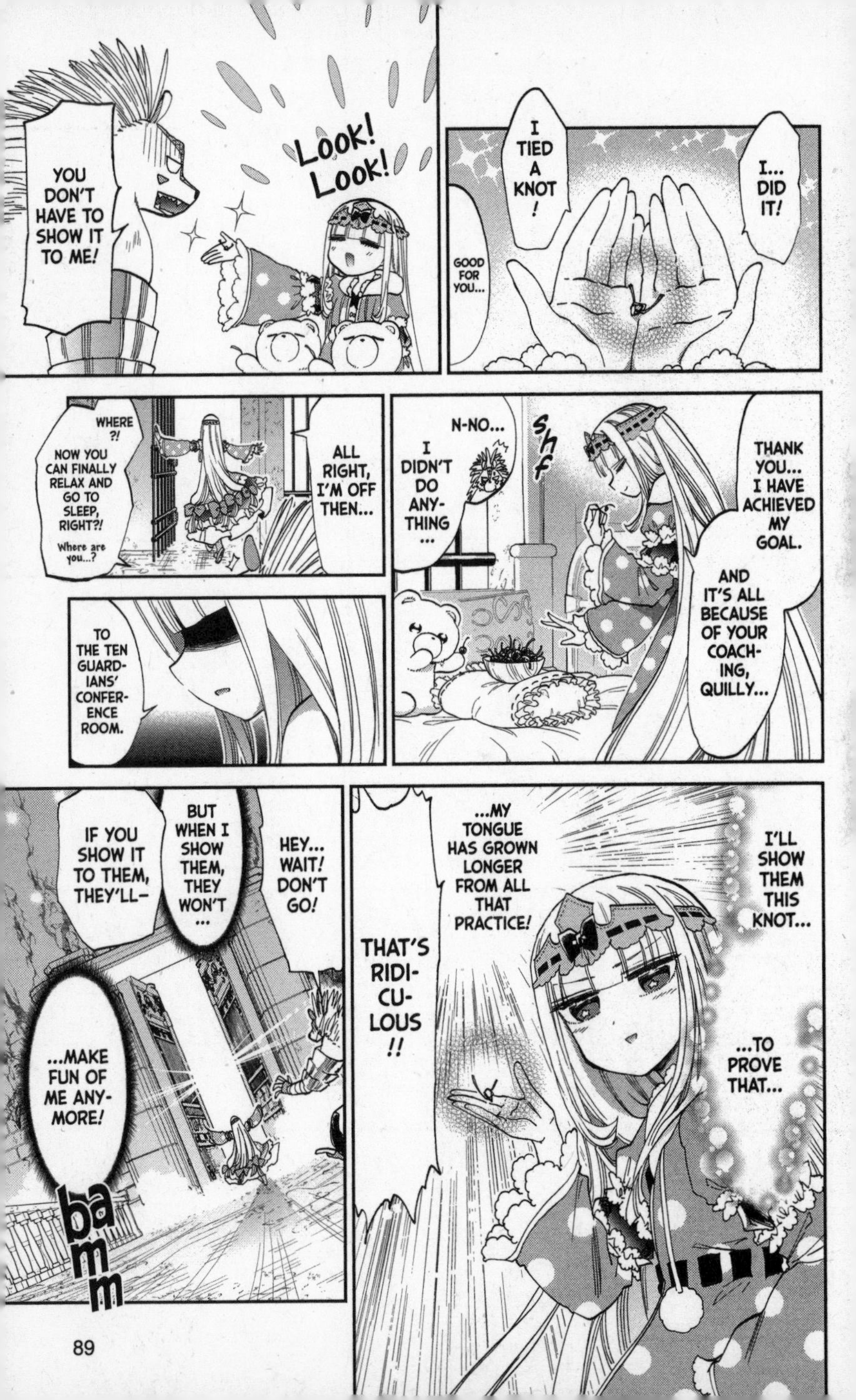
I... DID IT!
I TIED A KNOT!
GOOD FOR YOU...
LOOK! LOOK!
YOU DON'T HAVE TO SHOW IT TO ME!
THANK YOU... I HAVE ACHIEVED MY GOAL.
AND IT'S ALL BECAUSE OF YOUR COACHING, QUILLY...
SHF
N-NO...
I DIDN'T DO ANYTHING...
ALL RIGHT, I'M OFF THEN...
WHERE?!
NOW YOU CAN FINALLY RELAX AND GO TO SLEEP, RIGHT?!
Where are you...?
TO THE TEN GUARDIANS' CONFERENCE ROOM.
I'LL SHOW THEM THIS KNOT...
...TO PROVE THAT...
...MY TONGUE HAS GROWN LONGER FROM ALL THAT PRACTICE!
THAT'S RIDICULOUS!!
HEY... WAIT! DON'T GO!
BUT WHEN I SHOW THEM, THEY WON'T...
IF YOU SHOW IT TO THEM, THEY'LL–
...MAKE FUN OF ME ANYMORE!
bamm

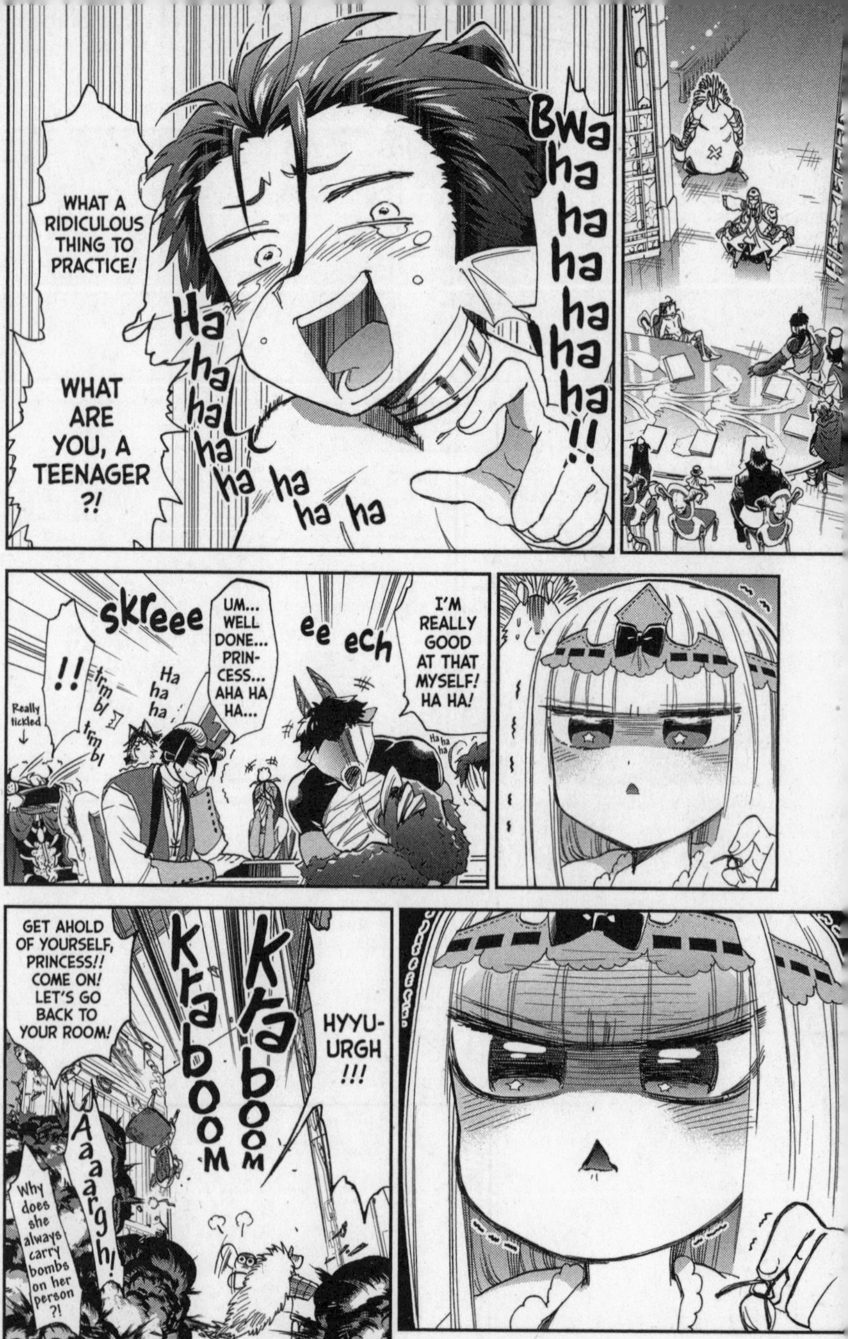
Bwahahahahahahaha!!
WHAT A RIDICULOUS THING TO PRACTICE!
Hahahahahahahaha
WHAT ARE YOU, A TEENAGER?!
I'M REALLY GOOD AT THAT MYSELF! HA HA!
ee ech
Ha ha ha
UM... WELL DONE... PRINCESS... AHA HA HA...
skreeee
Ha ha ha
!!
trmbl trmbl
Really tickled
HYYU-URGH!!!
Kraboom
Kraboom
GET AHOLD OF YOURSELF, PRINCESS!! COME ON! LET'S GO BACK TO YOUR ROOM!
Aaaargh!
Why does she always carry bombs on her person?!

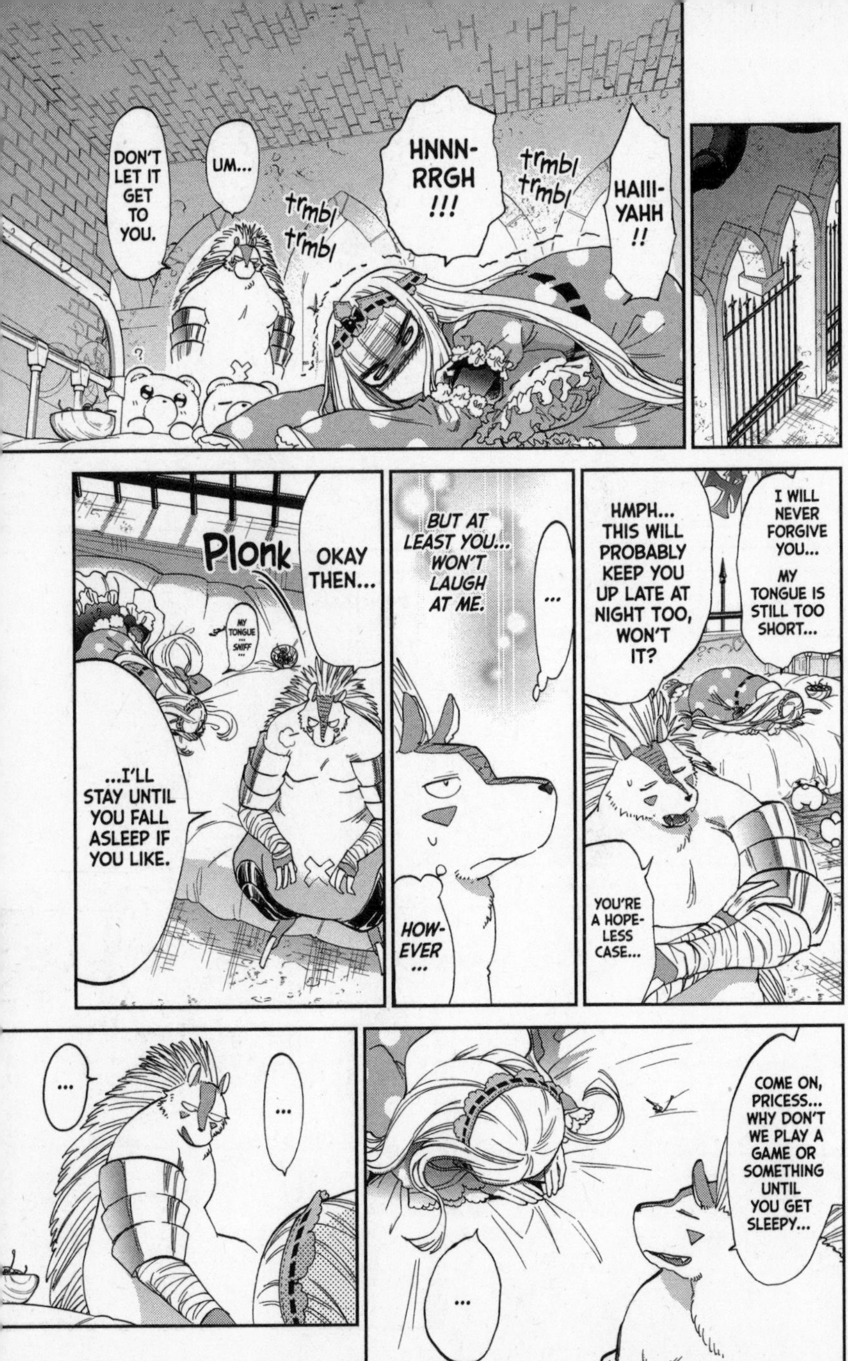
HAIII-YAHH!!
trmbl trmbl
HNNN-RRGH!!!
trmbl trmbl
UM...
DON'T LET IT GET TO YOU.
I WILL NEVER FORGIVE YOU... MY TONGUE IS STILL TOO SHORT...
HMPH... THIS WILL PROBABLY KEEP YOU UP LATE AT NIGHT TOO, WON'T IT?
YOU'RE A HOPE-LESS CASE...
...
BUT AT LEAST YOU... WON'T LAUGH AT ME.
HOW-EVER...
OKAY THEN...
Plonk
MY TONGUE ... SNIFF ...
...I'LL STAY UNTIL YOU FALL ASLEEP IF YOU LIKE.
COME ON, PRICESS... WHY DON'T WE PLAY A GAME OR SOMETHING UNTIL YOU GET SLEEPY...
...
...
...

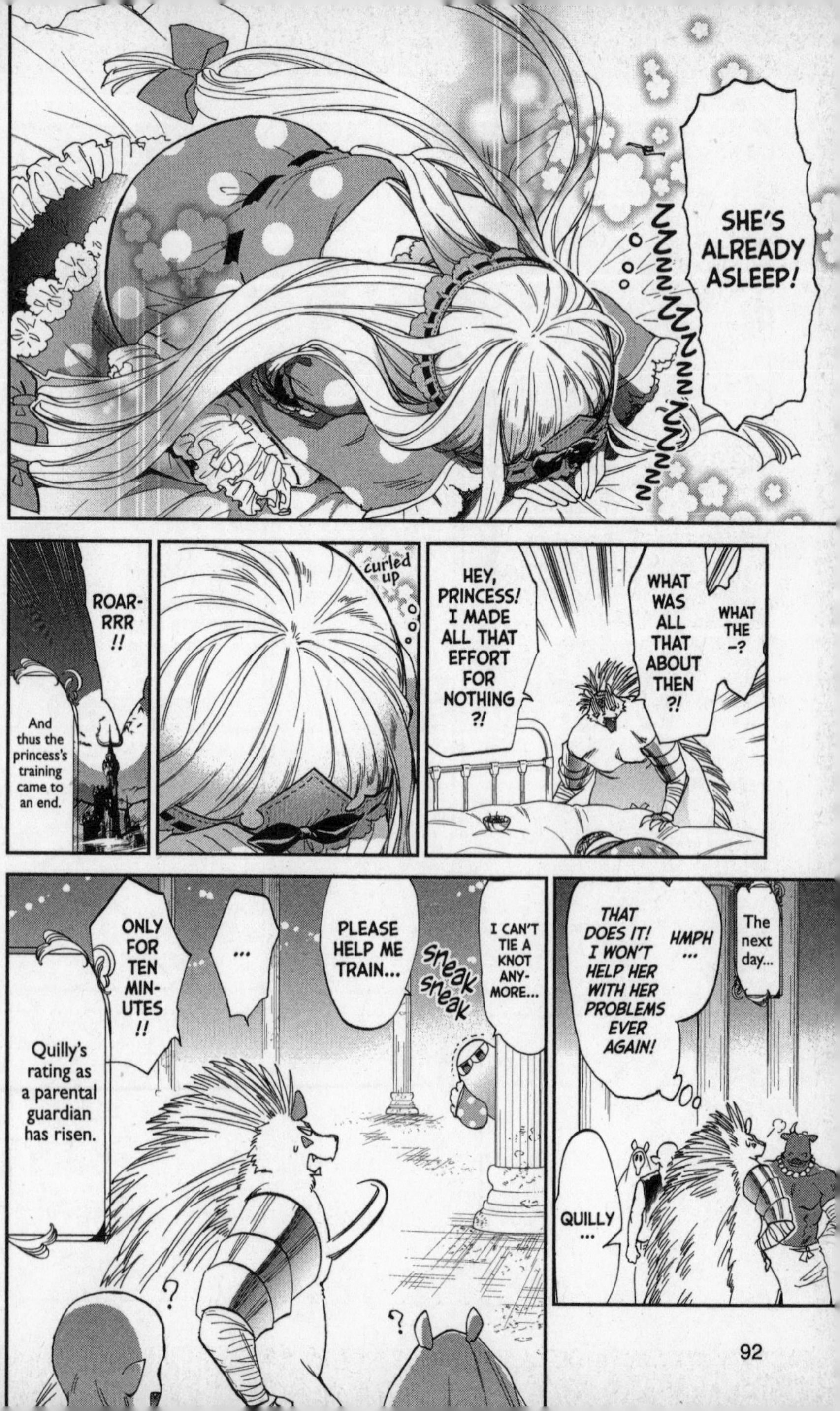
ZZZZ ZZZZ ZZZZ
SHE'S ALREADY ASLEEP!
WHAT THE –?
WHAT WAS ALL THAT ABOUT THEN?!
HEY, PRINCESS! I MADE ALL THAT EFFORT FOR NOTHING?!
curled up
ROAR-RRR!!
And thus the princess's training came to an end.
The next day...
HMPH...
THAT DOES IT! I WON'T HELP HER WITH HER PROBLEMS EVER AGAIN!
QUILLY...
I CAN'T TIE A KNOT ANY-MORE...
sneak sneak
PLEASE HELP ME TRAIN...
...
ONLY FOR TEN MIN-UTES!!
Quilly's rating as a parental guardian has risen.

Healing Cherry

Sweetness: ☆☆☆☆☆
Sourness: ☆☆☆☆

A must-have for topping pies and desserts.
▼

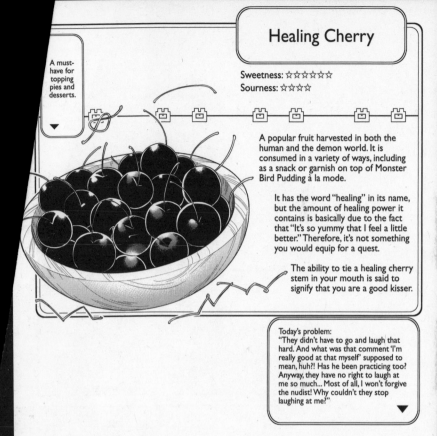

A popular fruit harvested in both the human and the demon world. It is consumed in a variety of ways, including as a snack or garnish on top of Monster Bird Pudding à la mode.

It has the word "healing" in its name, but the amount of healing power it contains is basically due to the fact that "It's so yummy that I feel a little better." Therefore, it's not something you would equip for a quest.

The ability to tie a healing cherry stem in your mouth is said to signify that you are a good kisser.

Today's problem:
"They didn't have to go and laugh that hard. And what was that comment 'I'm really good at that myself' supposed to mean, huh?! Has he been practicing too? Anyway, they have no right to laugh at me so much... Most of all, I won't forgive the nudist! Why couldn't they stop laughing at me?"
▼

BY THE WAY...

...CAN *YOU* TIE THIS IN YOUR MOUTH, QUILLY?

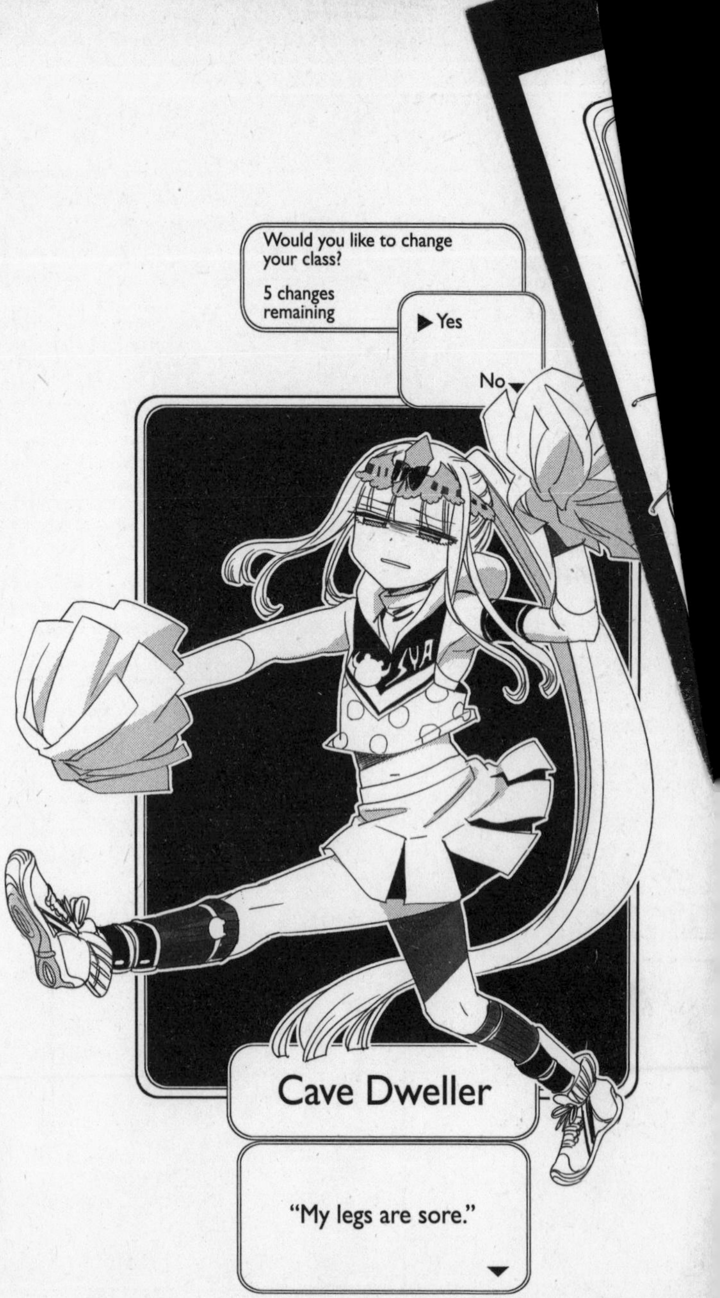

Would you like to change your class?
5 changes remaining
▶Yes
No
Cave Dweller
"My legs are sore."

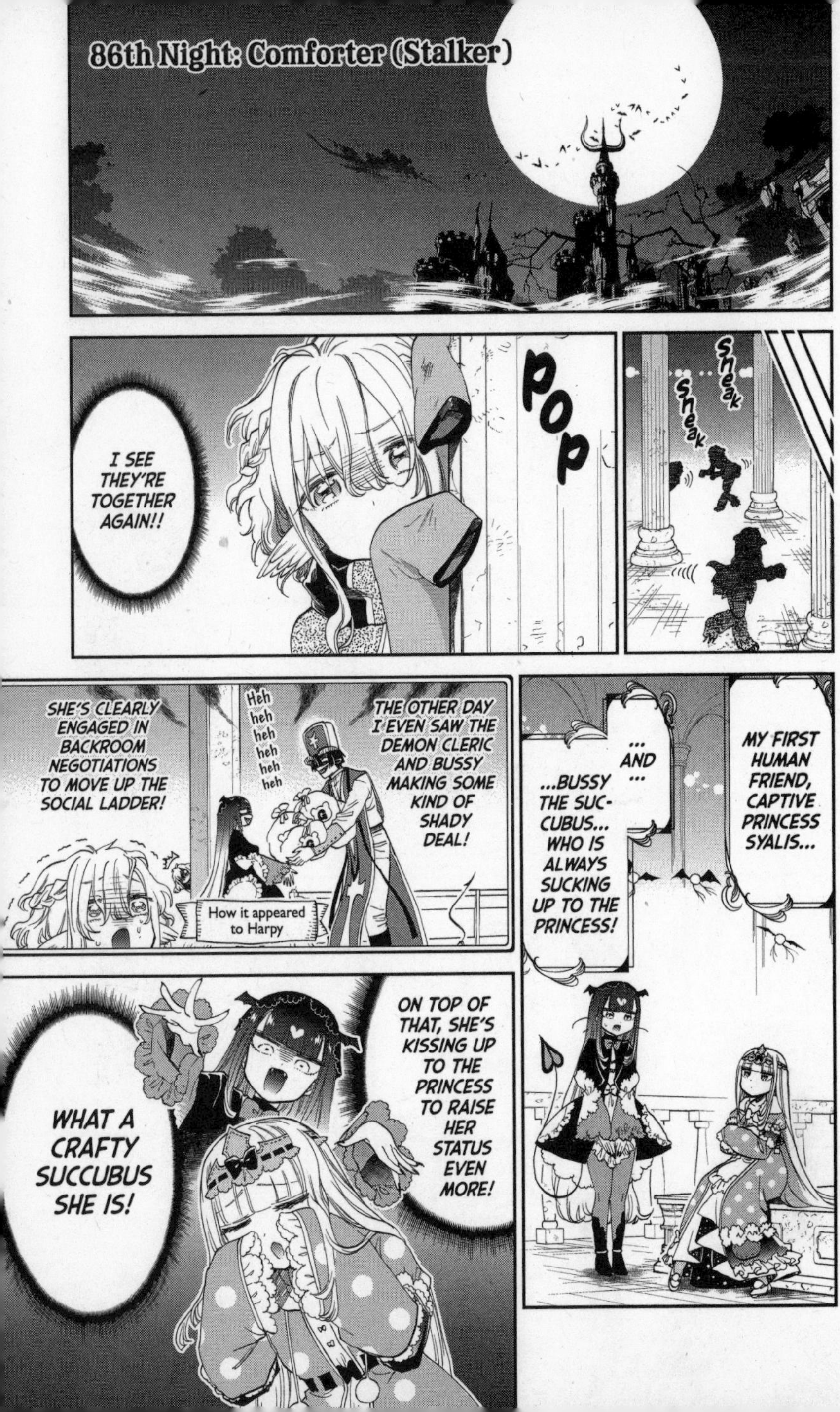
86th Night: Comforter (Stalker)
sneak
sneak
POP
I SEE THEY'RE TOGETHER AGAIN!!
MY FIRST HUMAN FRIEND, CAPTIVE PRINCESS SYALIS...
... AND ...
...BUSSY THE SUC-CUBUS... WHO IS ALWAYS SUCKING UP TO THE PRINCESS!
THE OTHER DAY I EVEN SAW THE DEMON CLERIC AND BUSSY MAKING SOME KIND OF SHADY DEAL!
Heh heh heh heh heh heh
SHE'S CLEARLY ENGAGED IN BACKROOM NEGOTIATIONS TO MOVE UP THE SOCIAL LADDER!
How it appeared to Harpy
ON TOP OF THAT, SHE'S KISSING UP TO THE PRINCESS TO RAISE HER STATUS EVEN MORE!
WHAT A CRAFTY SUCCUBUS SHE IS!

86th Night: Comforter (Stalker)

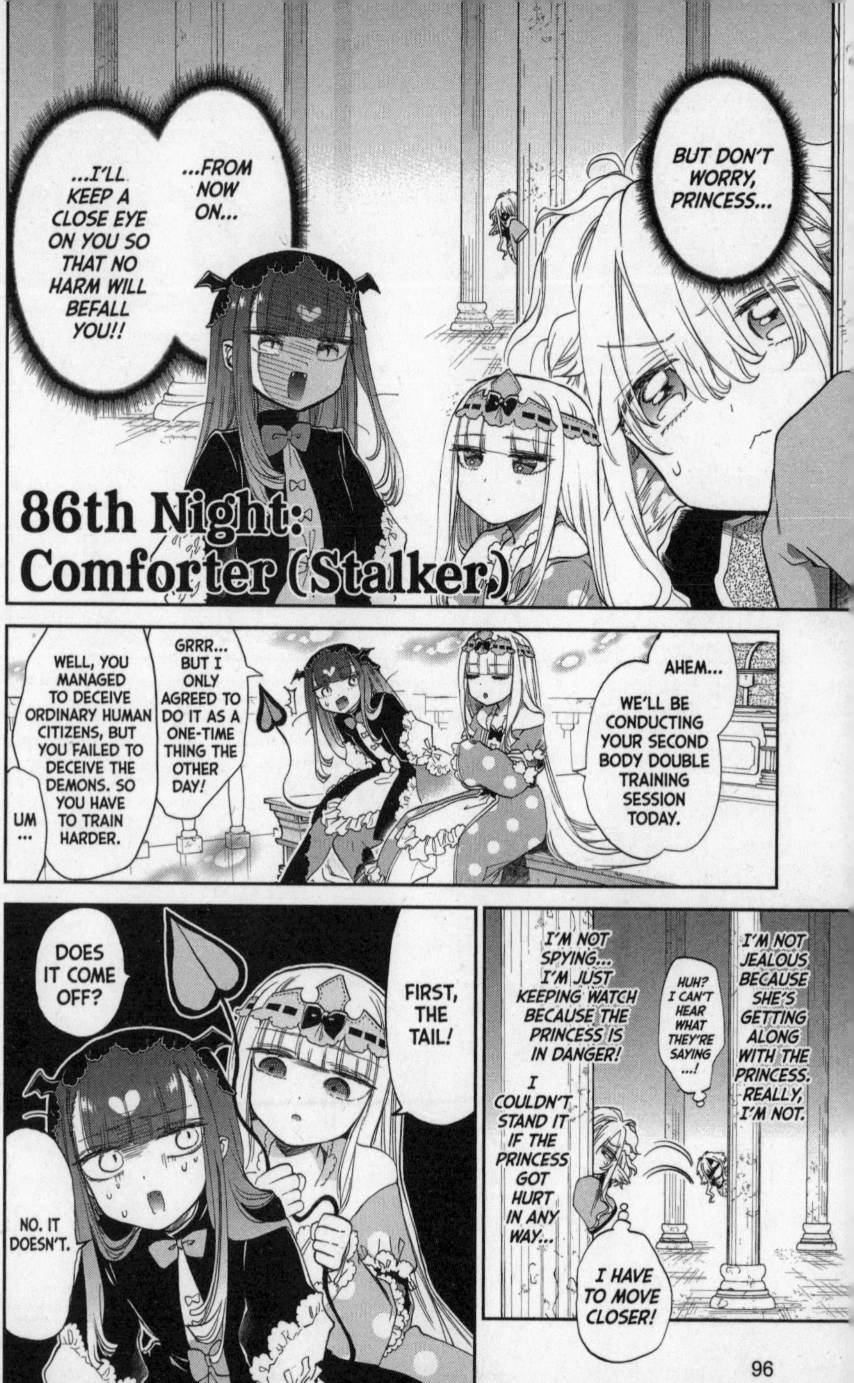
BUT DON'T WORRY, PRINCESS...
...FROM NOW ON...
...I'LL KEEP A CLOSE EYE ON YOU SO THAT NO HARM WILL BEFALL YOU!!
AHEM... WE'LL BE CONDUCTING YOUR SECOND BODY DOUBLE TRAINING SESSION TODAY.
GRRR... BUT I ONLY AGREED TO DO IT AS A ONE-TIME THING THE OTHER DAY!
WELL, YOU MANAGED TO DECEIVE ORDINARY HUMAN CITIZENS, BUT YOU FAILED TO DECEIVE THE DEMONS. SO YOU HAVE TO TRAIN HARDER.
UM ...
I'M NOT JEALOUS BECAUSE SHE'S GETTING ALONG WITH THE PRINCESS. REALLY, I'M NOT.
HUH? I CAN'T HEAR WHAT THEY'RE SAYING ...!
I'M NOT SPYING... I'M JUST KEEPING WATCH BECAUSE THE PRINCESS IS IN DANGER!
I COULDN'T STAND IT IF THE PRINCESS GOT HURT IN ANY WAY...
I HAVE TO MOVE CLOSER!
FIRST, THE TAIL!
DOES IT COME OFF?
NO. IT DOESN'T.

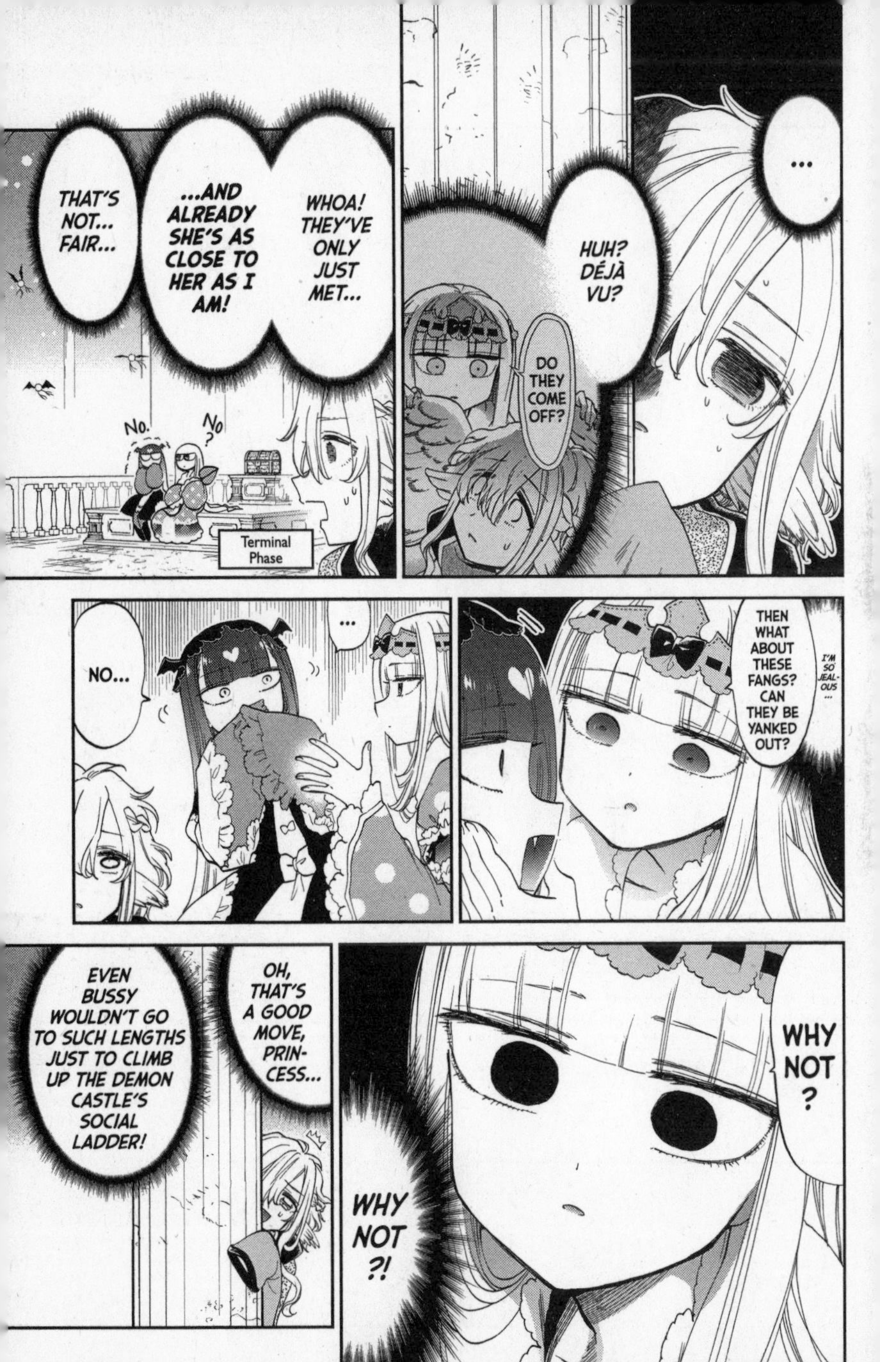
...
HUH? DÉJÀ VU?
DO THEY COME OFF?
WHOA! THEY'VE ONLY JUST MET...
...AND ALREADY SHE'S AS CLOSE TO HER AS I AM!
THAT'S NOT... FAIR...
No?
No.
Terminal Phase
THEN WHAT ABOUT THESE FANGS? CAN THEY BE YANKED OUT?
I'M SO JEALOUS...
...
NO...
WHY NOT?
WHY NOT?!
OH, THAT'S A GOOD MOVE, PRINCESS...
EVEN BUSSY WOULDN'T GO TO SUCH LENGTHS JUST TO CLIMB UP THE DEMON CASTLE'S SOCIAL LADDER!

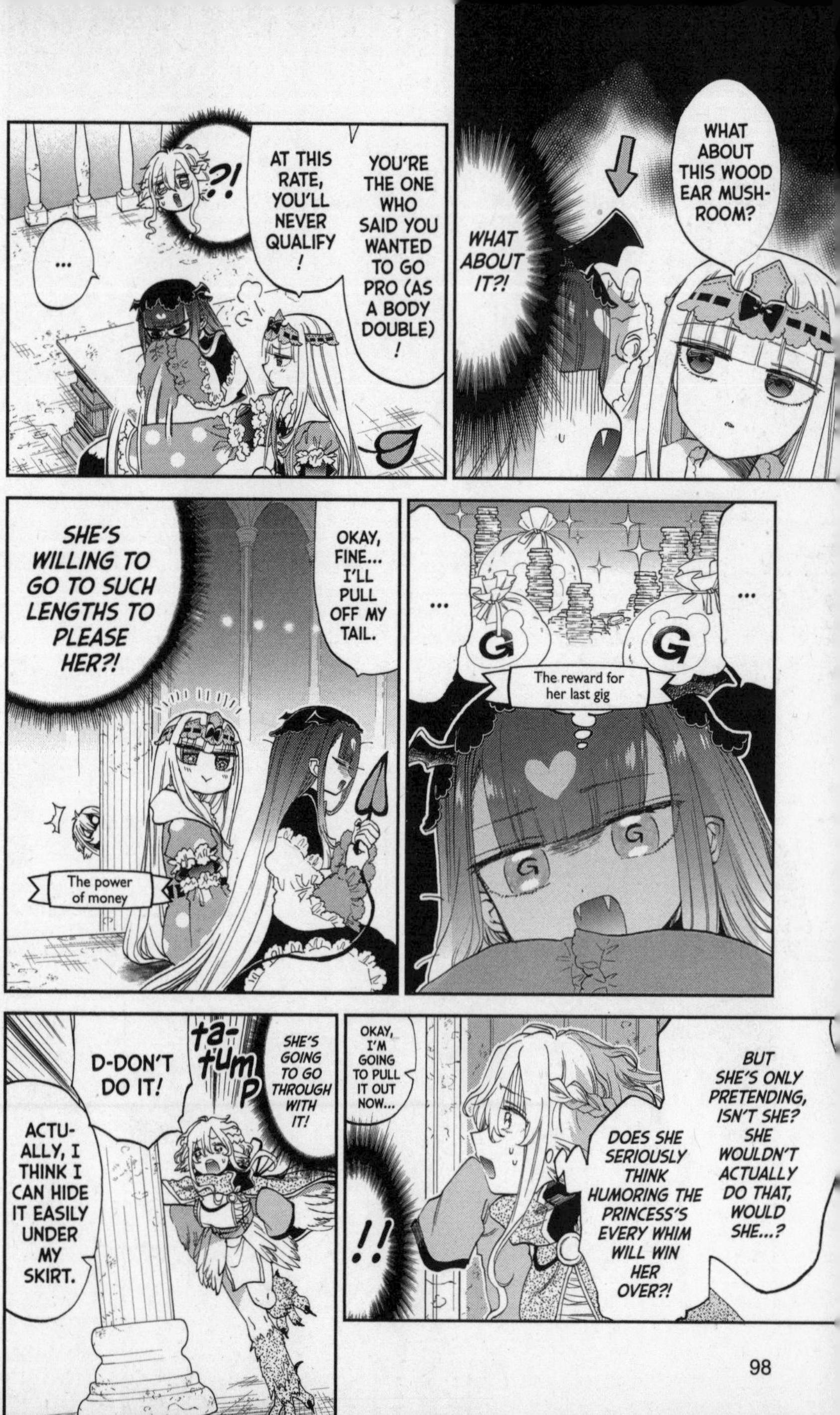
WHAT ABOUT THIS WOOD EAR MUSH-ROOM?
WHAT ABOUT IT?!
YOU'RE THE ONE WHO SAID YOU WANTED TO GO PRO (AS A BODY DOUBLE)!
AT THIS RATE, YOU'LL NEVER QUALIFY!
?!
...
...
...
The reward for her last gig
OKAY, FINE... I'LL PULL OFF MY TAIL.
SHE'S WILLING TO GO TO SUCH LENGTHS TO PLEASE HER?!
The power of money
BUT SHE'S ONLY PRETENDING, ISN'T SHE? SHE WOULDN'T ACTUALLY DO THAT, WOULD SHE...?
DOES SHE SERIOUSLY THINK HUMORING THE PRINCESS'S EVERY WHIM WILL WIN HER OVER?!
OKAY, I'M GOING TO PULL IT OUT NOW...
!!
SHE'S GOING TO GO THROUGH WITH IT!
ta-tump
D-DON'T DO IT!
ACTU-ALLY, I THINK I CAN HIDE IT EASILY UNDER MY SKIRT.

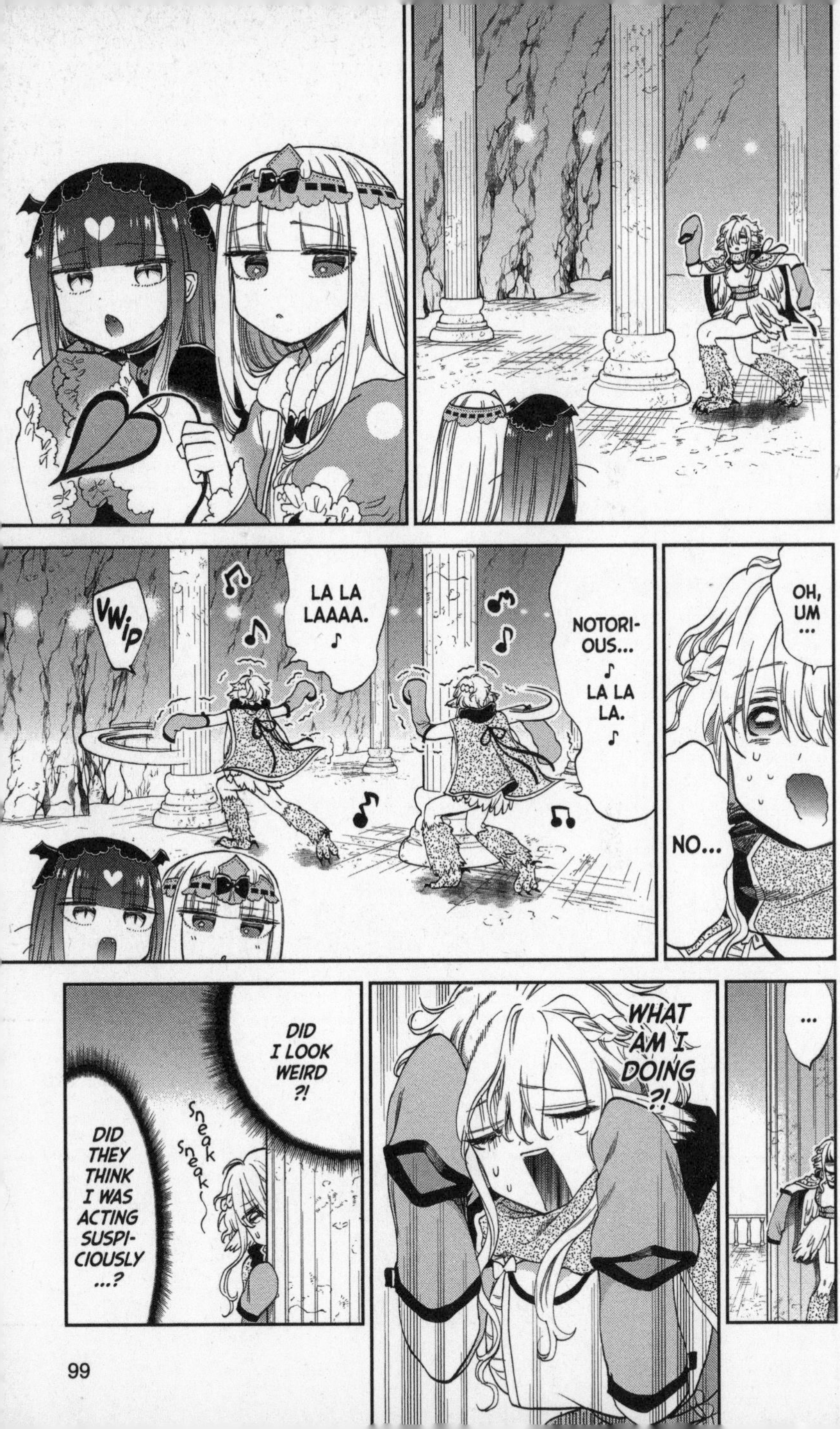
OH, UM...
NO...
NOTORI-OUS... ♪ LA LA LA. ♪
LA LA LAAAA. ♪
VWIP
...
WHAT AM I DOING?!
DID I LOOK WEIRD?!
DID THEY THINK I WAS ACTING SUSPI-CIOUSLY...?
sneak sneak

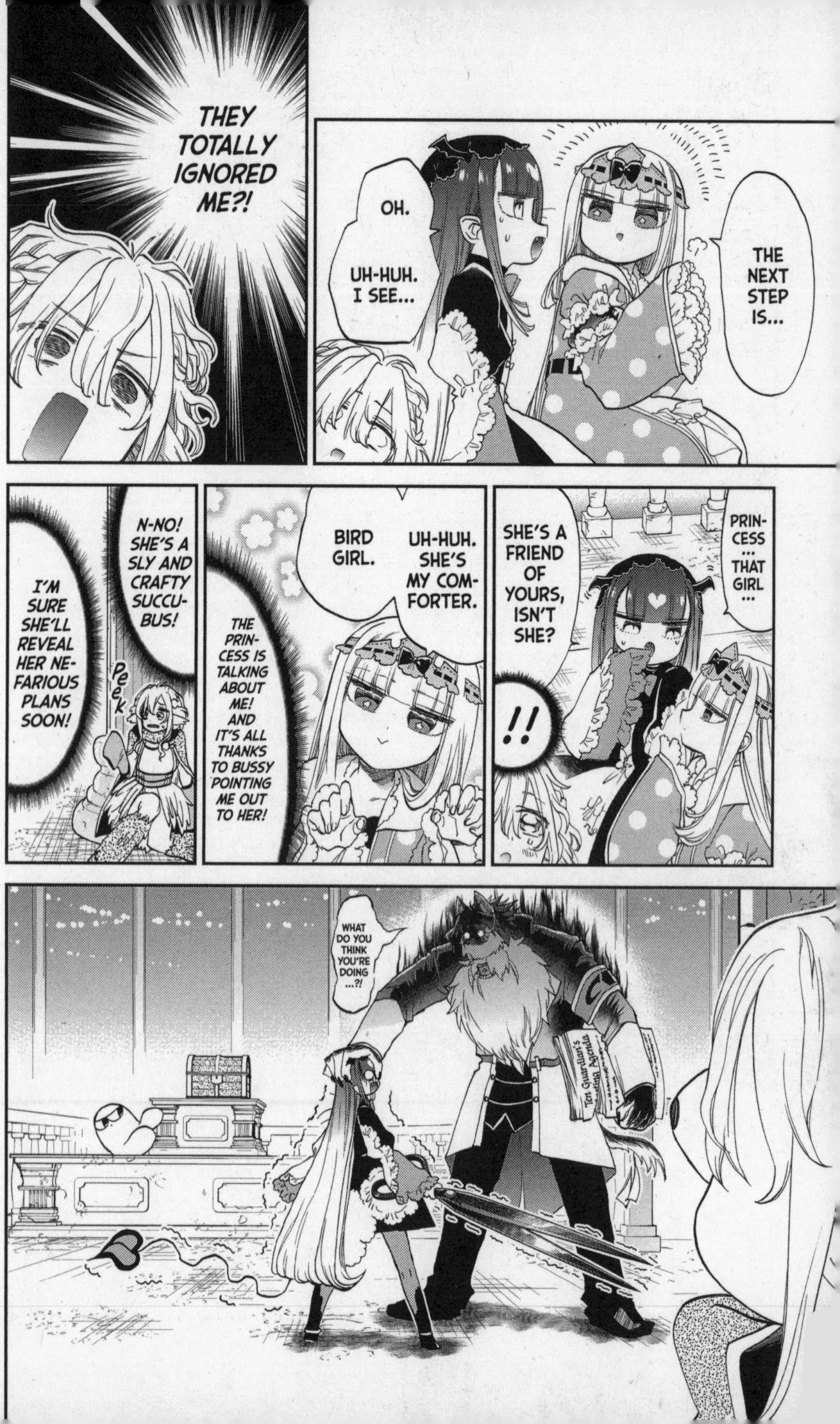
THE NEXT STEP IS...
OH.
UH-HUH. I SEE...
THEY TOTALLY IGNORED ME?!
PRINCESS... THAT GIRL...
SHE'S A FRIEND OF YOURS, ISN'T SHE?
!!
UH-HUH. SHE'S MY COMFORTER.
BIRD GIRL.
THE PRINCESS IS TALKING ABOUT ME! AND IT'S ALL THANKS TO BUSSY POINTING ME OUT TO HER!
N-NO! SHE'S A SLY AND CRAFTY SUCCUBUS!
I'M SURE SHE'LL REVEAL HER NEFARIOUS PLANS SOON!
Peek
WHAT DO YOU THINK YOU'RE DOING...?!
Ten Guardian's

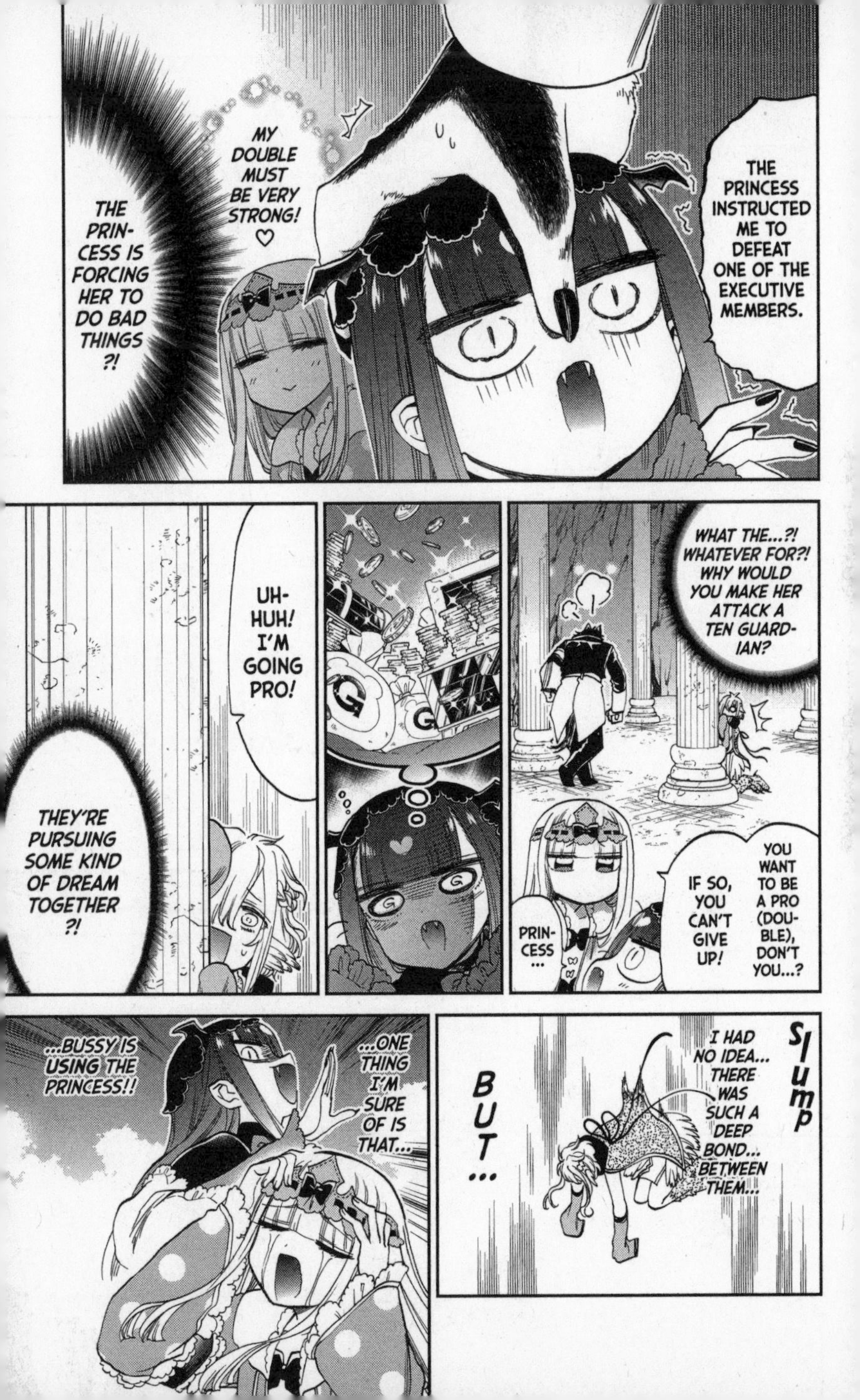
THE PRINCESS INSTRUCTED ME TO DEFEAT ONE OF THE EXECUTIVE MEMBERS.
MY DOUBLE MUST BE VERY STRONG! ♡
THE PRIN-CESS IS FORCING HER TO DO BAD THINGS?!
WHAT THE...?! WHATEVER FOR?! WHY WOULD YOU MAKE HER ATTACK A TEN GUARD-IAN?
YOU WANT TO BE A PRO (DOU-BLE), DON'T YOU...?
IF SO, YOU CAN'T GIVE UP!
PRIN-CESS...
UH-HUH! I'M GOING PRO!
THEY'RE PURSUING SOME KIND OF DREAM TOGETHER?!
Slump
I HAD NO IDEA... THERE WAS SUCH A DEEP BOND... BETWEEN THEM...
BUT...
...ONE THING I'M SURE OF IS THAT...
...BUSSY IS USING THE PRINCESS!!

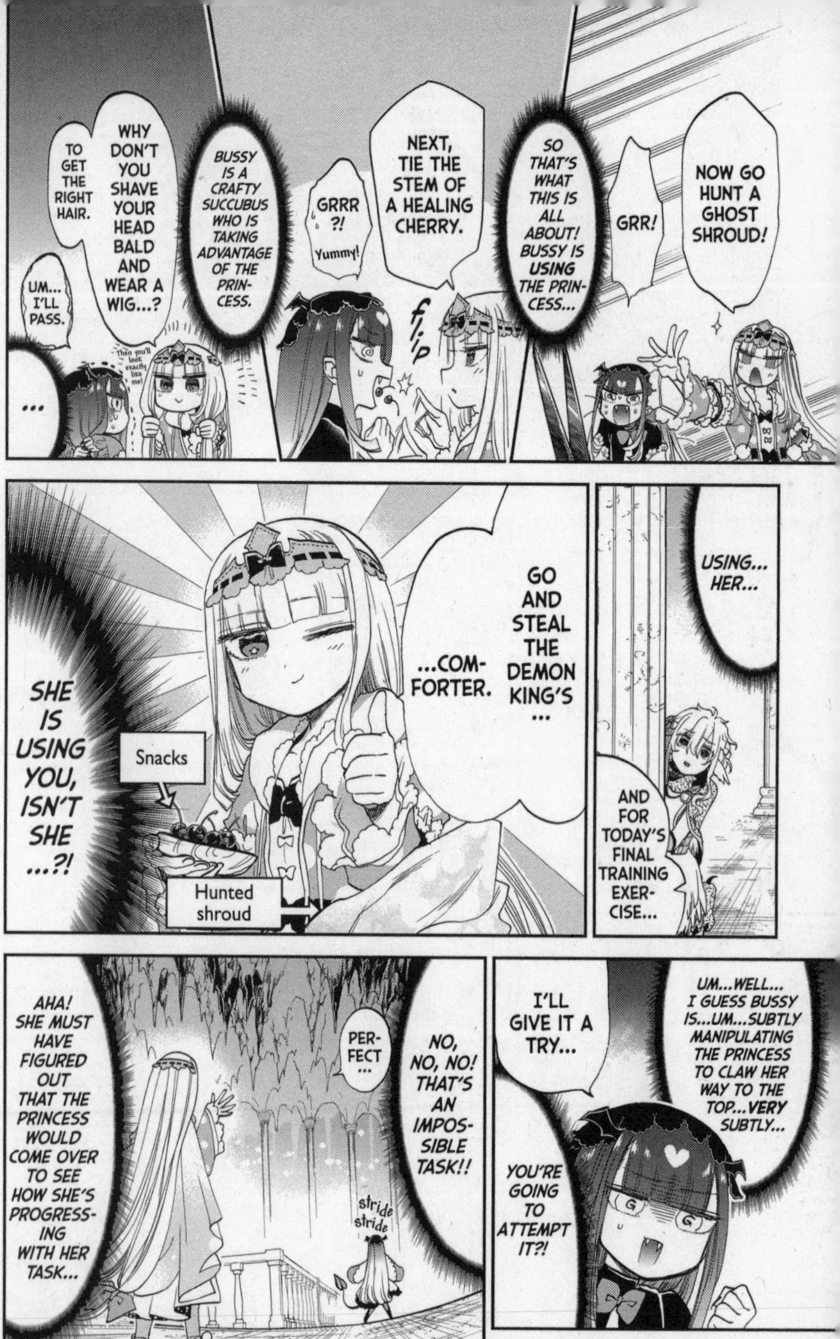
NOW GO HUNT A GHOST SHROUD!
GRR!
SO THAT'S WHAT THIS IS ALL ABOUT! BUSSY IS USING THE PRINCESS...
NEXT, TIE THE STEM OF A HEALING CHERRY.
flip
GRRR ?!
Yummy!
BUSSY IS A CRAFTY SUCCUBUS WHO IS TAKING ADVANTAGE OF THE PRINCESS.
WHY DON'T YOU SHAVE YOUR HEAD BALD AND WEAR A WIG...?
TO GET THE RIGHT HAIR.
Then you'll look exactly like me!
UM... I'LL PASS.
...
USING... HER...
AND FOR TODAY'S FINAL TRAINING EXERCISE...
GO AND STEAL THE DEMON KING'S...
...COMFORTER.
SHE IS USING YOU, ISN'T SHE ...?!
Snacks
Hunted shroud
UM...WELL... I GUESS BUSSY IS...UM...SUBTLY MANIPULATING THE PRINCESS TO CLAW HER WAY TO THE TOP...VERY SUBTLY...
I'LL GIVE IT A TRY...
YOU'RE GOING TO ATTEMPT IT?!
NO, NO, NO! THAT'S AN IMPOSSIBLE TASK!!
PERFECT...
stride stride
AHA! SHE MUST HAVE FIGURED OUT THAT THE PRINCESS WOULD COME OVER TO SEE HOW SHE'S PROGRESSING WITH HER TASK...

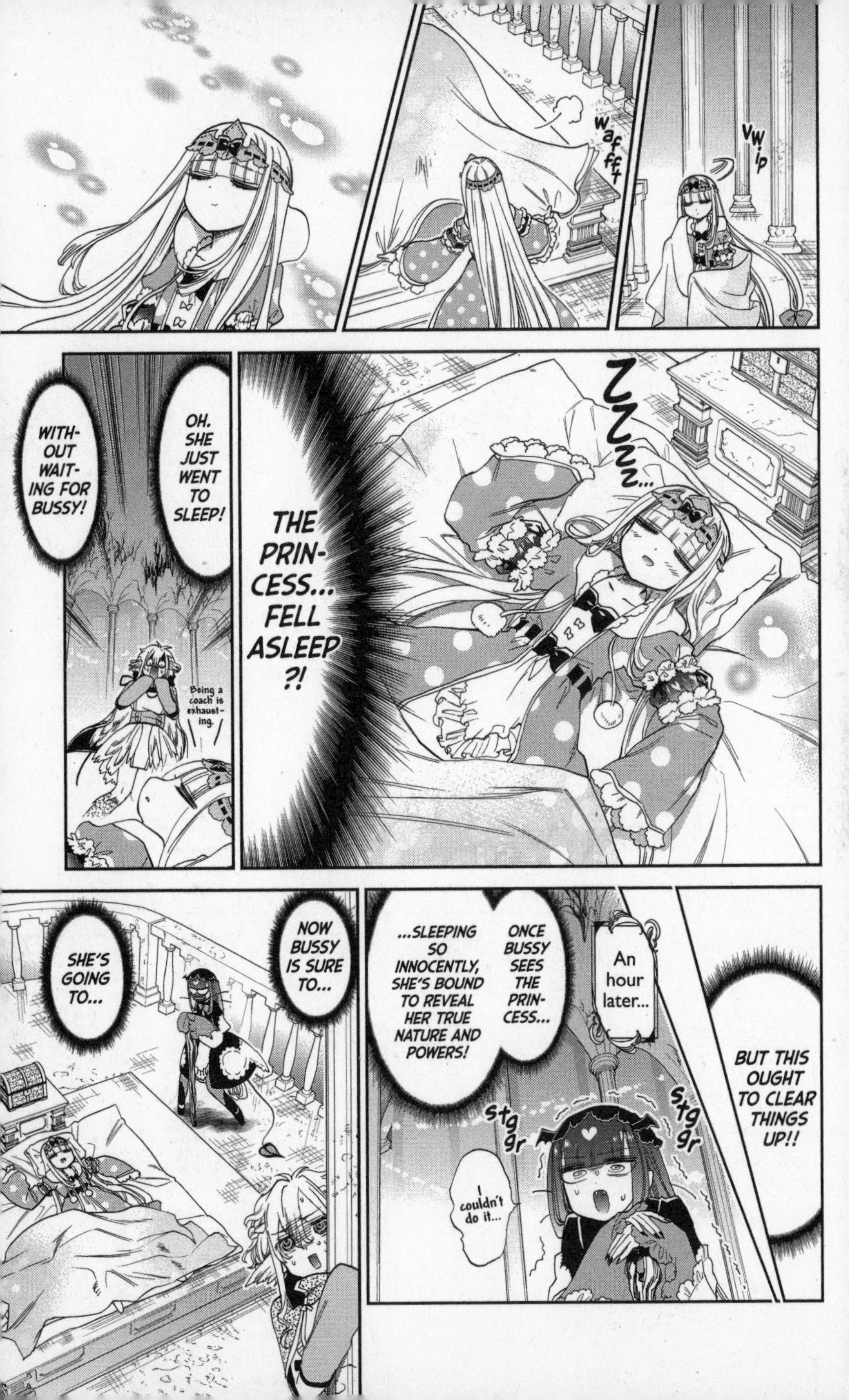
VWIP
WAFFFT
ZZZZ...
THE PRIN-CESS... FELL ASLEEP?!
OH. SHE JUST WENT TO SLEEP!
WITH-OUT WAIT-ING FOR BUSSY!
Being a coach is exhaust-ing.
BUT THIS OUGHT TO CLEAR THINGS UP!!
An hour later...
ONCE BUSSY SEES THE PRIN-CESS...
...SLEEPING SO INNOCENTLY, SHE'S BOUND TO REVEAL HER TRUE NATURE AND POWERS!
STGGR
STGGR
I couldn't do it...
NOW BUSSY IS SURE TO...
SHE'S GOING TO...

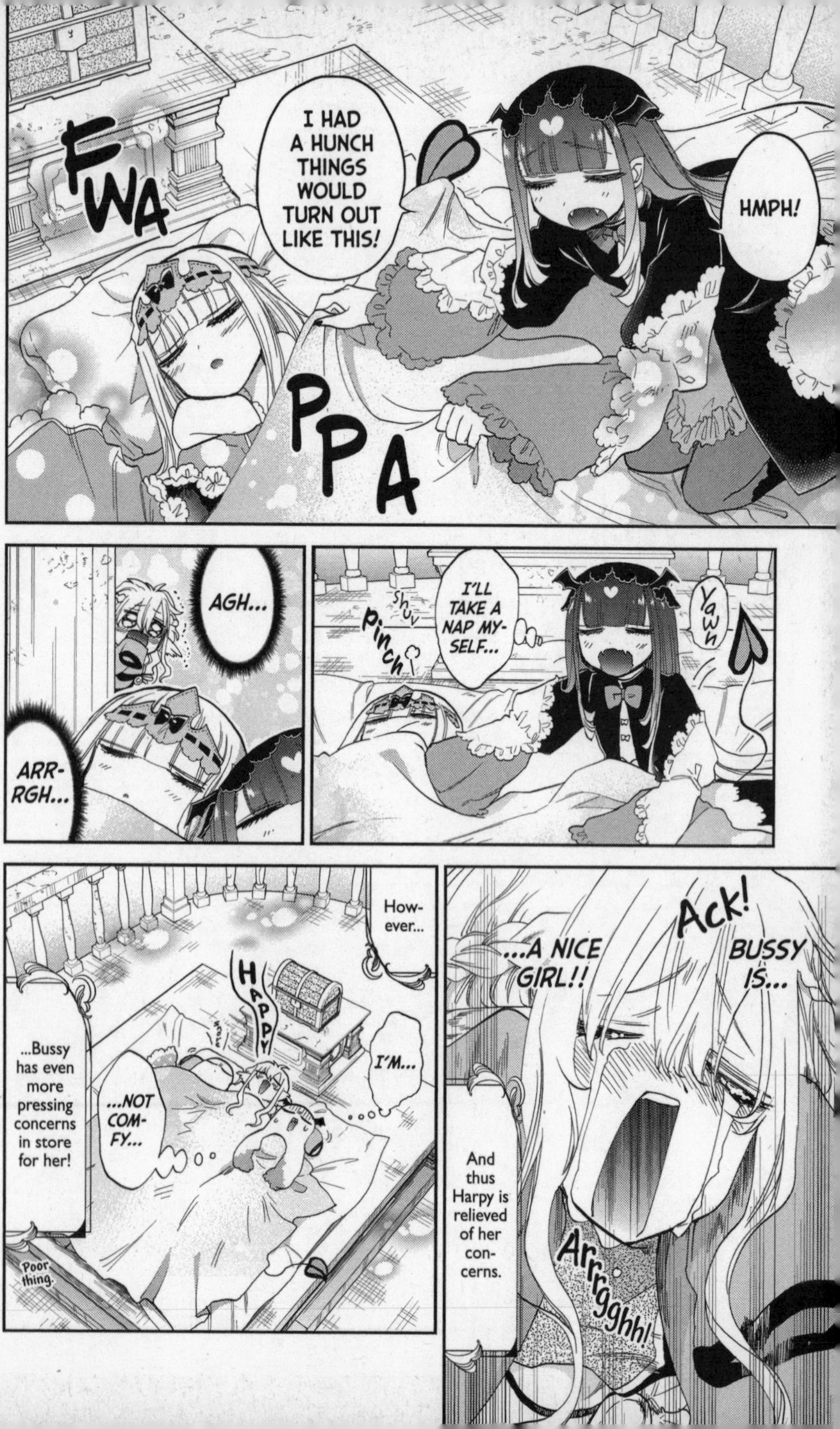
HMPH!
I HAD A HUNCH THINGS WOULD TURN OUT LIKE THIS!
FWA
PPA
Yawn
I'LL TAKE A NAP MY-SELF...
Shuv
pinch
AGH...
ARR-RGH...
Ack!
BUSSY IS...
...A NICE GIRL!!
And thus Harpy is relieved of her con-cerns.
Arrrgghh!
How-ever...
I'M...
HAPPY
...NOT COMF-FY...
...Bussy has even more pressing concerns in store for her!
Poor thing.

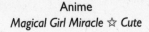

Anime
Magical Girl Miracle ☆ Cute

Strength and Seriousness: ☆☆☆☆☆☆☆☆☆☆
Cuteness and Invincibility: ☆☆☆☆☆☆☆☆☆☆

Miracle ☆ Cute! Wake ☆ uuuup !!

The princess was a huge fan of this show targeting girls.

Story Thus Far:
One day, Nagi Honoka meets a cat with a star-shaped mark on its forehead. The cat tells her to gather (capture) magic cards that have been scattered throughout the world in order to save it! Before Nagi knows it, she has transformed into Magical Girl Miracle ☆ Cute!

This slapstick comedy tells the tale of Nagi and her friends—how she became a pâtissier and ended up raising a mysterious baby. It turns out that Nagi Honoka is the daughter of a noble family! Tragedy strikes when the Apple Field Orphanage where she was raised is burned to the ground by an evil villain who is after Nagi's royal treasure. At the last second, Nagi is rescued by a traveling circus. How can she save the world now?! There are even romantic episodes featuring Nagi and the mysterious, handsome man known as the Masked Bear Ear...!

Former problem:
"How can this series continue for an entire year?"

Problem after the show ended:
"That wasn't the kind of story that could be squeezed into a yearlong series."

BUSSY!
PLEASE TELL ME THE SECRET OF HOW TO GET CLOSE TO THE PRINCESS!
What ...?
...
IN YOUR CASE, HARPY...
YOU'D BETTER START WITH SOME MAJOR BODY MODIFICATIONS...

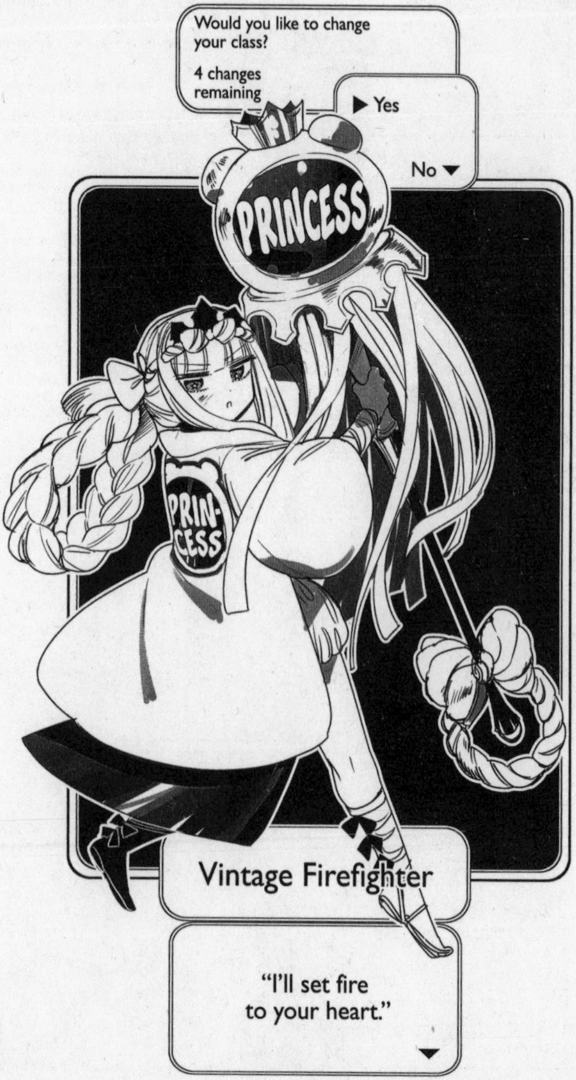
Would you like to change your class?
4 changes remaining
▶ Yes
No ▼
PRINCESS
PRIN-CESS
Vintage Firefighter
"I'll set fire to your heart."

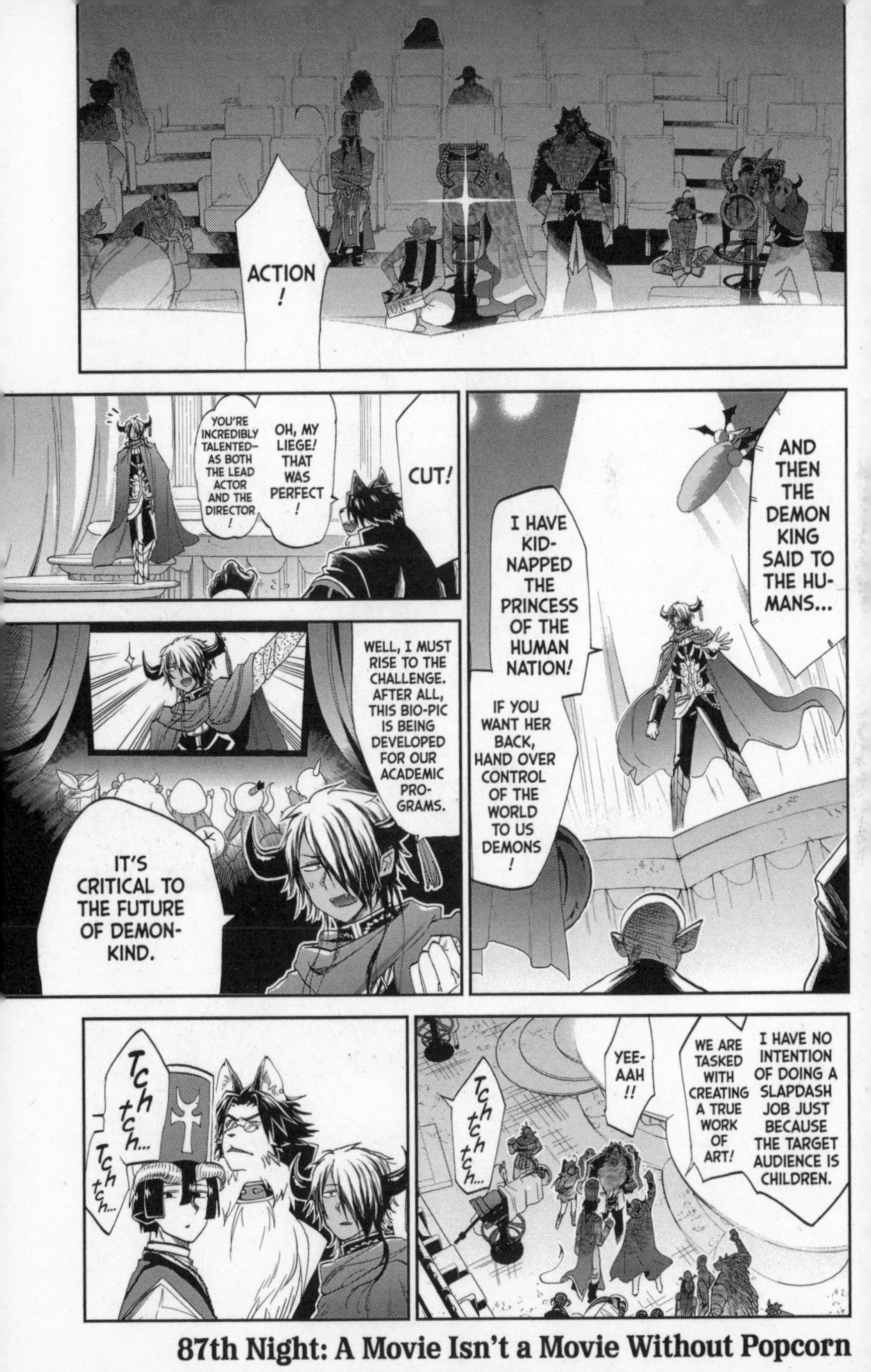
ACTION!
AND THEN THE DEMON KING SAID TO THE HUMANS...
I HAVE KIDNAPPED THE PRINCESS OF THE HUMAN NATION!
IF YOU WANT HER BACK, HAND OVER CONTROL OF THE WORLD TO US DEMONS!
CUT!
OH, MY LIEGE! THAT WAS PERFECT!
YOU'RE INCREDIBLY TALENTED—AS BOTH THE LEAD ACTOR AND THE DIRECTOR!
WELL, I MUST RISE TO THE CHALLENGE. AFTER ALL, THIS BIO-PIC IS BEING DEVELOPED FOR OUR ACADEMIC PROGRAMS.
IT'S CRITICAL TO THE FUTURE OF DEMONKIND.
I HAVE NO INTENTION OF DOING A SLAPDASH JOB JUST BECAUSE THE TARGET AUDIENCE IS CHILDREN.
WE ARE TASKED WITH CREATING A TRUE WORK OF ART!
YEE-AAH!!
Tch tch tch...
Tch tch...
Tch tch...

87th Night: A Movie Isn't a Movie Without Popcorn

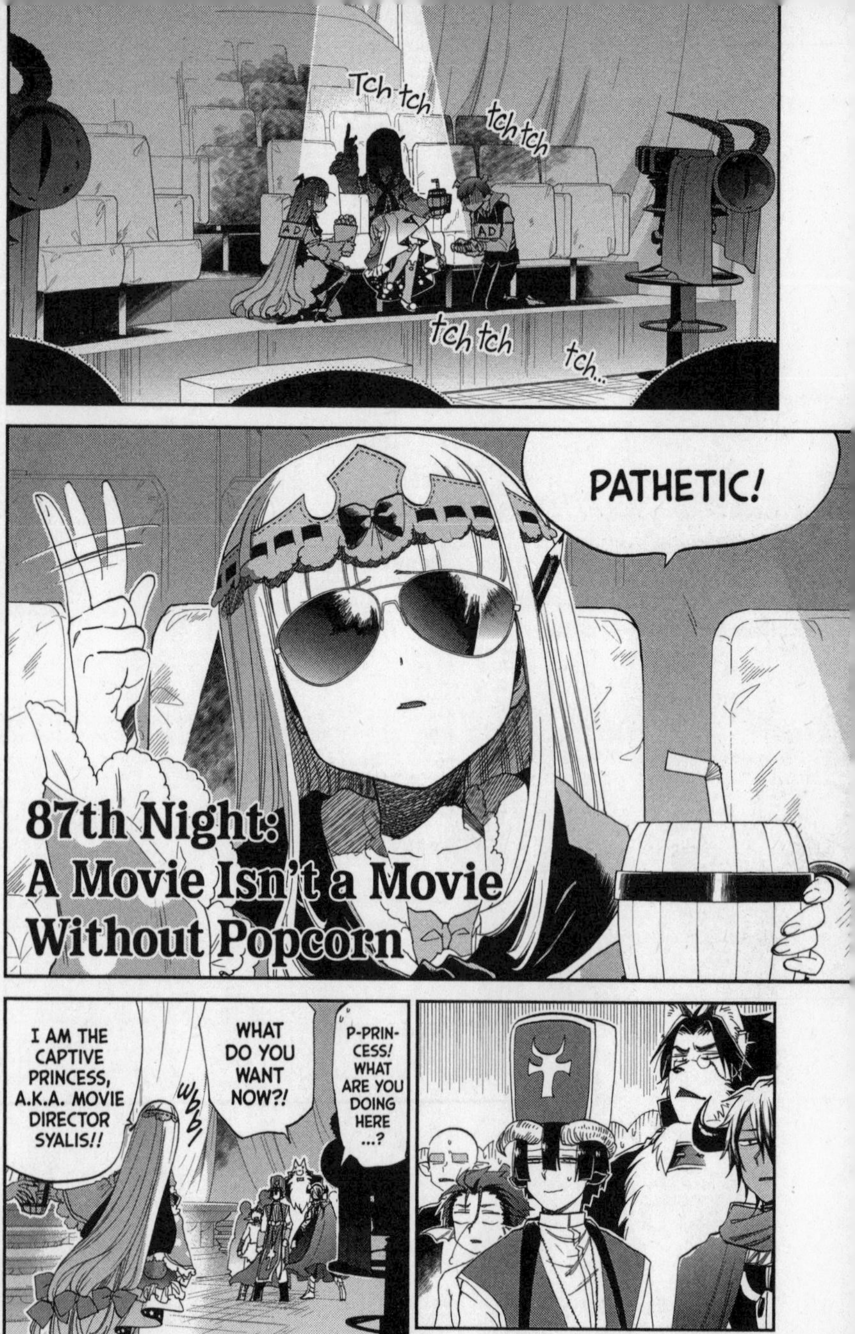
Tch tch
tch tch
tch tch
tch...
PATHETIC!
87th Night:
A Movie Isn't a Movie Without Popcorn
P-PRINCESS! WHAT ARE YOU DOING HERE...?
WHAT DO YOU WANT NOW?!
I AM THE CAPTIVE PRINCESS, A.K.A. MOVIE DIRECTOR SYALIS!!

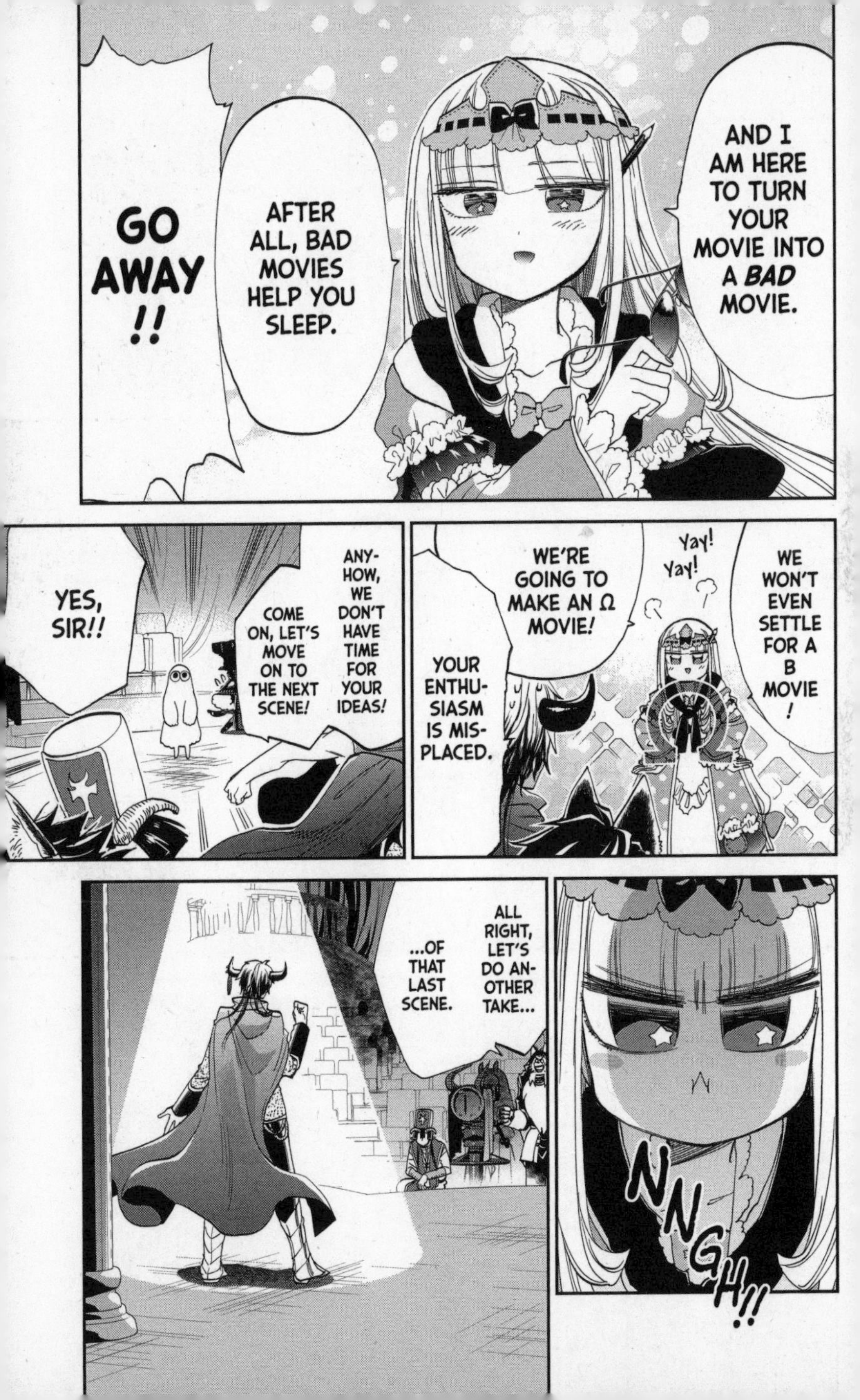
AND I AM HERE TO TURN YOUR MOVIE INTO A *BAD* MOVIE.
AFTER ALL, BAD MOVIES HELP YOU SLEEP.
GO AWAY!!
WE WON'T EVEN SETTLE FOR A B MOVIE!
Yay! Yay!
WE'RE GOING TO MAKE AN Ω MOVIE!
YOUR ENTHUSIASM IS MISPLACED.
ANYHOW, WE DON'T HAVE TIME FOR YOUR IDEAS!
COME ON, LET'S MOVE ON TO THE NEXT SCENE!
YES, SIR!!
NNGH!!
ALL RIGHT, LET'S DO ANOTHER TAKE...
...OF THAT LAST SCENE.

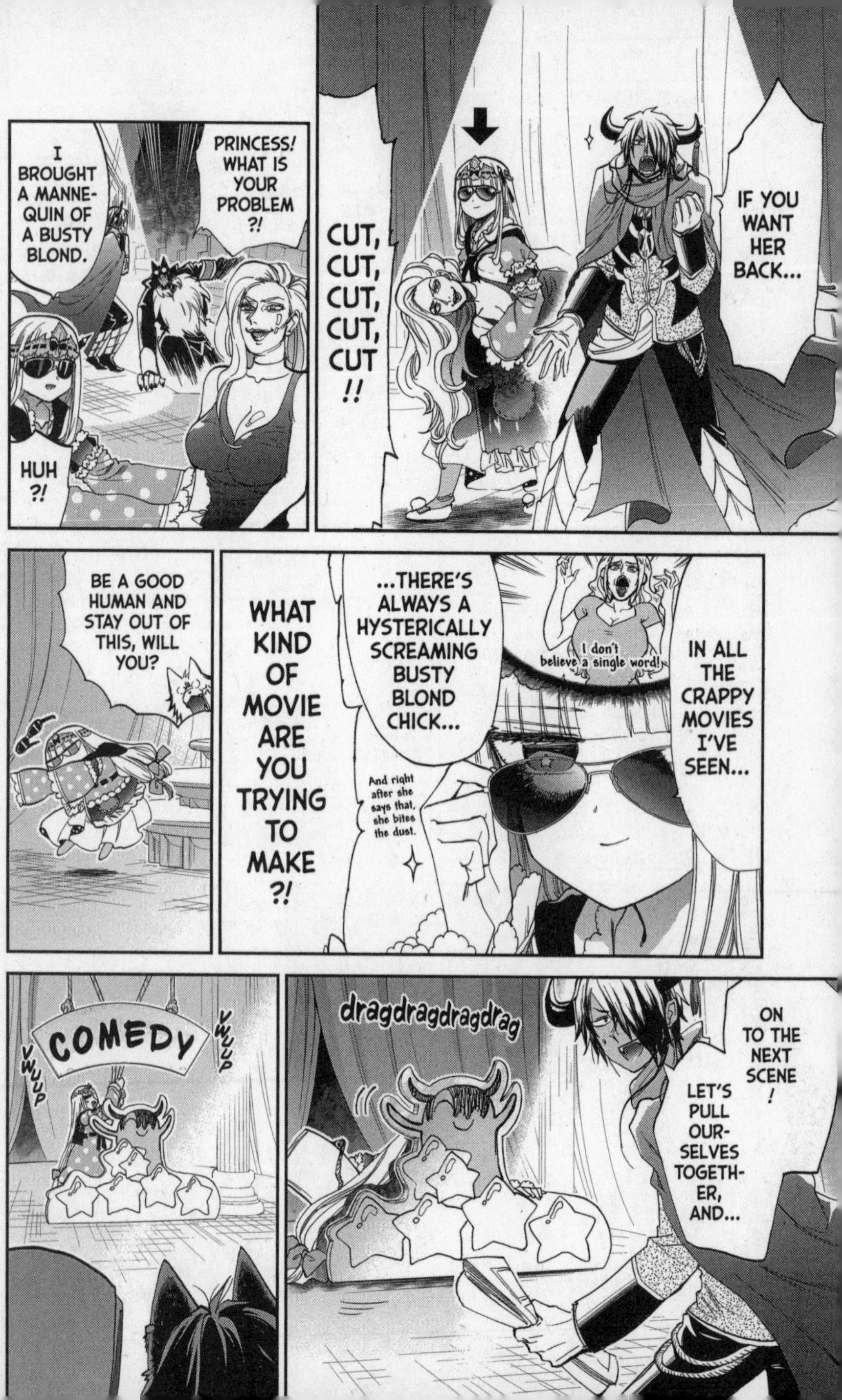
IF YOU WANT HER BACK...
CUT, CUT, CUT, CUT, CUT!!
PRINCESS! WHAT IS YOUR PROBLEM?!
I BROUGHT A MANNEQUIN OF A BUSTY BLOND.
HUH?!
IN ALL THE CRAPPY MOVIES I'VE SEEN...
I don't believe a single word!
...THERE'S ALWAYS A HYSTERICALLY SCREAMING BUSTY BLOND CHICK...
And right after she says that, she bites the dust.
WHAT KIND OF MOVIE ARE YOU TRYING TO MAKE?!
BE A GOOD HUMAN AND STAY OUT OF THIS, WILL YOU?
ON TO THE NEXT SCENE!
LET'S PULL OURSELVES TOGETHER, AND...
dragdragdragdrag
VWUUP
COMEDY
VWUUP

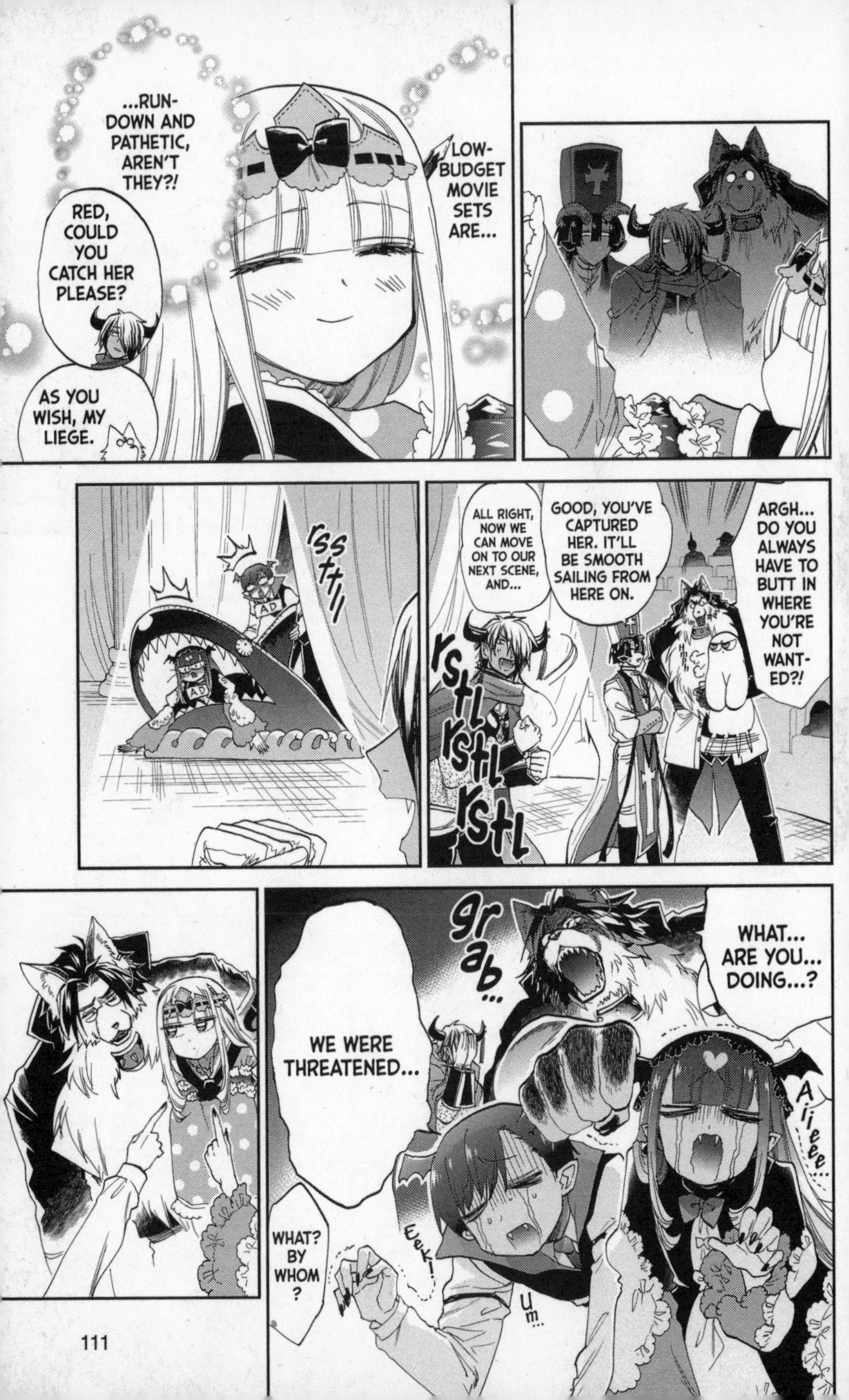
LOW-BUDGET MOVIE SETS ARE...
...RUN-DOWN AND PATHETIC, AREN'T THEY?!
RED, COULD YOU CATCH HER PLEASE?
AS YOU WISH, MY LIEGE.
ARGH... DO YOU ALWAYS HAVE TO BUTT IN WHERE YOU'RE NOT WANTED?!
Hmph
GOOD, YOU'VE CAPTURED HER. IT'LL BE SMOOTH SAILING FROM HERE ON.
ALL RIGHT, NOW WE CAN MOVE ON TO OUR NEXT SCENE, AND...
rstl rstl rstl
rsstll
WHAT... ARE YOU... DOING...?
Aiieee...
grab...
WE WERE THREATENED...
Eek!
Um...
WHAT? BY WHOM?

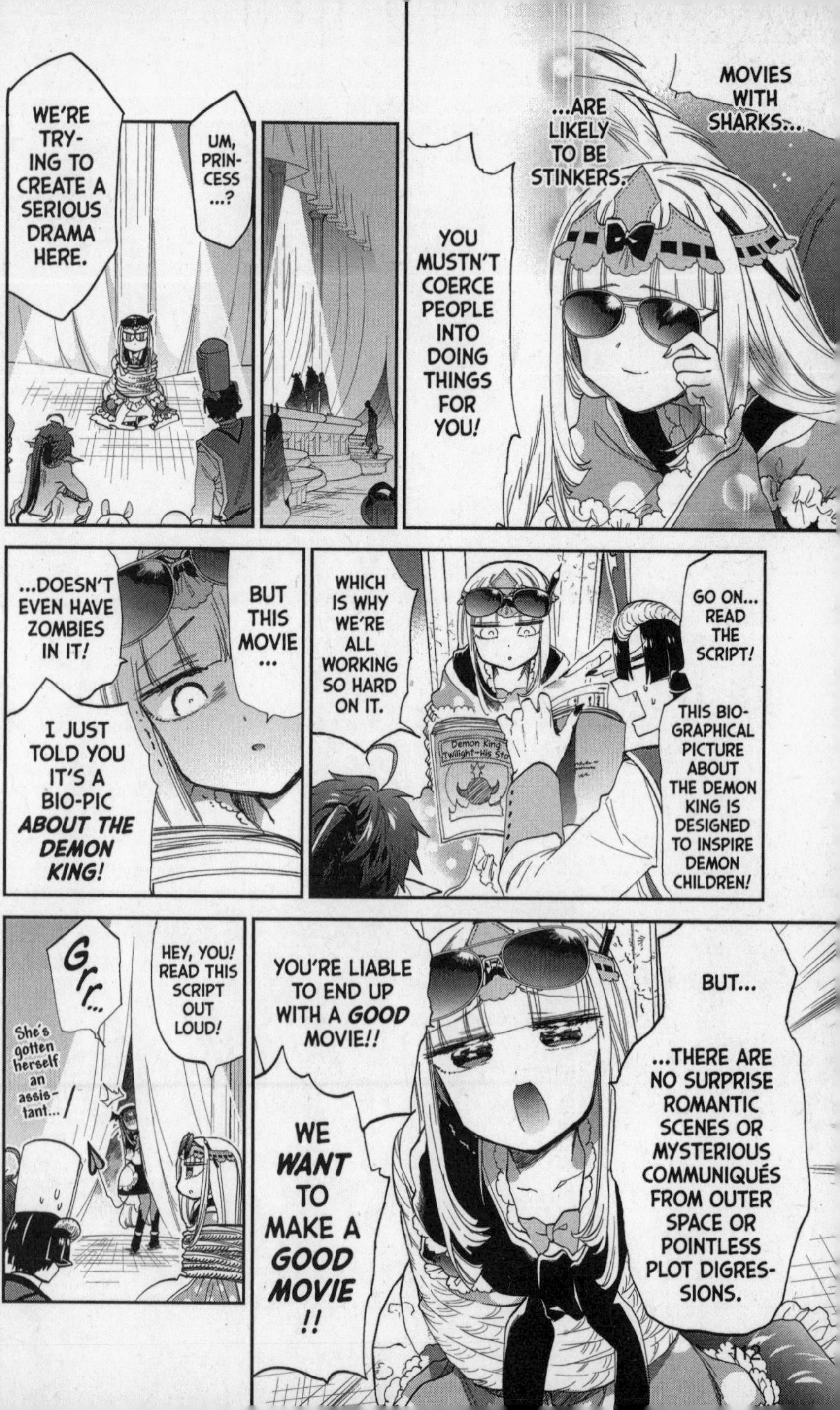
MOVIES WITH SHARKS...
...ARE LIKELY TO BE STINKERS.
YOU MUSTN'T COERCE PEOPLE INTO DOING THINGS FOR YOU!
UM, PRINCESS...?
WE'RE TRYING TO CREATE A SERIOUS DRAMA HERE.
GO ON... READ THE SCRIPT!
THIS BIOGRAPHICAL PICTURE ABOUT THE DEMON KING IS DESIGNED TO INSPIRE DEMON CHILDREN!
WHICH IS WHY WE'RE ALL WORKING SO HARD ON IT.
BUT THIS MOVIE...
...DOESN'T EVEN HAVE ZOMBIES IN IT!
I JUST TOLD YOU IT'S A BIO-PIC *ABOUT THE DEMON KING!*
BUT...
...THERE ARE NO SURPRISE ROMANTIC SCENES OR MYSTERIOUS COMMUNIQUÉS FROM OUTER SPACE OR POINTLESS PLOT DIGRESSIONS.
YOU'RE LIABLE TO END UP WITH A *GOOD* MOVIE!!
WE *WANT* TO MAKE A *GOOD MOVIE!!*
Grr...
HEY, YOU! READ THIS SCRIPT OUT LOUD!
She's gotten herself an assistant...

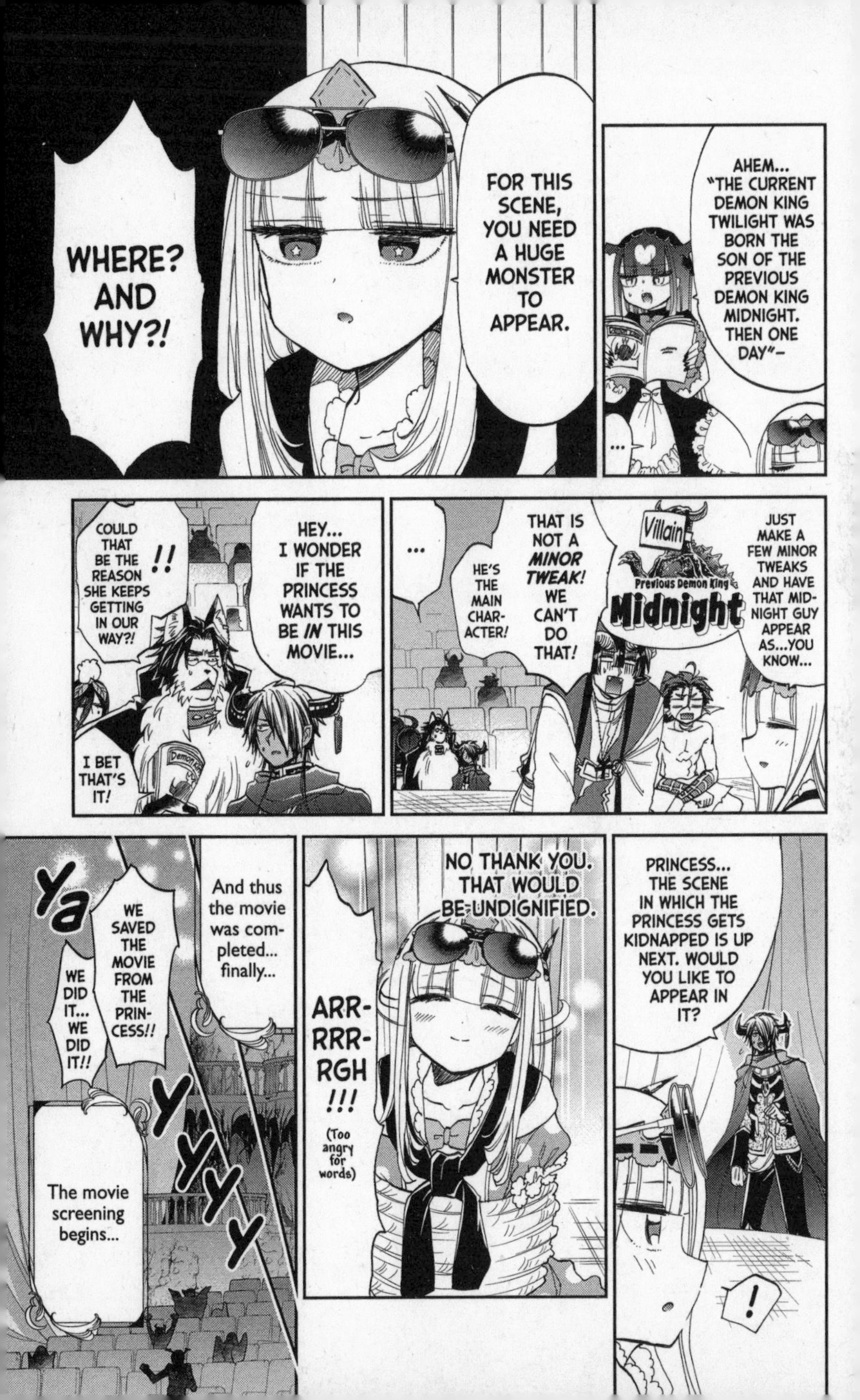

AHEM... "THE CURRENT DEMON KING TWILIGHT WAS BORN THE SON OF THE PREVIOUS DEMON KING MIDNIGHT. THEN ONE DAY"–
...
FOR THIS SCENE, YOU NEED A HUGE MONSTER TO APPEAR.
WHERE? AND WHY?!
JUST MAKE A FEW MINOR TWEAKS AND HAVE THAT MID-NIGHT GUY APPEAR AS...YOU KNOW...
Villain
Previous Demon King
Midnight
THAT IS NOT A *MINOR TWEAK*! WE CAN'T DO THAT!
HE'S THE MAIN CHAR-ACTER!
...
HEY... I WONDER IF THE PRINCESS WANTS TO BE *IN* THIS MOVIE...
!!
COULD THAT BE THE REASON SHE KEEPS GETTING IN OUR WAY?!
I BET THAT'S IT!
PRINCESS... THE SCENE IN WHICH THE PRINCESS GETS KIDNAPPED IS UP NEXT. WOULD YOU LIKE TO APPEAR IN IT?
!
NO THANK YOU. THAT WOULD BE UNDIGNIFIED.
ARR-RRR-RGH!!!
(Too angry for words)
And thus the movie was completed... finally...
WE SAVED THE MOVIE FROM THE PRIN-CESS!!
WE DID IT... WE DID IT!!
Yayyyyy
The movie screening begins...

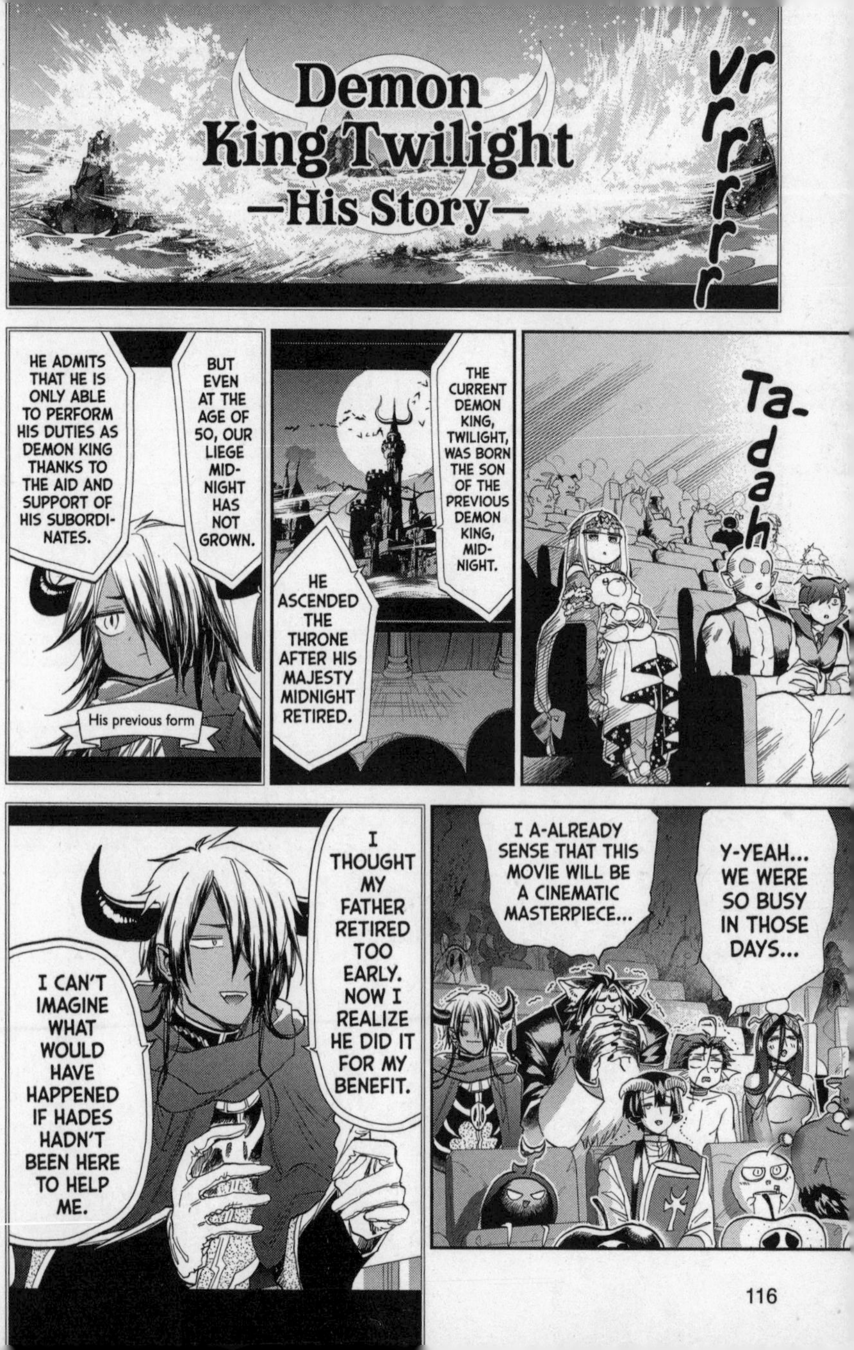
Demon King Twilight —His Story—
vrrrrrr
Ta-dah
THE CURRENT DEMON KING, TWILIGHT, WAS BORN THE SON OF THE PREVIOUS DEMON KING, MIDNIGHT.
HE ASCENDED THE THRONE AFTER HIS MAJESTY MIDNIGHT RETIRED.
BUT EVEN AT THE AGE OF 50, OUR LIEGE MIDNIGHT HAS NOT GROWN.
HE ADMITS THAT HE IS ONLY ABLE TO PERFORM HIS DUTIES AS DEMON KING THANKS TO THE AID AND SUPPORT OF HIS SUBORDINATES.
His previous form
Y-YEAH... WE WERE SO BUSY IN THOSE DAYS...
I A-ALREADY SENSE THAT THIS MOVIE WILL BE A CINEMATIC MASTERPIECE...
I THOUGHT MY FATHER RETIRED TOO EARLY. NOW I REALIZE HE DID IT FOR MY BENEFIT.
I CAN'T IMAGINE WHAT WOULD HAVE HAPPENED IF HADES HADN'T BEEN HERE TO HELP ME.

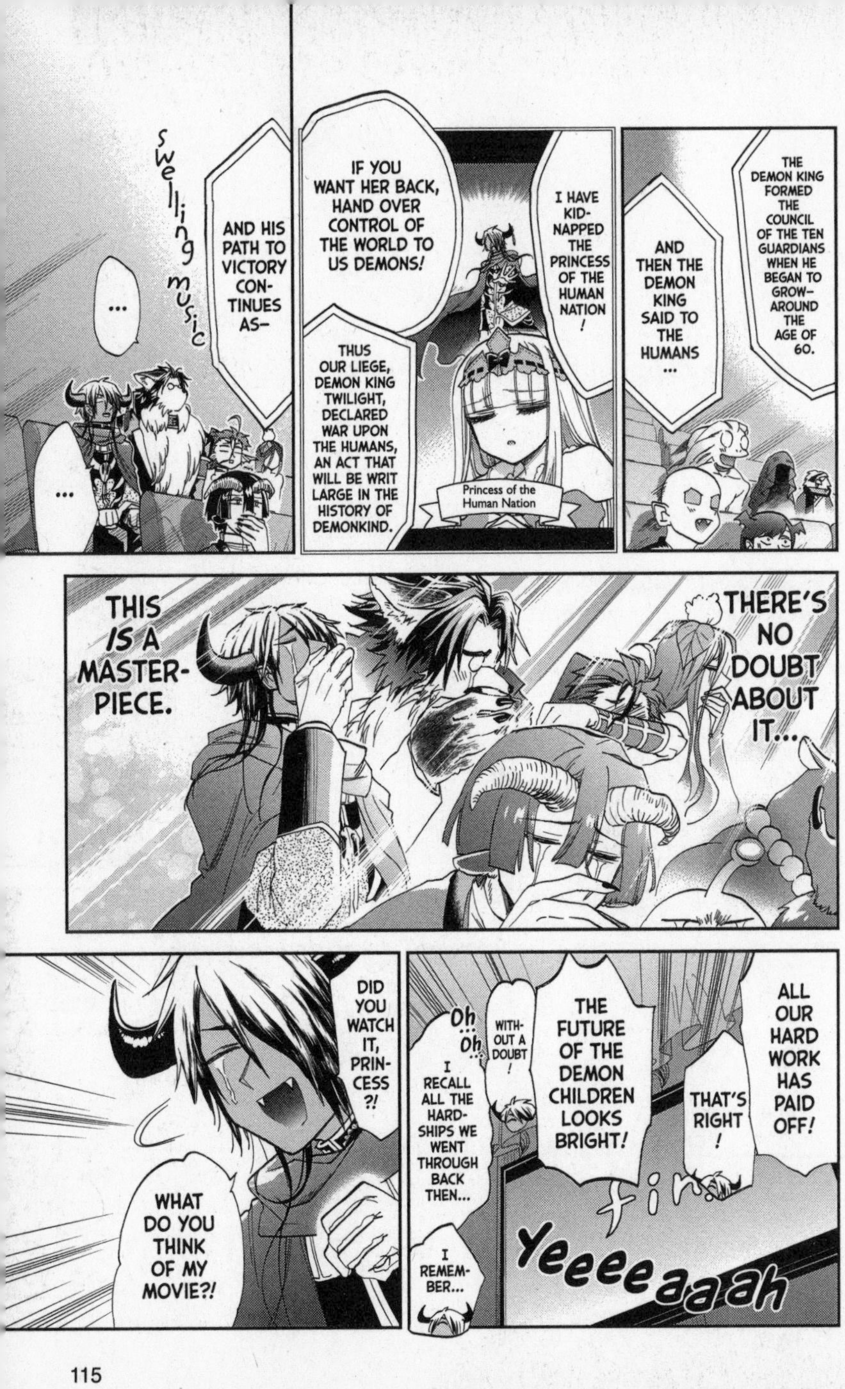

THE DEMON KING FORMED THE COUNCIL OF THE TEN GUARDIANS WHEN HE BEGAN TO GROW–AROUND THE AGE OF 60.
AND THEN THE DEMON KING SAID TO THE HUMANS...
I HAVE KIDNAPPED THE PRINCESS OF THE HUMAN NATION!
IF YOU WANT HER BACK, HAND OVER CONTROL OF THE WORLD TO US DEMONS!
THUS OUR LIEGE, DEMON KING TWILIGHT, DECLARED WAR UPON THE HUMANS, AN ACT THAT WILL BE WRIT LARGE IN THE HISTORY OF DEMONKIND.
Princess of the Human Nation
AND HIS PATH TO VICTORY CONTINUES AS–
swelling music
...
...
THERE'S NO DOUBT ABOUT IT...
THIS *IS* A MASTERPIECE.
ALL OUR HARD WORK HAS PAID OFF!
THAT'S RIGHT!
THE FUTURE OF THE DEMON CHILDREN LOOKS BRIGHT!
WITHOUT A DOUBT!
Oh... Oh...
I RECALL ALL THE HARDSHIPS WE WENT THROUGH BACK THEN...
fin
Yeeeeaaaah
I REMEMBER...
DID YOU WATCH IT, PRINCESS?!
WHAT DO YOU THINK OF MY MOVIE?!

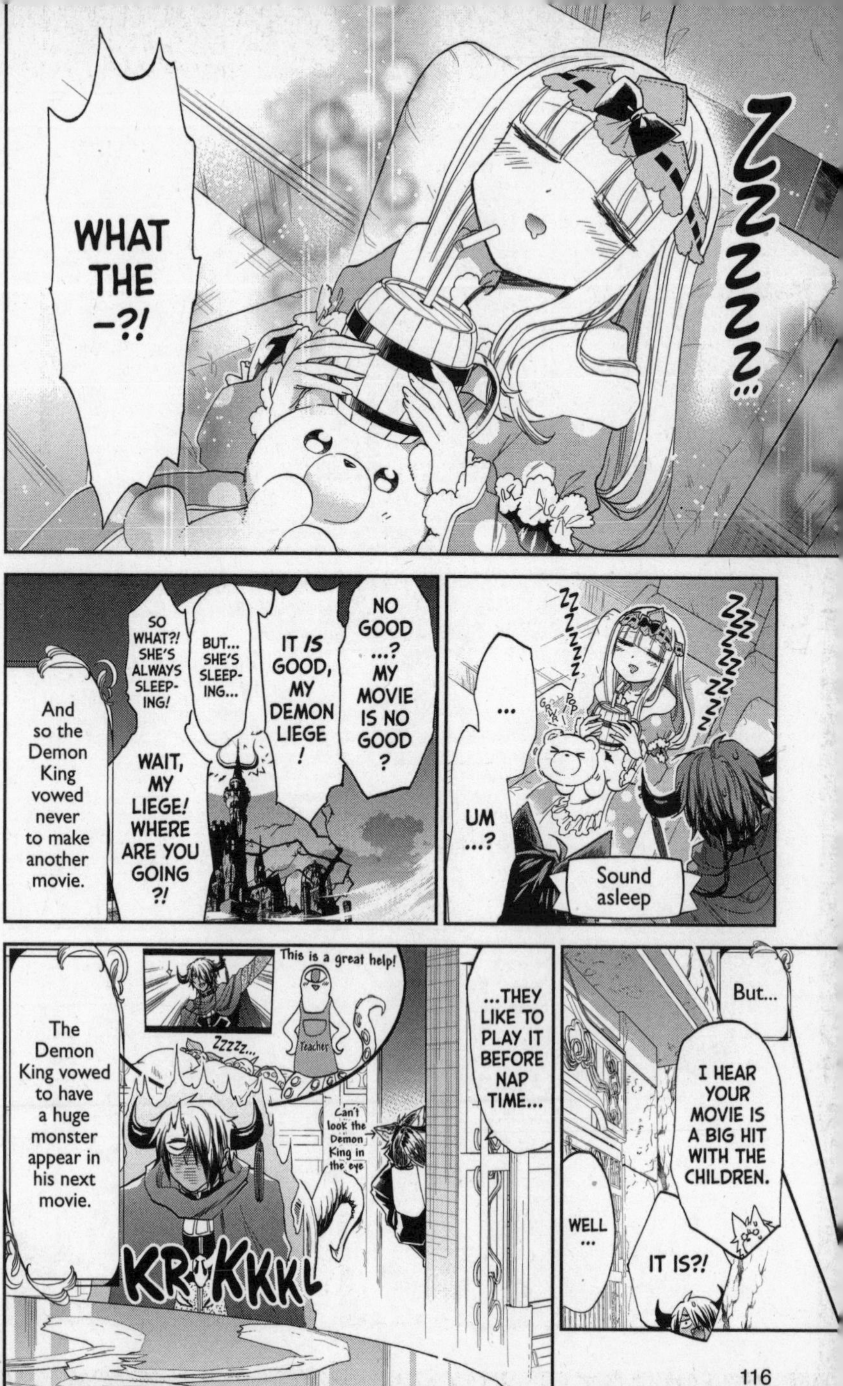
ZZZZZ...
WHAT THE —?!
ZZZZZZZZZ
ZZZZZZ
POP
...
UM ...?
Sound asleep
NO GOOD ...? MY MOVIE IS NO GOOD?
IT IS GOOD, MY DEMON LIEGE!
BUT... SHE'S SLEEPING...
SO WHAT?! SHE'S ALWAYS SLEEPING!
WAIT, MY LIEGE! WHERE ARE YOU GOING?!
And so the Demon King vowed never to make another movie.
But...
I HEAR YOUR MOVIE IS A BIG HIT WITH THE CHILDREN.
IT IS?!
WELL ...
...THEY LIKE TO PLAY IT BEFORE NAP TIME...
This is a great help!
Teacher
Zzzzz...
Can't look the Demon King in the eye
The Demon King vowed to have a huge monster appear in his next movie.
KRKKKL

Movie
Demon King Twilight: His Story

Effectiveness as a Sleep Aid: ☆☆☆☆☆
Budget: ☆☆☆☆

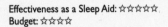

Three cheers for Demon King Twilight!!
Demon King Twilight —His Story—
♪
Now I realize he did it for my benefit.
What's going on? Are you filming us?!

A documentary created by the Demon King himself as an educational film for the children who are the demon future. The story unfolds as follows: the birth of Twilight, his succession to the demon throne, the present day.

They managed to keep the movie low-budget by incorporating archival footage.

The movie actually contained a lot of information that was new to the princess, including the age of the Demon King and the others, footage of Great Red Siberian traveling in his dog form, and depictions of Hades supporting his brother. However, none of these things interested her, so she fell sleep. This movie is actually quite popular with the (adult) demons.

Director's notes:
"I asked many demons to assist in the production of this movie, and they all generously agreed to contribute their time and talent. If not for their generosity and magnanimity of spirit, this film would never have come to be. But perhaps it would have been even better if I had created a random female character to play the heroine."

MAYBE I'LL SHOOT A SLASHER HORROR FILM NEXT...
...STARRING... GHOST SHROUD!
THAT WOULD BE A DOCU-MENTARY.
Snip Snip

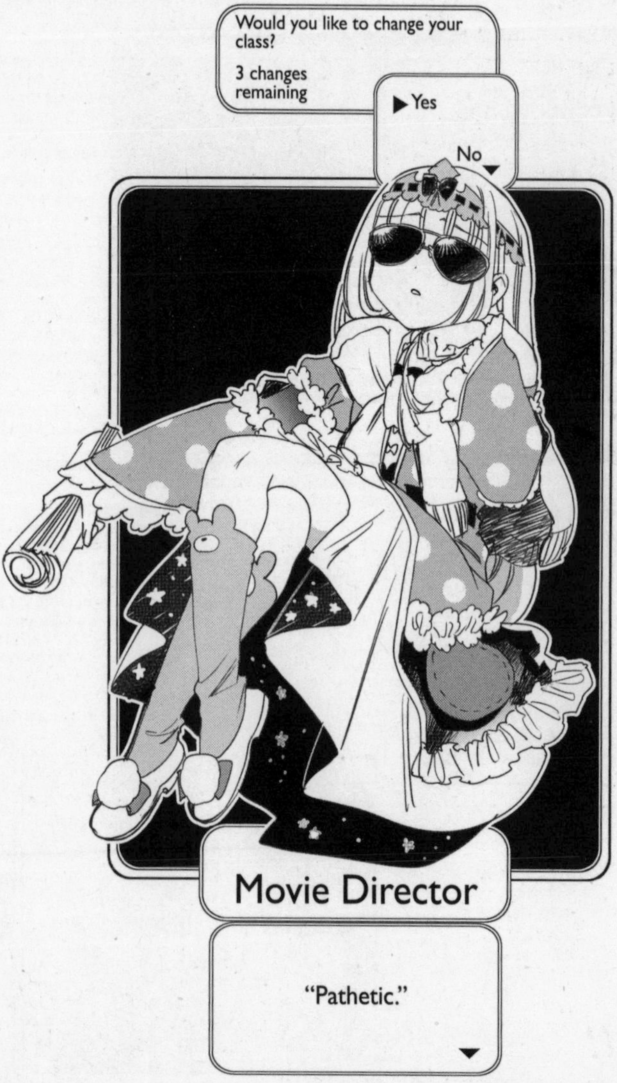
Would you like to change your class?
3 changes remaining
▶Yes
No
Movie Director
"Pathetic."

88th Night: Homemade Chocolate Pudding Inside ♡

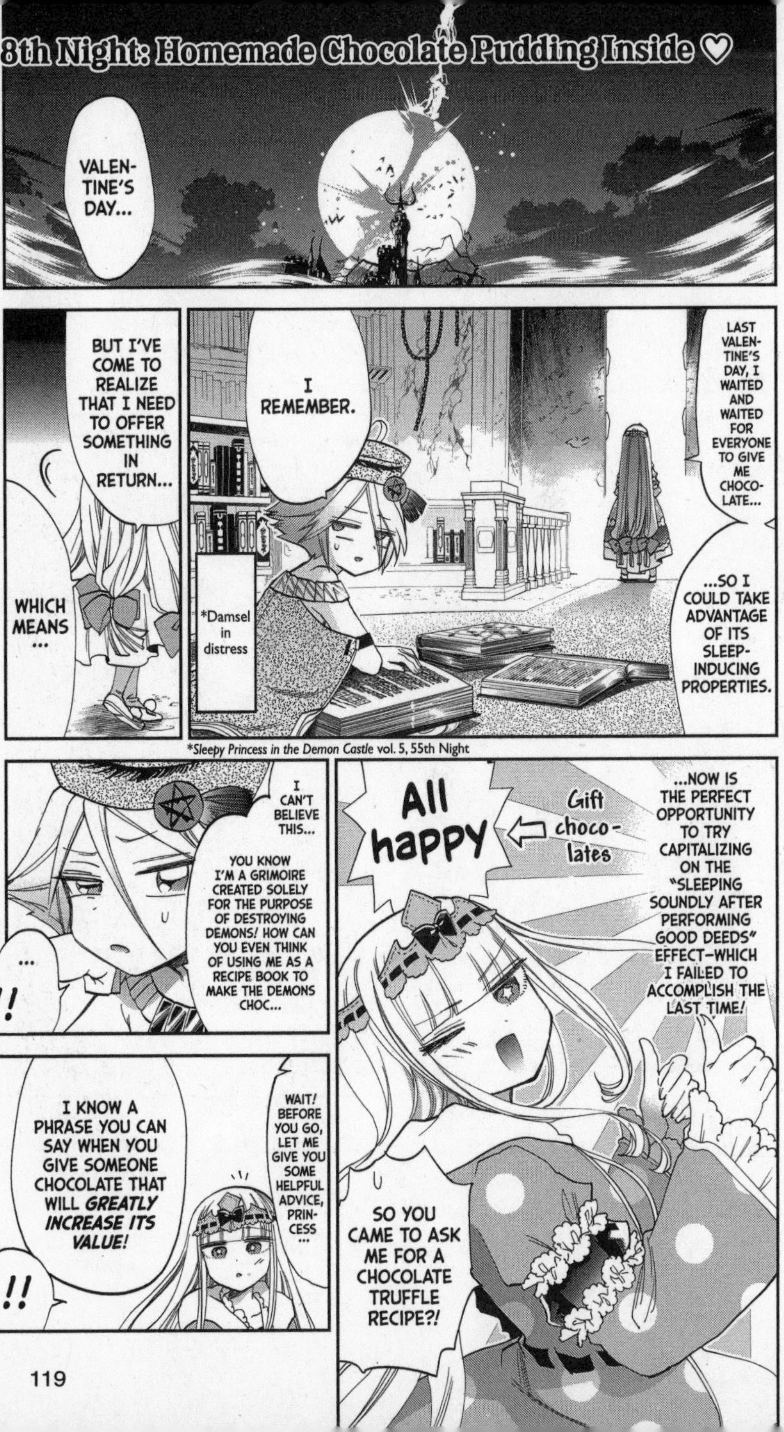
VALEN-TINE'S DAY...
LAST VALEN-TINE'S DAY, I WAITED AND WAITED FOR EVERYONE TO GIVE ME CHOCO-LATE...
...SO I COULD TAKE ADVANTAGE OF ITS SLEEP-INDUCING PROPERTIES.
I REMEMBER.
*Damsel in distress
BUT I'VE COME TO REALIZE THAT I NEED TO OFFER SOMETHING IN RETURN...
WHICH MEANS ...
...NOW IS THE PERFECT OPPORTUNITY TO TRY CAPITALIZING ON THE "SLEEPING SOUNDLY AFTER PERFORMING GOOD DEEDS" EFFECT—WHICH I FAILED TO ACCOMPLISH THE LAST TIME!
All happy
Gift choco-lates
SO YOU CAME TO ASK ME FOR A CHOCOLATE TRUFFLE RECIPE?!
I CAN'T BELIEVE THIS...
YOU KNOW I'M A GRIMOIRE CREATED SOLELY FOR THE PURPOSE OF DESTROYING DEMONS! HOW CAN YOU EVEN THINK OF USING ME AS A RECIPE BOOK TO MAKE THE DEMONS CHOC...
...
!!
WAIT! BEFORE YOU GO, LET ME GIVE YOU SOME HELPFUL ADVICE, PRIN-CESS ...
I KNOW A PHRASE YOU CAN SAY WHEN YOU GIVE SOMEONE CHOCOLATE THAT WILL *GREATLY INCREASE ITS VALUE!*
!!

**Sleepy Princess in the Demon Castle* vol. 5, 55th Night

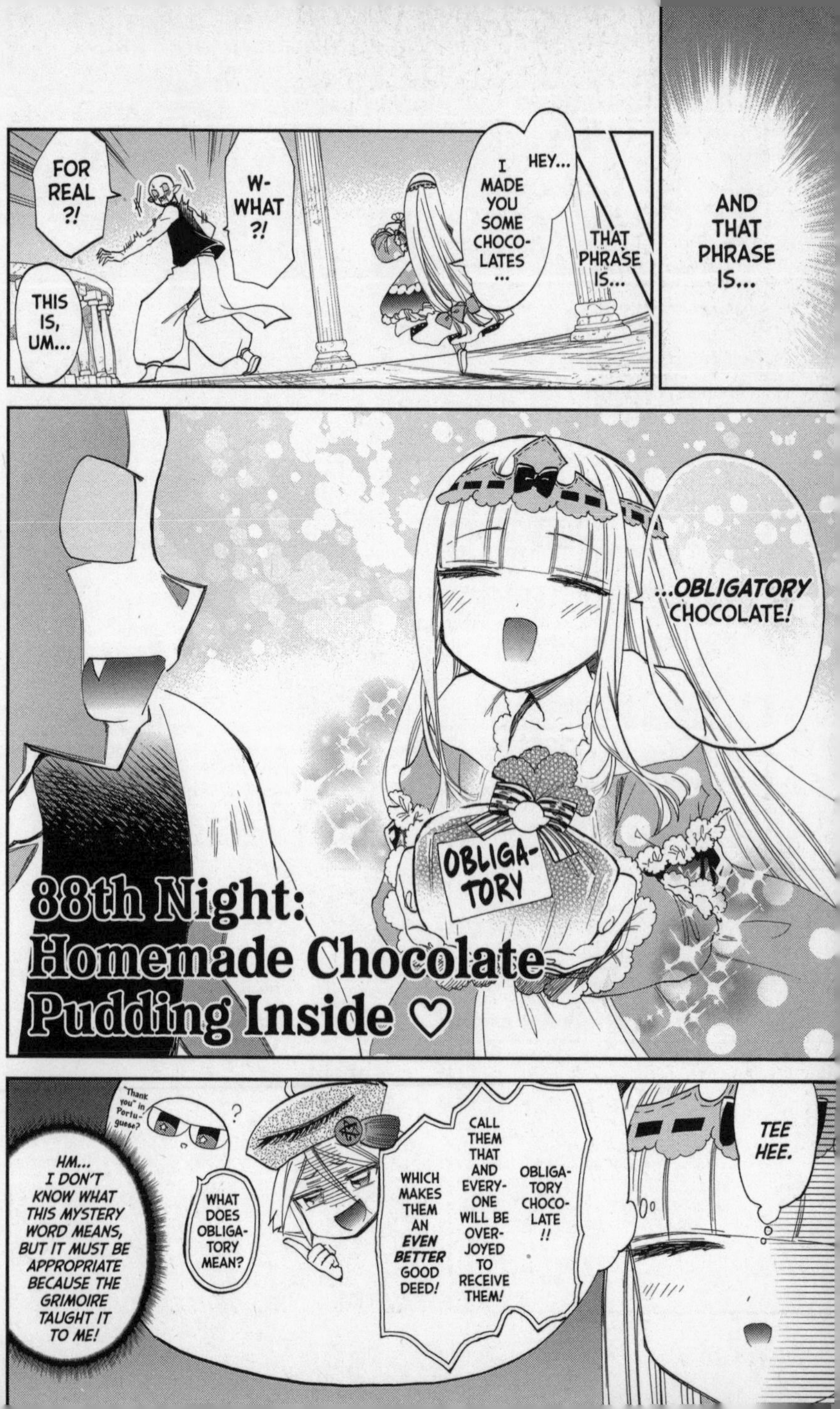
AND THAT PHRASE IS...
HEY... I MADE YOU SOME CHOCOLATES...
THAT PHRASE IS...
W-WHAT?!
FOR REAL?!
THIS IS, UM...
...OBLIGATORY CHOCOLATE!
OBLIGATORY
88th Night: Homemade Chocolate Pudding Inside ♡
TEE HEE.
OBLIGATORY CHOCOLATE!!
CALL THEM THAT AND EVERYONE WILL BE OVERJOYED TO RECEIVE THEM!
WHICH MAKES THEM AN EVEN BETTER GOOD DEED!
WHAT DOES OBLIGATORY MEAN?
"Thank you" in Portuguese?
?
HM... I DON'T KNOW WHAT THIS MYSTERY WORD MEANS, BUT IT MUST BE APPROPRIATE BECAUSE THE GRIMOIRE TAUGHT IT TO ME!

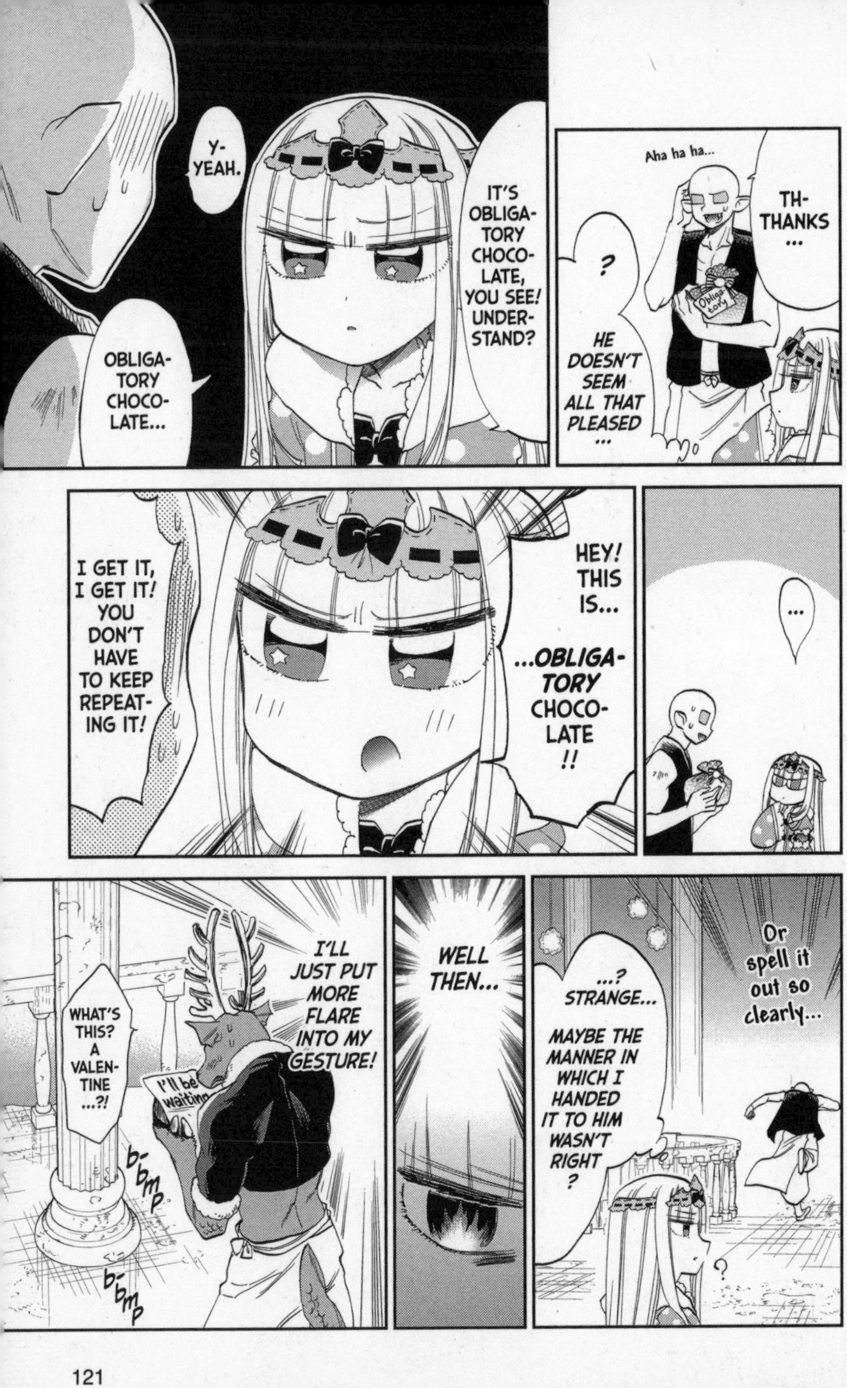
Aha ha ha...
TH-THANKS...
?
HE DOESN'T SEEM ALL THAT PLEASED...
IT'S OBLIGATORY CHOCOLATE, YOU SEE! UNDERSTAND?
Y-YEAH.
OBLIGATORY CHOCOLATE...
...
HEY! THIS IS...
...OBLIGATORY CHOCOLATE!!
I GET IT, I GET IT! YOU DON'T HAVE TO KEEP REPEATING IT!
Or spell it out so clearly...
...? STRANGE...
MAYBE THE MANNER IN WHICH I HANDED IT TO HIM WASN'T RIGHT?
WELL THEN...
I'LL JUST PUT MORE FLARE INTO MY GESTURE!
WHAT'S THIS? A VALENTINE...?!
I'll be waiting
b-bmp
b-bmp

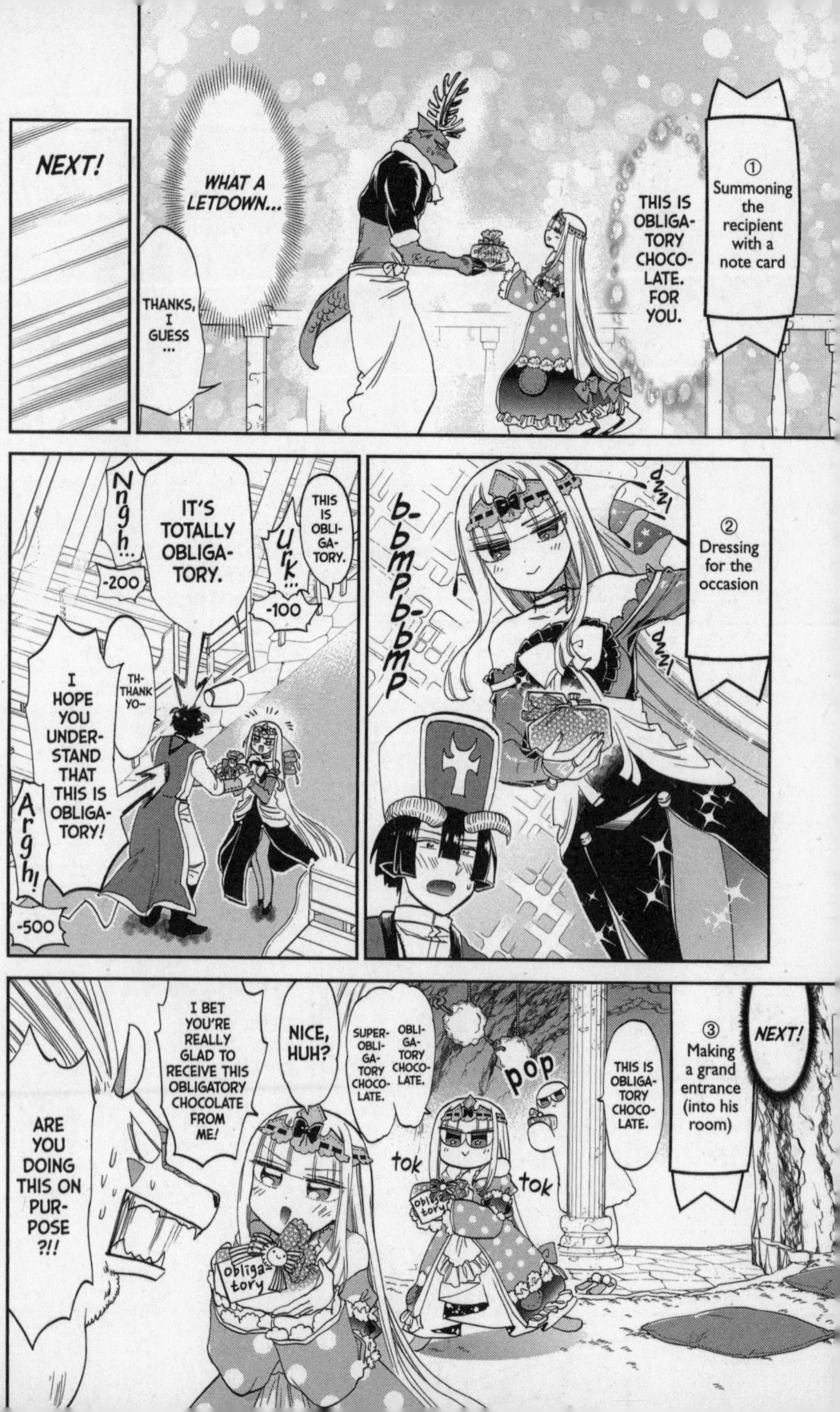
① Summoning the recipient with a note card
THIS IS OBLIGATORY CHOCOLATE. FOR YOU.
WHAT A LETDOWN...
THANKS, I GUESS...
NEXT!
② Dressing for the occasion
dzzl
b-bmpb-bmp
dzzl
THIS IS OBLIGATORY.
Urk...
-100
IT'S TOTALLY OBLIGATORY.
Ngh...
-200
TH-THANK YO-
I HOPE YOU UNDERSTAND THAT THIS IS OBLIGATORY!
Argh!
-500
NEXT!
③ Making a grand entrance (into his room)
THIS IS OBLIGATORY CHOCOLATE.
pop
OBLIGATORY CHOCOLATE.
SUPER-OBLIGATORY CHOCOLATE.
tok
tok
obligatory
NICE, HUH?
I BET YOU'RE REALLY GLAD TO RECEIVE THIS OBLIGATORY CHOCOLATE FROM ME!
obligatory
ARE YOU DOING THIS ON PURPOSE?!!

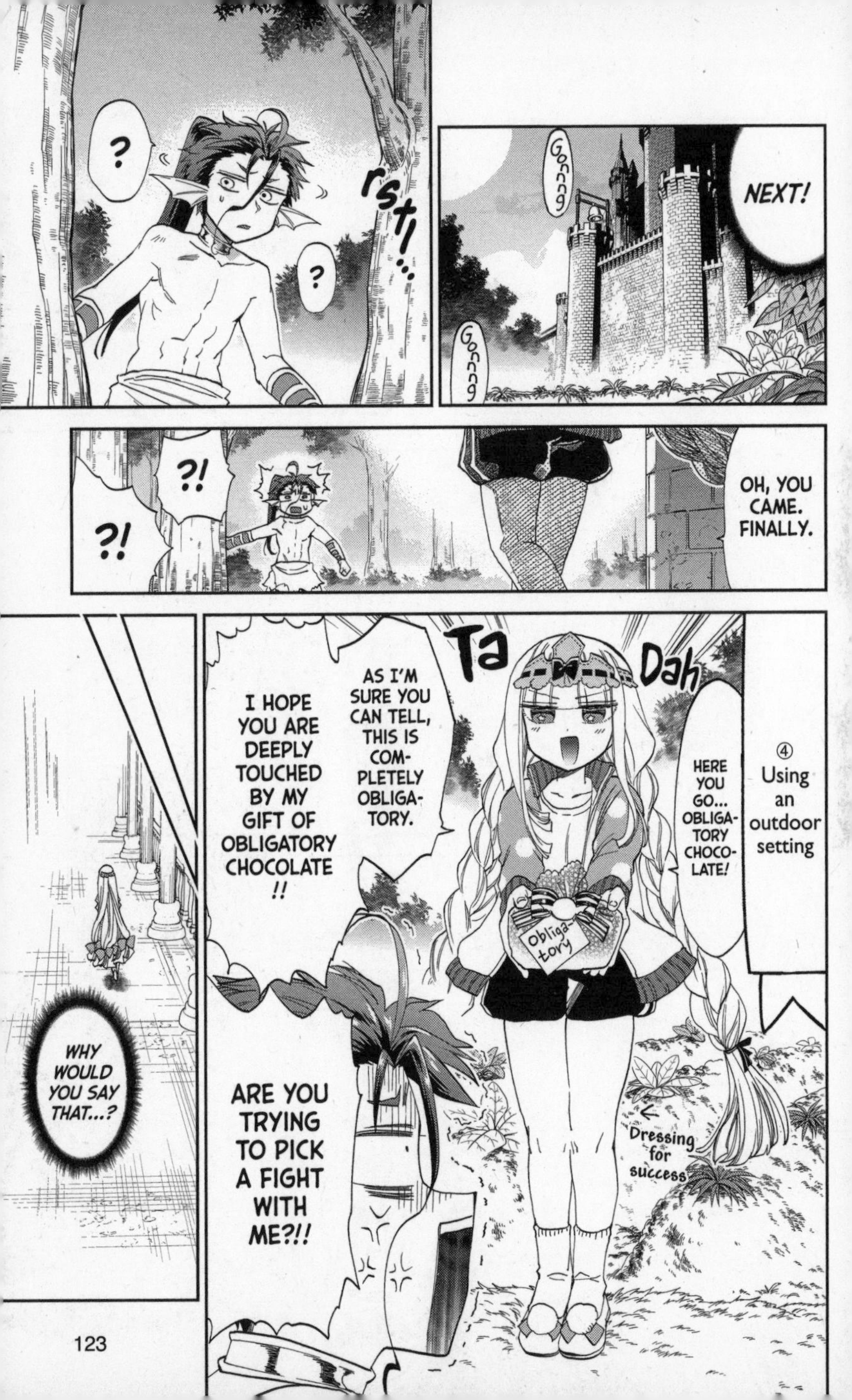
NEXT!
Gonnng
Gonnng
?
rstl...
?
OH, YOU CAME. FINALLY.
?!
?!
④ Using an outdoor setting
Ta Dah
HERE YOU GO... OBLIGATORY CHOCOLATE!
Obligatory
AS I'M SURE YOU CAN TELL, THIS IS COMPLETELY OBLIGATORY.
I HOPE YOU ARE DEEPLY TOUCHED BY MY GIFT OF OBLIGATORY CHOCOLATE!!
← Dressing for success
ARE YOU TRYING TO PICK A FIGHT WITH ME?!!
WHY WOULD YOU SAY THAT...?

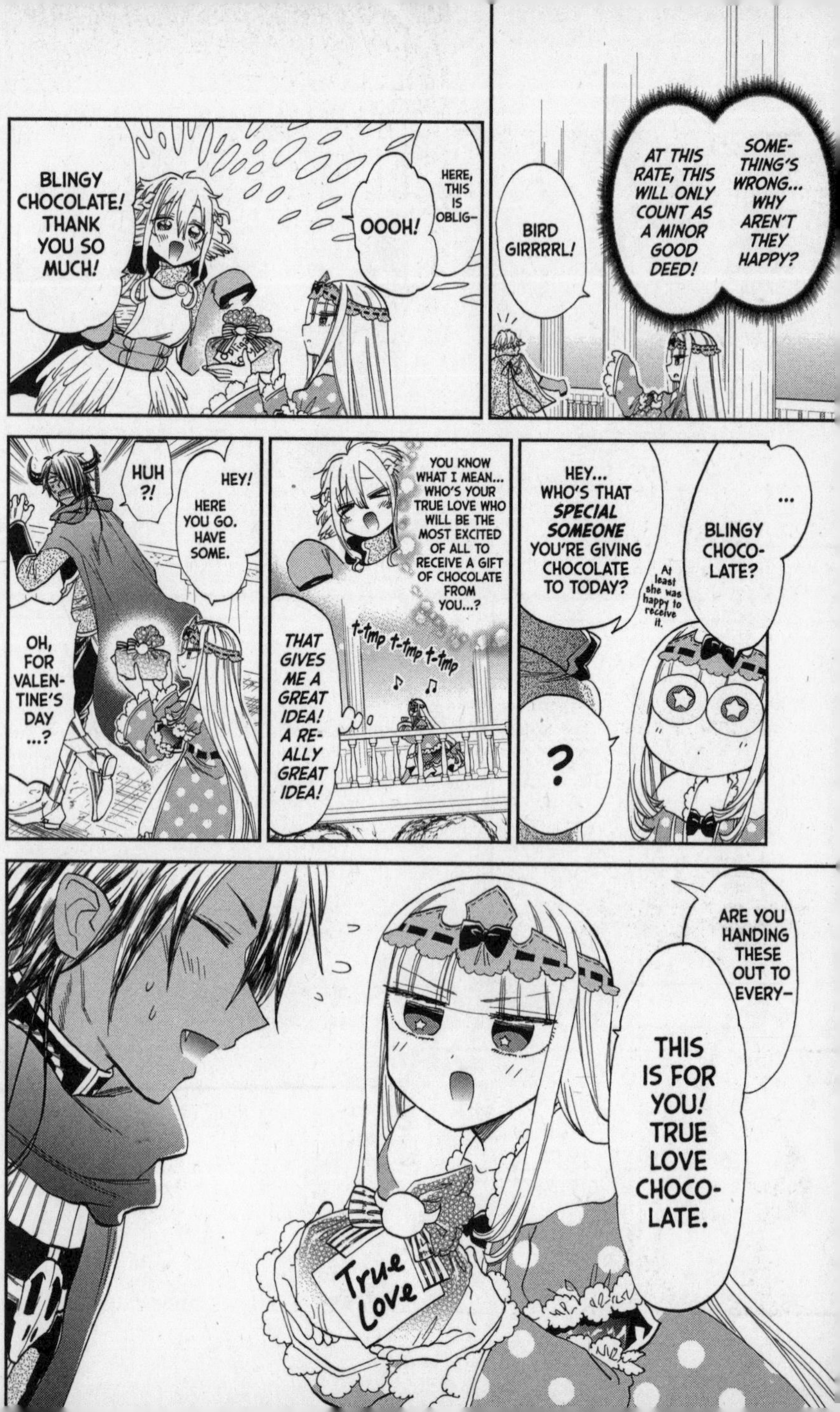
SOMETHING'S WRONG... WHY AREN'T THEY HAPPY?
AT THIS RATE, THIS WILL ONLY COUNT AS A MINOR GOOD DEED!
BIRD GIRRRRL!
HERE, THIS IS OBLIG—
OOOH!
BLINGY CHOCOLATE! THANK YOU SO MUCH!
...
BLINGY CHOCOLATE?
At least she was happy to receive it.
HEY... WHO'S THAT *SPECIAL SOMEONE* YOU'RE GIVING CHOCOLATE TO TODAY?
?
YOU KNOW WHAT I MEAN... WHO'S YOUR TRUE LOVE WHO WILL BE THE MOST EXCITED OF ALL TO RECEIVE A GIFT OF CHOCOLATE FROM YOU...?
THAT GIVES ME A GREAT IDEA! A REALLY GREAT IDEA!
t-tmp t-tmp t-tmp
HEY!
HERE YOU GO. HAVE SOME.
HUH?!
OH, FOR VALENTINE'S DAY ...?
ARE YOU HANDING THESE OUT TO EVERY—
THIS IS FOR YOU! TRUE LOVE CHOCOLATE.
True Love

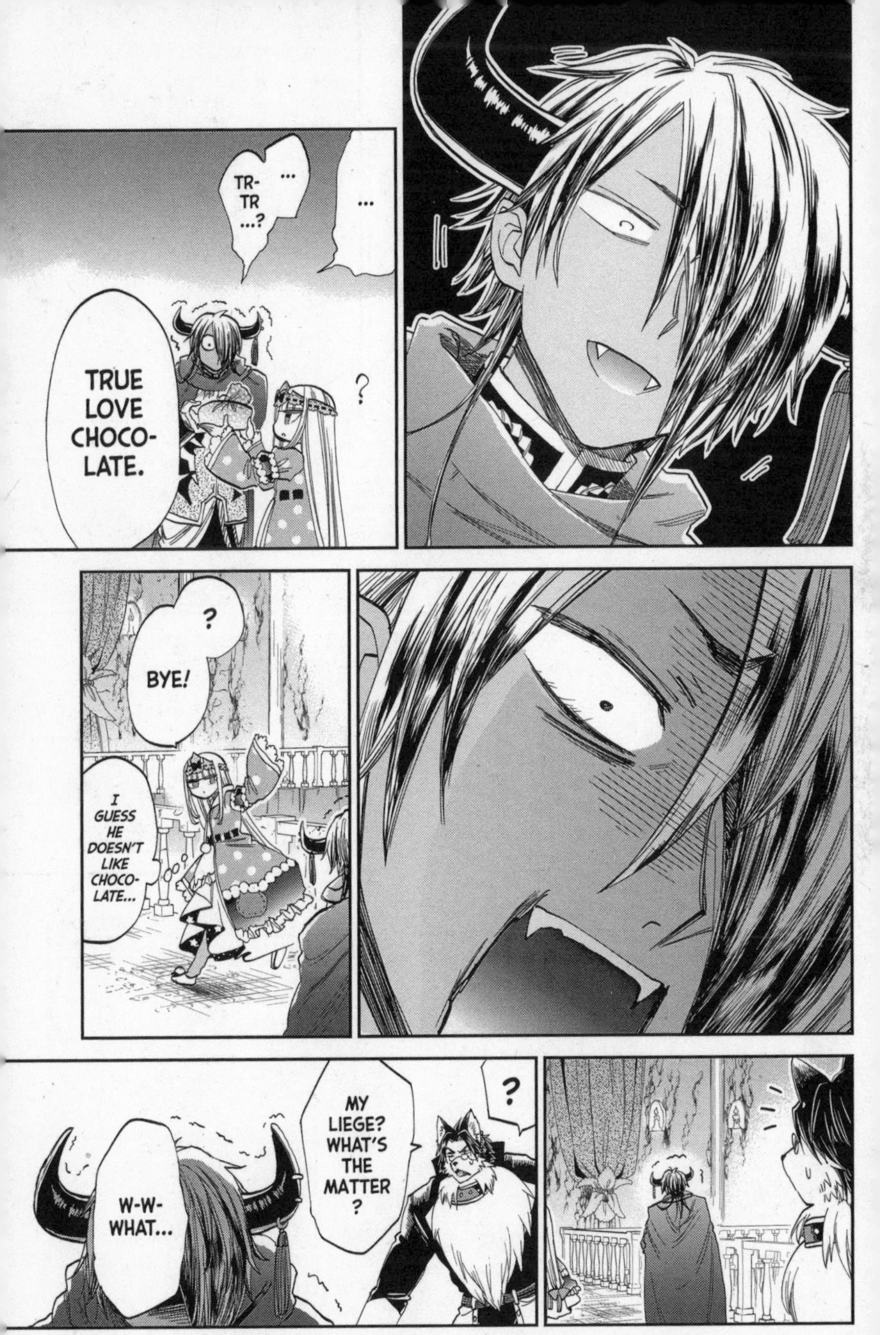
...
... TR-TR ...?
TRUE LOVE CHOCOLATE.
?
? BYE!
I GUESS HE DOESN'T LIKE CHOCOLATE...
?
MY LIEGE? WHAT'S THE MATTER?
W-W-WHAT...

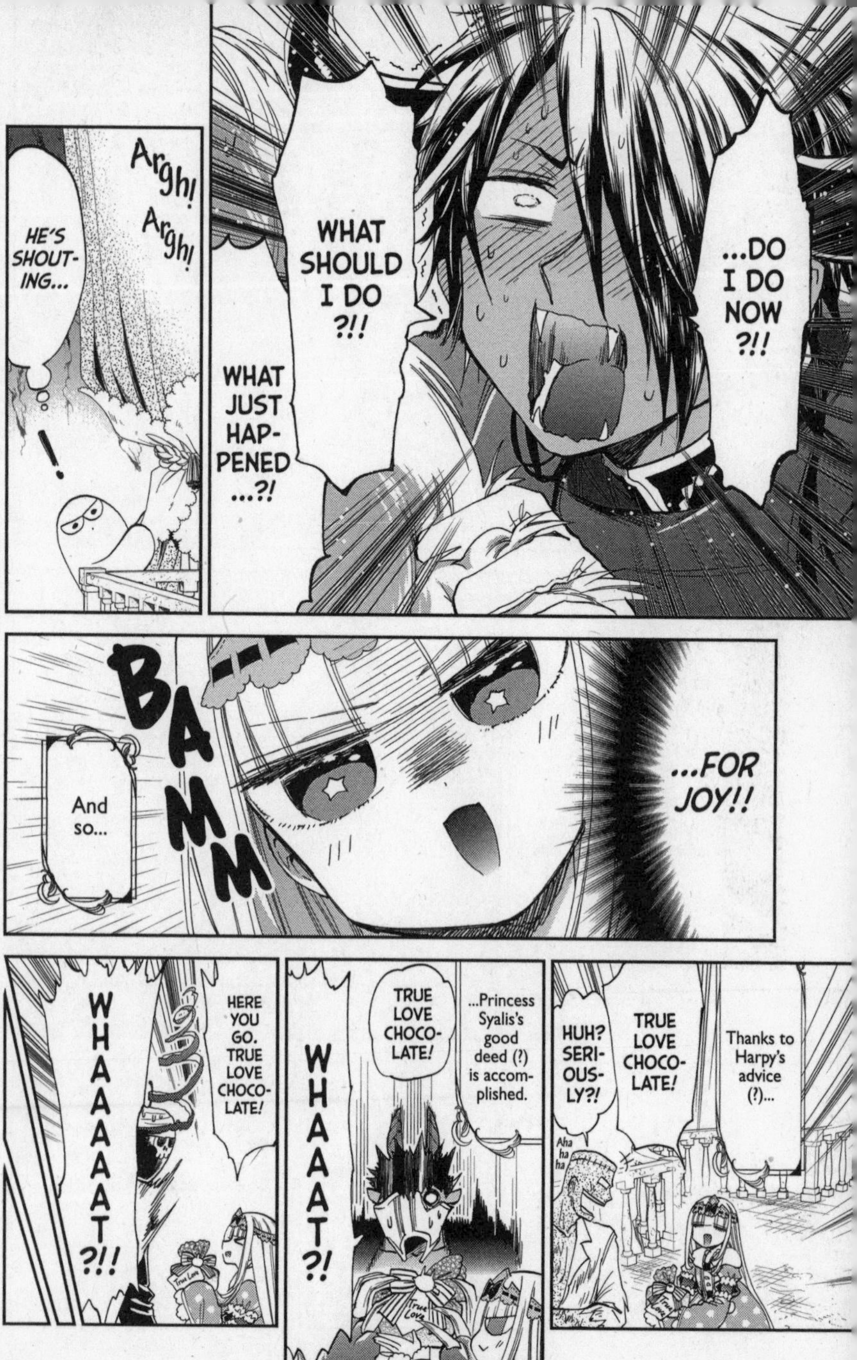
...DO I DO NOW ?!!
WHAT SHOULD I DO ?!!
WHAT JUST HAPPENED ...?!
Argh! Argh!
HE'S SHOUTING...
!
...FOR JOY!!
BAMM
And so...
Thanks to Harpy's advice (?)...
TRUE LOVE CHOCOLATE!
HUH? SERIOUSLY?!
Aha ha ha
...Princess Syalis's good deed (?) is accomplished.
TRUE LOVE CHOCOLATE!
WHAAAT ?!
True Love
HERE YOU GO. TRUE LOVE CHOCOLATE!
WHAAAAAT ?!!
True Love

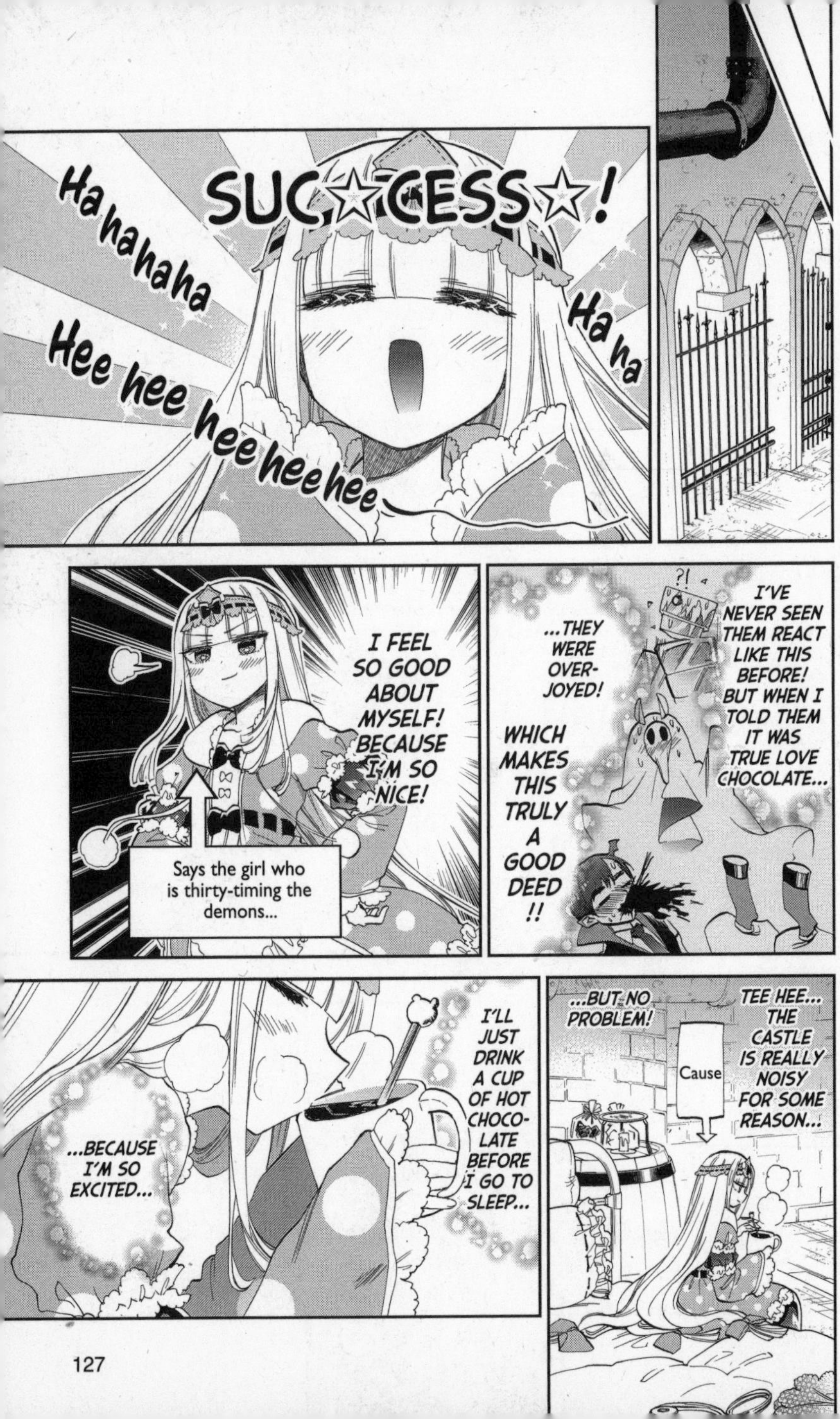
SUC☆CESS☆!
Ha ha
Hahahahaha
Hee hee hee hee hee
I'VE NEVER SEEN THEM REACT LIKE THIS BEFORE! BUT WHEN I TOLD THEM IT WAS TRUE LOVE CHOCOLATE...
?!
...THEY WERE OVER-JOYED!
WHICH MAKES THIS TRULY A GOOD DEED!!
I FEEL SO GOOD ABOUT MYSELF! BECAUSE I'M SO NICE!
Says the girl who is thirty-timing the demons...
TEE HEE... THE CASTLE IS REALLY NOISY FOR SOME REASON...
...BUT NO PROBLEM!
Cause
I'LL JUST DRINK A CUP OF HOT CHOCO-LATE BEFORE I GO TO SLEEP...
...BECAUSE I'M SO EXCITED...

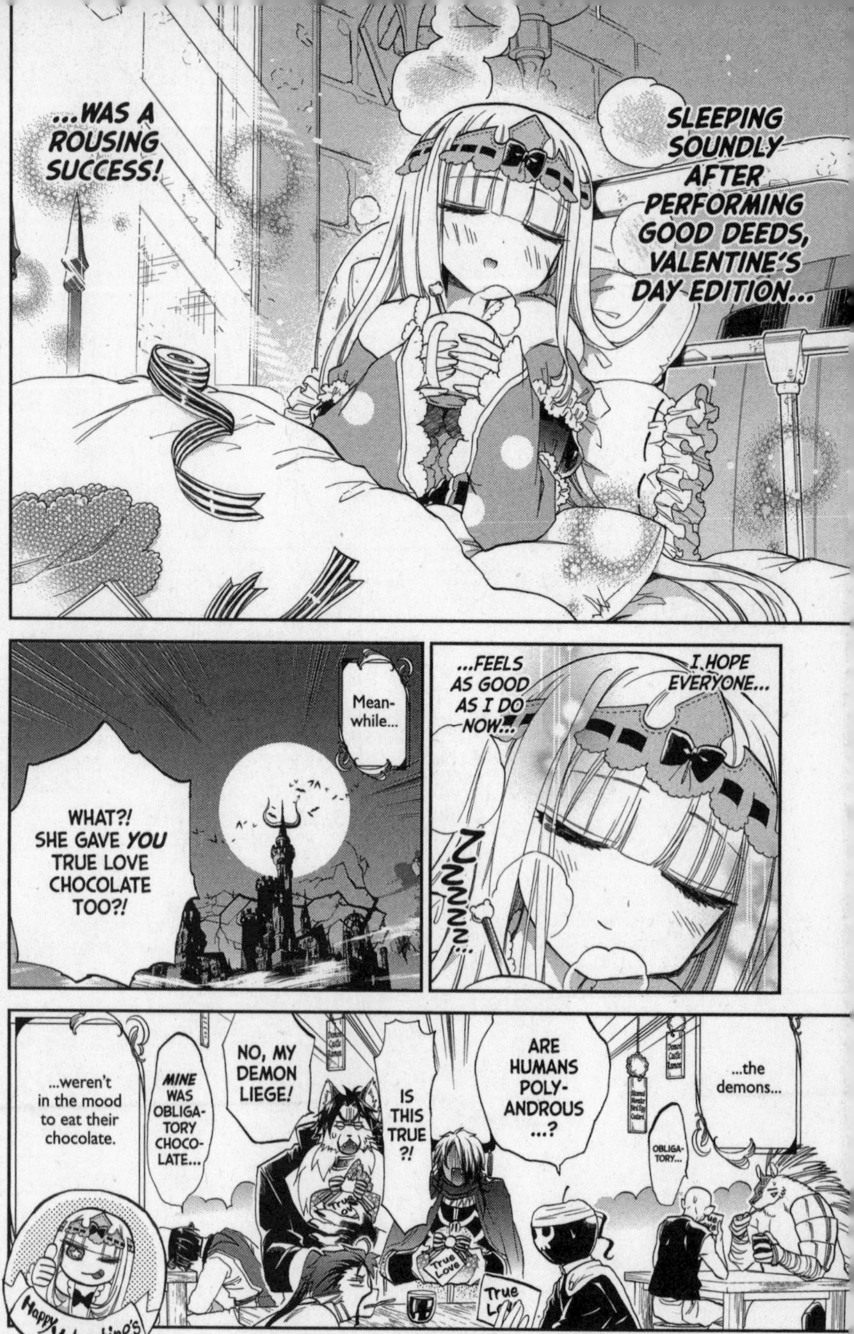
SLEEPING SOUNDLY AFTER PERFORMING GOOD DEEDS, VALENTINE'S DAY EDITION...
...WAS A ROUSING SUCCESS!
I HOPE EVERYONE...
...FEELS AS GOOD AS I DO NOW...
ZZZZZ...
Mean-while...
WHAT?! SHE GAVE *YOU* TRUE LOVE CHOCOLATE TOO?!
...the demons...
ARE HUMANS POLY-ANDROUS ...?
OBLIGA-TORY...
IS THIS TRUE ?!
NO, MY DEMON LIEGE!
MINE WAS OBLIGA-TORY CHOCO-LATE...
...weren't in the mood to eat their chocolate.
True Love
True Love
Happy Valentine's

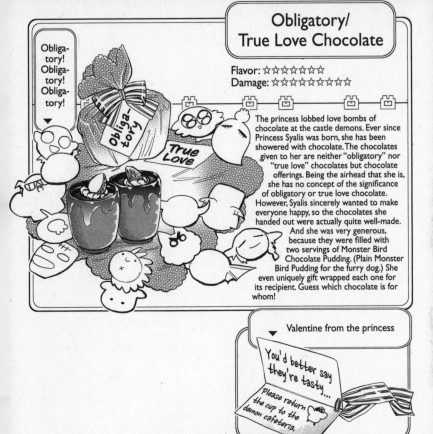

Obligatory/ True Love Chocolate

Flavor: ☆☆☆☆☆☆☆
Damage: ☆☆☆☆☆☆☆☆☆

The princess lobbed love bombs of chocolate at the castle demons. Ever since Princess Syalis was born, she has been showered with chocolate. The chocolates given to her are neither "obligatory" nor "true love" chocolates but chocolate offerings. Being the airhead that she is, she has no concept of the significance of obligatory or true love chocolate. However, Syalis sincerely wanted to make everyone happy, so the chocolates she handed out were actually quite well-made. And she was very generous, because they were filled with two servings of Monster Bird Chocolate Pudding. (Plain Monster Bird Pudding for the furry dog.) She even uniquely gift wrapped each one for its recipient. Guess which chocolate is for whom!

Obliga- tory! Obliga- tory! Obliga- tory!
Obliga- tory
True Love

▼ Valentine from the princess

You'd better say they're tasty...
Please return the cup to the demon cafeteria.

TH-THE DEMON CASTLE...
...HAS RECEIVED A DELIVERY OF CHOCO- LATES FROM SOME UNKNOWN ADMIRER AGAIN THIS YEAR!!
Really ?!
THANK YOU... YUM... THANK YOU...
Oh... Oh...
YOU SAID IT. THEY'RE SO GOOD.
Thanks!
YOU GOT SOME TOO, PRINCESS?! WOW, THIS ONE IS REALLY DELI- CIOUS!
Thank you!
Thank you very much!

Thank you for the chocolates for Kumanomata too!

Would you like to change
your class?

2 changes
remaining

▶ Yes

No ▼

Exorcist

"I need to sleep in
order to exorcise this evil
known as sleepiness."

▼

89th Night: You Didn't Create a Ko-tatsu, You Dug Your Own Grave

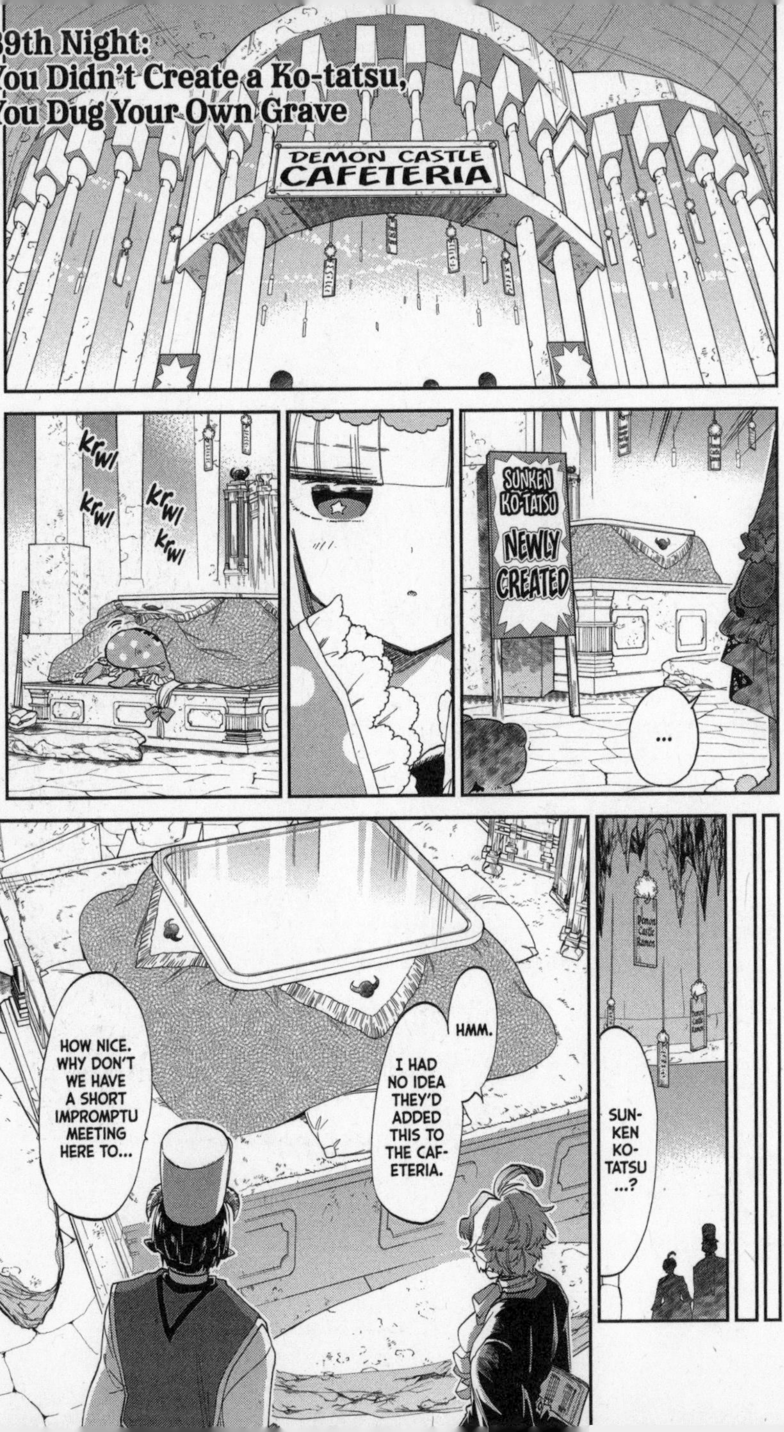
DEMON CASTLE CAFETERIA
SUNKEN KO-TATSU NEWLY CREATED
...
krwl krwl krwl krwl
Demon Castle Ramen
SUN-KEN KO-TATSU ...?
HMM.
I HAD NO IDEA THEY'D ADDED THIS TO THE CAF-ETERIA.
HOW NICE. WHY DON'T WE HAVE A SHORT IMPROMPTU MEETING HERE TO...

89th Night: You Didn't Create a Ko-tatsu, You Dug Your Own Grave

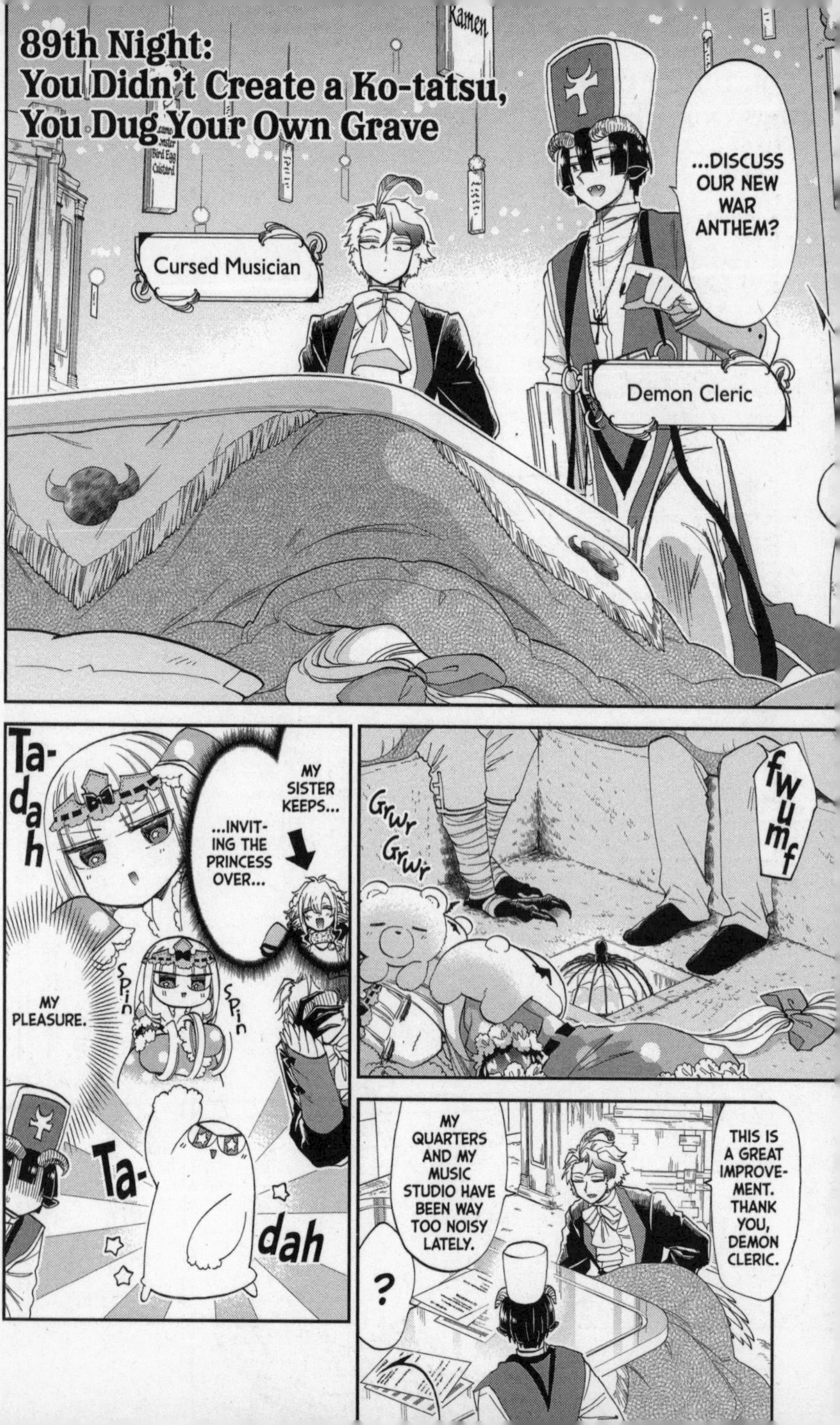
Ramen
Bird Egg Custard
...DISCUSS OUR NEW WAR ANTHEM?
Cursed Musician
Demon Cleric
fwumf
Grwr Grwr
THIS IS A GREAT IMPROVEMENT. THANK YOU, DEMON CLERIC.
MY QUARTERS AND MY MUSIC STUDIO HAVE BEEN WAY TOO NOISY LATELY.
?
Ta-dah
MY SISTER KEEPS...
...INVITING THE PRINCESS OVER...
MY PLEASURE.
Spin
Spin
Ta-dah

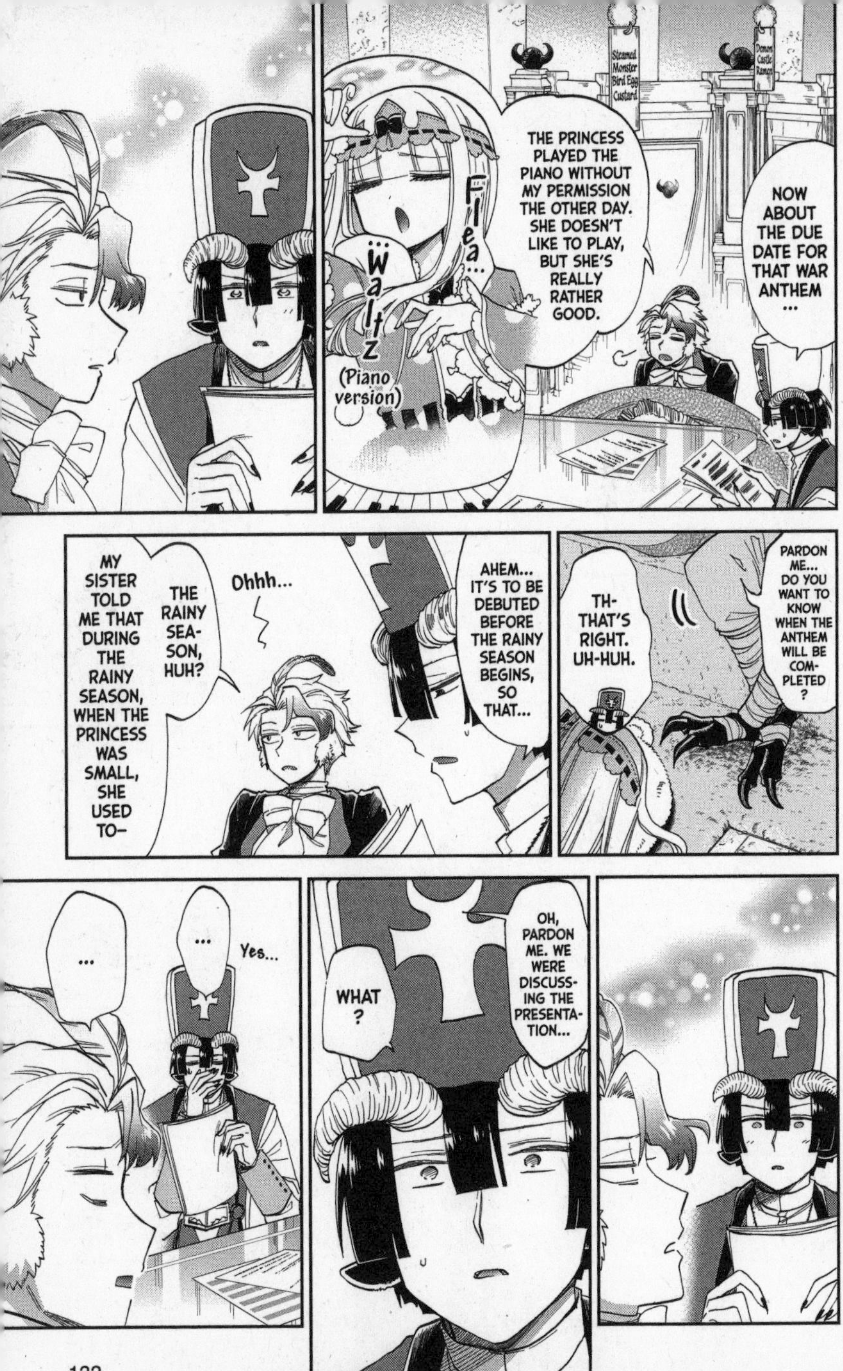
Demon Castle Ramen
Steamed Monster Bird Egg Custard
NOW ABOUT THE DUE DATE FOR THAT WAR ANTHEM...
THE PRINCESS PLAYED THE PIANO WITHOUT MY PERMISSION THE OTHER DAY. SHE DOESN'T LIKE TO PLAY, BUT SHE'S REALLY RATHER GOOD.
Flea...
...Waltz
(Piano version)
PARDON ME... DO YOU WANT TO KNOW WHEN THE ANTHEM WILL BE COMPLETED?
TH-THAT'S RIGHT. UH-HUH.
AHEM... IT'S TO BE DEBUTED BEFORE THE RAINY SEASON BEGINS, SO THAT...
Ohhh...
THE RAINY SEASON, HUH?
MY SISTER TOLD ME THAT DURING THE RAINY SEASON, WHEN THE PRINCESS WAS SMALL, SHE USED TO–
OH, PARDON ME. WE WERE DISCUSSING THE PRESENTATION...
WHAT?
Yes...
...
...

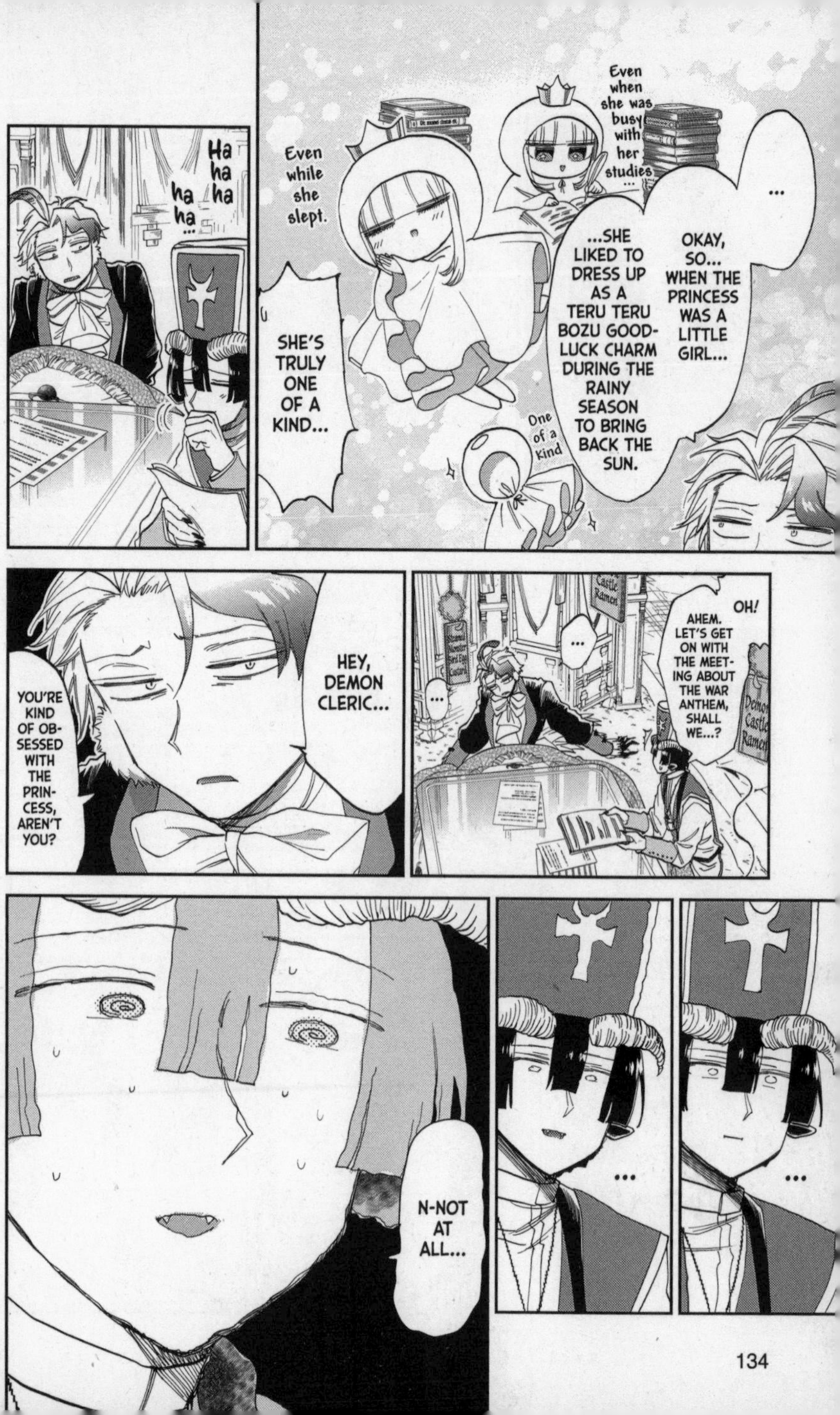
...
OKAY, SO... WHEN THE PRINCESS WAS A LITTLE GIRL...
...SHE LIKED TO DRESS UP AS A TERU TERU BOZU GOOD-LUCK CHARM DURING THE RAINY SEASON TO BRING BACK THE SUN.
Even when she was busy with her studies...
Even while she slept.
One of a Kind
SHE'S TRULY ONE OF A KIND...
Ha ha ha ha ha...
OH!
AHEM. LET'S GET ON WITH THE MEETING ABOUT THE WAR ANTHEM, SHALL WE...?
Demon Castle Ramen
...
...
HEY, DEMON CLERIC...
YOU'RE KIND OF OBSESSED WITH THE PRINCESS, AREN'T YOU?
...
...
N-NOT AT ALL...

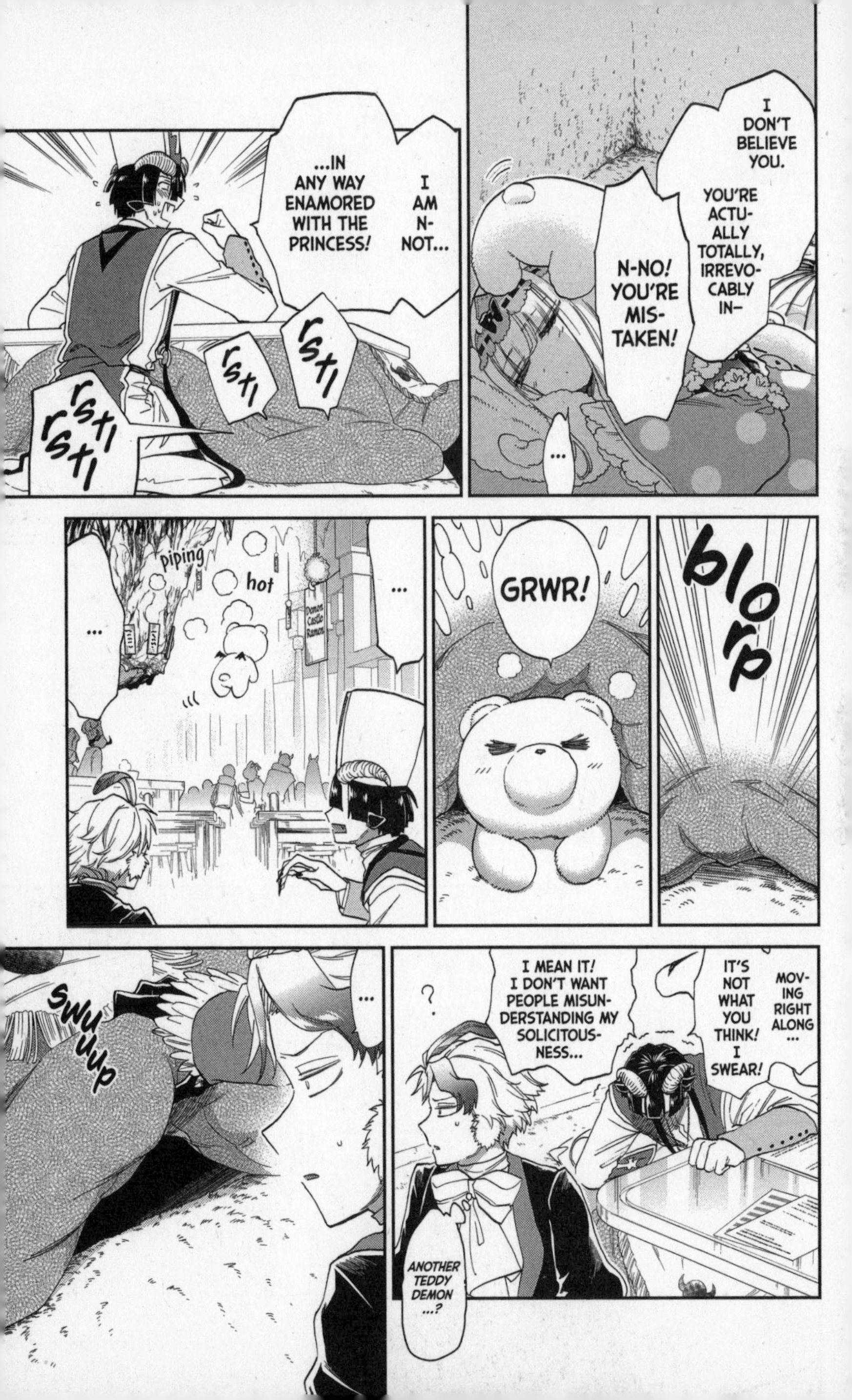
I DON'T BELIEVE YOU.
YOU'RE ACTUALLY TOTALLY, IRREVOCABLY IN–
N-NO! YOU'RE MISTAKEN!
...
I AM N-NOT...
...IN ANY WAY ENAMORED WITH THE PRINCESS!
rstl
rstl
rstl
rstl
blorp
GRWR!
...
piping hot
Demon Castle Ramen
...
MOVING RIGHT ALONG...
IT'S NOT WHAT YOU THINK! I SWEAR!
I MEAN IT! I DON'T WANT PEOPLE MISUNDERSTANDING MY SOLICITOUSNESS...
?
ANOTHER TEDDY DEMON...?
...
swuuup

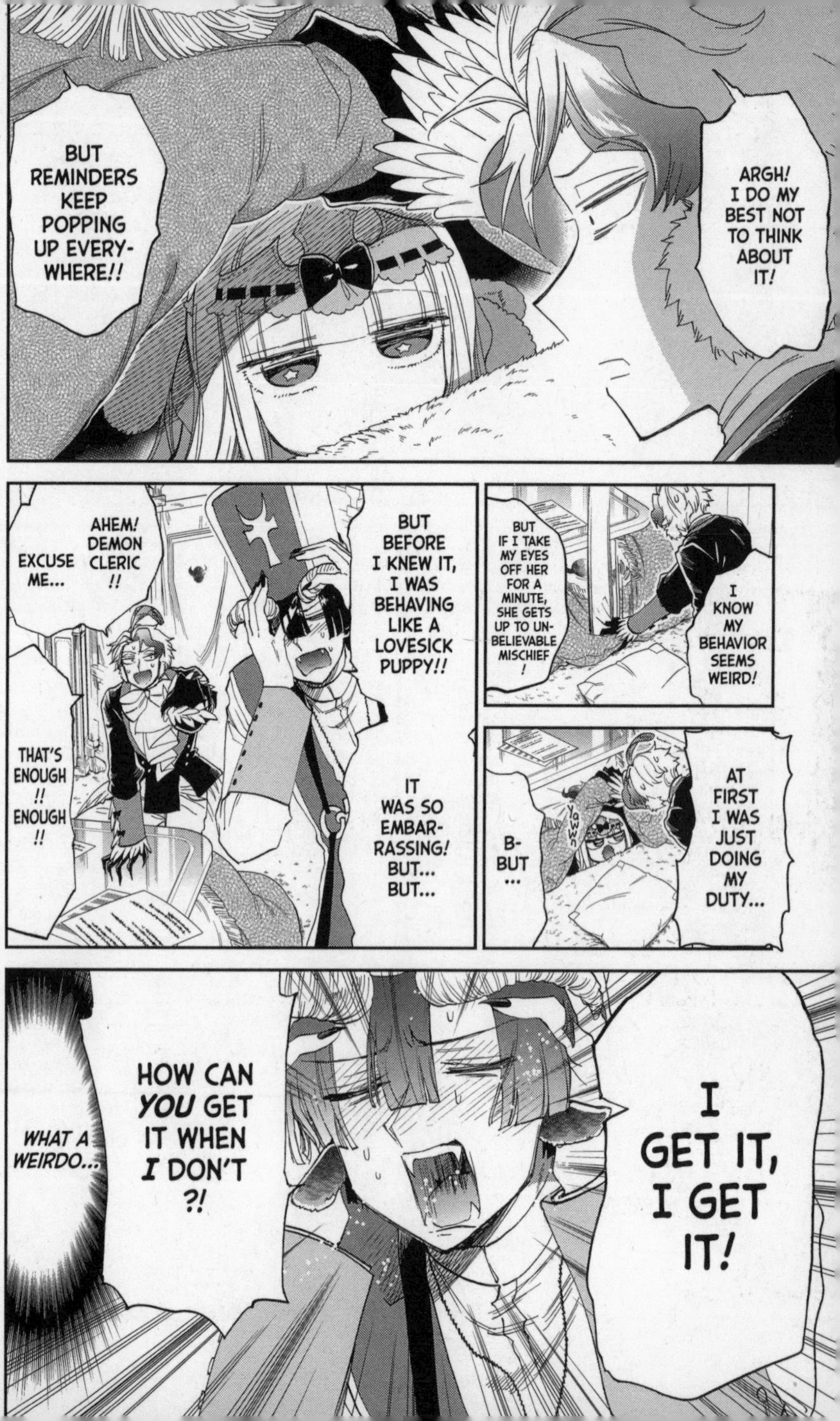
ARGH! I DO MY BEST NOT TO THINK ABOUT IT!
BUT REMINDERS KEEP POPPING UP EVERY-WHERE!!
I KNOW MY BEHAVIOR SEEMS WEIRD!
BUT IF I TAKE MY EYES OFF HER FOR A MINUTE, SHE GETS UP TO UN-BELIEVABLE MISCHIEF!
AT FIRST I WAS JUST DOING MY DUTY...
B-BUT...
BUT BEFORE I KNEW IT, I WAS BEHAVING LIKE A LOVESICK PUPPY!!
AHEM! DEMON CLERIC!!
EXCUSE ME...
IT WAS SO EMBARRASSING! BUT... BUT...
THAT'S ENOUGH!! ENOUGH!!
I GET IT, I GET IT!
HOW CAN *YOU* GET IT WHEN *I* DON'T?!
WHAT A WEIRDO...

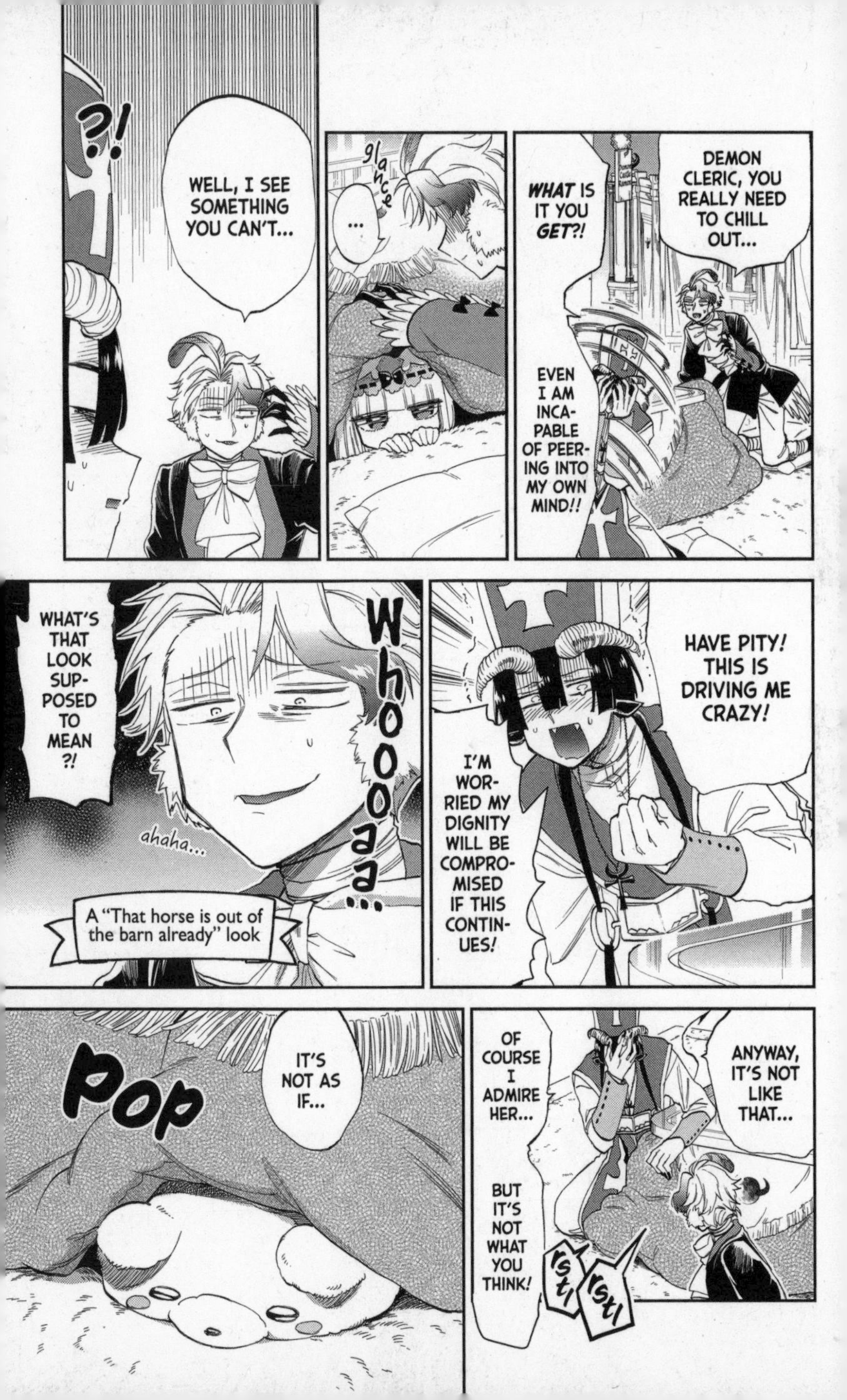
DEMON CLERIC, YOU REALLY NEED TO CHILL OUT...
WHAT IS IT YOU *GET*?!
EVEN I AM INCAPABLE OF PEERING INTO MY OWN MIND!!
glance
...
?!
WELL, I SEE SOMETHING YOU CAN'T...
HAVE PITY! THIS IS DRIVING ME CRAZY!
I'M WORRIED MY DIGNITY WILL BE COMPROMISED IF THIS CONTINUES!
Whoooaa...
WHAT'S THAT LOOK SUPPOSED TO MEAN?!
ahaha...
A "That horse is out of the barn already" look
ANYWAY, IT'S NOT LIKE THAT...
OF COURSE I ADMIRE HER...
BUT IT'S NOT WHAT YOU THINK!
rstl
rstl
IT'S NOT AS IF...
POP

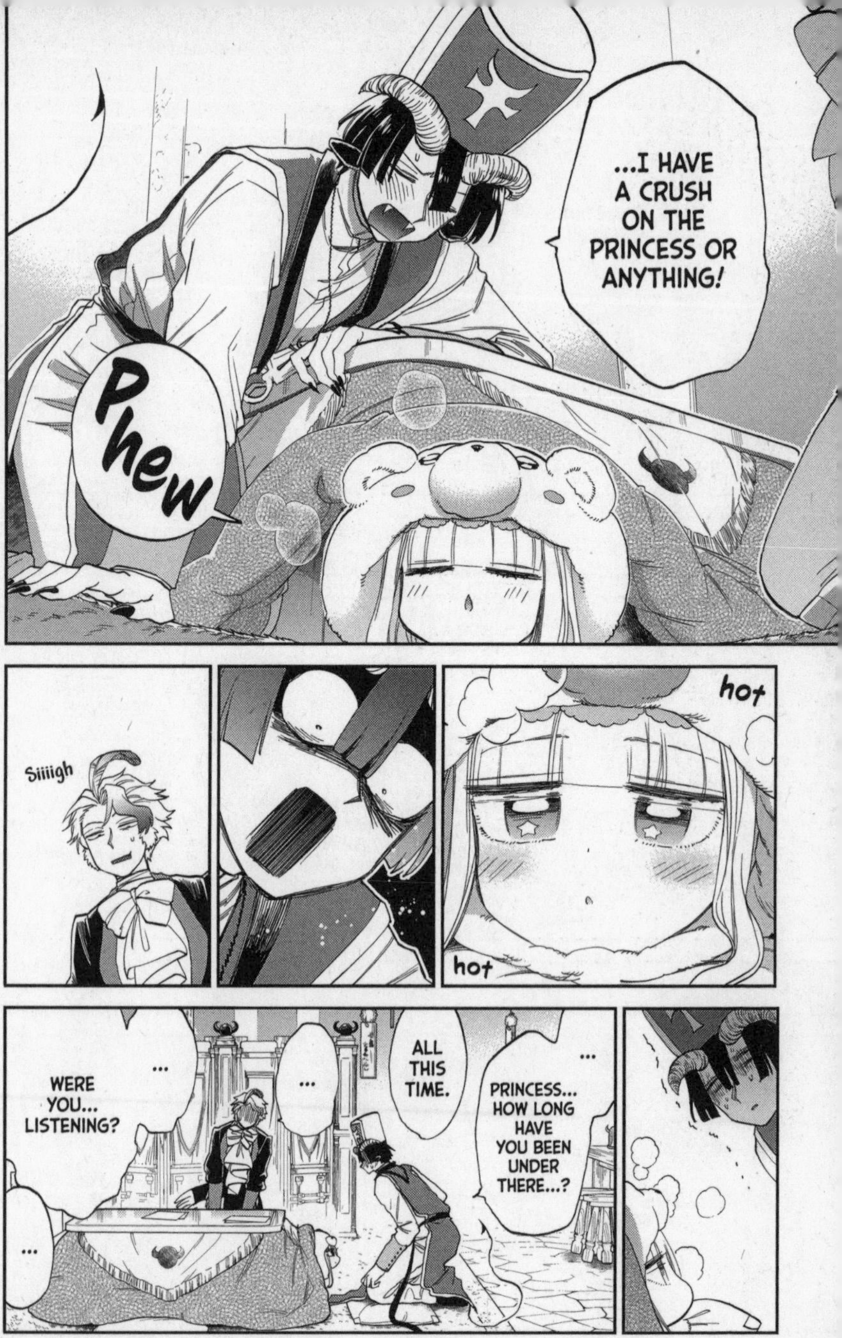
...I HAVE A CRUSH ON THE PRINCESS OR ANYTHING!
Phew
hot
hot
Siiiigh
...
PRINCESS... HOW LONG HAVE YOU BEEN UNDER THERE...?
ALL THIS TIME.
...
...
WERE YOU... LISTENING?
...

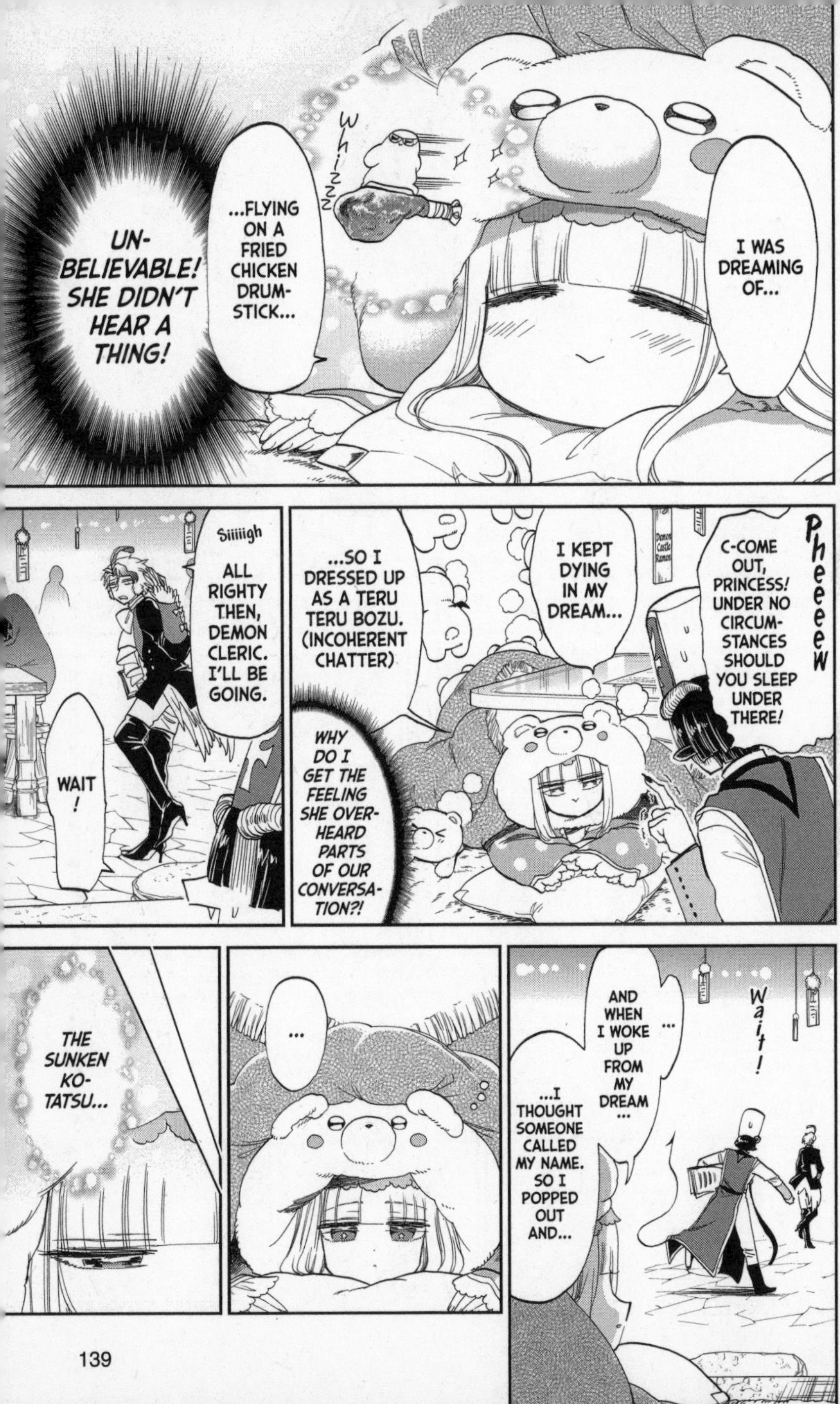
I WAS DREAMING OF...
...FLYING ON A FRIED CHICKEN DRUMSTICK...
Whizzz
UN-BELIEVABLE! SHE DIDN'T HEAR A THING!
Pheeeew
C-COME OUT, PRINCESS! UNDER NO CIRCUMSTANCES SHOULD YOU SLEEP UNDER THERE!
Demon Castle Ramen
I KEPT DYING IN MY DREAM...
...SO I DRESSED UP AS A TERU TERU BOZU. (INCOHERENT CHATTER)
WHY DO I GET THE FEELING SHE OVERHEARD PARTS OF OUR CONVERSATION?!
Siiiiigh
ALL RIGHTY THEN, DEMON CLERIC. I'LL BE GOING.
WAIT!
Wait!
AND WHEN I WOKE UP FROM MY DREAM...
...I THOUGHT SOMEONE CALLED MY NAME. SO I POPPED OUT AND...
...
THE SUNKEN KOTATSU...

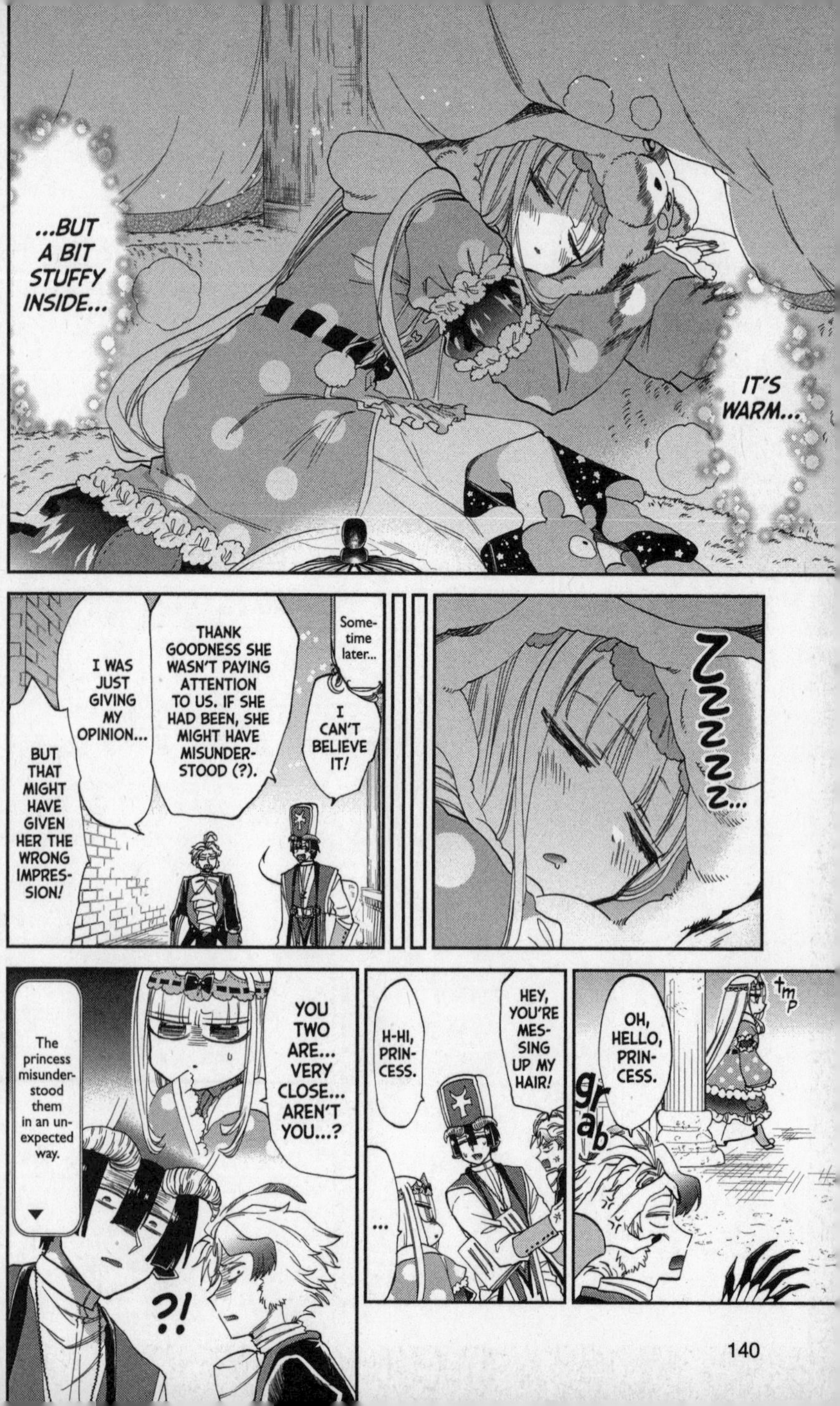
IT'S WARM...
...BUT A BIT STUFFY INSIDE...
ZZZZZZ...
Sometime later...
I CAN'T BELIEVE IT!
THANK GOODNESS SHE WASN'T PAYING ATTENTION TO US. IF SHE HAD BEEN, SHE MIGHT HAVE MISUNDERSTOOD (?).
I WAS JUST GIVING MY OPINION...
BUT THAT MIGHT HAVE GIVEN HER THE WRONG IMPRESSION!
tmp
OH, HELLO, PRINCESS.
grab
HEY, YOU'RE MESSING UP MY HAIR!
H-HI, PRINCESS.
...
YOU TWO ARE... VERY CLOSE... AREN'T YOU...?
?!
The princess misunderstood them in an unexpected way.

Sunken Ko-tatsu

Warm: ☆☆☆☆☆☆
Possibility of Bearlike Appearance: ☆☆☆☆☆☆☆☆☆

A heating apparatus inspired by the magical device of laziness, the Ko-tatsu, which Princess Syalis created. Several of them have been installed in the Demon Castle Cafeteria, and they are very popular! There is a small open space inside. Small demons often sneak into it and emerge steamy and warm. Teddy Demons are frequent visitors, and the current fad at the Demon Castle is to cuddle a warm Teddy Demon procured from inside the Ko-tatsu while chatting with friends. Peek inside before climbing in to make sure it's not already occupied by demons!

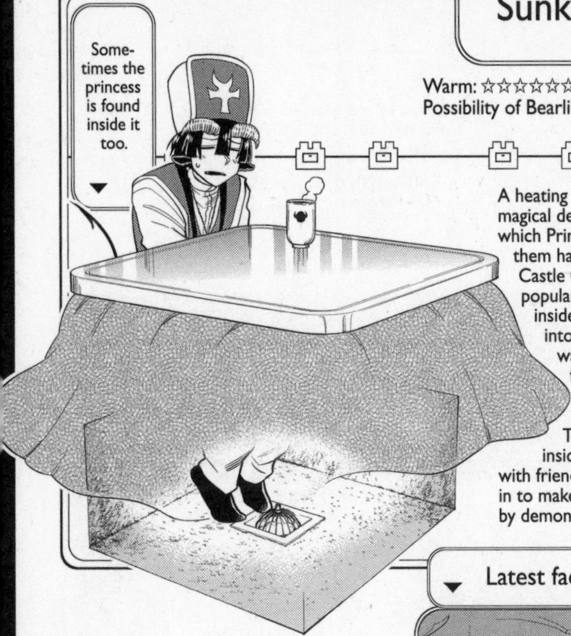
Sometimes the princess is found inside it too.

Latest fad: Hot Teddy Demon

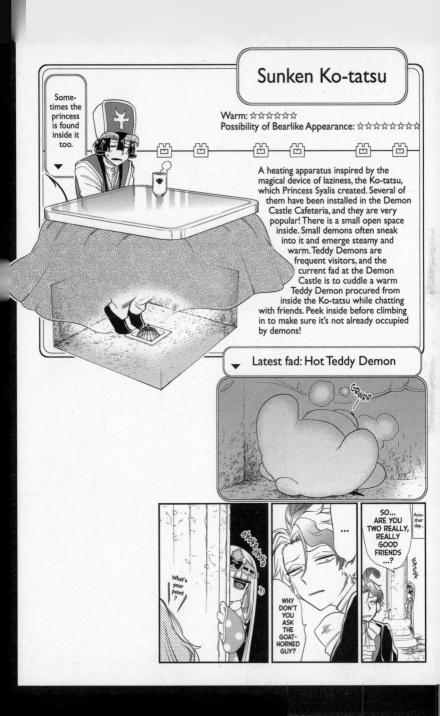

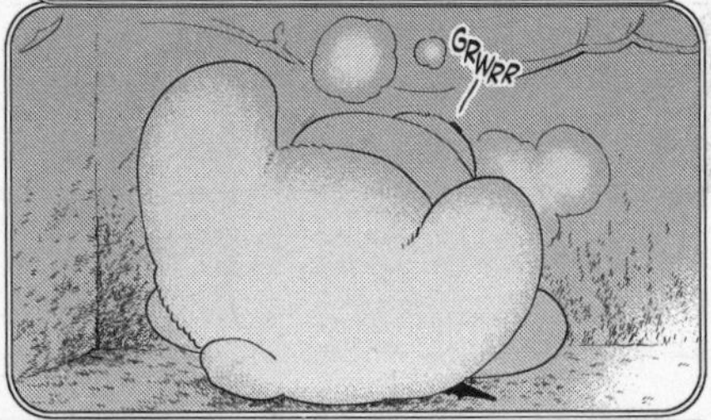
GRWRR

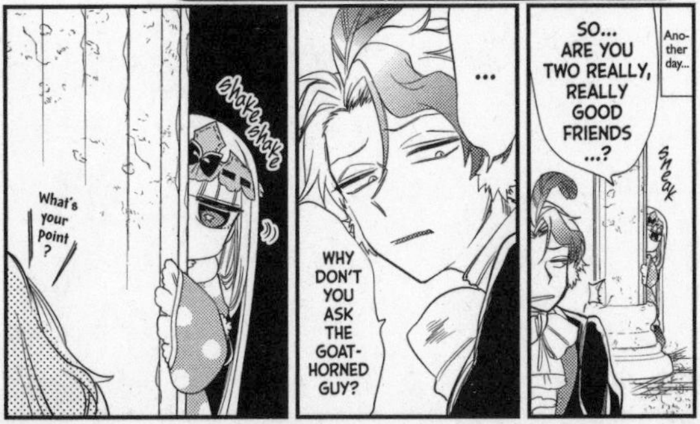
Another day...
SO... ARE YOU TWO REALLY, REALLY GOOD FRIENDS ...?
SNEAK
...
WHY DON'T YOU ASK THE GOAT-HORNED GUY?
Shake shake
What's your point?

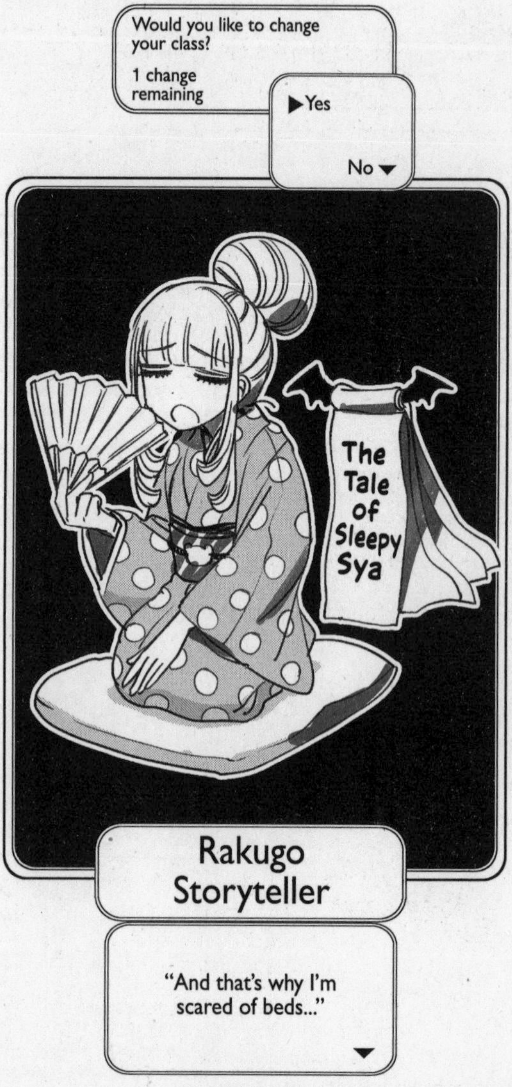
Would you like to change your class?
1 change remaining
▶Yes
No ▼
The Tale of Sleepy Sya
Rakugo Storyteller
"And that's why I'm scared of beds..."

90th Night: Don't You Dare "This May Sting a Bit" Me!

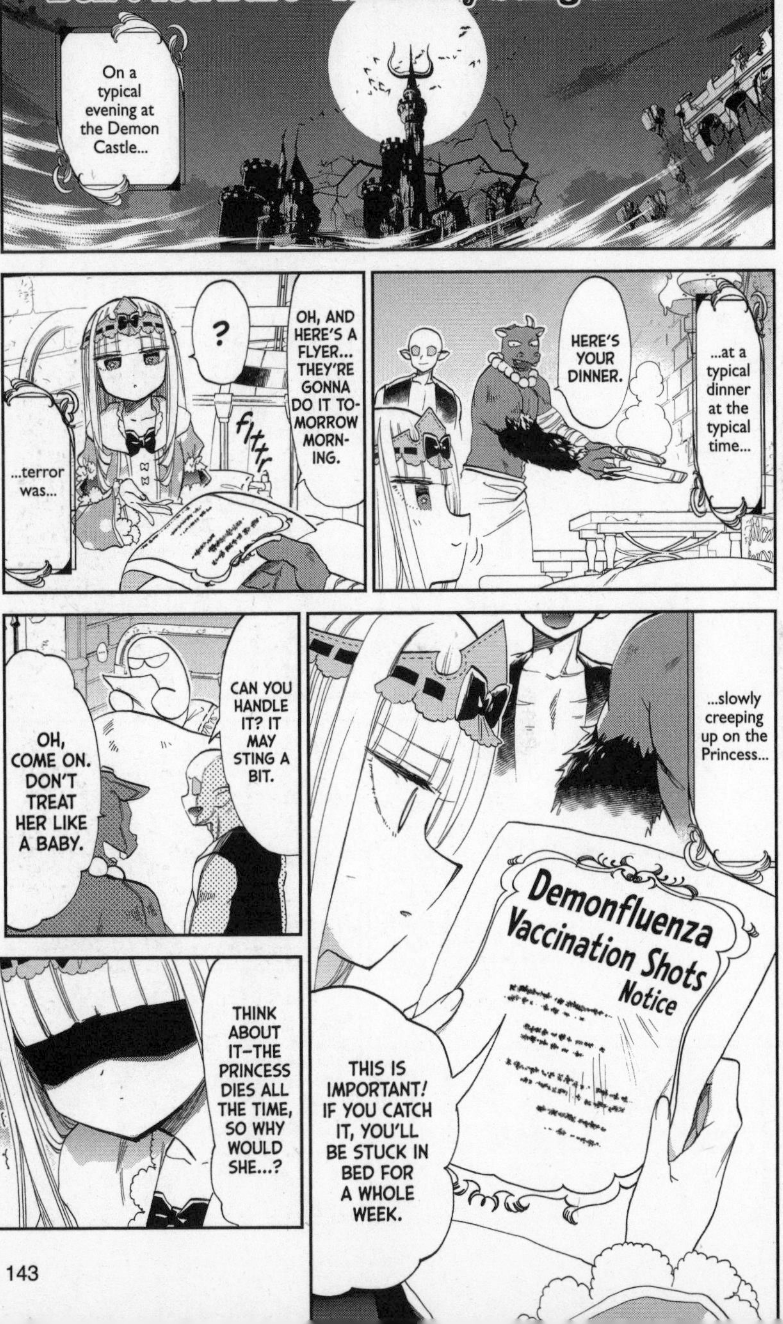

On a typical evening at the Demon Castle...
...at a typical dinner at the typical time...
HERE'S YOUR DINNER.
OH, AND HERE'S A FLYER... THEY'RE GONNA DO IT TO-MORROW MORNING.
?
fltxr
...terror was...
...slowly creeping up on the Princess...
Demonfluenza Vaccination Shots Notice
THIS IS IMPORTANT! IF YOU CATCH IT, YOU'LL BE STUCK IN BED FOR A WHOLE WEEK.
CAN YOU HANDLE IT? IT MAY STING A BIT.
OH, COME ON. DON'T TREAT HER LIKE A BABY.
THINK ABOUT IT—THE PRINCESS DIES ALL THE TIME, SO WHY WOULD SHE...?

THE PRINCESS HAS ARMED HERSELF AND IS MAKING A RUN FOR IT!!

To explain...

The princess has a phobia of needles!

I'm scared my eye will accidentally get poked out.

Okay	Quilly		Injection	Bee	Not okay

HNNNRRRGH!!!

ARMED

90th Night: Don't You Dare "This May Sting a Bit" Me!

WORST-CASE SCENARIO, I MIGHT HAVE TO CAMP OUTSIDE!!

BA
M

Their fears are justified.

DID YOU SEE THE LOOK IN HER EYES...? SHE'S SERIOUSLY GOING TO TRY TO ESCAPE FROM THE CASTLE NOW!

SHOOT! WE'VE GOT TO REPORT THIS TO OUR SUPERIORS!

HOW CAN I SLEEP WITH SUCH A SENSE OF DREAD HANGING OVER ME?!

A FLU SHOT?! TOMORROW MORNING?!

BUT IT'S JUST A FLU SHOT...

tump

tump

tump

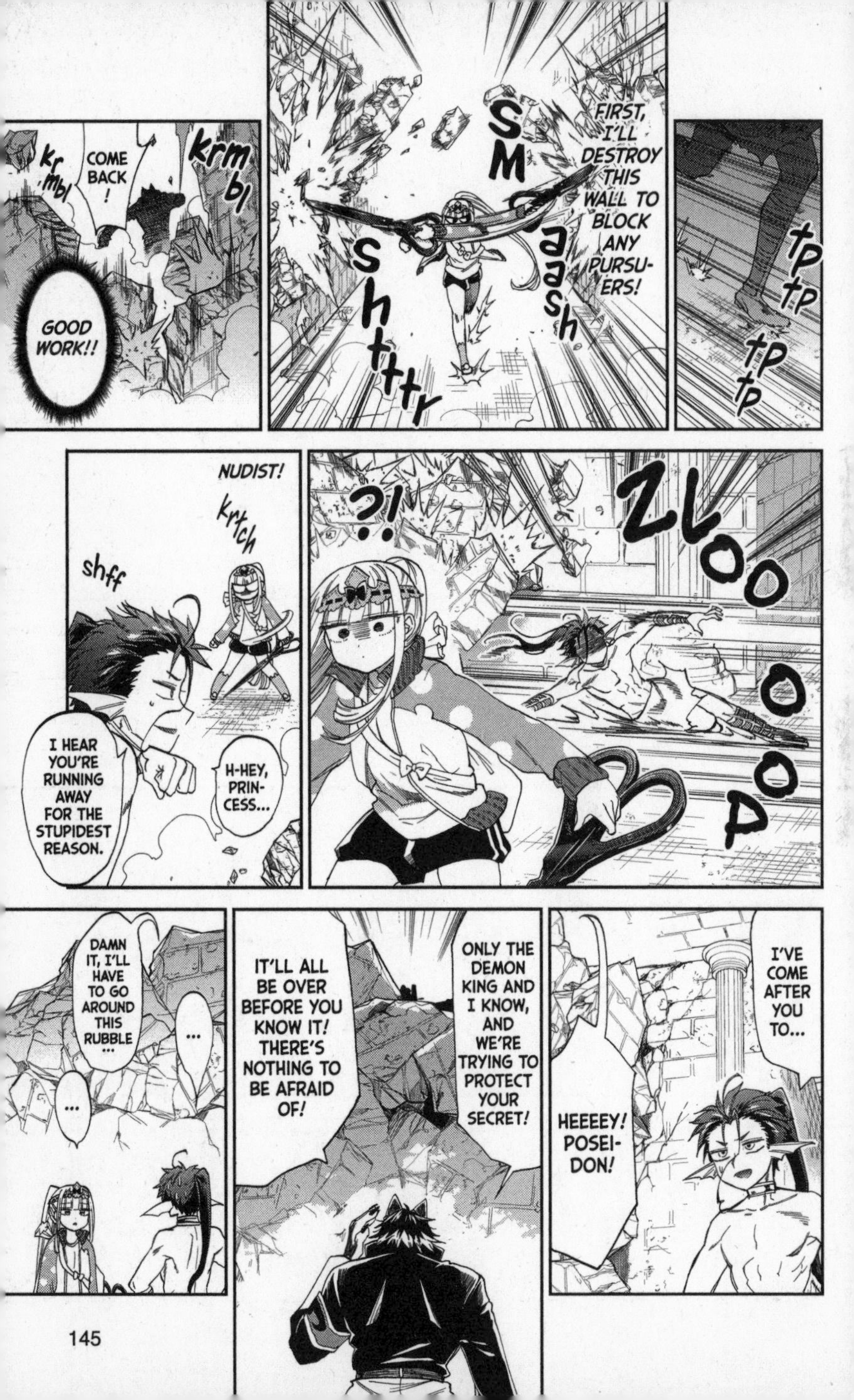
tp tp
tp tp
FIRST, I'LL DESTROY THIS WALL TO BLOCK ANY PURSUERS!
SMaaash
shtttr
krmbl
COME BACK!
krmbl
GOOD WORK!!
?!
ZLOOOOOP
NUDIST!
krtch
shff
H-HEY, PRINCESS...
I HEAR YOU'RE RUNNING AWAY FOR THE STUPIDEST REASON.
I'VE COME AFTER YOU TO...
HEEEEY! POSEIDON!
ONLY THE DEMON KING AND I KNOW, AND WE'RE TRYING TO PROTECT YOUR SECRET!
IT'LL ALL BE OVER BEFORE YOU KNOW IT! THERE'S NOTHING TO BE AFRAID OF!
DAMN IT, I'LL HAVE TO GO AROUND THIS RUBBLE...
...
...

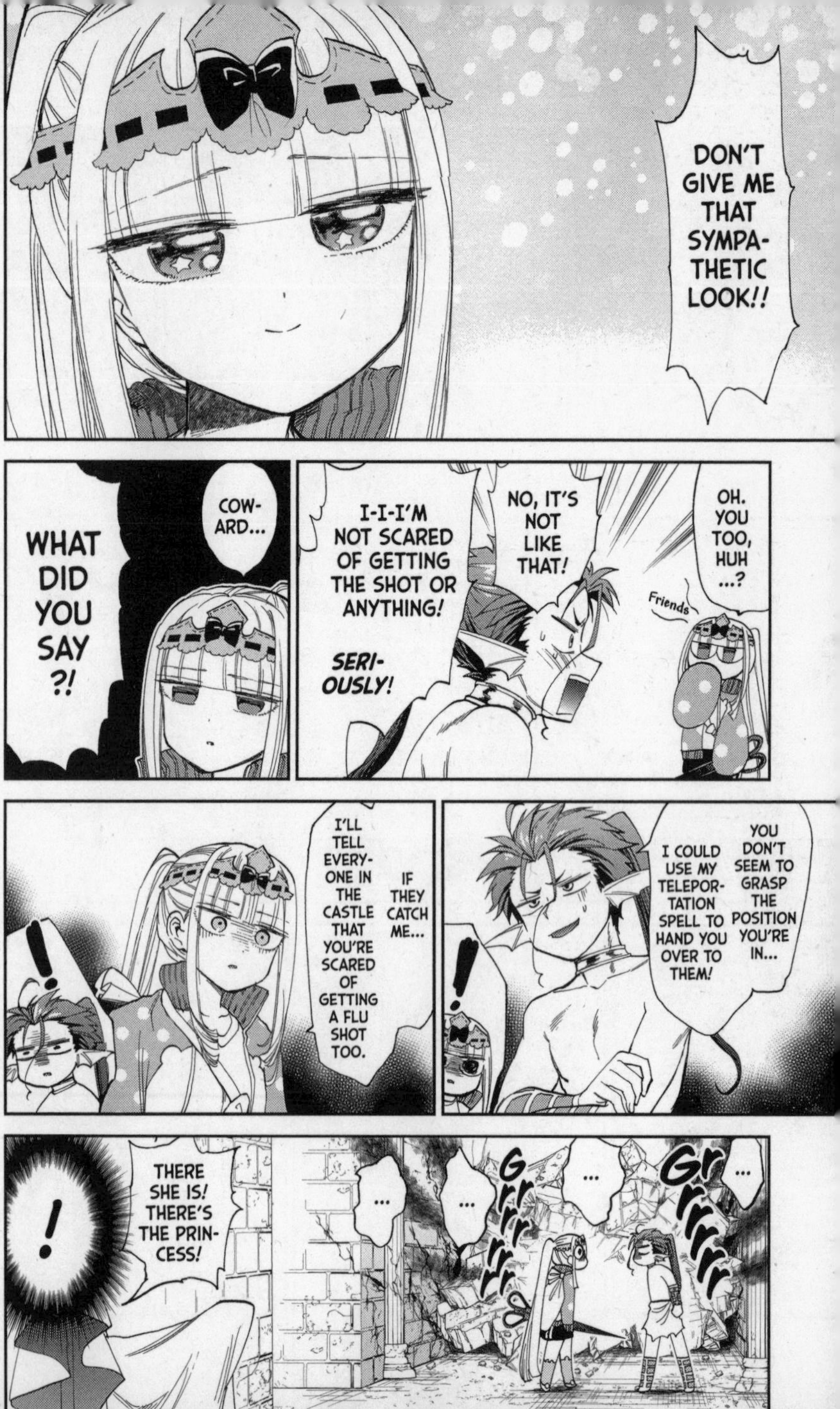
DON'T GIVE ME THAT SYMPA-THETIC LOOK!!
OH. YOU TOO, HUH ...?
Friends
NO, IT'S NOT LIKE THAT!
I-I-I'M NOT SCARED OF GETTING THE SHOT OR ANYTHING!
SERI-OUSLY!
COW-ARD...
WHAT DID YOU SAY ?!
YOU DON'T SEEM TO GRASP THE POSITION YOU'RE IN...
I COULD USE MY TELEPOR-TATION SPELL TO HAND YOU OVER TO THEM!
!
IF THEY CATCH ME...
I'LL TELL EVERY-ONE IN THE CASTLE THAT YOU'RE SCARED OF GETTING A FLU SHOT TOO.
!
...
Gr Grrrr
...
Gr Grrrrrr
...
...
THERE SHE IS! THERE'S THE PRIN-CESS!
!

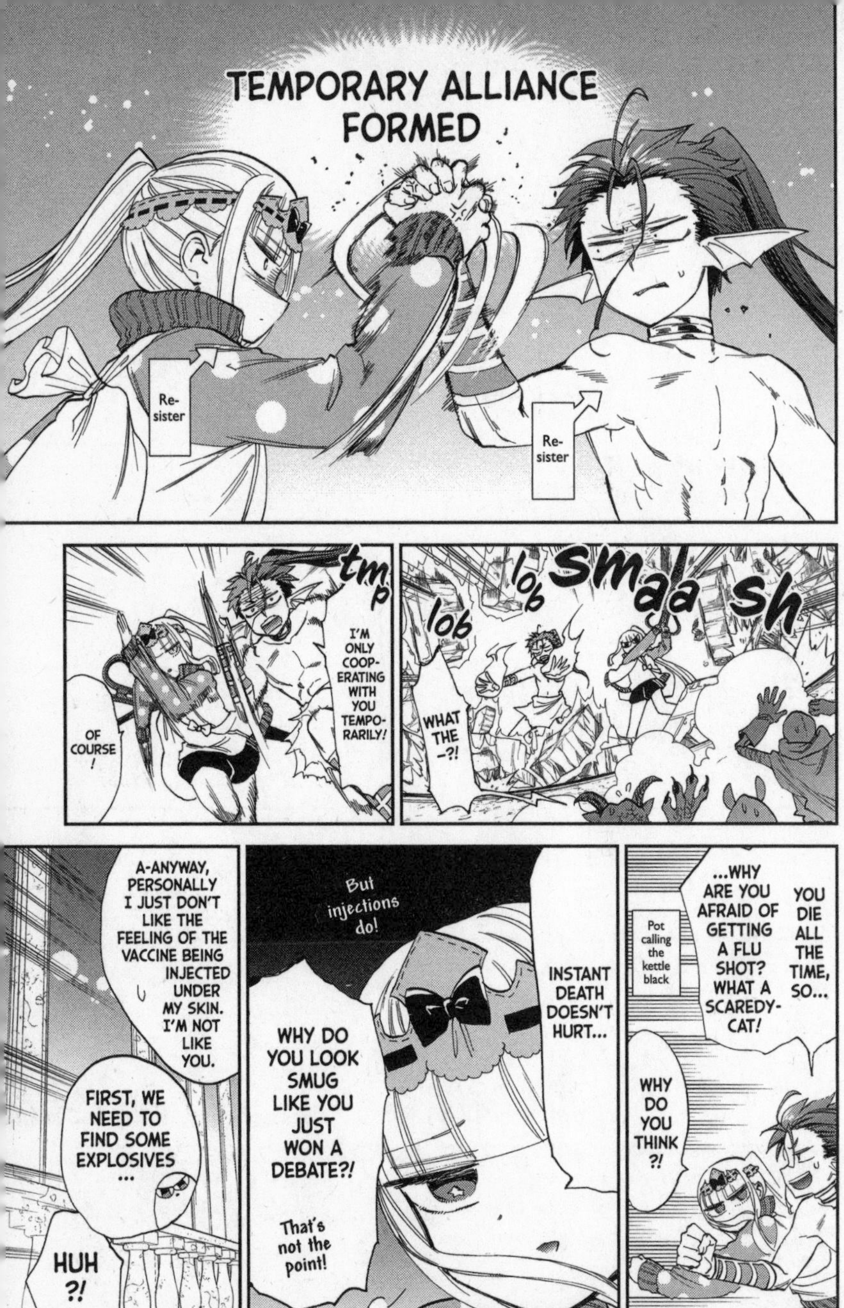
TEMPORARY ALLIANCE FORMED
Re-sister
Re-sister
lob lob Smaaash
WHAT THE—?!
tmp
I'M ONLY COOPERATING WITH YOU TEMPORARILY!
OF COURSE!
YOU DIE ALL THE TIME, SO...
...WHY ARE YOU AFRAID OF GETTING A FLU SHOT? WHAT A SCAREDY-CAT!
Pot calling the kettle black
WHY DO YOU THINK?!
INSTANT DEATH DOESN'T HURT...
But injections do!
WHY DO YOU LOOK SMUG LIKE YOU JUST WON A DEBATE?!
That's not the point!
A-ANYWAY, PERSONALLY I JUST DON'T LIKE THE FEELING OF THE VACCINE BEING INJECTED UNDER MY SKIN. I'M NOT LIKE YOU.
FIRST, WE NEED TO FIND SOME EXPLOSIVES...
HUH?!

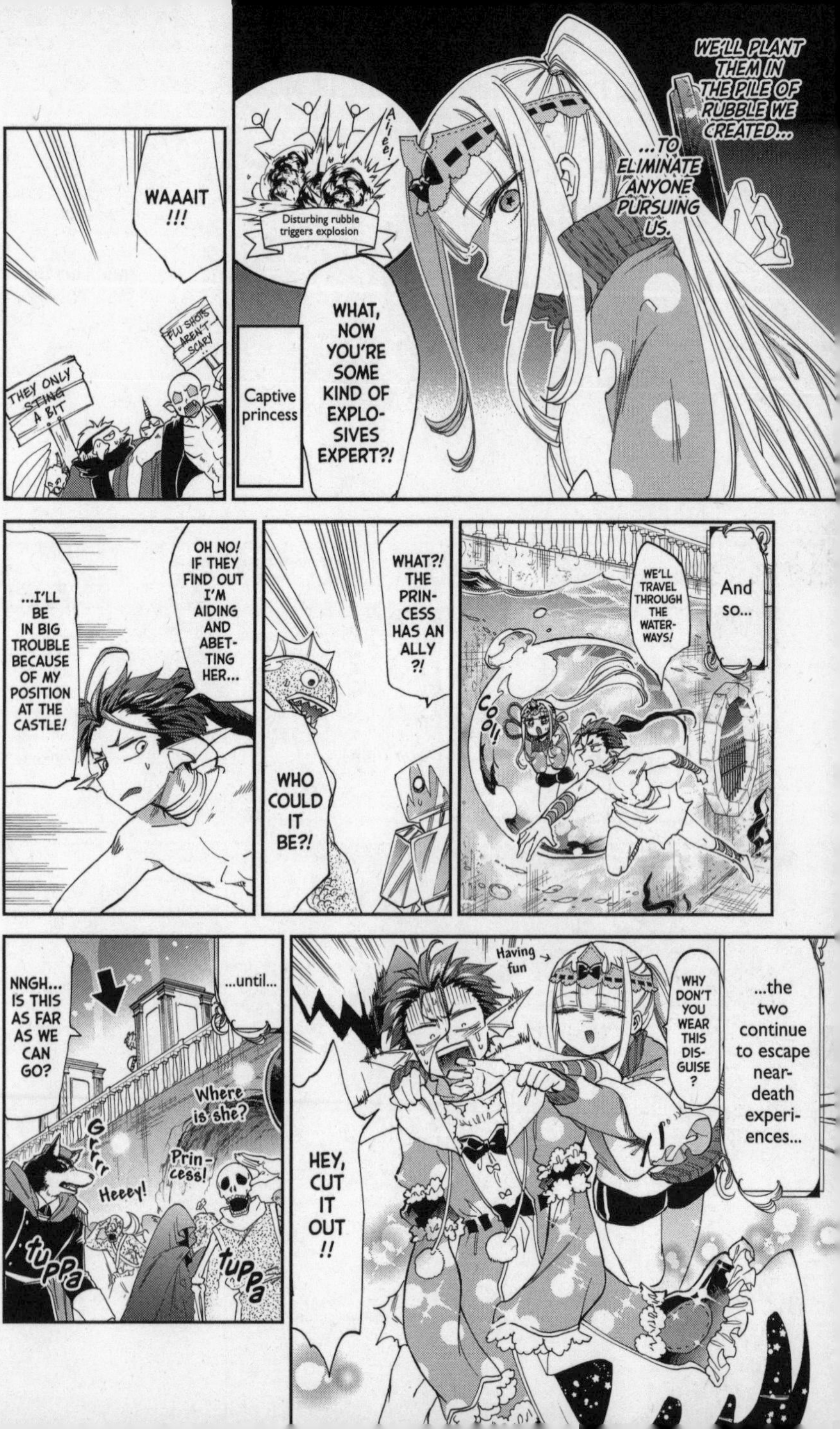
WE'LL PLANT THEM IN THE PILE OF RUBBLE WE CREATED...
...TO ELIMINATE ANYONE PURSUING US.
Aiiee!
Disturbing rubble triggers explosion
WHAT, NOW YOU'RE SOME KIND OF EXPLOSIVES EXPERT?!
Captive princess
WAAAIT !!!
FLU SHOTS AREN'T SCARY
THEY ONLY STING A BIT
And so...
WE'LL TRAVEL THROUGH THE WATERWAYS!
COO!!
WHAT?! THE PRINCESS HAS AN ALLY?!
WHO COULD IT BE?!
OH NO! IF THEY FIND OUT I'M AIDING AND ABETTING HER...
...I'LL BE IN BIG TROUBLE BECAUSE OF MY POSITION AT THE CASTLE!
...the two continue to escape near-death experiences...
WHY DON'T YOU WEAR THIS DISGUISE?
Having fun
HEY, CUT IT OUT!!
...until...
NNGH... IS THIS AS FAR AS WE CAN GO?
Where is she?
Prin-cess!
Heeey!
Grrr
tuppa
tuppa

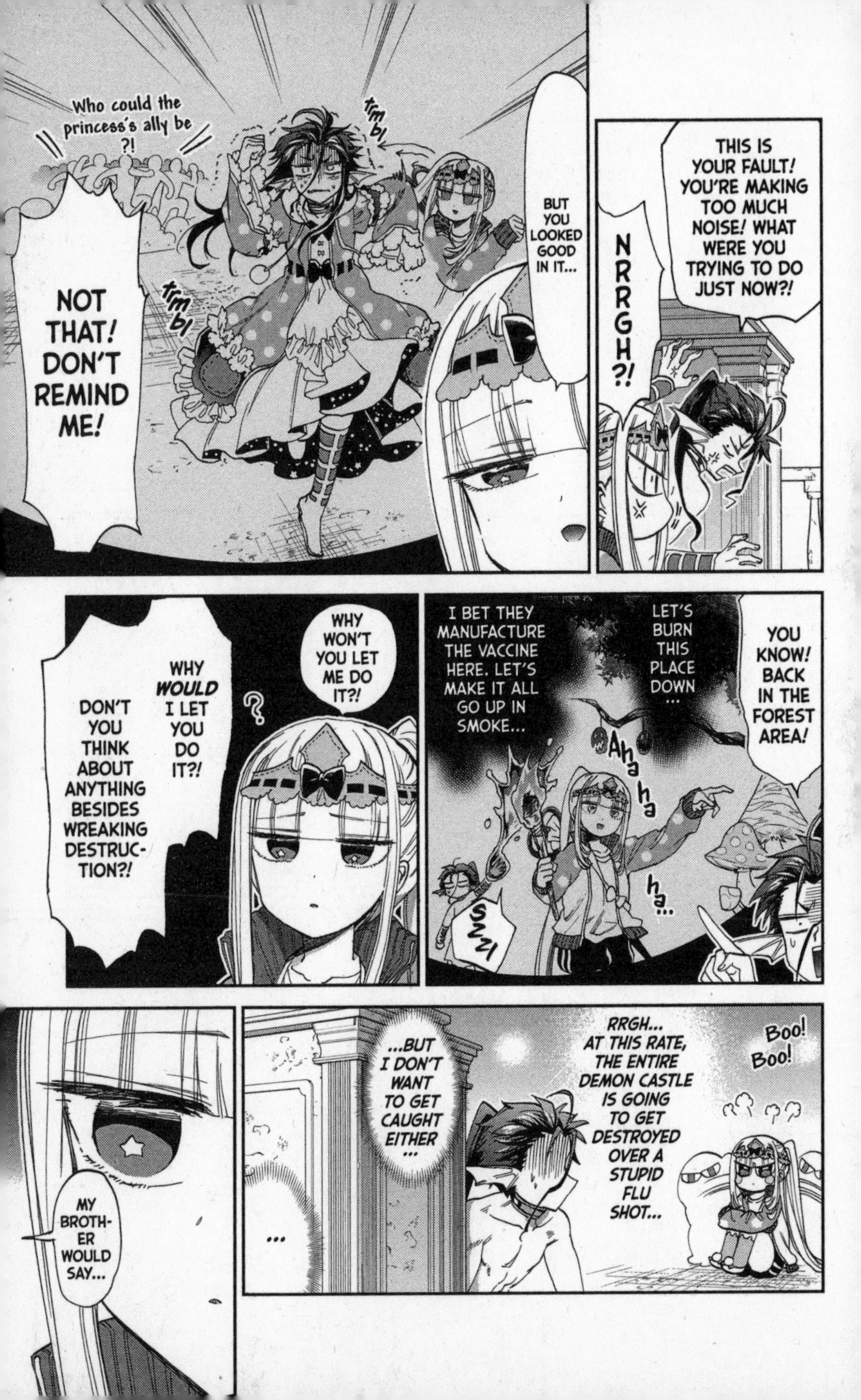
THIS IS YOUR FAULT! YOU'RE MAKING TOO MUCH NOISE! WHAT WERE YOU TRYING TO DO JUST NOW?!
NRRGH?!
BUT YOU LOOKED GOOD IN IT...
Who could the princess's ally be?!
trmbl
trmbl
NOT THAT! DON'T REMIND ME!
YOU KNOW! BACK IN THE FOREST AREA!
LET'S BURN THIS PLACE DOWN...
I BET THEY MANUFACTURE THE VACCINE HERE. LET'S MAKE IT ALL GO UP IN SMOKE...
Ahahaha
ha...
Szzz
WHY WON'T YOU LET ME DO IT?!
?
WHY *WOULD* I LET YOU DO IT?!
DON'T YOU THINK ABOUT ANYTHING BESIDES WREAKING DESTRUCTION?!
Boo! Boo!
RRGH... AT THIS RATE, THE ENTIRE DEMON CASTLE IS GOING TO GET DESTROYED OVER A STUPID FLU SHOT...
...BUT I DON'T WANT TO GET CAUGHT EITHER...
...
MY BROTHER WOULD SAY...

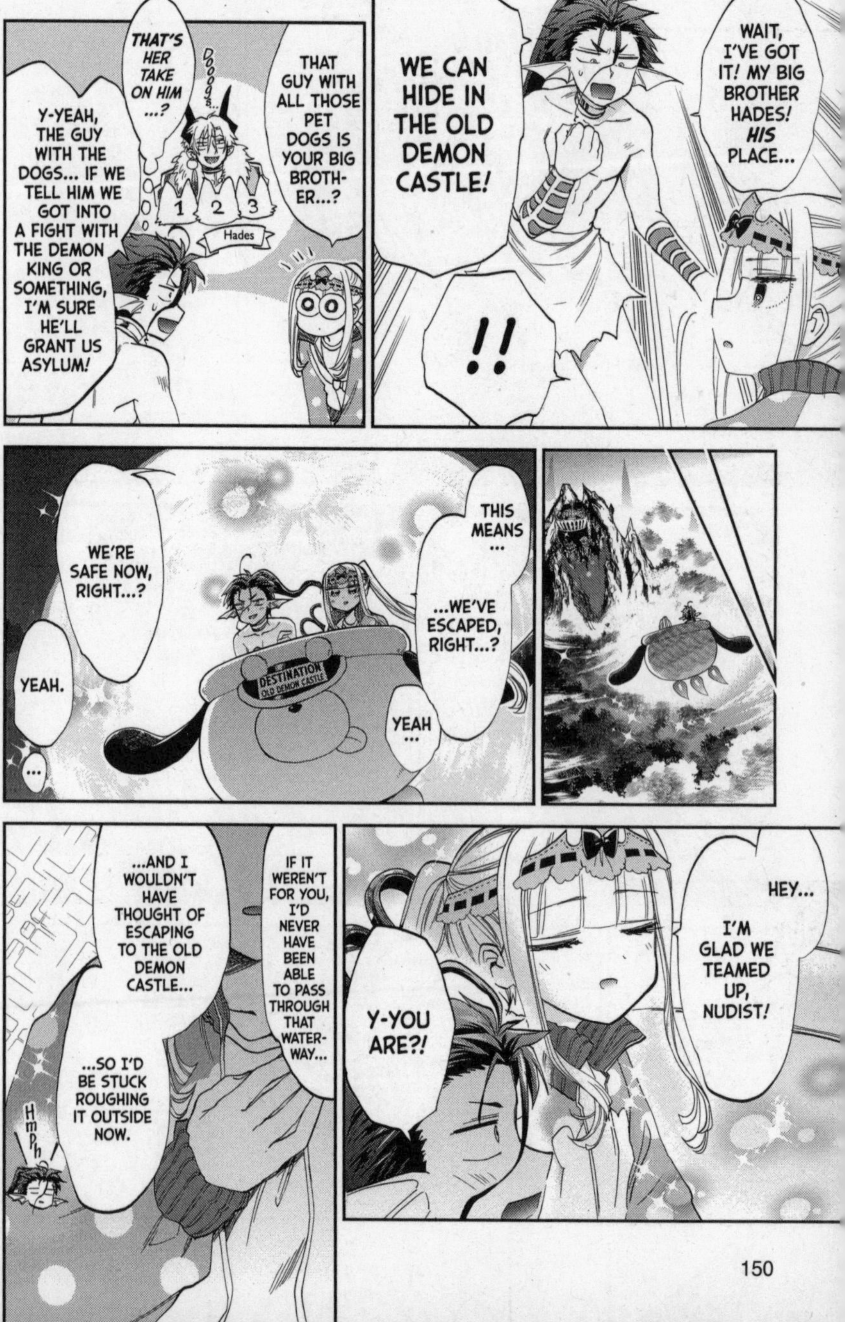
WAIT, I'VE GOT IT! MY BIG BROTHER HADES! HIS PLACE...
WE CAN HIDE IN THE OLD DEMON CASTLE!
!!
THAT GUY WITH ALL THOSE PET DOGS IS YOUR BIG BROTH-ER...?
THAT'S HER TAKE ON HIM ...?
Dooooogs...
1 2 3
Hades
Y-YEAH, THE GUY WITH THE DOGS... IF WE TELL HIM WE GOT INTO A FIGHT WITH THE DEMON KING OR SOMETHING, I'M SURE HE'LL GRANT US ASYLUM!
THIS MEANS ...
...WE'VE ESCAPED, RIGHT...?
YEAH ...
DESTINATION OLD DEMON CASTLE
WE'RE SAFE NOW, RIGHT...?
YEAH.
...
HEY...
I'M GLAD WE TEAMED UP, NUDIST!
Y-YOU ARE?!
IF IT WEREN'T FOR YOU, I'D NEVER HAVE BEEN ABLE TO PASS THROUGH THAT WATER-WAY...
...AND I WOULDN'T HAVE THOUGHT OF ESCAPING TO THE OLD DEMON CASTLE...
...SO I'D BE STUCK ROUGHING IT OUTSIDE NOW.
Hmph

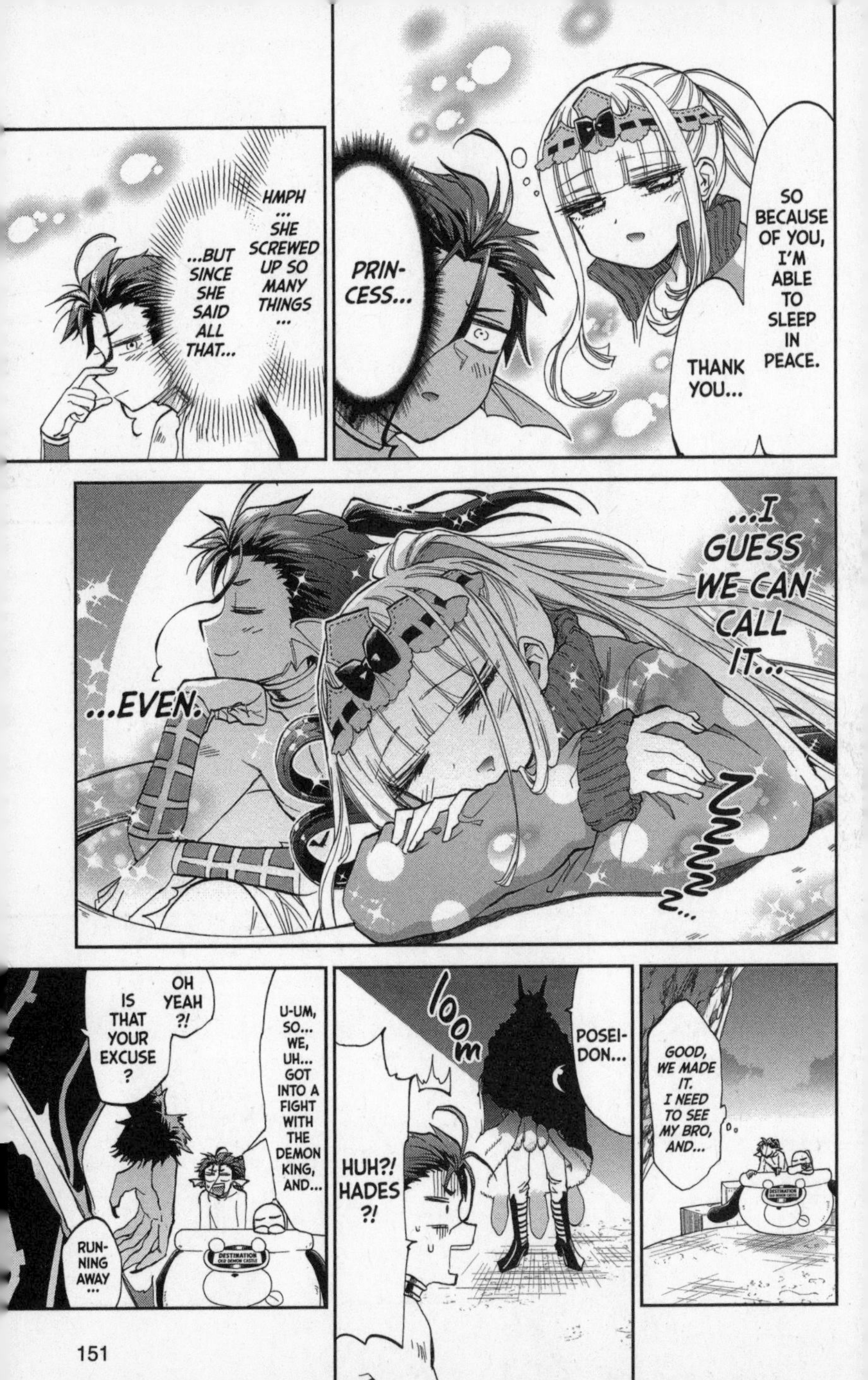
SO BECAUSE OF YOU, I'M ABLE TO SLEEP IN PEACE.
THANK YOU...
PRIN-CESS...
HMPH... SHE SCREWED UP SO MANY THINGS...
...BUT SINCE SHE SAID ALL THAT...
...I GUESS WE CAN CALL IT...
...EVEN.
ZZZZZ...
GOOD, WE MADE IT. I NEED TO SEE MY BRO, AND...
DESTINATION OLD DEMON CASTLE
POSEI-DON...
loom
HUH?! HADES?!
U-UM, SO... WE, UH... GOT INTO A FIGHT WITH THE DEMON KING, AND...
OH YEAH?!
IS THAT YOUR EXCUSE?
RUN-NING AWAY...
DESTINATION OLD DEMON CASTLE

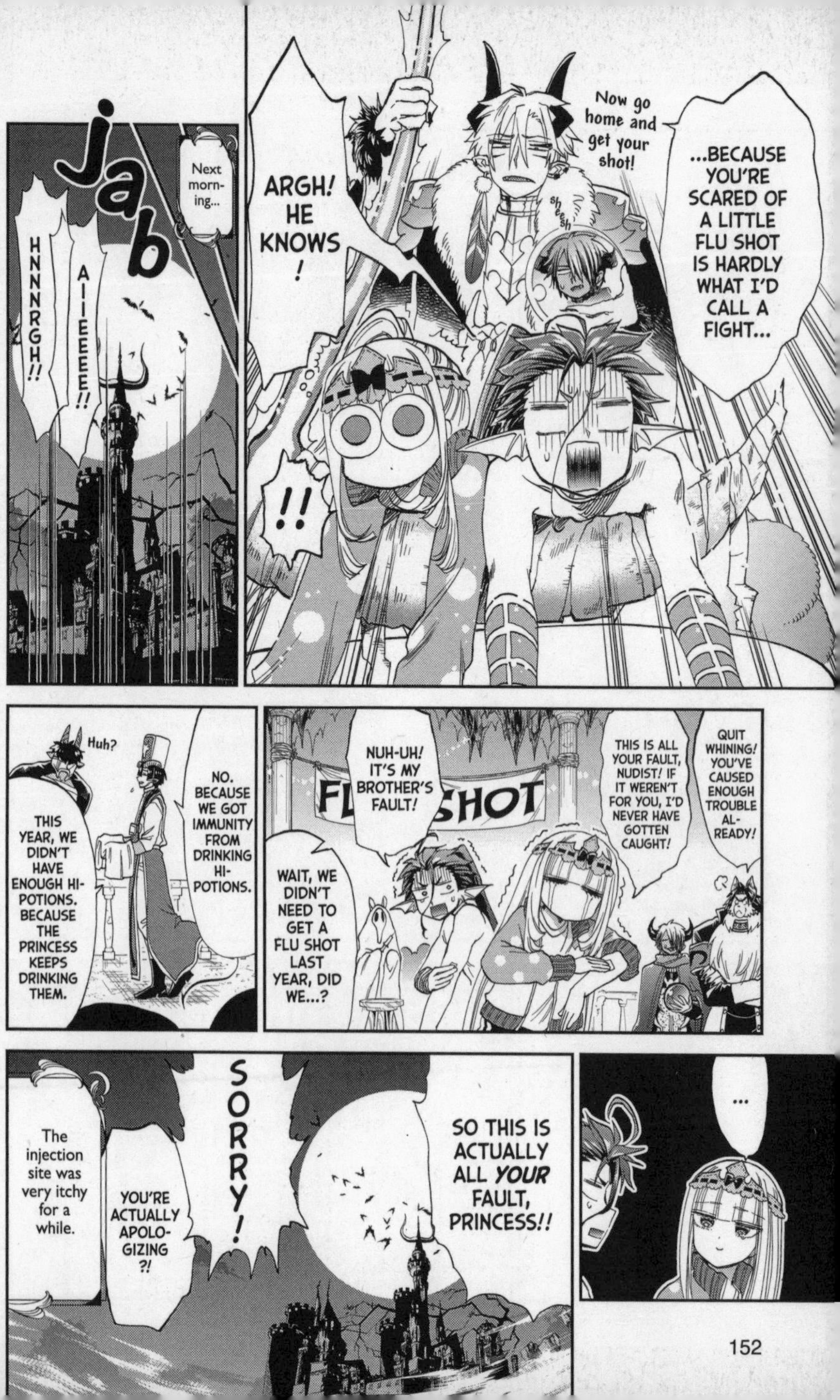

...BECAUSE YOU'RE SCARED OF A LITTLE FLU SHOT IS HARDLY WHAT I'D CALL A FIGHT...
Now go home and get your shot!
sheesh
ARGH! HE KNOWS!
!!
Next morning...
jab
AIIEEEE!!
HNNNRGH!!
QUIT WHINING! YOU'VE CAUSED ENOUGH TROUBLE AL-READY!
THIS IS ALL YOUR FAULT, NUDIST! IF IT WEREN'T FOR YOU, I'D NEVER HAVE GOTTEN CAUGHT!
FL SHOT
NUH-UH! IT'S MY BROTHER'S FAULT!
WAIT, WE DIDN'T NEED TO GET A FLU SHOT LAST YEAR, DID WE...?
NO. BECAUSE WE GOT IMMUNITY FROM DRINKING HI-POTIONS.
Huh?
THIS YEAR, WE DIDN'T HAVE ENOUGH HI-POTIONS. BECAUSE THE PRINCESS KEEPS DRINKING THEM.
...
SO THIS IS ACTUALLY ALL *YOUR* FAULT, PRINCESS!!
SORRY!
YOU'RE ACTUALLY APOLO-GIZING?!
The injection site was very itchy for a while.

Demonfluenza

High Fever: ☆☆☆☆☆☆
Danger: ☆☆☆☆☆☆☆

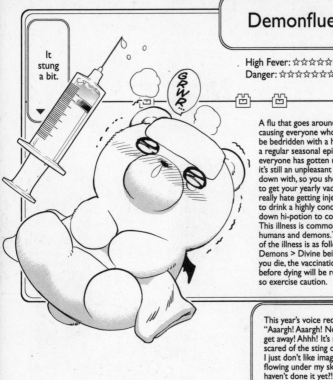

It stung a bit.

GRWR...

A flu that goes around every year causing everyone who catches it to be bedridden with a high fever. It's a regular seasonal epidemic, so everyone has gotten used to it. But it's still an unpleasant illness to come down with, so you shouldn't forget to get your yearly vaccination. If you really hate getting injections, it's easier to drink a highly concentrated, boiled-down hi-potion to confer immunity. This illness is common to both humans and demons. The intensity of the illness is as follows: Humans > Demons > Divine beings. By the way, if you die, the vaccination you received before dying will be rendered inactive, so exercise caution.

This year's voice recording:
"Aaargh! Aaargh! Nooo! I tried to get away! Ahhh! It's not that I'm scared of the sting of the needle! I just don't like imagining the vaccine flowing under my skin! What? You haven't done it yet?! When are you going to—?! Ouuuuuch!"

LOOK HERE, POSEIDON...
I KNOW YOU DON'T LIKE THIS, BUT EVEN CER, BER AND RUS GOT THEIR SHOTS!
YEAH...
AND IF YOU DON'T GET THE SHOT, YOU'RE THE ONE WHO'LL SUFFER IF YOU END UP CATCHING THE FLU.
I KNOW... UH-HUH...
DO YOU WANT TO EAT SOME FRIED CHICKEN FIRST TO HELP YOU MUSTER YOUR COURAGE? WOULD THAT HELP?
OKAY, I'LL EAT SOME CHICKEN.
She doesn't want to get the flu shot, but seeing the nudist get scolded amuses her so much that she is unable to escape.

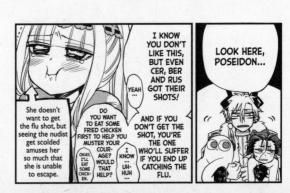

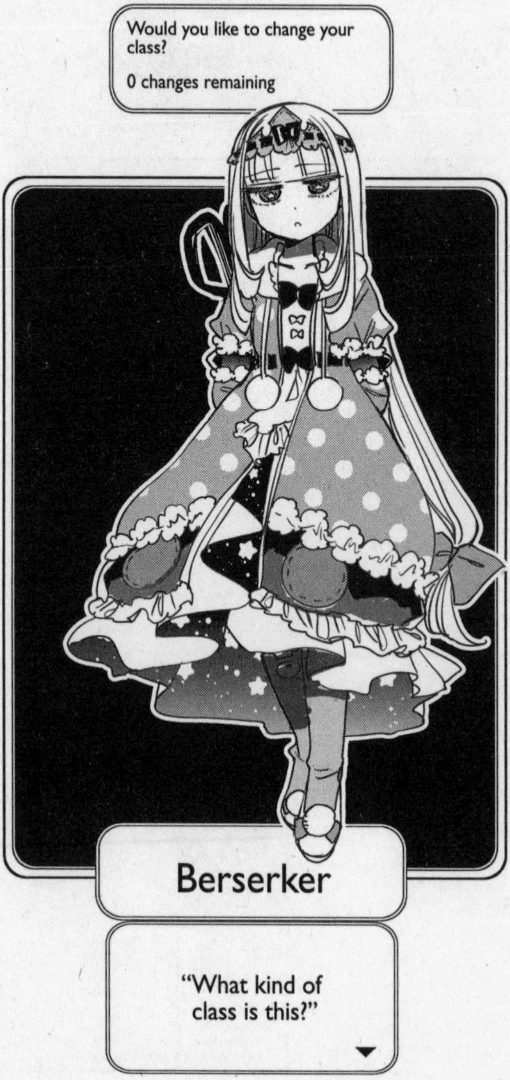
Would you like to change your class?
0 changes remaining
Berserker
"What kind of class is this?"

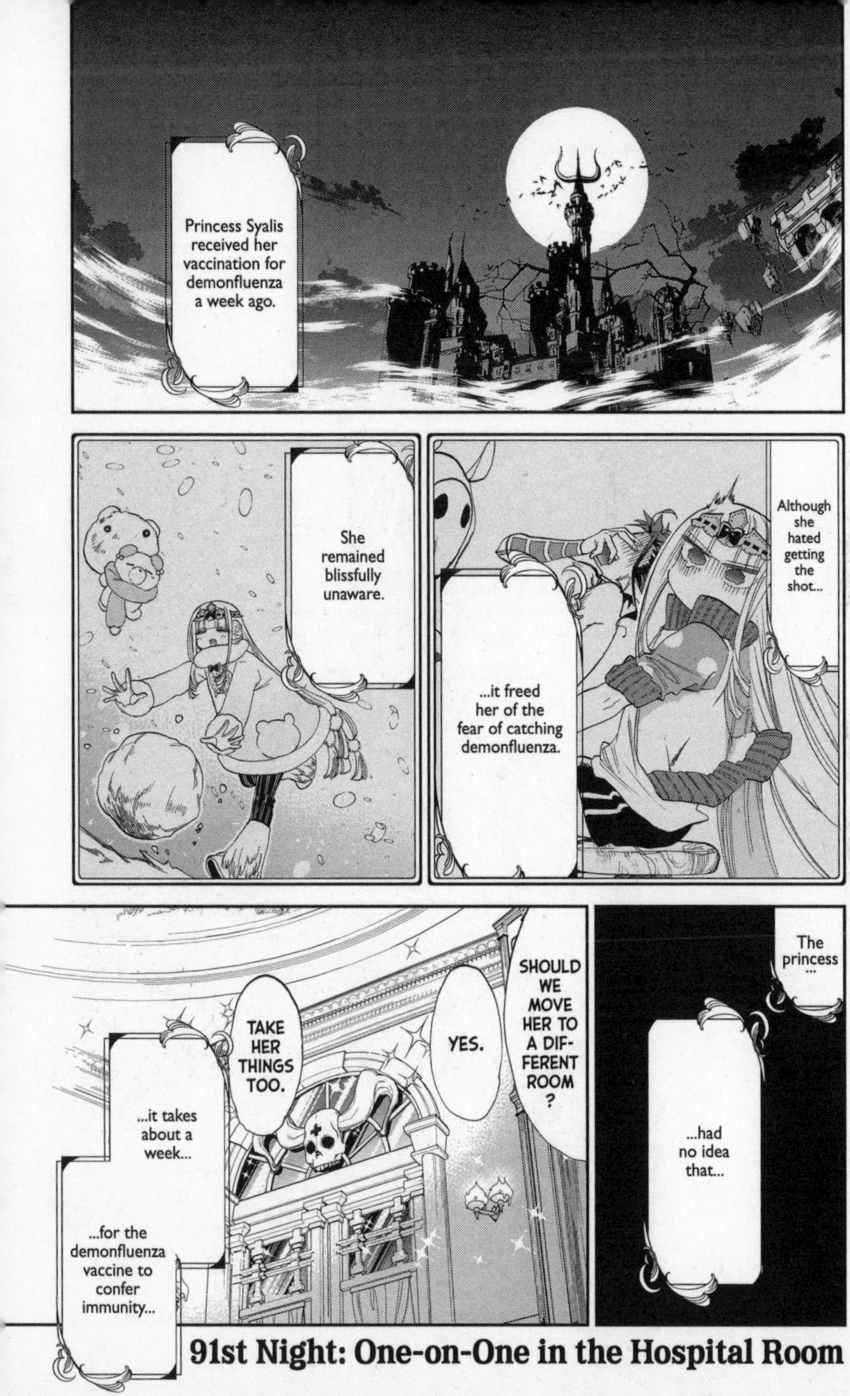
Princess Syalis received her vaccination for demonfluenza a week ago.
Although she hated getting the shot...
...it freed her of the fear of catching demonfluenza.
She remained blissfully unaware.
The princess...
...had no idea that...
SHOULD WE MOVE HER TO A DIF-FERENT ROOM?
YES.
TAKE HER THINGS TOO.
...it takes about a week...
...for the demonfluenza vaccine to confer immunity...

91st Night: One-on-One in the Hospital Room

91st Night: One-on-One in the Hospital Room

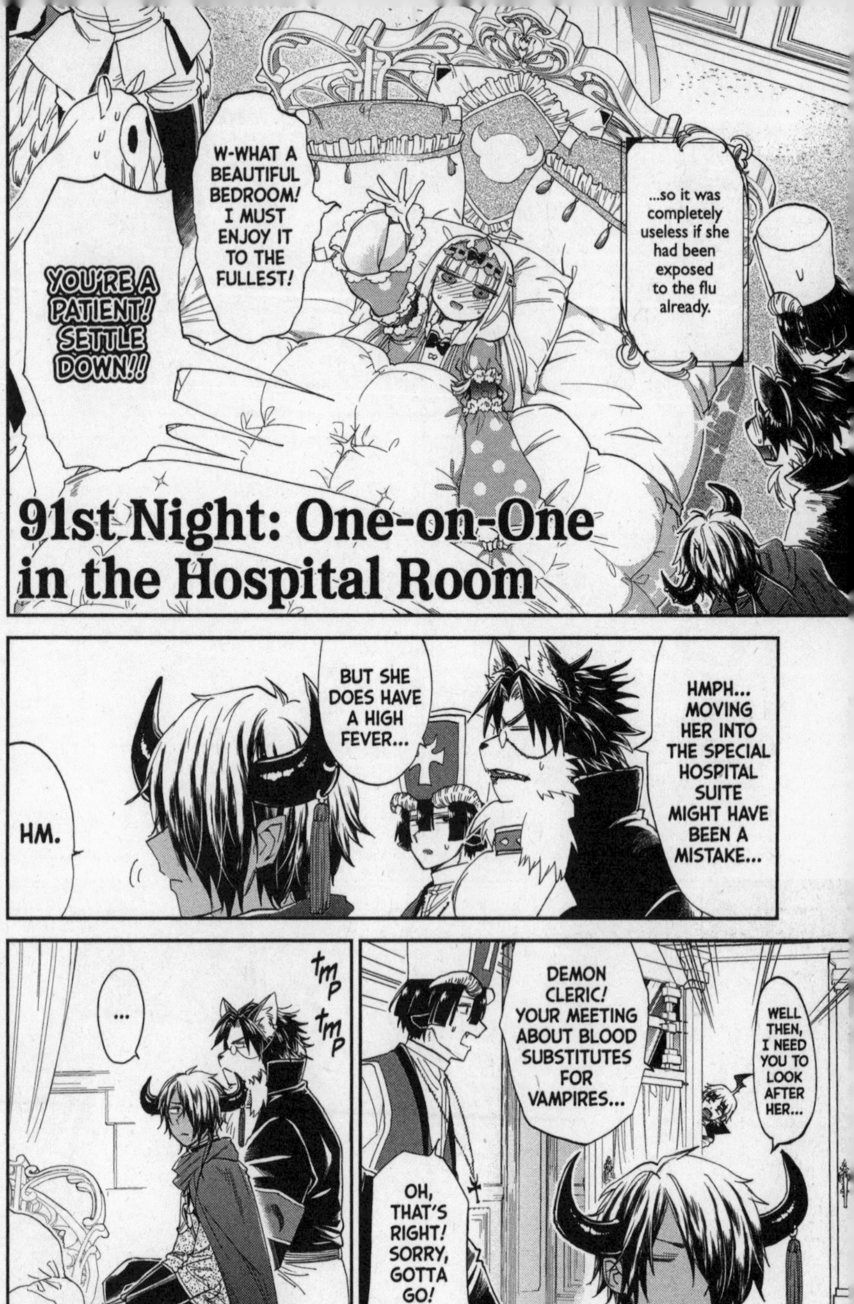

...so it was completely useless if she had been exposed to the flu already.
W-WHAT A BEAUTIFUL BEDROOM! I MUST ENJOY IT TO THE FULLEST!
YOU'RE A PATIENT! SETTLE DOWN!!
HMPH... MOVING HER INTO THE SPECIAL HOSPITAL SUITE MIGHT HAVE BEEN A MISTAKE...
BUT SHE DOES HAVE A HIGH FEVER...
HM.
WELL THEN, I NEED YOU TO LOOK AFTER HER...
DEMON CLERIC! YOUR MEETING ABOUT BLOOD SUBSTITUTES FOR VAMPIRES...
OH, THAT'S RIGHT! SORRY, GOTTA GO!
tmp tmp
...

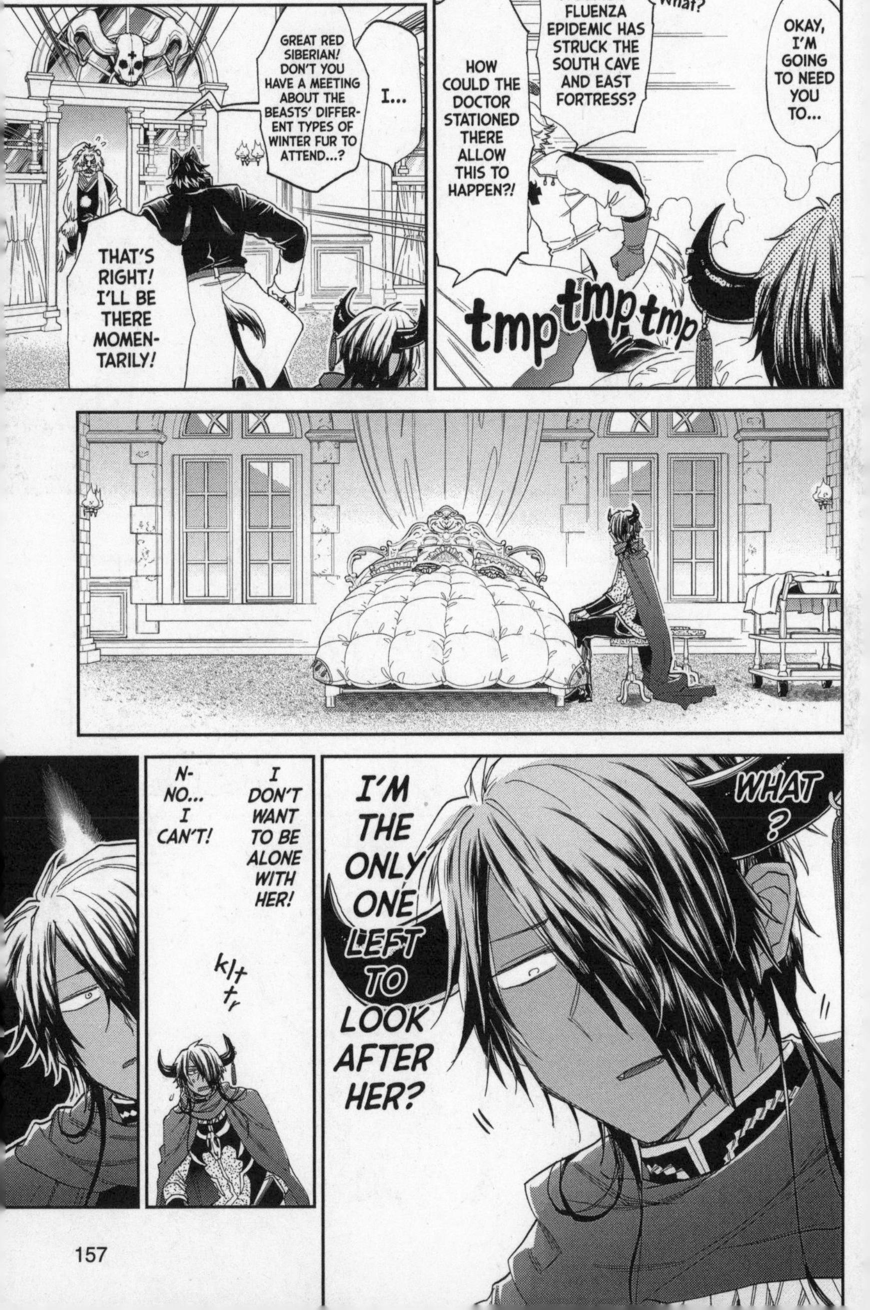
OKAY, I'M GOING TO NEED YOU TO...
What?
A DEMON-FLUENZA EPIDEMIC HAS STRUCK THE SOUTH CAVE AND EAST FORTRESS?
HOW COULD THE DOCTOR STATIONED THERE ALLOW THIS TO HAPPEN?!
tmp tmp tmp
I...
GREAT RED SIBERIAN! DON'T YOU HAVE A MEETING ABOUT THE BEASTS' DIFFERENT TYPES OF WINTER FUR TO ATTEND...?
THAT'S RIGHT! I'LL BE THERE MOMENTARILY!
WHAT?
I'M THE ONLY ONE LEFT TO LOOK AFTER HER?
I DON'T WANT TO BE ALONE WITH HER!
N-NO... I CAN'T!
kltttr

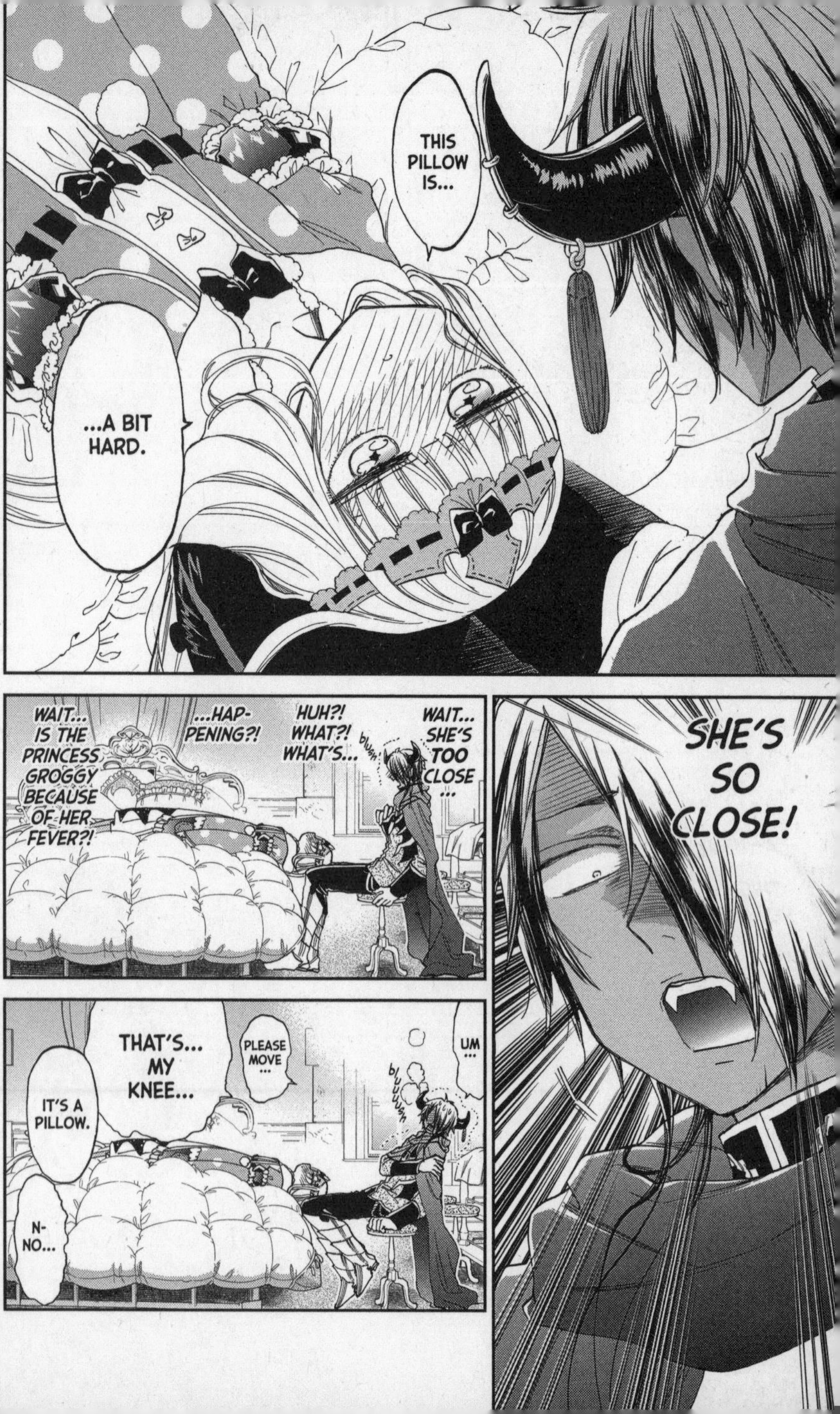
THIS PILLOW IS...
...A BIT HARD.
SHE'S SO CLOSE!
WAIT... SHE'S TOO CLOSE...
blush
HUH?! WHAT?! WHAT'S...
...HAP-PENING?!
WAIT... IS THE PRINCESS GROGGY BECAUSE OF HER FEVER?!
UM...
PLEASE MOVE...
THAT'S... MY KNEE...
IT'S A PILLOW.
N-NO...

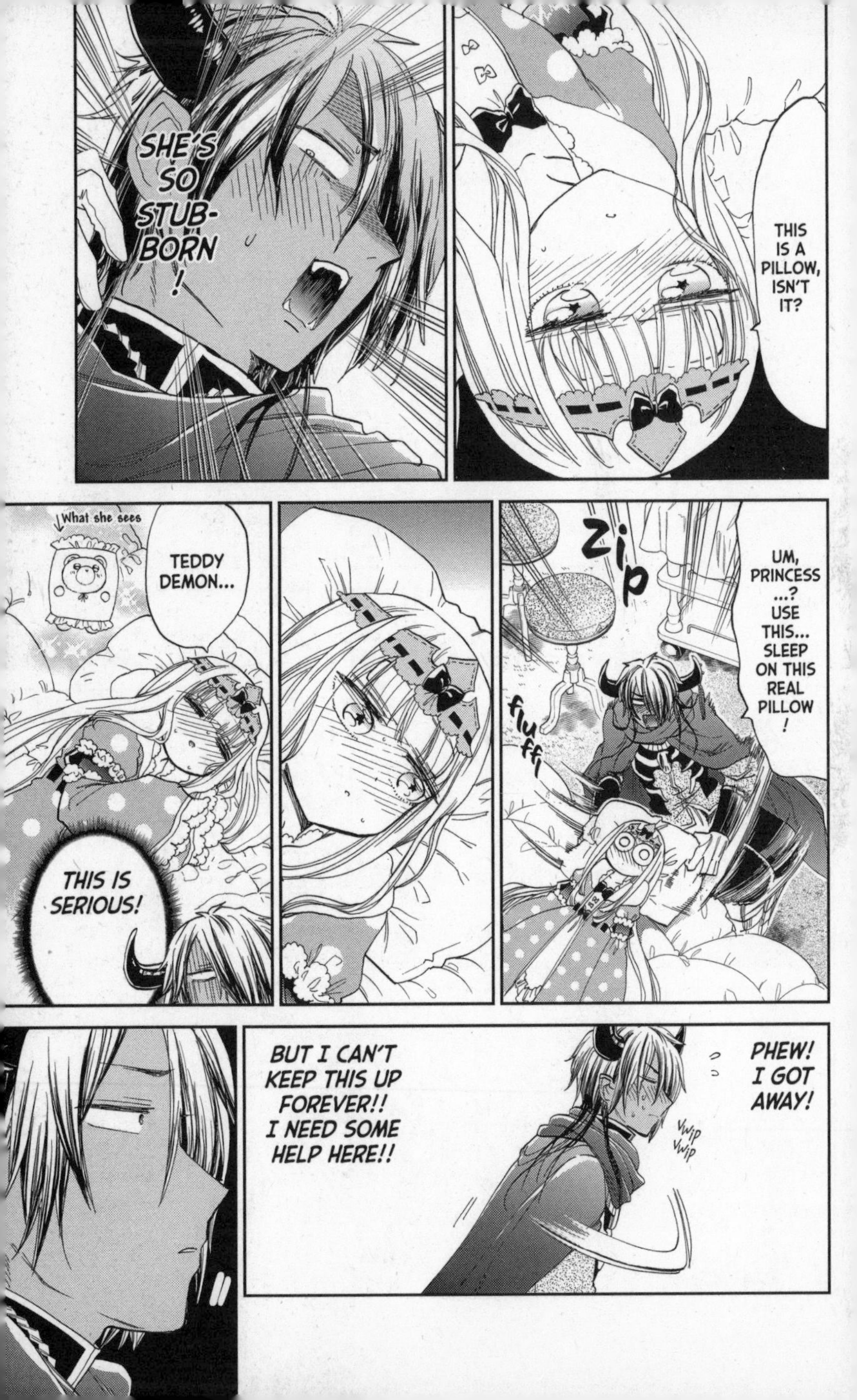
THIS IS A PILLOW, ISN'T IT?
SHE'S SO STUB-BORN!
Zip
UM, PRINCESS...? USE THIS... SLEEP ON THIS REAL PILLOW!
fluff
What she sees
TEDDY DEMON...
THIS IS SERIOUS!
PHEW! I GOT AWAY!
Vwip Vwip
BUT I CAN'T KEEP THIS UP FOREVER!! I NEED SOME HELP HERE!!

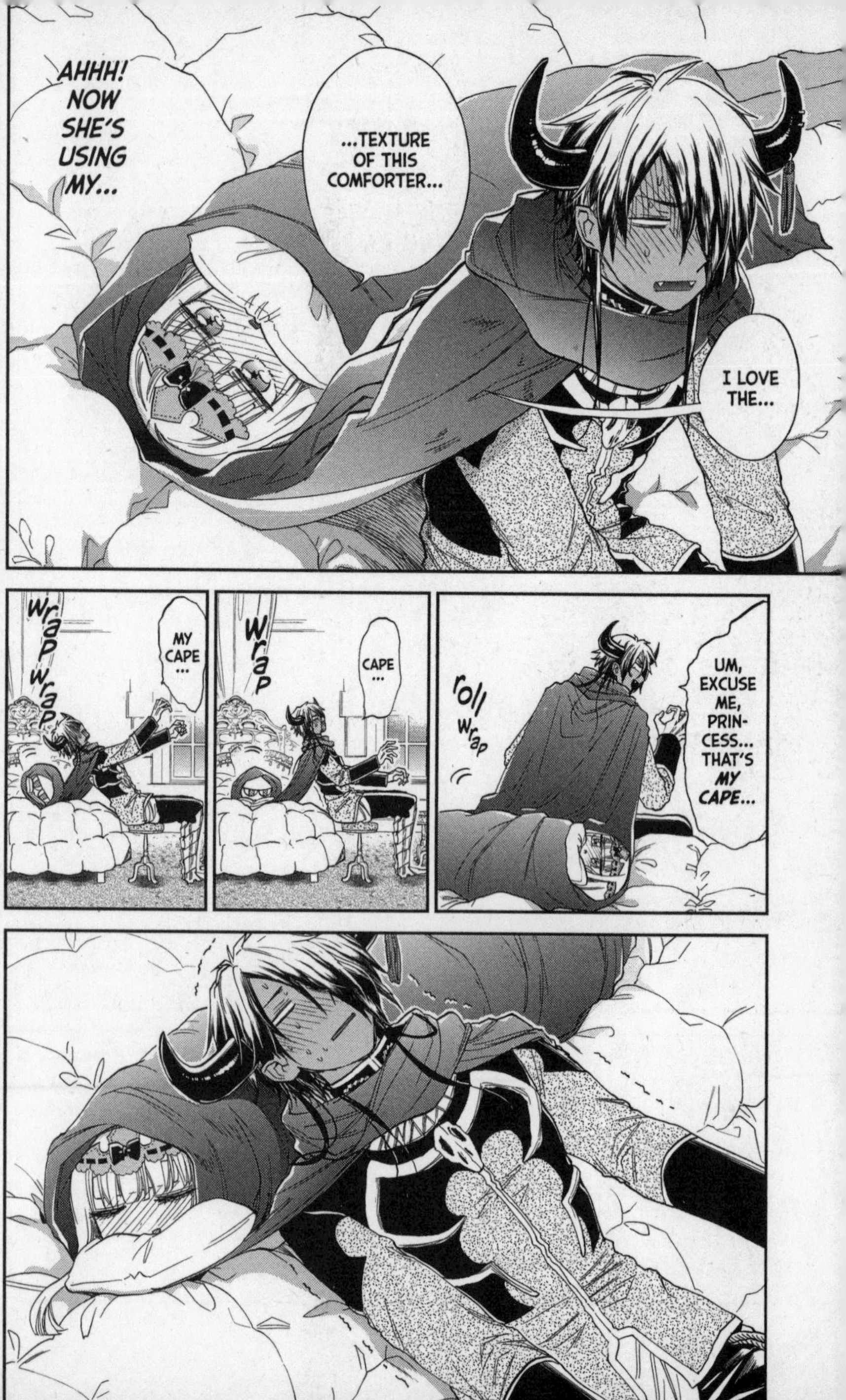
I LOVE THE...
...TEXTURE OF THIS COMFORTER...
AHHH! NOW SHE'S USING MY...
UM, EXCUSE ME, PRINCESS... THAT'S MY CAPE...
roll wrap
CAPE ...
Wrap
MY CAPE ...
wrap wrap wrap

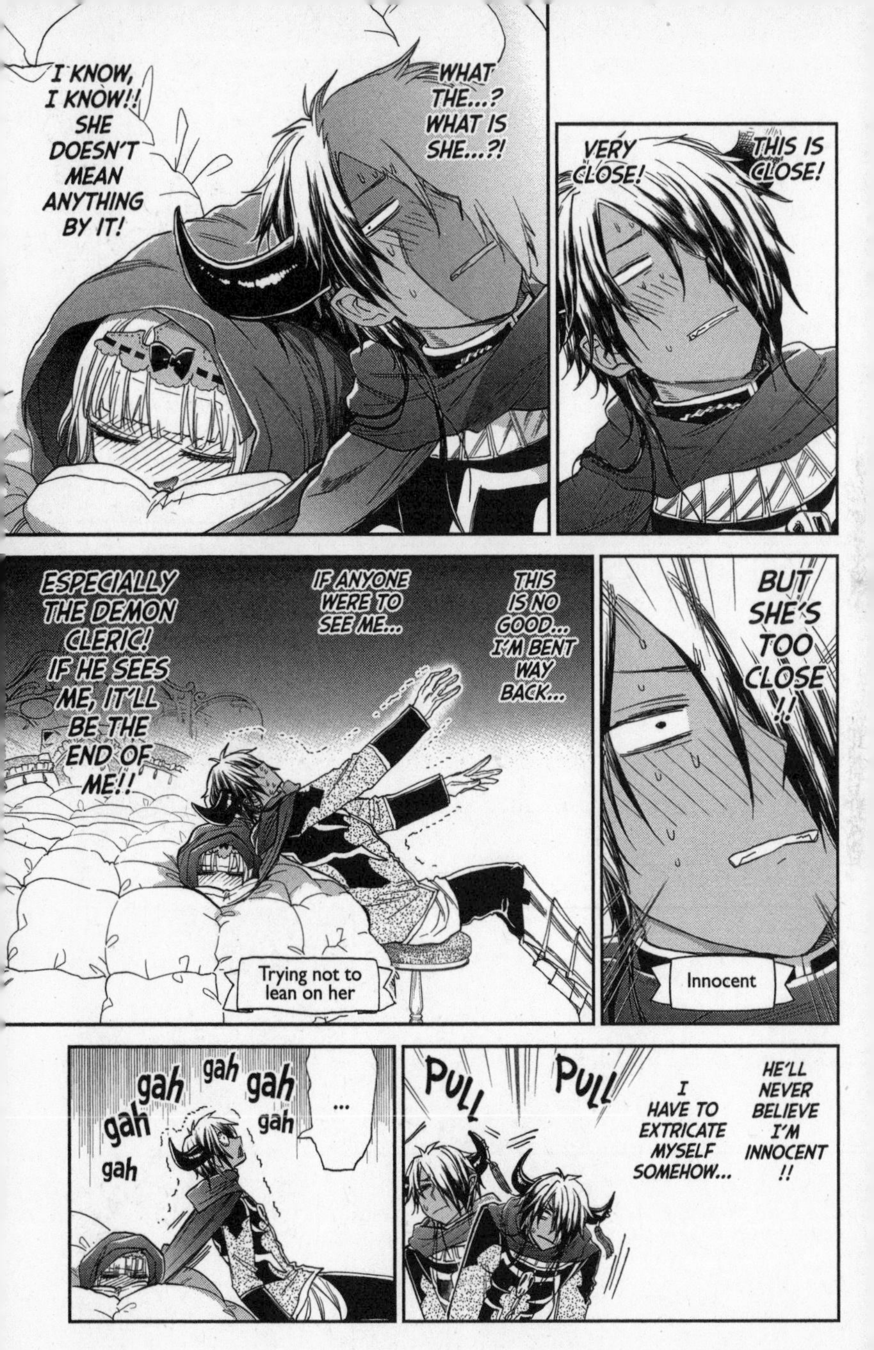
THIS IS CLOSE!
VERY CLOSE!
WHAT THE...? WHAT IS SHE...?!
I KNOW, I KNOW!! SHE DOESN'T MEAN ANYTHING BY IT!
BUT SHE'S TOO CLOSE!!
Innocent
THIS IS NO GOOD... I'M BENT WAY BACK...
IF ANYONE WERE TO SEE ME...
ESPECIALLY THE DEMON CLERIC! IF HE SEES ME, IT'LL BE THE END OF ME!!
Trying not to lean on her
HE'LL NEVER BELIEVE I'M INNOCENT!!
I HAVE TO EXTRICATE MYSELF SOMEHOW...
PULL
PULL
...
gah gah gah
gah gah gah

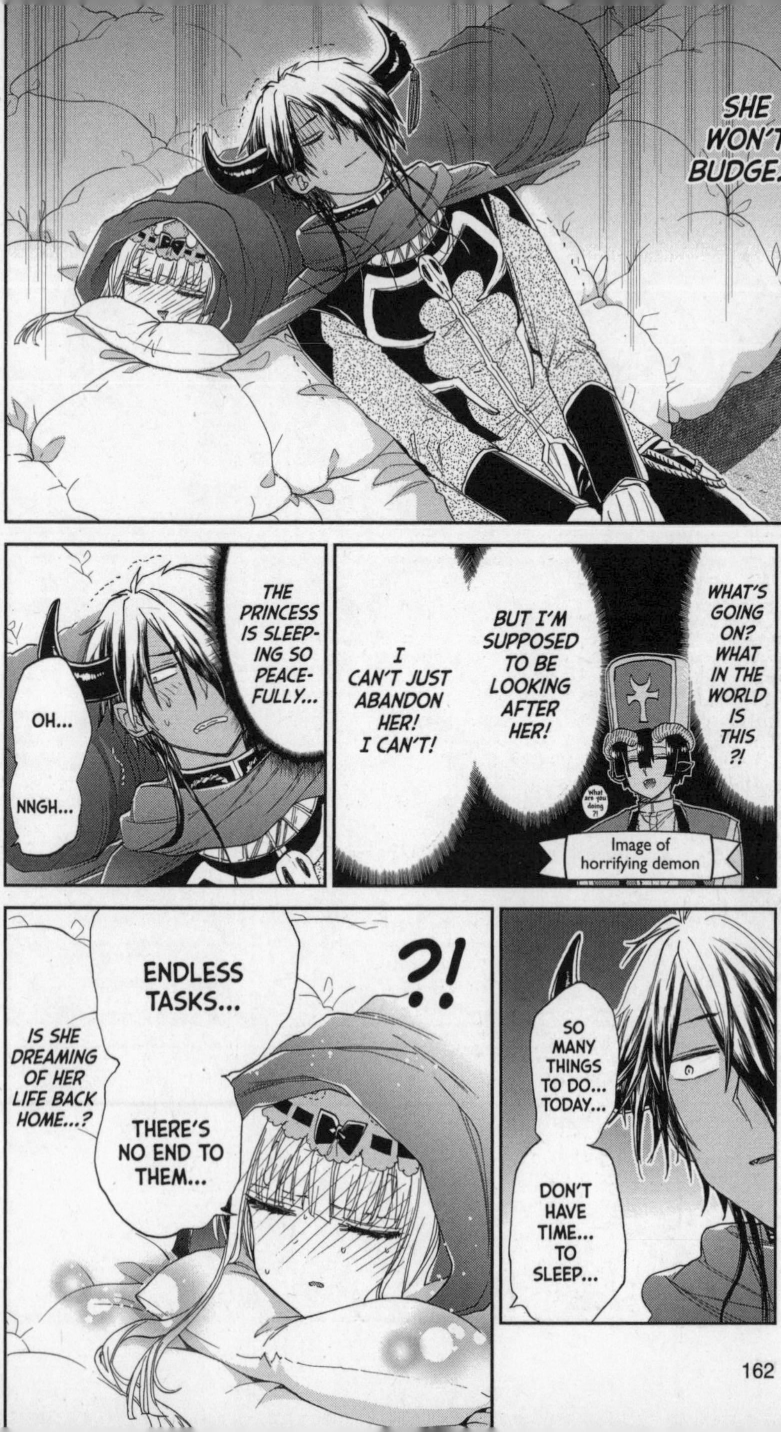
SHE WON'T BUDGE...
WHAT'S GOING ON? WHAT IN THE WORLD IS THIS?!
What are you doing?!
Image of horrifying demon
BUT I'M SUPPOSED TO BE LOOKING AFTER HER!
I CAN'T JUST ABANDON HER! I CAN'T!
THE PRINCESS IS SLEEPING SO PEACEFULLY...
OH...
NNGH...
SO MANY THINGS TO DO... TODAY...
DON'T HAVE TIME... TO SLEEP...
?!
ENDLESS TASKS...
THERE'S NO END TO THEM...
IS SHE DREAMING OF HER LIFE BACK HOME...?

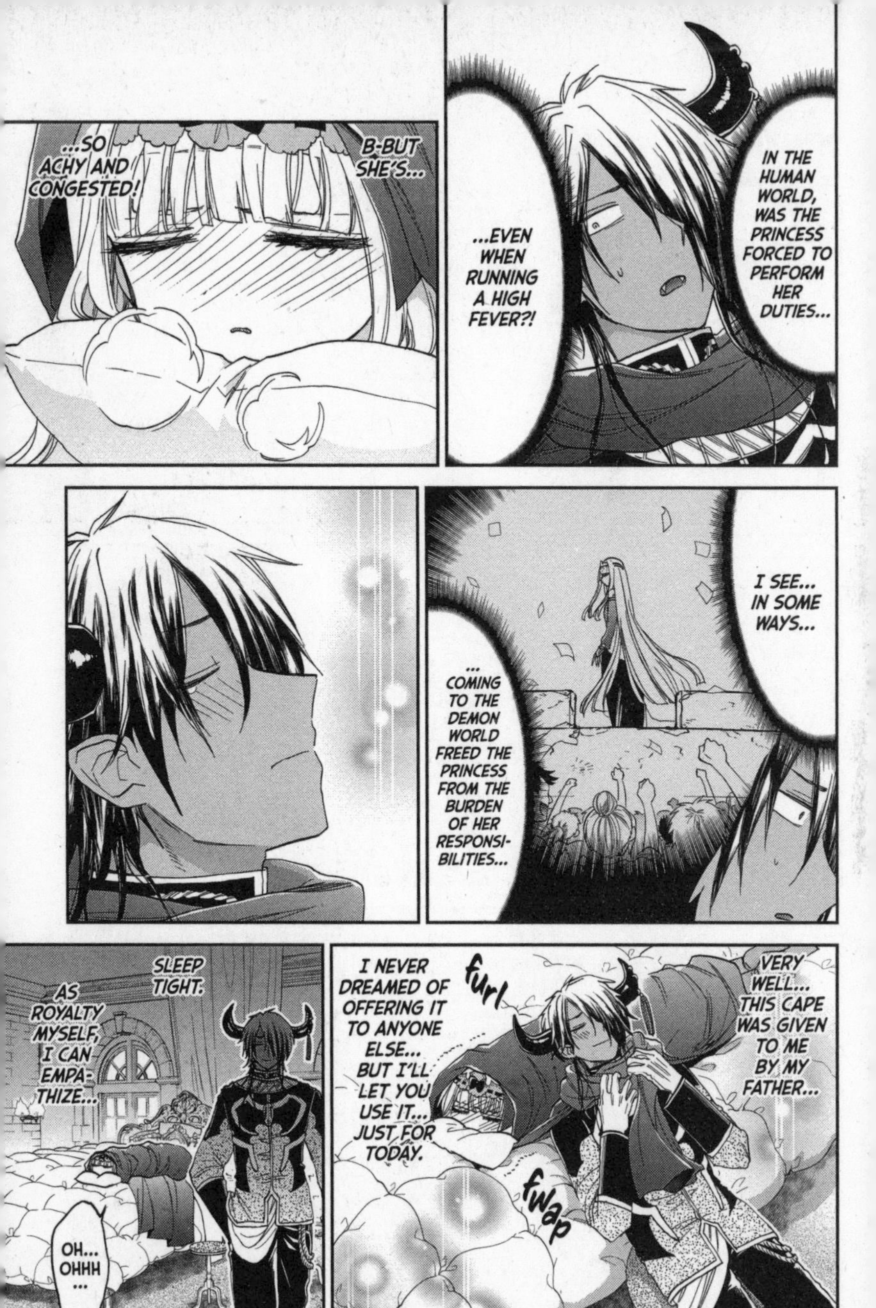

IN THE HUMAN WORLD, WAS THE PRINCESS FORCED TO PERFORM HER DUTIES...
...EVEN WHEN RUNNING A HIGH FEVER?!
B-BUT SHE'S...
...SO ACHY AND CONGESTED!
I SEE... IN SOME WAYS...
...COMING TO THE DEMON WORLD FREED THE PRINCESS FROM THE BURDEN OF HER RESPONSI-BILITIES...
VERY WELL... THIS CAPE WAS GIVEN TO ME BY MY FATHER...
furl
I NEVER DREAMED OF OFFERING IT TO ANYONE ELSE... BUT I'LL LET YOU USE IT... JUST FOR TODAY.
fwap
SLEEP TIGHT.
AS ROYALTY MYSELF, I CAN EMPA-THIZE...
OH... OHHH...

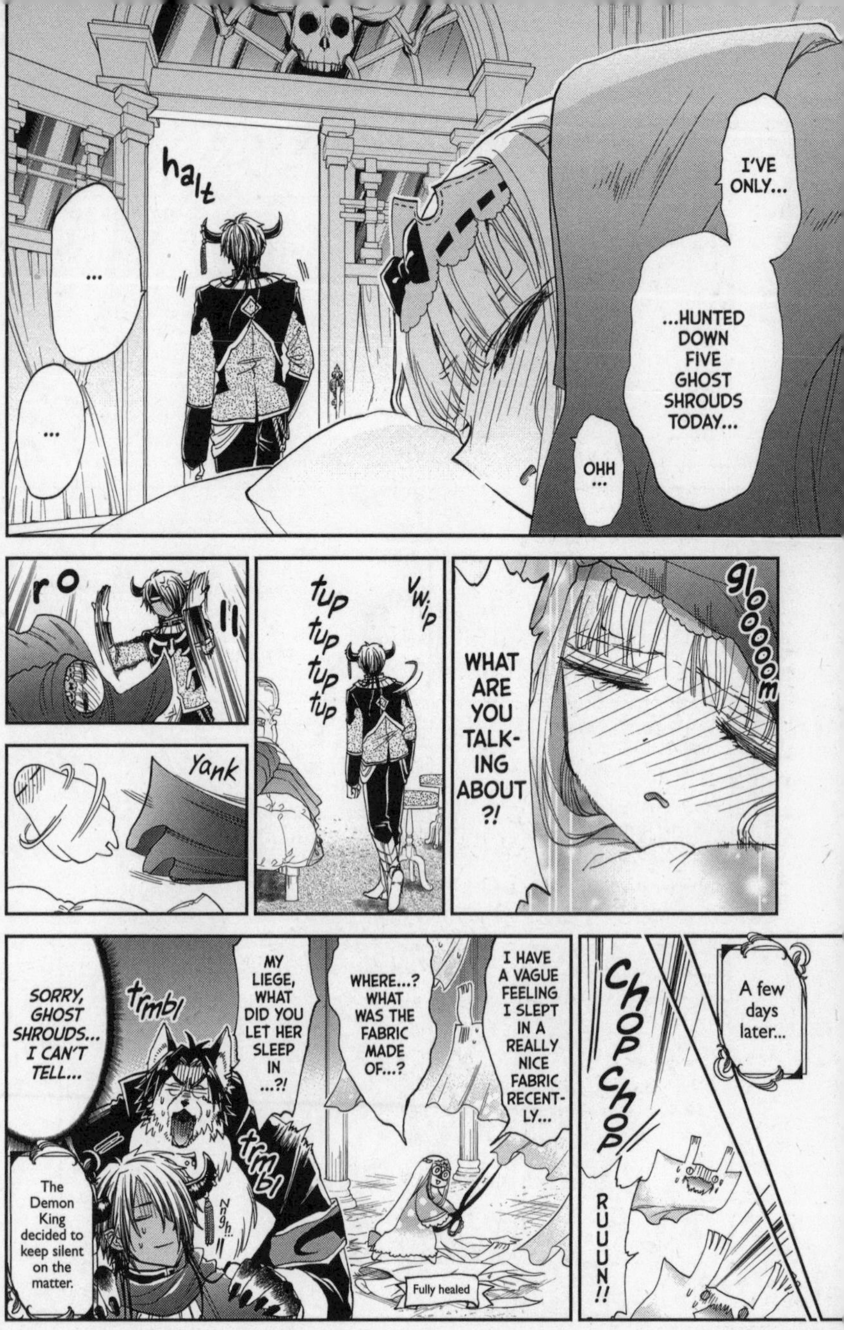
I'VE ONLY...
...HUNTED DOWN FIVE GHOST SHROUDS TODAY...
OHH...
halt
...
...
gloooooom
WHAT ARE YOU TALKING ABOUT?!
vwip
tup tup tup tup
ro
Yank
A few days later...
CHOP CHOP CHOP
RUUUN!!
I HAVE A VAGUE FEELING I SLEPT IN A REALLY NICE FABRIC RECENTLY...
WHERE...? WHAT WAS THE FABRIC MADE OF...?
Fully healed
MY LIEGE, WHAT DID YOU LET HER SLEEP IN...?!
trmbl
trmbl
SORRY, GHOST SHROUDS... I CAN'T TELL...
Nngh...!!
The Demon King decided to keep silent on the matter.

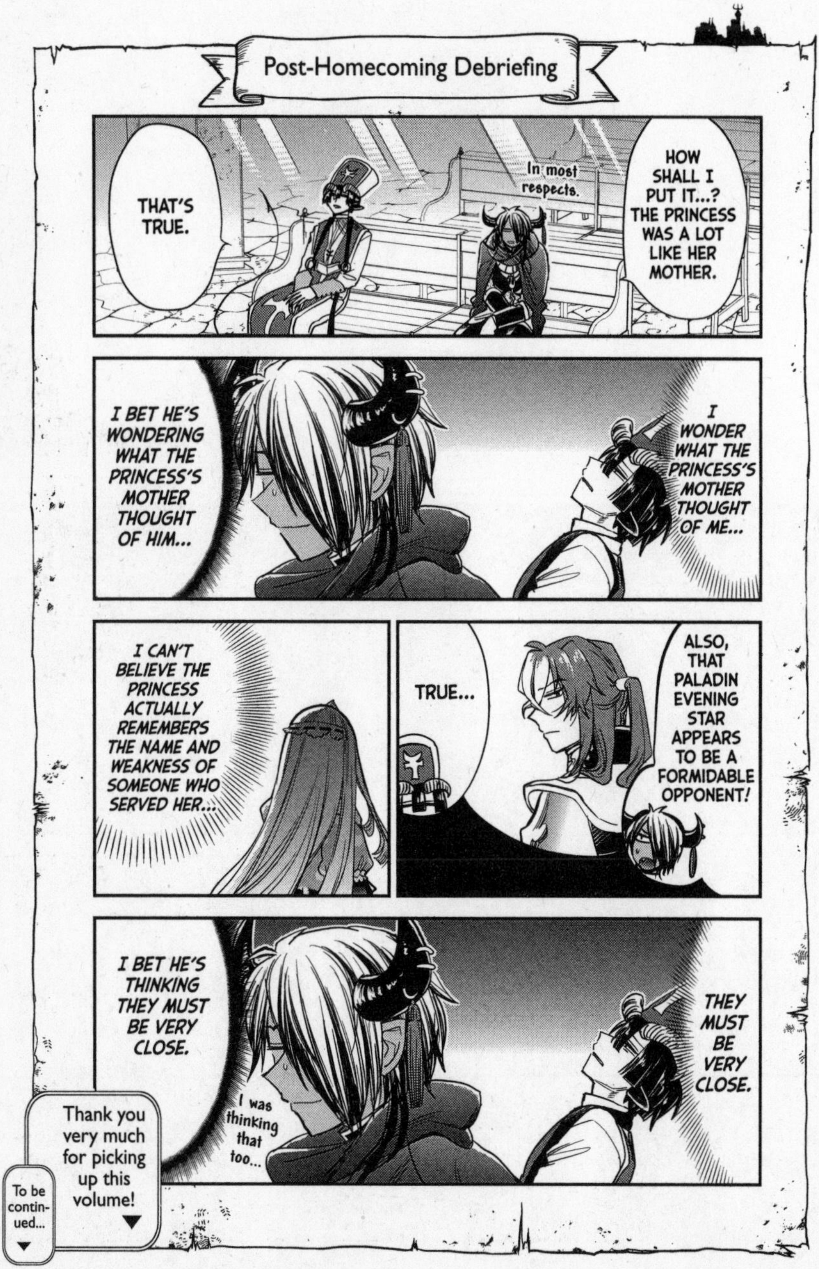
Post-Homecoming Debriefing
HOW SHALL I PUT IT...? THE PRINCESS WAS A LOT LIKE HER MOTHER.
In most respects.
THAT'S TRUE.
I WONDER WHAT THE PRINCESS'S MOTHER THOUGHT OF ME...
I BET HE'S WONDERING WHAT THE PRINCESS'S MOTHER THOUGHT OF HIM...
ALSO, THAT PALADIN EVENING STAR APPEARS TO BE A FORMIDABLE OPPONENT!
TRUE...
I CAN'T BELIEVE THE PRINCESS ACTUALLY REMEMBERS THE NAME AND WEAKNESS OF SOMEONE WHO SERVED HER...
THEY MUST BE VERY CLOSE.
I BET HE'S THINKING THEY MUST BE VERY CLOSE.
I was thinking that too...
Thank you very much for picking up this volume!
To be continued...

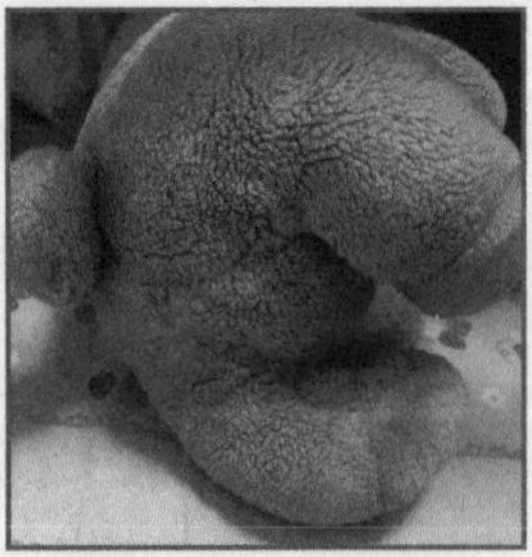

The seventh volume of a manga about sleeping!!!
Wow!! Amazing!!

– KAGIJI KUMANOMATA

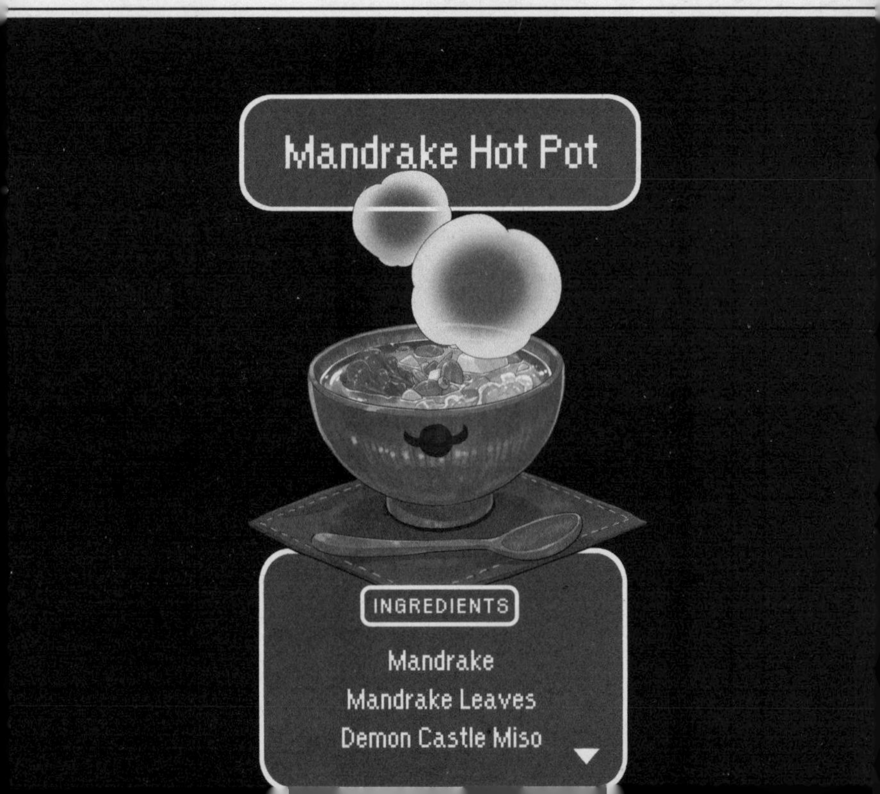

Mandrake Hot Pot
INGREDIENTS
Mandrake
Mandrake Leaves
Demon Castle Miso

Those who lurk b

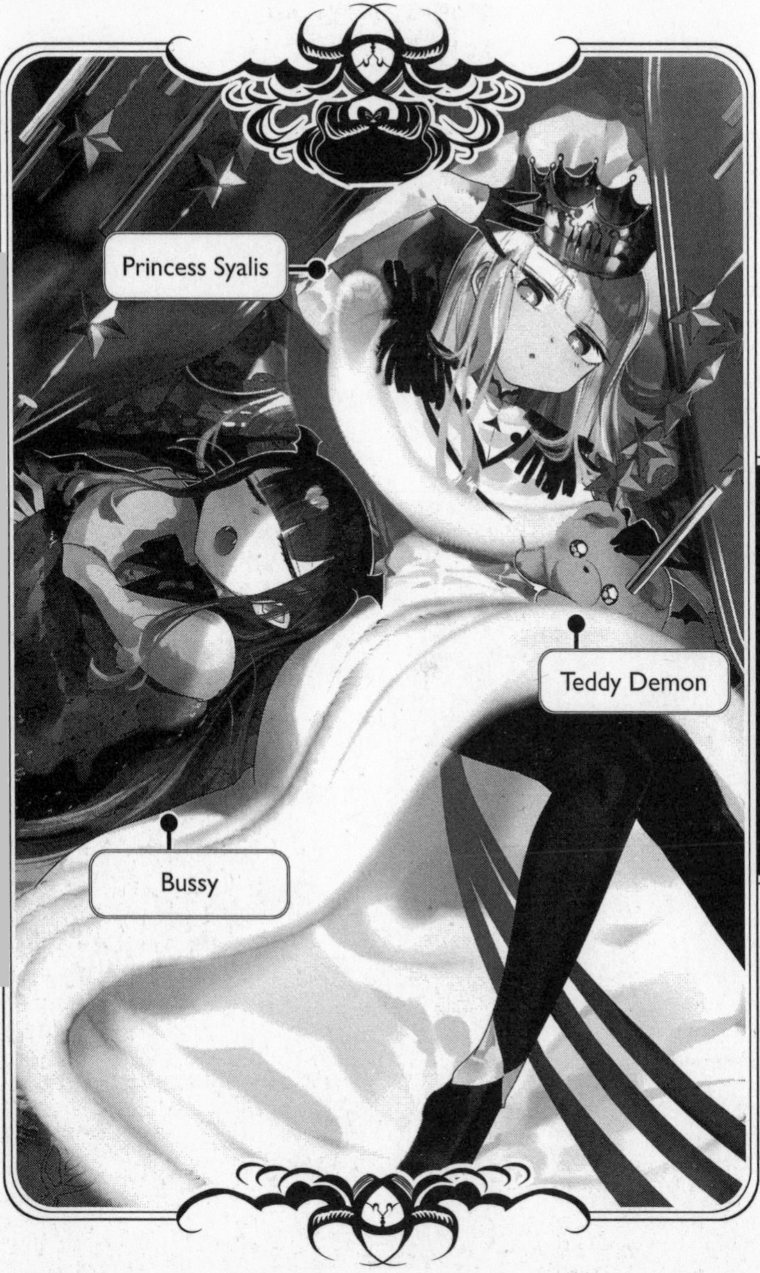
Princess Syalis
Teddy Demon
Bussy

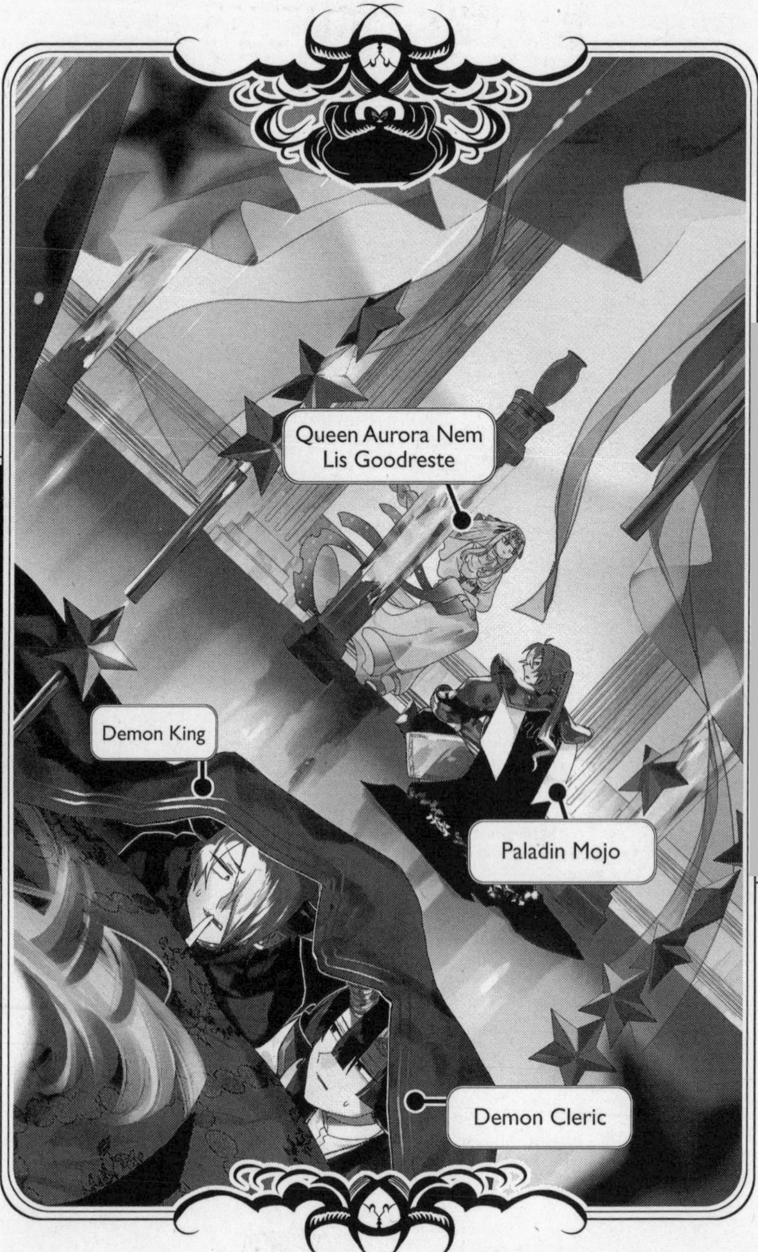
Queen Aurora Nem
Lis Goodreste
Demon King
Paladin Mojo
Demon Cleric

SLEEPY PRINCESS IN THE DEMON CASTLE

7

Shonen Sunday Edition

STORY AND ART BY

KAGIJI KUMANOMATA

MAOUJO DE OYASUMI Vol. 7
by Kagiji KUMANOMATA
© 2016 Kagiji KUMANOMATA
All rights reserved.
Original Japanese edition published by SHOGAKUKAN.
English translation rights in the United States of America, Canada,
the United Kingdom, Ireland, Australia and New Zealand arranged
with SHOGAKUKAN.

TRANSLATION **TETSUICHIRO MIYAKI**

ENGLISH ADAPTATION **ANNETTE ROMAN**

TOUCH-UP ART & LETTERING **SUSAN DAIGLE-LEACH**

COVER & INTERIOR DESIGN **ALICE LEWIS**

EDITOR **ANNETTE ROMAN**

Printed in the U.S.A.

Published by VIZ Media, LLC
P.O. Box 77010
San Francisco, CA 94107

10 9 8 7 6 5 4 3 2 1
First printing, June 2019

VIZ MEDIA
viz.com

SHONEN SUNDAY
shonensunday.com

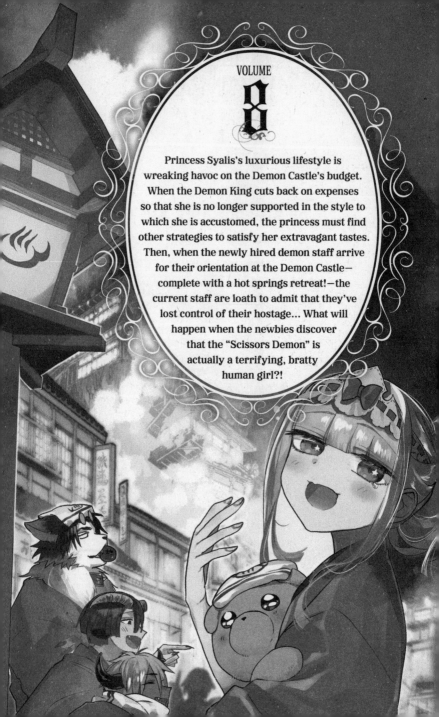

VOLUME

8

Princess Syalis's luxurious lifestyle is wreaking havoc on the Demon Castle's budget. When the Demon King cuts back on expenses so that she is no longer supported in the style to which she is accustomed, the princess must find other strategies to satisfy her extravagant tastes. Then, when the newly hired demon staff arrive for their orientation at the Demon Castle—complete with a hot springs retreat!—the current staff are loath to admit that they've lost control of their hostage... What will happen when the newbies discover that the "Scissors Demon" is actually a terrifying, bratty human girl?!

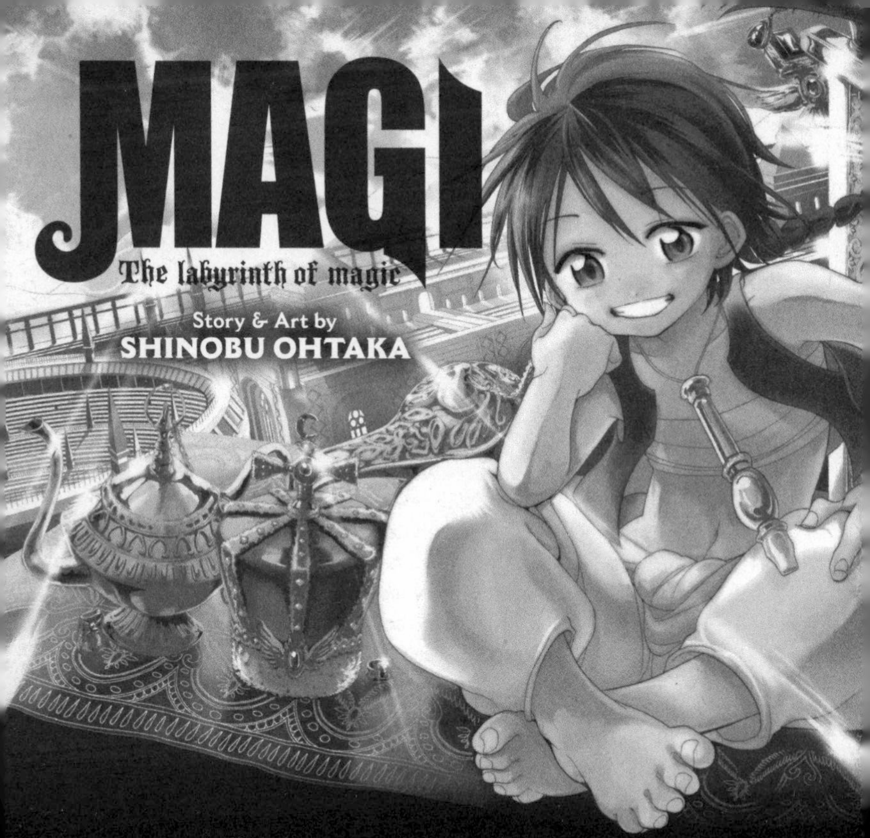
MAGI
The labyrinth of magic
Story & Art by
SHINOBU OHTAKA

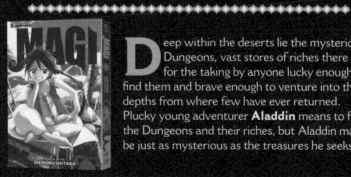

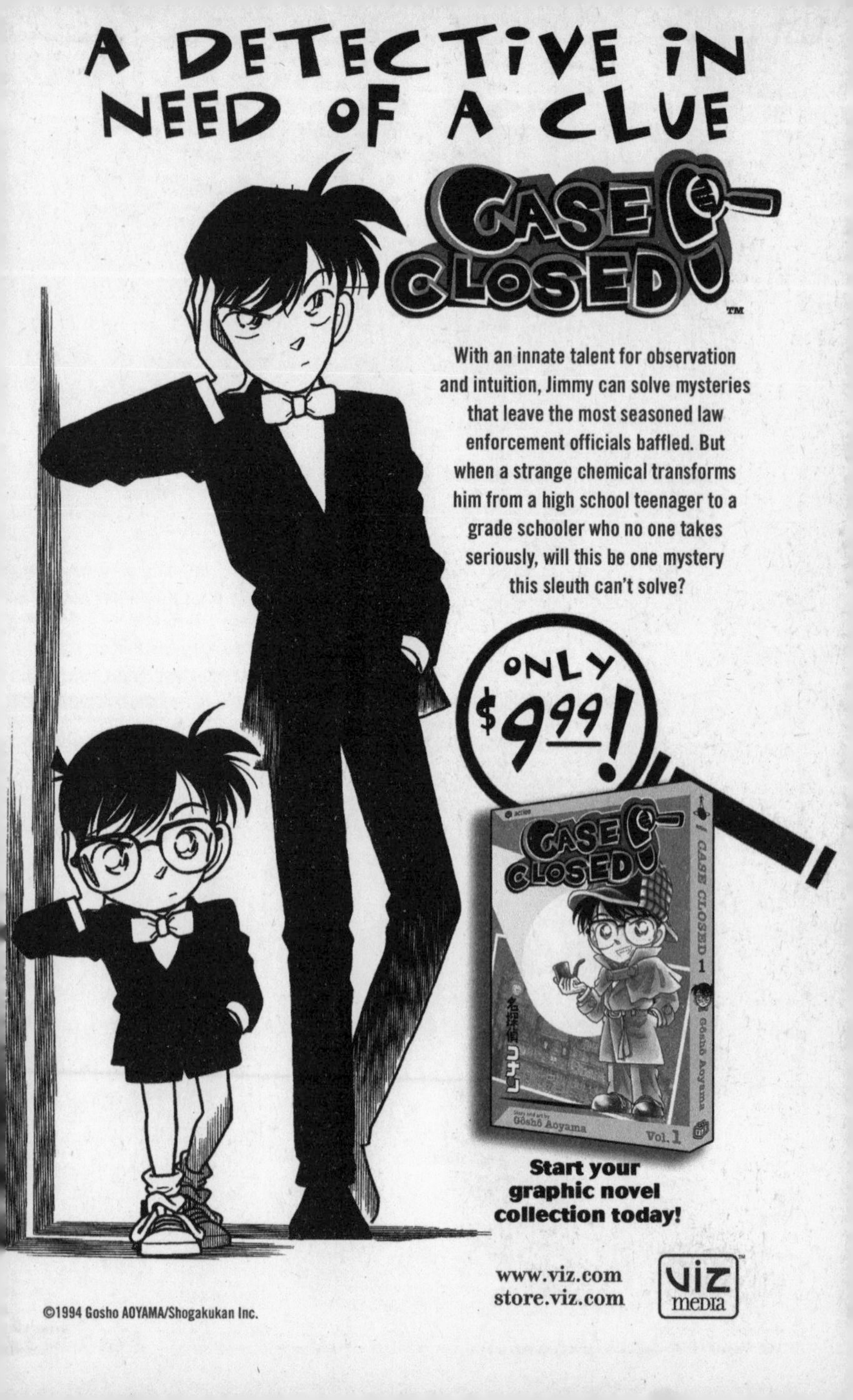
A DETECTIVE IN NEED OF A CLUE
CASE CLOSED™
With an innate talent for observation and intuition, Jimmy can solve mysteries that leave the most seasoned law enforcement officials baffled. But when a strange chemical transforms him from a high school teenager to a grade schooler who no one takes seriously, will this be one mystery this sleuth can't solve?
ONLY $9.99!
CASE CLOSED
CASE CLOSED 1
Gōshō Aoyama
名探偵コナン
Vol. 1
Start your graphic novel collection today!
www.viz.com
store.viz.com
VIZ MEDIA
©1994 Gosho AOYAMA/Shogakukan Inc.

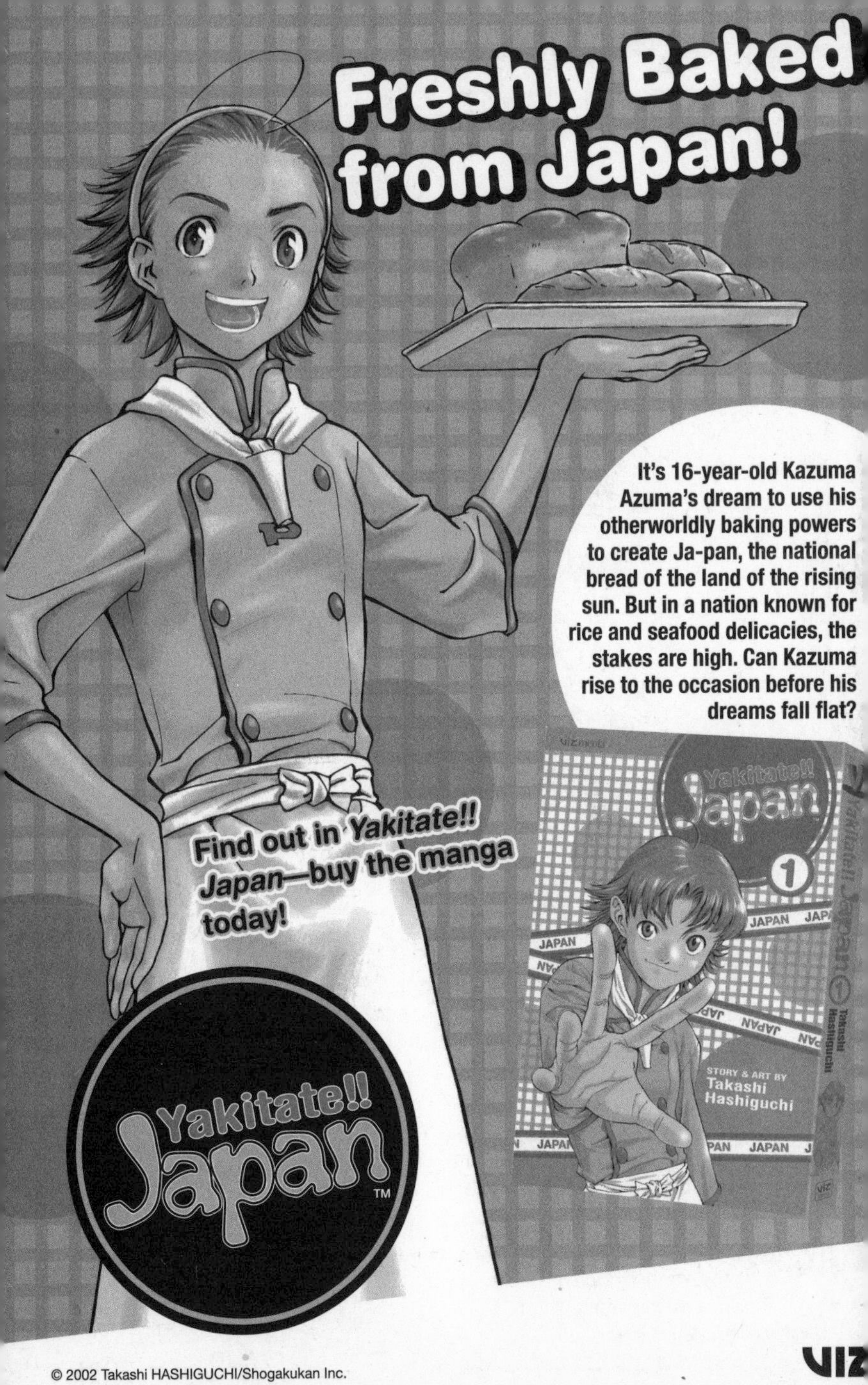

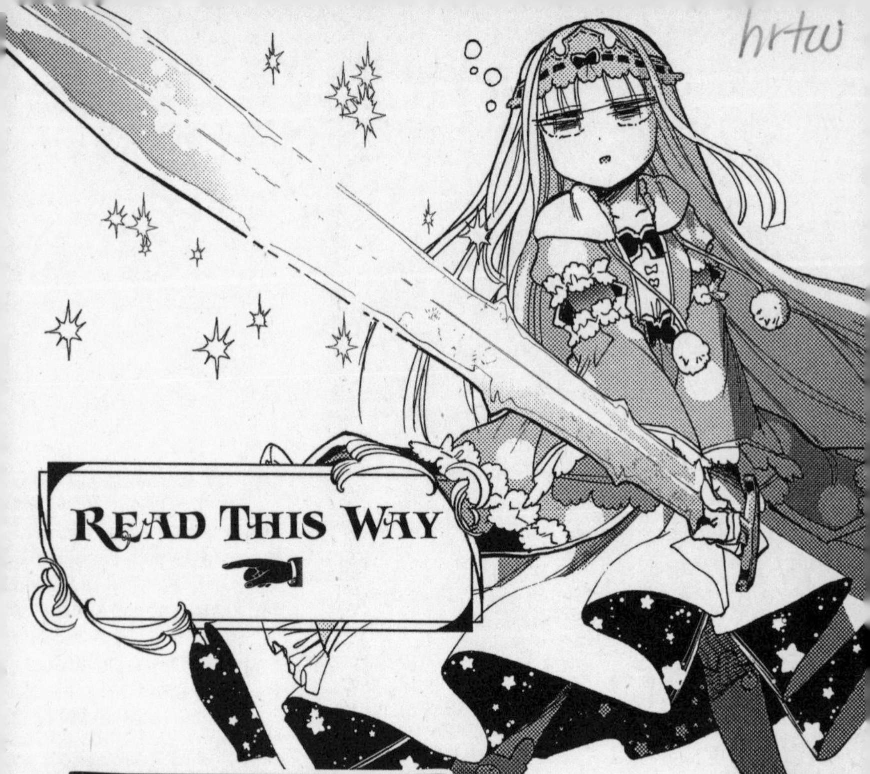
READ THIS WAY

STOP!

You may be reading the wrong way!

In keeping with the original Japanese comic format, this book reads from right to left—so action, sound effects and word balloons are completely reversed to preserve the orientation of the original artwork.

Check out the diagram shown here to get the hang of things, and then turn to the other side of the book to get started!

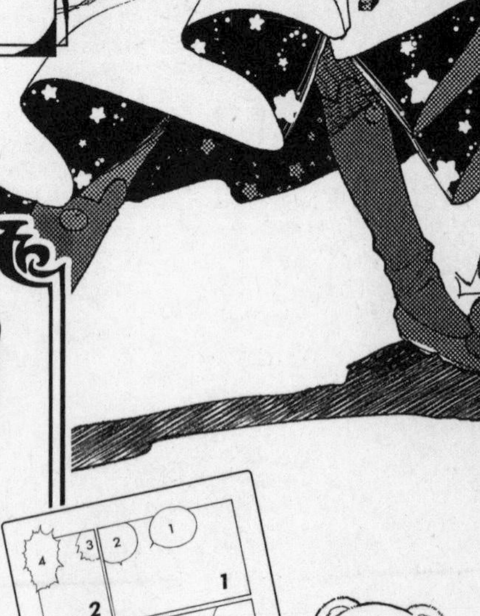
1
2
3
4
5